Confronting Sexual Assault in Canada
A Decade of Legal and Social Change

In 1983 reform legislation was introduced in Canada with the purpose of changing the treatment of victims of sexual assault and the processing of cases in the courts. The 1983 legislation was, however, only the beginning, not the end of reform. The essays in this volume address the power that legislative reform has to structure our understanding of, and our response to, crimes of sexual aggression.

The subjects explored include the origins of the 1983 legislation, recent national trends in criminal justice statistics relating to sexual assault, cultural bias, alternatives to sentencing, and the provision of civil compensation for the victims of sexual assault. Essays also analyse how cases are processed, how judges have constructed sexual assault, and how the level of harm caused is determined. The concluding chapters discuss the struggle between the courts and Parliament in determining the admissibility of sexual history evidence (before and after the *Seaboyer* decision) and the consultation process that contributed to the 1992 legislative changes.

Several common themes emerge. One is that statutory revisions can effect changes in the behaviour of criminal justice personnel only to a limited extent. Another is the need for explicit guidance in – and perhaps limits on – the exercise of discretion by these personnel in their handling of sexual assault cases. Finally, this volume makes it clear that the issue of criminal sexual aggression can be understood and dealt with effectively only through an integrated approach, incorporating both sociological and legal perspectives.

JULIAN V. ROBERTS is a member of the Department of Criminology, University of Ottawa, and is editor of *Canadian Journal of Criminology*.

RENATE M. MOHR is a member of the Department of Law, Carleton University, and is on the editorial board of *Canadian Journal of Women and the Law*.

Edited by

Julian V. Roberts and Renate M. Mohr

Confronting Sexual Assault:
A Decade of Legal
and Social Change

UNIVERSITY OF TORONTO PRESS
Toronto Buffalo London

©University of Toronto Press Incorporated 1994
Toronto Buffalo London
Printed in Canada

ISBN 0-8020-5928-7 (cloth)
ISBN 0-8020-6868-5 (paper)

Printed on acid-free paper

Canadian Cataloguing in Publication Data

Main entry under title:

Confronting sexual assault : a decade of legal
and social change

ISBN 0-8020-5928-7 (bound). – ISBN 0-8020-6868-5 (pbk.)

1. Sex crimes – Canada.   2. Rape – Canada.
3. Sex crimes – Law and legislation – Canada.
4. Rape – Law and legislation – Canada.   I. Roberts,
Julian V.   II. Mohr, Renate M., 1954–.

KE8928.C65 1994   364.1'53'0971   C93-095272-3
KF9325.C65 1994

This book has been published with the help of a grant from the Social Science Federation of Canada, using funds provided by the Social Sciences and Humanities Research Council of Canada.

Contents

Acknowledgments

This volume could not have been prepared without the generous assistance of the following individuals and organizations. First and foremost, we would like to acknowledge the assistance and advice offered by Virgil Duff, Executive Editor at the University of Toronto Press. We would also like to acknowledge the feedback provided by the anonymous reviewers who read an earlier draft of this manuscript. We gratefully acknowledge the financial contribution of the Department of Justice Canada. As well, we would like to acknowledge the support of the Social Science Federation of Canada. Financial assistance for the contributing authors' conference was provided by the Social Sciences and Humanities Research Council of Canada (Aid to Occasional Scholarly Conferences in Canada Fund). We would also like to acknowledge the assistance of the Faculty of Social Sciences at Carleton University, the Department of Criminology at the University of Ottawa, and the Sustaining Grants Program of the Ministry of the Solicitor General Canada to the Department of Criminology at the University of Ottawa. We would like to express our gratitude to Lisa Clement and particularly to Jean-Paul Prieur for technical assistance in preparing the manuscript. Finally, the editors dedicate their work on this project to V.M.-B. and M.K.R.

Contributors

Adelyn L. Bowland is a lawyer working in Toronto.

Christine Boyle is a professor in the Faculty of Law at the University of British Columbia.

Scott Clark is Chief of the Criminal Law Research Unit, Research Section, Department of Justice Canada.

Michelle Grossman is a graduate student in Social Work at the University of Toronto and a researcher working in the area of sexual assault and child sexual abuse.

Rita Gunn is a research consultant and lecturer in the Department of Sociology at the University of Manitoba.

Dorothy Hepworth is Director of Research, Department of Justice Canada.

Rick Linden is a professor in the Department of Sociology at the University of Manitoba.

Maria Łoś is a professor in the Department of Criminology at the University of Ottawa.

Sheila McIntyre is an associate professor in the Faculty of Law at Queen's University.

Diana Majury is an associate professor in the Department of Law at Carleton University.

Renate M. Mohr is an associate professor in the Department of Law at Carleton University.

Teressa Nahanee is a graduate student in the Faculty of Law, Queen's University.

Julian V. Roberts is an associate professor in the Department of Criminology at the University of Ottawa.

Elizabeth A. Sheehy is an associate professor in the Faculty of Law at the University of Ottawa.

CONFRONTING SEXUAL ASSAULT

1

RENATE M. MOHR AND
JULIAN V. ROBERTS

Sexual Assault in Canada: Recent Developments

Introduction: The Social Context of Sexual Assault Legislation

This book is about the phenomenon of criminal sexual aggression, and the criminal justice response to the crimes of sexual assault. In the last decade, we have witnessed a phenomenal growth in awareness of, and concern about, the pervasive and painful issue of sexual assault in Canada. The response of the criminal justice system to acts of violence, particularly the violence of sexual assault, is a response that affects the lives of the women and children who are almost invariably the victims of this violence, the lives of the men who are almost invariably the perpetrators of this violence and the lives of women, children, and men who live in a society that countenances coercive sexuality. The recent dramatic increase in scholarship – both legal and socio-logical – on this topic received its impetus in large part from the passage of the 1983 Canadian legislation and comparable law reform efforts in other countries, notably the United States. At the same time, contributions to the literature by feminist writers have greatly influenced both scholarship and public awareness of violence against women. In fact, the broader issue of vio-lence against women has recently reached a wider audience than at any point in the past. A recent nation-wide survey of the Canadian public found that sexual assault generated more concern than any other crime, with the sole exception of homicide. In short, this is a propitious time to write a book upon the topic of sexual assault.

Sexual Assault: Some Recent Cases

The attention of the news media to issues surrounding sexual assault cannot be overlooked. Stories about sexual assault and the treatment of sexual assault cases sell newspapers. Recently, through print and electronic media, the Canadian public has learned of the prevalence of sexual assaults involving children, perpetrated by men in positions of authority. The stories paint a picture (long familiar to victims) of what can only be called institutionalized sexual aggression. The stories take place in rural and urban settings from British Columbia to Newfoundland. The abusers include clergymen while the abused include Native Canadians in residential schools and economically disadvantaged children in orphanages. Perhaps more than ever before, the term sexual assault evokes the image of children – children abused by their fathers, stepfathers, uncles, social workers, teachers, doctors, and priests.

The stories also concern adult victims and their treatment at the hands of the criminal justice system. Kitty Nowdluk-Reynolds' story is one that has outraged many, but surprised few. For this Inuit woman, being raped and beaten in a small community on Baffin Island was merely the beginning of her humiliation. She was later arrested by the RCMP in British Columbia, handcuffed, jailed, and flown to various locations across the country, finally returning to Baffin Island, in order to ensure that she, the victim of a sexual assault, would testify at the trial. The ordeal ended only after the police drove her to the courthouse, handcuffed, in the same van as the man whom she had identified as the rapist. These cases, and others like them, have prompted pressure on the government to conduct public inquiries into the treatment of victims of sexual assault.

The media coverage of the consultations leading up to the 1992 legislation had an extremely valuable educative effect on the public. The issue of consent in sexual assault cases raised public awareness to many existing problems with the judicial interpretation of consent. Following coverage of 'no means no' campaigns launched to educate students at Canadian universities and high schools about date rape, the proposed 'no means no' definition of consent became a hotly debated topic in newspapers, classrooms, and homes across the country.

It does not take a book on sexual assault to report that the 1983 rape reform legislation has failed to eradicate sexual assault. Nor does it take a book to make the claim that changing the language surrounding sexual aggression, from rape to sexual assault, did not result in a corresponding change of attitudes on the part of those who were and are in a position to develop legal definitions. Although judicial interpretations of the 1992 legislation are now starting to appear in the case reports, it may be a long while before the 'no means no' intent of the law is understood by judges and lawyers alike. Indeed, an impressive body of literature[1] exists that reveals the way in which law-making is influenced by the gender, race, class, and sexual orientation of the law-maker. The drafters of the 1983 sexual assault provisions did not define 'sexual assault.' It is judges who, by default, become the law-makers as far as the definition of the offence itself is concerned. In *R. v. Chase*,[2] an early case in which the New Brunswick Court of Appeal had to determine whether grabbing a woman's breasts constituted a 'sexual assault,' Mr. Justice Angers determined that the assaultive behaviour was not sexual since breasts, 'like a man's beard,' were merely secondary sexual characteristics. As Brettel Dawson (1985) wrote, 'the proliferation and fetishization of breasts which is so abundantly clear in images of women in the media, advertising and pornography, renders the assumption [breasts as a secondary sexual characteristic] absurd.' The Supreme Court of Canada ultimately overturned the Court of Appeal ruling in *Chase*[3] and held that non-consensual grabbing of breasts does in fact constitute a sexual assault.

In another publicized and controversial decision that revealed important underlying assumptions about sexual assault held by some judges, an Ottawa District Court judge acquitted a man on a charge of uttering threats to commit a serious bodily injury. In *McCraw*,[4] Judge Keith Flanigan held that a threat to rape does not necessarily involve 'serious bodily harm.' The accused had sent letters to three women describing his intentions to force them to submit to a number of acts including fellatio, cunnilingus, vaginal and anal penetration. Judge Flanigan wrote that these letters 'while immature and disgusting, reveal more of an adoring fantasy than a threat to cause serious bodily harm.' Although the decision was subsequently overturned by the Ontario Court of Appeal, one of three appeal court judges agreed with Flanigan's construction of the letters as an 'adoring fantasy.' The Supreme Court of Canada upheld the majority decision of the Court of Appeal by finding that a threat to rape is in fact a threat that falls within the legislative requirement of 'serious bodily harm.'[5]

In spite of the 1983 legislation, it is clear that Canadian society continues to pay the price of coercive sexuality. This volume addresses the role that legislative reform can play in reducing, and ultimately eliminating, those costs. In order to provide the reader with a framework within which to assess the different aspects of the 1983 legislation, some highlights of the legislative changes will be provided below. Our aim in this chapter is not to provide a lengthy discussion of the current sexual assault provisions in the Criminal Code, but rather to provide readers with a brief description of the offences of sexual aggression as they now exist, and of the offences that were eliminated by the Criminal Code revision of 1983. As well, we aim to inform readers of the recent developments leading up to the 1992 amendments to the Criminal Code.

Twenty years ago this was a criminal justice issue of concern primarily to researchers, policy-makers, rape crisis centre professionals, and of course the victims of the crime. Times have changed, and today sexual assault concerns not just these groups but also the judiciary, the general public, politicians, law-makers, as well as many special-interest groups such as the National Association of Women and the Law, the National Action Committee, and the Canadian Civil Liberties Association. In fact, sexual assault concerns all who belong to a Canadian society in which sexual assault takes place. In this introductory chapter, we briefly review the most important events that have taken place in the area of sexual assault over the past ten years.

Recent Developments

The decade of social and legal change documented in this volume began with the passage of rape reform legislation ten years ago. In 1983, Canadian criminal laws governing acts of sexual aggression were repealed and amended and new offences were legislated.

BILL C-127: THE 1983 LEGISLATIVE AMENDMENTS

In 1982, the last year under the old legislation, the principal offences of sexual aggression were the following: rape and attempted rape (s. 143), indecent assault against a female (s. 156), and indecent assault against a male (s. 156). These offences were not the only sexual offences contained in the Criminal Code; there were many others, but these four offences were the ones replaced by the three new sexual assault sections. Bill C-127 introduced three new offences: sexual assault (s. 271); sexual assault with a weapon, threats to a third party or causing bodily harm (s. 272); and aggravated sexual assault (s. 273). The maximum penalties prescribed by the Code for these three offences are, respectively, 10 years' imprisonment, 14 years' imprisonment; and life imprisonment. Level I sexual assault (s. 271) is in fact a hybrid offence, and this has consequences for the maximum penalty. If the Crown proceeds by way of summary conviction, the maximum penalty is six months' imprisonment or a $2000 fine. If the Crown elects to proceed by way of indictment, the maximum penalty is imprisonment for 10 years. (See Boyle 1984 and Watt 1984 for further description of the sexual assault offences created in 1983.) The 1983 legislative amendments are set out in chart form in Table 1.1. This table provides an overview of the principal offences of sexual aggression as they existed before 1983 and as they exist in the current Criminal Code.

Since the sexual assault offences mirror closely in structure the assault offences, it is worth noting them as well. There are three levels of assault[6]: assault (s. 266), assault with a weapon or causing bodily harm (s. 267), and aggravated assault (s. 268). The maximum penalties for assault offences are, respectively, 5, 10, and 14 years' imprisonment. (As with the first level of sexual assault, the first level of assault is a hybrid offence, with the same implications in terms of the maximum penalty that can be imposed.)

Bill C-127 was passed and proclaimed in force on 4 January 1983. The major changes included replacing the offences of rape, attempted rape, and indecent assault by three new crimes: sexual assault; sexual assault with a weapon/threats to a third party/causing bodily harm; and aggravated sexual assault. Unlike rape, which was found in Part IV of the Criminal Code (under the heading 'Sexual Offences, Public Morals and Disorderly Conduct'), the sexual assault offences were located in Part VI (entitled 'Offences against the Person and Reputation').

Concern with criminal sexual aggression was not restricted to adult victims. In 1980, the federal government announced the establishment of the Committee on Sexual Offences Against Children and Youths. This committee conducted a national fact-finding study of sexual crimes against children, and studied recommendations aimed at protecting juvenile victims. Headed by Robin Badgley, the Committee released its report four years later (Badgley 1984). This initiative was followed by the passage, in 1988, of legislation relating to sexual offences involving children (Bill C-15). The next important piece of legislation relating to the treatment of cases of sexual aggression was provoked by an appeal to the Supreme Court of Canada.

THE 'RAPE SHIELD' LAW

The first draft of this book was completed in August 1991. The original intention was to provide the first multidisciplinary exploration of the 1983 sexual assault legislation and its impact upon the criminal justice system, victims of sexual assault, and Canadian society in general. Then, in late August 1991, the Supreme Court of Canada shifted the legal terrain and raised serious concerns about the legal construction of sexual assault. In *Seaboyer and Gayme*,[7] the Supreme Court struck down s. 276 of the Criminal Code, which limited the questioning of victims in sexual assault trials about their sexual history. Steven Seaboyer and Nigel Gayme, two men accused of rape, successfully argued that these 'rape shield' laws violated their rights, as accused persons, to a fair trial. Although the Supreme Court upheld s. 277 of the Criminal Code, which excludes evidence of a victim's

TABLE 1.1
Offences of Sexual Aggression

Pre-1983			1983			1985–present		
Section #	Offence	Maximum Penalty	Section #	Offence	Maximum Penalty	Section #	Offence	Maximum Penalty
143	Rape	Life						
145	Attempt rape	10 years	246.1	Sexual Assault I	10 years*	271	Sexual Assault I	10 years*
149	Indecent assault female	5 years	246.2	Sexual Assault II	14 years	272	Sexual Assault II	14 years
156	Indecent assault male	10 years	246.3	Sexual Assault III	Life	273	Sexual Assault III	Life
155	Buggery/bestiality	14 years	155	Buggery/bestiality	14 years	160	Bestiality	10 years*
157	Acts of gross indecency	5 years	157	Acts of gross indecency	5 years	159	Anal intercourse	10 years*
150	Incest	14 years	150	Incest	14 years	155	Incest	14 years*
						151	Sexual interference under 14	10 years*
						152	Invitation to sexual touching under 14	10 years*
						153	Sexual exploitation 14–18	5 years*
146	Sexual intercourse with female under 14	Life	146(1)	Sexual intercourse with female under 14	Life			
146	Sexual intercourse with female 14–16	5 years	146(2)	Sexual intercourse with female 14–18	5 years			
148	Sexual intercourse with feeble-minded	5 years						

*This is a hybrid offence. If the Crown proceeds by way of summary conviction, the maximum penalty is six months or a $2000 fine.

TABLE 1.1 (concluded)
Offences of Sexual Aggression

Pre-1983			1983			1985–present		
Section #	Offence	Maximum Penalty	Section #	Offence	Maximum Penalty	Section #	Offence	Maximum Penalty
151	Seduction of a female 16–18	2 years	151	Seduction of female 16–18	2 years			
152	Seduction under promise of marriage	2 years	152	Seduction under promise of marriage	2 years			
153	Sexual intercourse with stepdaughter or female employee	2 years	153	Sexual intercourse with stepdaughter or female employee	2 years			
154	Seduction of female passengers on vessels	2 years	154	Seduction of female passengers on vessels	2 years			
166	Parent or guardian (<14) under defilement (14+)	14 years	166	Parent or guardian procuring defilement (< 14) (14+)	14 years / 5 years	170	Parent or guardian procuring sexual activity (<14) (14–18)	5 years / 2 years
167	Householder permitting defilement	2 years	167	Householder permitting defilement	2 years	171	Householder permitting sexual activity (<14) (14–18)	2 years / 5 years / 2 years
			169	Indecent acts	6 months	173	Indecent acts	6 months
			170	Nudity	6 months	174	Nudity	6 months
			171	Causing disturbance, Indecent exhibition		175	Causing disturbance /Indecent exhibition	6 months
						172	Corrupting children	2 years

sexual reputation for purposes of questioning her credibility, the decision to strike down s. 276 was felt by many women's groups across the country to strike a devastating blow to women's rights in Canada. In striking down existing protections for women from cross-examination on their past sexual history, the majority decision set out broad guidelines to be used by judges when determining whether to admit evidence about a victim's sexual history. In other words, the decision as to whether to admit or exclude evidence of past sexual history would no longer be strictly constrained by the Criminal Code but would instead be left largely to the discretion of individual trial judges. As the executive director of the national organization that promotes equality for women through legal action and public education (LEAF) stated, 'The guidelines provide women no certainty at the time they must decide whether to use the criminal justice system that their cases will be decided based on what happened to them and not on their sexual history.'[8]

Although the *Seaboyer* decision signalled an end to what many women had seen as a decade of important changes in attitudes and perceptions surrounding the 'new' sexual assault laws, it also inaugurated an active new phase of redefining and restructuring the legal terrain.[9] The 80-page dissenting judgment in *Seaboyer*, written by Madame Justice L'Heureux-Dubé, provided a strong and passionate argument against the striking down of the rape shield laws. Her dissent provided the grounds for perhaps the strongest and most effective lobby effort by women's groups that Canada has ever witnessed.

Within a year of this important Supreme Court decision, the minister of Justice, Kim Campbell, responded with new legislation. In August 1992, new legislation amending the sexual assault provisions in the Criminal Code came into force. Bill C-49 provides the legal parameters for determining the admissibility of a victim's past sexual history as evidence in sexual assault trials. It also provides – for the first time in Canadian legal history – a definition of the concept of 'consent' as it applies to sexual assault. The minister acknowledged the role that women's voices played in forming the substance of the new legislation. As she noted in a speech accompanying the second reading of the Bill in April 1992:[10]

The input I have received from Canadian women has been very troubling: They have very little confidence in the Canadian justice system as it deals with sexual assault. They have indicated that the admissibility of evidence of a complainant's past sexual history is one, albeit, important aspect of the inadequacy of our sexual assault laws.

BILL C-49: THE 1992 LEGISLATIVE AMENDMENTS

The 1992 legislative amendments did not affect the structure of the sexual assault offences created in 1983. Instead, the 1992 amendments focused on three main issues: first, Bill C-49 set out a new test that judges will use to determine whether a complainant's sexual history may be admitted at trial; second, it provided a definition of 'consent' for the purpose of sexual assault offences; and third, it restricted the defence of mistaken belief in consent as it concerns sexual assault offences. Bill C-49, which contains the 1992 legislative amendments, is set out in full in Appendix B.

Two final non-legislative steps have been taken which will contribute to our understanding of the phenomenon of sexual assault. First, in 1991 the federal government created the Canadian Panel on Violence Against Women. This panel spent most of the year touring the country and listening to the voices of women who had been subjected to abuse, including sexual violence. It was the first time that a major government commission had addressed the issue of violence against women in Canadian society. A preliminary report was released in the summer of 1991; a final report was published in 1993.

VICTIM SURVEYS

In addition to the Canadian Panel, another initiative will also provide a unique research base on which to found further legislative reform. In 1993, the federal government conducted a major survey of women across Canada. The survey explored all forms of violence against women, including sexual assault.[11] The results of this Violence Against Women survey are to be published in 1994, and will provide sound empirical data regarding the nature and extent of aggression against women. As well, the Canadian Centre for Justice Statistics (located in Statistics Canada) recently released a report containing national sentencing statistics in the area of sexual assault (see Roberts and Grossman 1993). This is significant because Statistics Canada has not published sentencing statistics for some years now. In light of the extreme interest in sentencing practices, it is to be hoped that further publications containing sentencing information will follow.

Perhaps one of the most significant changes in this decade of lobbying and reform has been the recognition on the part of women's groups and legislators that there is no single voice that can express the concerns of all women. Although male violence against women may be universal, the reality of how that violence is lived is greatly affected by other factors including a woman's skin colour, economic status, sexual orientation, and physical and mental ability. The intense lobby efforts that followed the *Seaboyer* decision challenged the historically dominant voices of white middle-class, able-bodied women. The result was that immigrant women, sex-trade workers, women of colour, and women with disabilities were included in the decision-making process. The inclusion of these women ensured recognition of otherwise ignored realities. One such reality, long neglected by criminal justice professionals and academics, is the impact of sexual assault on women (as well as children and men) with disabilities. A study published by the Disabled Women's Network in the fall of 1991 found that '96.4% of women with disabilities who responded to the[ir] survey had been sexually assaulted and 42% had been sexually assaulted more than once.' Women with disabilities not only experience sexual assault more often than able-bodied women, but are also less likely to be believed by actors in the criminal justice system (charges were laid in only 14 per cent of these cases; 8 per cent of the cases went to court; 5 per cent of the accused were found guilty). It doesn't end there; as of 1990, only 14 per cent of transition houses and rape crisis centres in Canada were accessible to women who use wheelchairs and none were accessible to women with other types of disabilities.[12]

The decade that began in 1983 with the repeal of the rape laws and the creation of sexual assault legislation ended in 1992 with the legislative amendments defining consent and redefining when the victim's sexual history is relevant to the issue of whether she consented to the sexual act in question. The focus of this book therefore has been widened to include the significant changes that occurred within the last two years of this decade. New chapters were added and others substantially revised in order that this collection of work on sexual assault will reflect the changes that have taken place since 1983.

Contributions to This Volume

In this volume we have attempted to provide the reader with an idea of where things stand now, how we have come to this point, and where we should be going next to address the issue of sexual assault in Canada. The approach we have adopted is clearly multidisciplinary. The problems associated with sexual assault are not exclusively legal in nature. Accordingly the contributing authors in this volume represent the fields of law, sociology, criminology, and psychology – all have made significant contributions to an understanding of the phenomenon of sexual aggression. This is particularly important when one evaluates the impact of the 1983 reform legislation and the recent lobby efforts that followed the Supreme Court of Canada decision in *Seaboyer* in

1991. Understanding how the last decade of law reform has changed and will continue to change the processing of sexual assault cases requires a truly multidisciplinary approach.

It was not, nor could it have been, our intention to survey all the issues that have arisen since 1983. Given the number of issues and the complexities of the problems, that task would require several volumes. A recent bibliography (Roberts and Grossman 1991) of the sexual assault literature reveals the volume of work that has been written on this topic since 1977. Rather than survey the area, it was our intention to assemble a team of contributing authors who could write about the central issues in the field, and also discuss some issues that have to date received insufficient attention.

Although the contributing authors have approached the issue of sexual assault from a variety of perspectives, several common themes emerge. One of these is that there are clear limitations on the degree to which statutory revisions (such as Bill C-127) can effect changes in the behaviour of criminal justice personnel. Or, to place a more optimistic interpretation upon the research findings, it is clear that changes in responding to criminal sexual aggression cannot be wrought within a few years. Attitudes (and consequently, behaviour) take longer to change and may require efforts on a broader scale. That is to say, society itself must change before the criminal justice system will respond in a more positive way to cases of sexual assault.

It is also clear that according a wide degree of latitude to actors in the criminal justice system without clear guidance as to how to exercise that discretion has adverse consequences. We can see this occurring at all stages of the criminal justice system, beginning with the police and ending with the judiciary. The police, for example, are given few guidelines as to the initial classification of reports of sexual assault. And the judiciary exercise even more discretion at the sentencing stage, but without a great deal of guidance from the Criminal Code or the appellate courts.

Finally, it is obvious from almost every chapter in this volume that the issue of criminal sexual aggression can only be understood through an integrated approach that incorporates the sociological and legal perspectives. Future research and writing on this topic is, we believe, destined to approach sexual violence from a multidisciplinary perspective to a far greater extent than has been the case in the past.

One of the central aims of our collaborative effort in producing this volume has been to effect a rapprochement between different groups working in the area of sexual assault. All too frequently there is little dialogue between and among activists, academics, and policy-makers. And yet the struggle against sexual violence can only advance when there is a coordinated response from all these groups. Unless we hear the voices of women themselves, the sociolegal research can only tell us so much about the phenomenology of sexual violence and sexual exploitation. On the other hand, rigorous scientific research is also necessary both to inform policy-making and to ensure that resources are directed where the need is greatest. This volume contains contributions from a diversity of perspectives.

One of the central questions addressed in several chapters concerns the impact of the 1983 reform legislation. Rape reforms have now been implemented in a number of American states (see Galvin 1985). As well, in several of these jurisdictions evaluation research has been conducted (e.g., Horney and Spohn 1990; Marsh, Geist, and Caplan 1982). In this volume we present the results of systematic evaluation research on the Canadian reforms.

The chapters are the result of an iterative process of writing, consulting, and revising. In April 1991, a conference of the contributing authors was held in Ottawa. This meeting permitted participants to make contributions to other chapters, and to receive feedback upon their own chapters. After the meeting the process of revision and integration continued. The final versions reflect this process of integration.

The order of the chapters reflects our intention to present in sequence: the origins of the 1983 legislation; recent national trends in criminal justice statistics relating to sexual assault; how cases are processed; how judges have constructed 'sexual assault'; how judges determine the level of harm caused for purposes of sentencing; the particular problem of cultural bias in the sentencing of Inuit men convicted of sexual assault; and an alternative to relying on sentencing – the provision of civil compensation for people who have been sexually assaulted. The next three chapters describe the struggle between the courts and Parliament in determining the admissibility of sexual history evidence (before and after *Seaboyer*); provide an examination of sexual assault as an equality issue; and explore the consultation process that contributed to the 1992 legislative changes. The final chapter identifies research issues that should be given priority in future work on this topic.

In Chapter 2, Maria Łoś focuses on the origins of the 1983 legislation: she describes the struggle to redefine the offences of sexual aggression in Canada. In particular, her chapter details the role of women's groups in lobbying for change in this area. Łoś has examined policy briefs, as well as other official documents and transcripts of parliamentary debates. The role and image of women's groups as agents of social change are scrutinized. This chapter provides a thorough exploration of the process that eventually resulted in the sexual assault offences contained in the Criminal Code.

The next chapter, by Julian Roberts and Michelle Grossman, examines sexual assaults reported to the police across Canada. One of the most well-documented findings in the pre-reform era was the under-reporting of sexual offences. A clear goal of the 1983 legislation was to encourage a greater number of victims to report to the police. The national statistics presented in this chapter show that a significant increase in reporting took place at the time the legislation was passed. It appears then that the legislation was successful in achieving one of its aims, although as subsequent chapters reveal, the legislation has been less successful in terms of its other objectives, such as increasing the efficiency of the criminal justice response to cases of sexual aggression.

As noted earlier in this introduction, a topic that has attracted a great deal of public and professional attention recently is the issue of sexual assaults involving children. There has been a dramatic increase in the numbers of cases involving children reported to the police. In Chapter 4, Rita Gunn and Rick Linden report the results of a recent empirical study conducted in Manitoba on the processing of cases of child sexual abuse. While Bill C-127 was directed mainly at the treatment of adult victims of sexual assault, we clearly need to know more about offences against children. Gunn and Linden discuss some critical issues, such as the attrition rate of such cases as they proceed through the criminal justice system.

Scott Clark and Dorothy Hepworth, in Chapter 5, summarize some of the findings from the sexual assault evaluation conducted by the federal Department of Justice. As already noted, rape reform evaluations have been conducted in several American states. However, the Canadian research program was far broader and addressed more issues than any other evaluation to date. The Department of Justice conducted or commissioned research on the processing of sexual assault cases, on public knowledge of the new legislation, on sentencing patterns, on the reactions of victims, and on many other topics. The results indicate that while the criminal justice treatment of victims has improved, some critical statistics – such as the conviction rates – have not been affected by the reforms introduced in 1983.

Christine Boyle focuses upon the substantive law of sexual assault, that is, the judicial interpretations of the sexual assault sections contained in the Criminal Code. Her book, entitled *Sexual Assault* (1984), identified a number of issues that warranted exploring in the years following the passage of Bill C-127. In Chapter 6 of the present volume, she follows up some of the questions she raised regarding the substantive laws of sexual assault and considers judicial responses to those questions. Her legal analysis is explicitly rooted in its social context: she examines the meaning of sexuality or the meaning of consent in a world where heterosexual activity between social and economic unequals is the norm.

Although sentencing was not central to the 1983 reforms, it has dominated the public debate about sexual assault in the past few years. Unfortunately, we know little about sentencing in cases of sexual assault: national sentencing statistics have not been publicly available for several years now.[13] Chapter 7, by Renate Mohr, examines, for the first time, sentencing appeals in cases of sexual assault. These decisions can tell us a great deal about the kinds of sentences viewed as appropriate by courts of appeal across the country. As well, the analysis of the cases provides insight into the kinds of aggravating and mitigating factors endorsed at the appellate level.

The sentencing practices of some judges in courts in northern Canada have received considerable media attention over the past few years. In Chapter 8, Teressa Nahanee comments on some of the troubling issues surrounding the sexual assault of Inuit women and children in northern communities. In particular she looks at the judicial construction of a 'cultural defence' that has been challenged by Paktuutit, an organization representing Inuit women in Canada.

In Chapter 9, Elizabeth Sheehy discusses an important avenue of redress open to victims of sexual assault: compensation. The criminal law process, with its focus on the relationship between the state and the wrongdoer, rarely results in a compensation award for victims of crime. The chapter discusses the two avenues of redress that may result in monetary compensation for victims of sexual assault (civil litigation/'tort' and provincial criminal injuries compensation boards).

Adelyn Bowland, in Chapter 10, examines the issues surrounding the admissibility of evidence of the victim's sexual history in a sexual assault trial. She first reviews the history of the judge-made sexual character rules, then examines legislative amendments to these rules, and finally examines how *Seaboyer* and the most recent legislative amendments (1992) have again shifted the legal terrain.

In *Seaboyer*, the Supreme Court of Canada held that the legislative restrictions on past sexual history evidence breached an accused's section 7 Charter right to life, liberty, and security of the person and her or his section 11(d) right to a fair trial and that the breaches were not justified under section 1 of the Charter. In Chapter 11, Diana Majury explores the language of the majority and dissenting judgments in order to reveal the sex equality implications of the decision. The chapter reveals the limitations of traditional legal analysis in uncovering and challenging underlying assumptions of sexual equality.

Chapter 12 explores the historical consultation process that was initiated by the decision in *Seaboyer* and resulted in the 1992 legislative amendments.

Sheila McIntyre, as counsel for the Women's Legal Education and Action Fund (LEAF), was an active participant in the process, and in this chapter she provides her perspective on the consultation process. The story of the coalition of Canadian women is told in the hope that it will provoke new thinking about old debates concerning whether (and how) women and other historically disempowered groups should pursue egalitarian social change through law. She also brings back into the public view the fundamental basis of the coalition's approach – an approach rooted in and justified by Charter equality guarantees. One decade of reform ends with the efforts of this coalition, but another is about to begin.

In the last chapter, we provide some indication of what remains to be done in the area of sexual assault in Canada. As noted earlier, Bill C-127 was the first step toward reform, rather than the last word. Chapter 13 sets out some pressing research priorities in the hope of stimulating further research upon this vital topic.

Our volume concludes with a bibliography of recent publications on sexual assault in Canada (Appendix A), and a copy of the rape shield legislation (Bill C-49), which is contained in Appendix B. It is our intention that these documents will prove useful to researchers, practitioners, and anyone actively involved in the study of sexual assault.

Conclusion

Many aspects of the 1983 legislative reforms require further research and study. At the same time there are many implications of the 1992 reforms that need to be explored through careful sociolegal scholarship. This volume represents but one step in a lengthy process of evaluations and analysis. Although we fully recognize that legislative reform will never, in and of itself, eradicate sexual assault, we are conscious of the power of law and law reform to structure our understanding of, and our response to, crimes of sexual aggression. In this book we hope to raise some questions about the power of law and provide some 'answers' and empirical information wherever possible. We offer no solutions, but rather some suggestions as to how the law may ultimately work to help women and children 'take back the night' ... and the day.

Notes

1 For bibliographies, see for example, Lorna Doerkson, 'Women and Crime: A Bibli-

ography,' *Resources for Feminist Research* 13 (1985–6): 60; Susan Boyd and Elizabeth Sheehy, 'Feminist Perspectives on Law: Canadian Theory and Practice' *Canadian Journal of Women and the Law* 2 (1986): 1–52

2 (1984), 55 N.B.R. (2d) 97

3 (1987), 37 C.C.C. (3d) 97 (S.C.C.)

4 (1989), 51 C.C.C. (3d) 239

5 (1991), 3 S.C.R. 72 (S.C.C.)

6 There are of course other assault offences as well, including unlawfully causing bodily harm (s. 269) and assaulting a police officer (s. 270), but these account for a small percentage of the total number of assaults (see Canadian Centre for Justice Statistics 1992).

7 (1991), 66 C.C.C. (3d) 321 (S.C.C.)

8 Christie Jefferson, LEAF Lines, January 1992

9 See, for example, Martha Shaffer, '*Seaboyer* v. *R.*: A Case Comment,' *Canadian Journal of Women and the Law* 5(1) (1992).

10 Notes for an Address by the Honourable Kim Campbell, Minister of Justice on the Occasion of the Second Reading of Bill C-49, Ottawa, Ontario, 8 April 1992

11 For further information about the Violence against Women Survey, the reader is advised to contact Ms. Holly Johnson, at the Canadian Centre for Justice Statistics.

12 Disabled Women's Network Canada, 'Disabled Women and Bill C-49,' submitted to The Legislative Committee of Parliament on Bill C-49, 20 May 1992.

13 This is now changing. Two databases located at the Canadian Centre for Justice Statistics (The Adult Criminal Court Survey and the Youth Court Survey) collect dispositional data from several provinces, with the remainder to be added in the near future.

References

Badgley, R., et al. 1984. *Report of the Committee on Sexual Offences Against Children and Youths.* Ottawa: Supply and Services Canada

Boyle, C. 1984. *Sexual Assault.* Toronto: Carswell

Canadian Centre for Justice Statistics. 1992. *Canadian Crime Statistics. 1991.* Ottawa: Supply and Services Canada

Clark, L., and D. Lewis. 1977. *Rape: The Price of Coercive Sexuality.* Toronto: The Women's Press

Dawson, T.B. 1985. 'Legal Structures: A Feminist Critique of Sexual Assault Reform' *Resources for Feminist Research* 14:40

Galvin, J. 1985. 'Rape: A Decade of Reform'. *Crime and Delinquency* 31:163–9

Horney, J., and C. Spohn. 1990. *The Impact of Rape Reform Legislation*. Washington, DC: National Institute of Justice

Marsh, J., A. Geist, and N. Caplan. 1982. *Rape and the Limits of Law Reform*. Boston: Auburn House

Roberts, J., and M. Grossman. 1991. *Sexual Assault: An Annotated Bibliography with Special Emphasis on Canadian Research*. Ottawa: Crime and Justice Research Centre

Watt, D. 1984. *The New Offences Against the Person: The Provisions of Bill C-127*. Toronto: Butterworths

2

MARIA ŁOŚ

The Struggle to Redefine Rape
in the Early 1980s[1]

Several of the chapters in this volume deal with the effects of the 1983 reform legislation (Bill C-127 – see Chapter 1 of this volume). For example, Scott Clark and Dorothy Hepworth (Chapter 5) examine the impact of the reform upon the processing, by the Canadian criminal justice system, of sexual assault cases. It is important, however, to understand first the nature of the law reform, and the sociolegal context from which the reform emerged. This is the purpose of the present chapter. Maria Łoś examines the pre-reform legislation, and then presents an analysis of the actual rape reform, based upon her study of background documents, parliamentary debates, committee testimony, and related materials. She focuses upon the struggle that emerged as various groups attempted to redefine the crime of rape. Łoś concludes that, on balance, the rape reform has neither facilitated the task of dismantling the patriarchal society, nor seriously prejudiced it.

Like any other crime, rape is socially constructed. It has been assigned different definitions across time, space, and diverse cultures, and it is being constructed daily through multiple interpretations by the victims, police, lawyers, juries, judges, the mass media, and many other actors and agencies. While all socially constructed reality is influenced by past and present gender relations, dominant definitions of rape are likely to epitomize the key features of historically specific relations of gender domination and subordination.

It says volumes about our forefathers and their relative position to our foremothers, that they used to define rape as a property crime whereby compensation was paid to the woman's rightful owner, be it her father, or her husband. Their evaluation of a woman's worth and their attitudes toward women's feelings are revealed through such cultural practices as the duty imposed on the assailant (in the Hebrew tradition) to marry his previously chaste victim (see, for example, Brownmiller 1975, Clark and Lewis 1977, Schwendinger and Schwendinger 1982). Even when rape was eventually recognized as a crime against the woman, the binding codes of language and etiquette often prevented victims from giving testimony in court as it was not proper for women to refer to human anatomy and sexual matters in public (Clark 1987).

As has already been well documented, the history of rape is also a history of the devaluation and stigmatization of the victim. Modern-day rape laws and cultural interpretations appear to carry the vestiges of old traditions. In this chapter, the law reform process in Canada in the early 1980s will be examined in order to assess whether a clean break with the past can in fact be achieved within the legal discourse of a gender-stratified society.

Being an ultimate expression of gender conflict, the act of rape is particularly susceptible to cultural-ideological interpretations instrumental to the interests of the gender groups involved. One of the most powerful ways of symbolically defining an act is to include it in the body of the official law. In this way it helps protect, reinforce, and sometimes change prevailing sociopolitical relations. Given the fact that legal language, the legislature, and the judiciary have traditionally been a male domain, it can safely be assumed that the process of the legal construction of the crime of rape has been shaped by ideological and cultural perceptions and assumptions that are shared by men rather than by both men and women. It is, therefore, the interests of men rather than women that are likely to be addressed by the resultant legal definitions. These interests can be conceptualized in terms of strategies that maintain a group's status.

The maintenance of the dominant group's status requires the utilization of cultural and political resources (including law) to project the notion of legitimacy and natural permanency of the group's position within the existing power structure as well as the rectitude and benevolence of the power itself. The group's image (consistent with its rank within the hierarchy) must be symbolically affirmed, possibly through conveying an impression that the subordinate group – due to its special deficiencies or dispositions – has justifiably been relegated to a lower status.

A number of feminist scholars have explored the dichotomous mode of thinking prevalent in traditional philosophy and science (especially since the Enlightenment) (see, for example Griffin 1978, Harding 1986, Hartsock 1987). They have traced some typical expressions of this dualism, in the dominant (male) scholarly discourse: mind/body, abstract/concrete, culture/nature, rational/irrational, truth/falsehood, objective/ subjective, independent/dependent, knower/known, self/other, subject/object, active/passive, free-will/predestination. Maleness and femaleness have been systematically constructed in reference to these dual principles, whereby the first feature in each pair has been assigned superiority and associated with maleness.[2] In each dichotomy, 'the former is to control the latter lest the latter threaten to overwhelm the former' (Harding 1986, 165).

These dichotomous mental patterns have structured and conditioned our way of thinking and – even more important – our ways of knowing.[3] Within the Western tradition it has been a male task to explore, describe, and subjugate the external world. The very goal of science – to enable men to manage diverse and scarce resources – has led to the hegemony of epistemological positivism in social and human sciences. An external efficacy of an order based on subjugation became a proof of the 'objective' truth on which it was founded. Accordingly, women's relegation to the 'wrong' side of the human dichotomy became, in turn, a source of 'objective' data on the fruitfulness and correctness of dichotomous thinking.

In rape, both the male side of the dichotomy (the man as a free-willed subject, active, independent, knower) and the female side (the woman as body, object, known (carnally), passive, dependent) are clearly apparent. With the social construct of rape approaching so closely the fundamental gender dichotomy on which the whole modern patriarchal culture rests, a task of devising a suitable interpretation must have presented a considerable challenge to male moralists, legislators, and politicians. Quite ingeniously, an understanding has been advanced of rape as a mindless act, brought about by lust and passion, which, when not controlled by reason, reduces a man to the level of an animal. The rapist has been defined as belonging to a separate species, a mad or feeble-minded creature, profoundly sick, pathological, monstrous. The rape victim has also had to be constructed, her subjectivity engineered for her, her social status defined. If the woman is her body, then rape devalues her as a woman. If rape is an animal act, the female must have sent some sexual signals – common in animal mating practices – which stirred the attacker's primitive instincts. If she has been sexually penetrated by a beast, she becomes impure, less human herself.

There can be no doubt that the ramifications of any culturally accepted definition of rape are far-reaching. But no definition can stand on its own. It must be validated by the prevailing ways in which gender is constructed, and thus masculinity and femininity defined, in the given society. Consequently, the efforts of women's groups to redefine rape are not really about the relabelling of crimes of sexual aggression, but about the conceptual underpinnings that have sustained old definitions of rape, the rapist, and the victim.

In this chapter, I describe first the definition of rape and legal concepts contained in the Canadian Criminal Code's sections on sexual aggression prior to their reform in 1983. I try to assess whether and in what explicit and implicit ways this law projected images and symbolic messages instrumental to the male status maintenance. In the second section I examine the debates preceding the enactment of the new law on sexual assault introduced *inter alia* to satisfy demands of the feminist lobby. The third section explores the philosophy and expectations of the latter and attempts to assess the outcomes of the reform process. In the fourth section, I analyse the efforts of women's groups to redefine rape on their own terms and try to assess the viability of utilizing the law on rape to project women's interests and enhance their status. I point to several reasons why women's groups were not able to detach the issue of rape from the dominant male gender ideology.

The Canadian Rape Law Prior to the 1983 Reform: Its Symbolic Content

The normative messages projected by the law dealing with sexual aggression prior to 1983[4] reflect the gender dichotomy and cultural perceptions of gender relations that were functional to the male status maintenance. The most important of these messages are listed below. They are only briefly discussed because there already exists an abundance of publications on the sexist nature of Canadian rape laws and similar legal enactments in other countries (for example, Borgida 1981, Boyle 1984, Brownmiller 1975, Clark and Lewis 1977, Goldsmith Kasinsky 1978, Le Grand 1973, Schwartz and Clear 1980, Snider 1985).

THE PATRIARCHAL MARRIAGE MUST BE PROTECTED

This was reflected in four ways:

(a) Husbands were granted unlimited access to their wives' sexuality/body.[5]

(b) To qualify as rape, a sexual attack had to involve a heterosexual penetration. This requirement suggests that within the old law the loss of virginity or the possibility that the woman (i.e., wife, daughter) might conceive a child outside marriage was more important than her own definition of sexual violence, which could include forced oral sexual acts, penetration with foreign objects, and so forth.

(c) The law penalized sexual intercourse with a female of 14 to 16 years of age, of previously chaste character (s. 146), and seduction of a female of 16 to 18 years of age, of previously chaste character (s. 151). The harm was thus measured in terms of the loss of virginity, thereby reinforcing the assumption that the latter determines women's bargaining power in the marital market.

(d)   A man who seduced a young virgin under a false promise of marriage was guilty of an indictable offence (s. 152). This implies that women were presumed to be weaker and dependent partners in a relationship and that marriage presented to them a supreme opportunity. While historically true, the reality of women's subordinate status was presented in this law as unproblematic, a fact of life to be taken into consideration in order to protect (and maintain) the delicate balance between unequal gender positions.

WOMEN ARE MORALLY UNDERDEVELOPED

This was reflected in two ways:

(a)   Women's testimony under oath could not be trusted. Thus, the judge was obliged to inform the jury that it would not be safe to convict solely on the basis of the rape complainant's testimony; such warnings were required otherwise only in cases of testimony by children (for interesting examples of such warnings, see Temkin 1987, 133–7).

(b)   A peculiar clause of the recent complaint requirement invalidated rape complaints that were not made immediately after the attack, since otherwise the woman would have had enough time to fabricate the incident. This supported a stereotype of women as being by nature deceitful and manipulative (Pollak, 1961:8-10). It also reflected the prevailing moral double standard which lent credibility to the suspicion that women would rather 'cry rape' than have their reputation tarnished by allegations of consensual, but extramarital sex.

WOMEN'S CREDIBILITY DEPENDS ON HER SEXUAL REPUTATION, WHILE MEN'S DOES NOT

Before 1983, it was possible to use information on the complainant's sexual conduct and reputation in assessing her credibility.[6] On the other hand, information about the accused's past convictions – including those for rape and other sexual offences – was inadmissible when evaluating his testimony unless he took the stand. While the latter is of course a standard provision in criminal trials, one may ask why the past sexual activity of the woman was considered more relevant to her credibility than the history of sexual violence was to the accused's credibility. This imbalance is of tremendous consequence in rape trials where the case often rests on 'her word against his.'

SOME WOMEN DO NOT DESERVE LEGAL PROTECTION, AND MEN ARE ENTITLED TO TAKE ADVANTAGE OF THIS

Prior to the 1975–76 amendments,[7] women were in practice deprived of a right to refuse sexual access to some men if they had granted it liberally to others. The complainant's sexual conduct with men other than the accused was considered crucial in establishing whether she had in fact consented to the act. The underlying rationale appears to be that men should be able to safely assume that some women are available to all of them without discrimination, that they are in fact common male property. Once a woman is believed to have crossed the symbolic 'madonna–whore' line, her body is to serve men in the ways functional to maintaining the existing familial and gender arrangements.

FEMALE SEXUALITY IS COMPLEMENTARY TO, AND DEFINED BY, MALE SEXUALITY

This was reflected in three ways:

(a) The requirement of penetration by the man's sexual organ defined it as the only instrument with which a woman's body could be sexually violated.

(b) A unique usage of the legal concept of consent underlines the pre-1983 law's definition of intercourse as rape when the woman's consent was 'extorted by threats or fear of bodily harm' (s. 143). Insistence on using the term 'consent' to describe 'non-consent' reflected well the stereotypical male perception that a woman could not really be raped totally against her will: she must somehow have consented, even if out of fear. Implicitly, every rape victim is thus perceived as a participant in sexual intercourse rather than a victim of coercive violation.[8]

(c) The very definition of rape as sexual intercourse suggests a purely male perspective. For women, intercourse requires mutuality, which by defi-

nition is absent in rape. Its victims are unlikely to call their victimization
an example of intercourse. Yet the inclusion of the term in the definition
of rape warranted interrogation of the complainant by defence lawyers
as to the amount of pleasure she experienced and the extent of her cooperation.

These symbolic messages were further reinforced in the course of the interpretation and implementation of the rape law, which allowed for the dismissal
of a majority of complaints (CACSW 1981, 3, 28–35; Clark and Lewis 1977;
Minch et al. 1987; for non-Canadian sources, see Box 1983, 120–64; Chappell
et al. 1977; Hindelang and Davis 1977; LaFree 1980, 1989; Renner and Sahjpaul 1986; Temkin 1986, 20–4). They also allowed selection for prosecution
of those cases principally where the accused could be classified as a sexual
deviant or an outright social misfit. Consequently, any suggestion of a possible connection between rape and the culturally prescribed male sexuality was
easily countered with legally produced 'facts.'

In short, instead of controlling sexual violence against women, the law
reinforced the informal control of women and helped to perpetuate the ideological premises of the traditional gender-based order.

The Sexual Assault Law of 1983: Its Ultimate Purpose

The sexual assault law, promulgated on 1 January 1983, was preceded by a
prolonged campaign by feminist writers and women's organizations. Despite
frequent official references to women's demands as a uniform entity[9] – as if
women could speak only with a single voice and were not capable of disagreements – several women's groups put forward different proposals that varied
in their degree of adherence to the internal conventions and principles of the
extant legal system. Eventually, however, most groups accepted the proposal
submitted to Parliament by the National Association of Women and the Law
(NAWL) (Macdonald 1982, 13–16), which had the endorsement of the
National Action Committee on the Status of Women (NAC). The Association
supported in principle Bill C-53[10] introduced by the minister of Justice in January 1981, but strongly disagreed with several specific clauses both in the initial bill and in its final, amended version (Bill C-127) (see NAWL 1979, 1981,
1982a, b).

The sudden pressure from the Department of Justice to reform the law on
rape after years of inaction may be explained by factors other than a belated
but genuine recognition of the demands of the women's lobby. The enactment, in 1982, of the Canadian Charter of Rights and Freedoms (as part of

the Constitution Act) was bound to lead to constitutional challenges to those parts of the law that were likely to fail the equal rights test. In particular, section 15 of the Charter granted right to equality without discrimination on the basis of sex, and section 28 determined that 'notwithstanding anything in this Charter, the rights and freedoms referred to in it are guaranteed equally to male and female persons.' The Criminal Code had to be carefully screened and all signs of sex discrimination corrected before the three-year moratorium on section 15 expired. The Criminal Code's sections on sexual aggression were an obvious area of concern, with their clearly discriminatory vocabulary and unusual procedures. Furthermore, the existence of an organized women's movement made challenges under the new Charter virtually inevitable. The new sophistication and strength of the movement were demonstrated convincingly in the lobbying effort to ensure the passage of section 28 of the Charter (Baines 1988, de Jong 1985, Hosek 1983, Keet 1985).

Following the failure in 1978 of an earlier bill (C-52), drafted by the Progressive Conservative Cabinet, and prior to the enactment of the Charter, the issue of a new rape law seemed to have disappeared from the agenda of the Department of Justice in spite of intensive pressure from women lobbyists and the release of a major report by the Law Reform Commission of Canada (1978b). With the change of government, a new bill was promised in the Speech from the Throne in April 1980; the promise was repeated later by the minister of Justice in the House of Commons on several occasions (House of Commons Debates 1980, 1741, 3685). It was, however, only in January 1981 that Bill C-53 was introduced in the House. Moreover, it proved to be an exceptionally chaotic and inconsistent document. Six months passed before the motion to proceed to second reading was made on behalf of the minister of Justice (Jean Chrétien), on 7 July 1981, literally in the last days before the summer recess. The minister, who did not present the motion in person, was also absent during most of the subsequent debates. This created a negative climate and some scepticism concerning the federal Department's commitment. Ray Hnatyshyn, Justice Critic for the Official Opposition (Progressive Conseratives), described the bill as 'a kind of sausage factory production' (House of Commons Debates 1981, 11,305) and attacked the Department for the low priority it gave to the long-awaited legislation:

I am very much concerned that what is happening here is somewhat of a charade. The government has introduced this bill in the dying moments of this part of the session, late at night, an afterthought after a number of less important bills ... I really wonder whether this will get the attention it should get in terms of the public media ... I am very disappointed in the way it has been handled and in the lack of priority ... That the minister did not even think it important enough to appear in the House at any time that this matter has been discussed (11,345).

While the Department of Justice presented the reform as legally necessary, it kept changing and amending the bill throughout the parliamentary process, thereby generating much confusion and dissatisfaction among the members. On some occasions, they were even unsure which version they were discussing. It was also extremely difficult for outside groups and organizations to monitor the process and exert pressure. This was brought to the attention of the minister by Margaret Mitchell (New Democratic Party) during the debates of the Standing Committee on Justice and Legal Affairs on 22 April 1982:

I think it should be noted that the National Action Committee on the Status of Women ... – and that group represents well over 200 women's organizations across Canada – had a very serious concern that there would be enough time allowed for women's groups to be involved as witnesses in the discussions (House of Commons Standing Committee 1982, vol. 77, 55).

Parliamentary debates on Bill C-53 were only in part devoted to the reform of rape and indecent assault sections. The bill also included certain other sexual offences, offences against young persons, procuring, and vagrancy. Speakers tended to shift from one issue to another and many did not comment on the proposed sexual assault sections at all. As a result, debates in the House of Commons and parliamentary committees were unfocused and confusing. Not surprisingly, a great deal of parliamentary time was taken up by postulates to split the original bill into more coherent and manageable pieces, complaints about the irresponsibility of the minister of Justice, and disagreements about procedure. In the end, however, no agreement was achieved on those other sections of the proposed bill, and a new bill (C-127) was introduced that focused mostly on (sexual) assault offences that were deemed less controversial. Compared with the highly morally charged issues of child pornography, group sex, buggery, or bestiality, the proposed rape law reform appeared to be of a more technical, legal nature.

It may be argued that the amendments finally enacted consisted of the necessary minimum required to make the law on sexual aggression compatible with the Charter rather than being a sincere attempt to address the concerns of women. The underlying motive for the proposed reform was explained in the Standing Senate Committee by the legal counsel to the Department of Justice:

The bill attempts to reconcile the law on sexual offences with the rest of the criminal law and to bring it back into keeping or into the same stream with the rest of the criminal law (Senate of Canada 1982, vol. 2, 19).

The elimination of sex discrimination was one of the two basic principles of Bill C-53 in so far as it dealt with sexual aggression against adults (the other one being the protection of the integrity of the person) (House of Commons Debates 1981, 11,300).[11] Accordingly, as explained by Mr. Chrétien,

an effort has been made throughout the bill to degenderize the Criminal Code provisions relating to sexual offences in keeping with the equality rights guaranteed by the Charter of Rights (House of Commons Debates 1982, 20039).

Therefore, by including female offenders but, more important, male homosexual rape, the definition of sexual violation had to be changed and could no longer be limited to the traditional understanding of sexual intercourse.[12] Since a whole range of sexual activities had to be covered, the term 'rape' was no longer appropriate, and 'sexual assault' – suggested by both women's groups and the Law Reform Commission – appeared to be a good substitute. It allowed for a multi-tiered offence to account for different degrees of severity.[13]

Furthermore, with rape classified as a type of assault, inquiries into the complainant's sexual conduct with people other than the accused became harder to justify. They were, therefore, further restricted in response to the pressure from the women's lobby and persistent efforts by the NDP Justice Critic, Svend Robinson.[14]. As well, under the Charter, it was clearly no longer feasible to discriminate against married women. And this is exactly how the minister of Justice introduced in the House of Commons the proposal to repeal the 'spousal immunity':

The Criminal Code must not continue to deny persons equal protection because of their marital status especially in light of the new Charter of Rights and Freedoms (House of Commons Standing Committee 1982, 29).

The peculiar usage of the term 'consent' had to be corrected simply because – as explained by the federal Department of Justice representative – 'at common law you do not have consent if it is not predicated upon a voluntary act' (Senate of Canada 1982, 35). Similarly, the rules of evidence had to be made consistent with those for comparable offences. The 'recent complaint' requirement and the special rules of corroboration could no longer be sustained. The legal inconsistency of the latter rules were highlighted in the Senate by the departmental official:

Generally speaking, in our criminal law if a crime is committed and there is just one witness to the crime, then the evidence of that one witness is sufficient, if believed, to convict. But in the past the idea developed that in certain circumstances a rule should be applied that there had to be evidence tending to support the evidence of the witness ... Unfortunately, classified or lumped together under that heading were children ... people of limited capacity, and complainants in sexual cases, which usually meant women (Senate of Canada 1982, vol. 25, 19).

Likewise, he called the 'recent complaint' doctrine an anomaly, 'because such a doctrine is not required for any other type of criminal offence' (Senate of Canada 1982, vol. 25, 20).

However, neither he nor anyone else recorded in the hundreds of pages of the minutes of the parliamentary debates made an attempt to address the question of why it was that women happened to be 'lumped together' with children and the mentally retarded, and why all these blatantly discriminatory rules were applied to them in a country proud of its egalitarian traditions. And no one asked what kind of damage was done to *women as a group* as a result of the bias in the law, quite explicit in its design to enforce the gender hierarchy.

The Problems and Promises of the Rape Law Reform

Once the rape law reform campaign was over and the new sexual assault law promulgated, an old problem resurfaced: What could be done about rape (see, for example, Heald 1985)? If the law reform addressed this issue at all, it was in a very indirect way. A reasonable argument can be made that in the long run, the change of a sexist law contributes to a reduction in the overall sexism within the society and thus erodes the misogynistic culture that contributes to male violence and sexual aggression toward women. On the other hand, the claim most often made by women's groups – that the law reform will increase the willingness of victims to report and enhance successful prosecution – does not seem to be in any obvious way related to a likely reduction in sexual victimization of women.

This leads to an intriguing question: If criminal law reform cannot really make any difference in terms of victimization levels (at least for such crimes as rape), is it worthwhile – or is it even justified – to engage in it? Clearly, the answer depends on the definition of the problem that campaigners want to address. What was perhaps misleading in the lobbying process preceding the rape law reform of the early 1980s was the crime prevention rhetoric. This created an impression that something was actually being done about rape itself and might even have diverted attention and resources from relevant social and educational policies that had been advanced by many feminists.

Rape cannot be explained apart from the dominant culture and structure with their distinct gender roles and power relations. The focus of women's groups on the criminal law reform blurred this connection and reinforced an individualized view of rape. While the feminist campaign gave sexual violence against women new visibility, its legal objectives might have distorted the message. To the extent, however, that the law itself was defined as a part of the problem, the legal reform stood on a firmer ground. If a law is positively harmful it is quite logical to try either to abolish or change it. Since it would be quite hazardous to start the dismantling of the criminal law by decriminalizing those offences that victimize predominantly women, a revision of the existing law may be the only option. This can only be achieved through the legal, legislative channels, a longstanding male domain, permeated by symbols of male culture and deep-seated hostility toward women. The viability of such a project can be assessed through an analysis of women's involvement in the rape law reform campaign from a perspective that views the specific law itself as a problem and a source of harm, quite apart from the crime problem it purports to address.

Women's groups criticized the pre-1983 law on at least three grounds:

1 It sent symbolic messages that contributed to the maintenance of patriarchy.
2 It was biased against victims (women).
3 It precluded efficient enforcement.

The actual reform addressed all these aspects.

SYMBOLIC MESSAGES

On the symbolic level, a change in terminology from rape and indecent assault to sexual assault was designed to send a message that sexual aggression toward women should be viewed as a crime of violence and domination rather than lust or passion. This was also underscored by the transfer of these crimes from the Criminal Code's part on sexual offences and public morals to the part dealing with offences against the person. These changes have a particular importance as indicative of a shift from viewing the woman as body to perceiving her as a person.

The focus on the legal relabelling, however, may create a fiction that somehow the sexual degradation of women, integral to the traditional notion of rape, has been reduced, or is going to be reduced, by the changed label. On the one hand, it is true that the new label more easily locates the offender within the broader culture that promotes and perpetuates patterns of male domination over women and increasingly associates sex with violence. On the other hand, however, through this concept, women's experience of rape as a *sexual* violation is deliberately minimized.[15]

Following Foucault, many feminist writers point to the socially constructed nature of sexuality. Winifred Woodhull (1988) notes that

the experience of rape as a *sexual* assault is inevitable in a culture where many forces converge to define women as essentially sexual beings. Because women do not merely apprehend this definition as something alien imposed from the outside, but live it concretely, sexuality, like power, is central to the experience of rape (172; italics in original).

In fact, sexuality is saturated with power, while being overtly culturally defined as a sphere of natural, free, spontaneous, personal expression (Foucault 1978). The social perception of rape necessarily depends on a social construction of sexuality. By implication, the victim's feelings are a part of her concrete cultural experience and participation in the world, shaped by certain historically specific institutions and discourses. It has been amply documented how contemporary woman's relation to her body has been influenced and indeed manufactured by modern professional and commercial discourses. Perhaps now more than ever women are identified and identify themselves as bodies despite their struggle against the constraints of the traditional opposition between mind (the masculine) and body (the feminine). Sandra Lee Bartky (1988) points to some aspects of this problem:

As modern industrial societies change and as women themselves offer resistance to patriarchy, older forms of domination are eroded. But new forms arise, spread, and become consolidated ... normative femininity is coming more and more to be centered on woman's body – not its duties and obligations or even its capacity to bear children, but its sexuality, more precisely, its presumed heterosexuality and its appearance. There is of course nothing new in women's preoccupation with youth and beauty. What is new is the growing power of the image in a society increasingly oriented toward the visual media ... New too is the spread of this discipline to all classes of women and its deployment throughout the life cycle (81).

The change of terminology from the gender-specific rape to gender-neutral sexual assault may be interpreted as a conscious attempt to reorient not only the manner in which sexual aggression is perceived but also the way in which it is experienced. This approach can hardly be seen solely as an attempt to educate men. It inevitably redefines the subjective experience of victims, by recognizing that their sexuality and femininity have been socially constructed in a way that makes them particularly vulnerable to sexual objectification and stigmatization. This is a precarious stand in so far as it questions or even disqualifies the woman's subjectivity, and therefore – unwittingly – may heighten her alienation and self-perception as mindless object, victim, body.

But for women to refrain from any influence upon cultural construction and deployment of sexuality may not be a good option either. Vikki Bell (1991) makes an interesting observation about the difference between the approach elaborated by Foucault and that adopted by feminists involved in rape law reforms:

Foucault seems to be arguing in the debate on rape that we should refuse to see the sex of our bodies, i.e. the genitalia, as anything more than or different from another part of the body ... To treat rape as a sexual crime separates it out from other crimes of violence against the body and colludes in this sense with the deployment of sexuality (Bell 1991, 87). Whereas Foucault argues that rape is not about sex in order to *escape* power's operations which, he argues, are discursively marking the body, the feminist work in the 1970s argued that rape was not about sex in order to *reveal* and *highlight* the power relations and politics that are involved in rape ... They argued that rape is not about sex but is, instead, about power (90, italics added).

While this is an important concern, the élitist tendency to impose the concepts worked out by a few feminists upon all women remains questionable and may add to the oppression and devaluation of some women. Furthermore, a systematic desexualization of rape might actually obscure the relationship between male power, violence, and sex so actively promoted and glorified by modern media culture.

As well, a one-sided stress on the violence involved might inadvertently send a message that only really brutal attacks are criminal and that sexual imposition itself is of little consequence. The purely physical harm may become the measure of crime seriousness.[16] Yet feminist reformers themselves, aware of the reality of the male control of the courts of law, felt compelled to argue against the inclusion of psychological or emotional harm as a part – alongside bodily harm – of the definition of the second (and possibly third) level of sexual assault. The argument presented in the Senate by the spokesperson for the NAC illustrates well this attitude: 'It would be a woman again who was put through all kinds of psychological tests and again put on trial' (Senate of Canada 1982, vol. 27, 24). These fears are echoed by the speaker for a rape crisis centre:

Although ... there are some psychologically very serious consequences of rape, where some women take many years to recover, for the purpose of the criminal justice system I think that to include psychological damage would be more of a problem than a benefit (Senate of Canada 1982, vol. 27, 24).

Paradoxically, just when feminist research on the rape trauma has finally brought to light its horrifying dimensions, the biases of the legal system moved women to deny its suitability as a factor in assessing the level of seriousness of the offence.[17]

Another powerful message sent by the sexual assault legislation is that of sexual assault as a gender-neutral crime. This is consistent with the feminist reformers' wish to challenge the tendency to perceive women as the only possible victims of sexual aggression, as if their sexuality predestined them and only them for the fate of rape victims.

Yet the new degenderized approach negates an argument that many women feel comfortable with, namely that rape is a very unique crime in that it involves predominately victimization of members of one gender group by members of the other. It is intrinsic to the broader structure of culturally legitimized gender hierarchy. The eradication of the explicit male bias is thus achieved at the cost of the preservation of the implicit, historically entrenched bias and the exclusion of a possibility of exceptional affirmative measures needed to secure a fair treatment of women. Women's perception of the world as gender-stratified is replaced by the legal construct of the gender-neutral world.[18]

A narrower reading of the degenderization effort may imply that all that the reform has achieved was the extension of the scope of the law to include the possibility of convicting women for all offences of sexual aggression, making them more, not less vulnerable to social control.[19] It is noteworthy that homosexual assault was only vaguely alluded to in Parliament,[20] while the applicability of the new law to female offenders was emphasized by the minister of Justice on several occasions, especially to counter any proposals that would allegedly limit the rights of the accused (House of Commons Standing Committee 1982, vol. 77, 39, 46).

The degenderization of the rape law was an easy way to comply with the equality clauses of the Charter. As suggested by Christine Boyle (1984, 31–42), however, a more difficult and ambitious interpretation of the latter may be imagined, whereby the law would actually undertake to provide equal protection of men and women from unwanted interference. Under this understanding, the gender-specific reality of actual risk would have to be recognized and the causes of the prevailing pattern of victimization addressed. It is unlikely, however, that this could be achieved through the criminal law. Its repressive nature hardly allows for positive action. Attempts to account for the actually existing inequality through formal constructs of the criminal law would only petrify this inequality into a formula legitimating it as a natural frame of reference.[21]

In sum, the law on sexual assault refrains from the overt sexism characteristic of the former rape law. Married women are no longer presented as the sexual property of their husbands.[22] Neither are sexually liberated women assumed to be a common male property (although the new law continued to allow some evidence as to the sexual conduct of the victim). Complainants are not presumed *a priori* to be mendacious and morally suspect. Victims of sexual aggression are not automatically assumed to be female. And female sexuality is no longer defined exclusively by male sexuality. This new, nonsexist image of sexual aggression has come at some cost, however. It may be argued that the degenderization and partial desexualization of the former crime of rape have disguised the omnipresent reality of fear of rape among women (almost nonexistent among heterosexual men) and put into question the validity of rape victims' subjective sense of their femininity and sexual identity. Moreover, through the artificial, legal construct of gender-neutrality, the actual economic and social content of heterosexual relations and the related victimization of women have been effectively obscured.

BIAS AGAINST VICTIMS

Another problem the rape law reform attempted to correct was the cruel treatment of victims by the criminal justice system, which was not only permitted but even encouraged by the old law. For most women's groups as well as for the Department of Justice officials (and many legislators) this appeared to be a major concern. All records studied (briefs, minutes of parliamentary debates, etc.) show a relatively high level of sensitivity to victims' ordeal in court.

In so far as sexual assault offences are defined mostly in nonsexual terms and are analogous to nonsexual assault offences, the reformed law was supposed to put less pressure on the victim, and reduce the humiliation and sexual objectification she was bound to suffer under the old law. Moreover, while

rape was socially constructed as a shameful crime, which devalued and stigmatized the victim, the changed definition conceptualized sexual aggression
as an attack against the person, a violent act that happened to be expressed in
sexual terms.

There was some disagreement, also among women's groups, whether a
definition of the adjective 'sexual' should be provided by the law to assure
consistent application. Many members of Parliament found it unacceptable to
leave the crucial word undefined, and some suggested that a suitable definition could be relatively easily devised. Mr. Blaine A. Thacker argued, for
example, that in the absence of an explicit definition,

many situations ... might arise that may result in convictions that Parliament would
not want, or vice versa. Surely with the collective wisdom of cabinet, Parliament and
the skilled bureaucracy, along with all the witnesses who come forward, we should be
able to arrive at a proper definition (House of Commons Debates 1981, 14,188).

Women's groups were facing a frustrating choice between a possible definition devised by almost exclusively male government officials and legislators, on the one hand, and courtroom interpretations developed by judges,[23]
almost all of whom were male. There was, however strong scepticism about
the feasibility of formulating an *a priori* definition. From the woman's perspective, the sexual aspects of behaviour cannot be defined by body parts or
the purely physical characteristics of the acts performed. What makes an
assault sexual is not intrinsic to the act, but is derived from the specific circumstances and the interpretation of the processes involved.

Despite the lack of a formal definition of sexual assault in the 1983 law,
however, the specific nature of sexual acts remains extremely important in
the practice of the courts and the complainant has to answer questions
focused directly on those aspects. The presence or absence of vaginal penetration remains an extremly important consideration in sentencing (Baril et al.
1989, 64, 138, 190). Evidence of the complainant's sexual conduct with people
other than the accused may still be allowed under certain circumstances[24]
(which have been further expanded in 1992 – see Chapter 1) and there are
virtually no restrictions on evidence related to previous sexual relations with
the accused. The lack of consent must be proven, and the accused may still be
acquitted if the jury decides that he honestly, even if mistakenly, believed
that the victim consented.[25]

The victim's experience in court continues to depend on the nature and circumstances of the case. It may still be extremely humiliating and traumatic,
especially when her sense of having been sexually assaulted does not fit the

'common (male) sense' perception of the 'real' victim and 'real' sexual assault. The changed rules do not automatically remove the blame and the stigma traditionally attached to the victim, because they cannot change the way women, and not just rape victims, are viewed within the institutional culture of the society. Far from being neutral, the law remains a vehicle for expression of the dominant cultural patterns that identify male sexuality with female subordination.

Susan Estrich (1987) commented on the post-reform experience in the United States:

Many courts remain suspicious of women victims and protective of male defendants in ... cases that do not involve weapons or beatings; that are concerned with friends, neighbours, or pickups: the cases of simple rape (57–8).

The force doctrine is so efficient a vehicle for screening out the simple rape and imposing blame on the woman victim that it leads one to question whether the reform effort wasn't limited to preventing humiliating questions (80).

The changed wording and procedures of the law cannot bridge the historical chasm between male and female subjectivities:

Gender neutrality suggests that rape law can be made and enforced without regard to the different ways men and women understand force and consent ... But all experience suggests that if there is only one standard, it will be a male standard (82).

Even before the reform, women victims of 'real rapes' (see Estrich 1987, LaFree 1989, Sebba and Cahan 1973) were treated by the justice system with some restraint, and the question of consent or desire to be raped were usually deemed inappropriate in cases of brutal attacks by strangers against 'respectable' women. It was in 'other' rapes that women complainants were submitted to much harsher treatment and persistently branded as liars. By promoting reporting and thus encouraging a greater number of such cases to enter the criminal justice system, the reform has perhaps increased rather than decreased the overall victim exposure to the humiliating police and court tactics, the new rules on evidence and procedure notwithstanding. While the police statistics show a dramatic increase in sexual assault reports in the years following the overhaul of the rape law, they also show that the percentage of reports treated as unfounded has remained constant and considerably higher than for other crimes against the person (15 per cent compared with 7 per cent – see Roberts 1990, 33). Translated into real numbers, this means that many more complainants now face suspicion, rejection and the stigma of being branded false accusers.

In sum, while the increased reporting rates indicate sexual assault victims' greater faith in the fairness of the criminal justice system, this does not necessarily benefit individual victims. Indeed, it may be detrimental to women in general, because, as Carol Smart (1989) claims, 'in the symbolic sense, every rape case that fails is a victory for phallocentric values' (34). Smart's argument is as follows: 'The only alternative when non-consent is not established is to presume consent – and hence innocence of the accused ... The woman must have lied. In this way the phallocentric view of women's capricious sexuality is confirmed' (34).

EFFICIENT ENFORCEMENT

When women's groups and other actors involved in the law reform process referred to the need to alleviate the suffering inflicted by the criminal justice system upon victims of sexual aggression, they normally saw it as a precondition for an increase in conviction rates. The revised offence categories and rules of evidence were also designed to allow for more effective enforcement of the law. Such a rationale for the law reform presupposes some faith in the prevailing system of punishment.

While some women's groups recommended moderation in penalties, they did it only to increase juries' readiness to convict (NAWL 1981, 13; 1982a, 2; 1982b, 6; Snider 1985, 343; *Toronto Star* 1981). Moreover, a number of feminists explicitly opposed lowering of the maximum penalties, warning that this would symbolically downgrade the seriousness of the crime of sexual assault relative to other crimes (for example, CACSW 1982, 9; Chase 1983, 54; Cohen and Backhouse 1980, 102-3).

In their legal proposals, the unresolved dilemmas of the criminal justice system were glossed over and the well-documented class and race biases in the application of the penal law were overlooked due to the exclusive concern with gender-based discrimination.[26] As Snider (1985) summed it up:

This reform initiative went forth because the old laws seemed to threaten the principles of universality and equality which the Anglo-American legal system purports to embody ... the result will be most likely to reinforce state control over the large and impotent underclass (352–3).

The hope that increasing the severity of the law on sexual assault and enhancing its enforcement would at least send an appropriate symbolic message to society is also questionable. It is either unrealistic or, more critically, misguided. Tamar Pitch (1985) has pointed to the dubious wisdom of 'the attribution to the penal system of the function of symbolic organiser of the hierarchy of general goods' (43). Commenting on Italian feminists' proposals for rape law reform, Pitch wondered how – given the existing reality of conflict and inequality – penal law could be expected 'to perform the symbolic function of establishing and supporting universal values, to provide a focus for political and cultural consensus' (44). However, a number of statements by Canadian women's groups betray this illusory longing for a legal formula that would facilitate and symbolize a fair societal consensus. A rape crisis centre's representative, for instance, argued before the Senate Legal and Constitutional Affairs Committee that:

This bill has important implications not only in terms of the relatively few cases which actually make it to trial, but in terms of the attitude of the people of this country to rape and their faith or lack of it in the criminal justice system (Senate of Canada 1982, vol. 27, 12).

An early brief by the Canadian Advisory Council on the Status of Women (1975) provides another illustration of this consensual vision of law reform:

There is a need to rationalize these crimes in relation to social values ... The laws are reviewed in an attempt to suggest changes which would a) be consistent with certain principles which reflect present norms, and b) make men and women equal under the law (1).

However, such a consensus on social values and norms is a fiction, and the law not only disguises the existing differences, but is likely – through selective enforcement – to legitimate certain interpretations and 'de-legitimate' others. By participating in the law reform process together with the minister of Justice and Parliament, women created an impression of a shared definition of sexual aggression. All those participating appeared to agree that it is a very serious, coercive, usually violent crime that occurs mainly against women. Nevertheless, they might all have had in mind quite different images. The prevailing ideology still assumes that a certain measure of male domination and coercion is normal in sexual relations and that it would be ridiculous to try to criminalize it. This ideology is no longer shared by an increasingly large number of women, who want a recognition of their right to sexual autonomy.

The multi-tiered offences of sexual assault seem to acknowledge the existence of a continuum of sexual coercion. But it would be unrealistic to expect any significant changes in law enforcement with respect to sexual assault in the dating and marital relationships. The unrestricted right of the defence to introduce evidence concerning the victim's past sexual activities with the accused may actually serve as a 'natural' deterrent for women to report this type of act of sexual abuse and rape. Indeed, it has been argued already that 'one of the problems in "proving" rape in a court is that, forced or coerced sex are common experiences for women' (Kelly, 1987, 55). Law-makers and law-enforcers are thus likely to 'endorse' the lines that demarcate uncommon forms of sexual coercion from those practised almost routinely in contemporary societies.

Feminist analysis has demonstrated quite convincingly that sexual violence and internalized fear of violence constitute an integral part of the social control of women (see, for example, Brownmiller 1975, Smart and Smart 1978, Edwards 1987, Radford 1987). It also shows that some types of violence have in practice been legitimated by the refusal of the criminal justice system to intervene, or by its displacement of the blame from the offender to the victim. Indeed, it has been suggested that as long as the state is guided by male ideology and interests, it will continue to define 'the limits of violence appropriate for the control of women' (Radford 1987, 43). What the women's lobby was able to do was to negotiate these limits, but not the principle itself.

It remains an open question whether the Canadian rape law reform has led to any increase in conviction rates. The incomplete research evidence has not so far brought any decisive answer to this question (see Chapter 4). Given a sharp increase in reporting rates, a lack of corresponding increase in conviction rates would be most troubling. A number of studies from the United States (and some from Canada) suggest that the impact of rape law revisions on the courts is rather limited (see, for example, Caringella-MacDonald 1985, Estrich 1987, Horney and Spohn 1987, LaFree 1989, Loh 1980, Marsh, Geist, and Caplan 1982, Polk 1985, Renner and Sahjpaul 1986). An inquiry into the effects of Michigan's criminal sexual conduct (CSC) law (Marsh et al. 1982) showed an increase in effectiveness of case processing 'without concomitant "symbolic" changes such as a redefinition of the crime' (65). Moreover,

neither prosecutors nor defence attorneys have substantially altered their courtroom tactics ... The victim's character and credibility remain the central focus of the CSC case. In general, the findings from interviews with officials suggest that the law has very little impact on the system's approach to sexual assault cases, despite statistical improvements in conviction rates (65).

Caringella-MacDonald (1985), in her study in Michigan, established that attrition and non-conviction persisted. There was however, an increase in cases solved by plea-bargaining, facilitated by multilevel sexual assault legislation. This produced more lenient sentences, but spared the victim the ordeal of a court appearance and increased slightly the likelihood of conviction (79).

LaFree (1989), in his very thorough research in Indiana, found that 'expectations about how jurors are likely to respond to cases ... influence[d] decisions throughout the selection process' (153). His research also demonstrated that – especially in the cases where either consent or the performance of the sexual acts was disputed – 'measures of the victim's gender-role behavior were more important than measures of physical evidence and seriousness of offence in predicting jurors' case evaluation' (226). The new rules thus seem to serve old stereotypes.

An interview study (based on responses of court officials to hypothetical cases involving sexual aggression) in six jurisdictions in the United States concluded that

officials, in their own minds, may no longer equate chastity and credibility, but they may still require a woman's sexual relationships to be within an acceptable 'normal range.' Social mores may have changed, but the line may have simply been redrawn in a new place (Spohn and Horney 1991, 155).

The authors found, however, that the exact nature of rape shield laws had an impact on the officials' (judges', prosecutors', and defence attorneys') perceptions of what was in practical terms likely to happen in court as far as sexual history evidence was concerned. They all believed that the law can be stretched and circumvented, but the wording of the law did influence somewhat their perceptions of how far they could go. Spohn and Horney also found that the whole system was biased against the victim:

If a defendant is acquitted because the judge ignored the law and either admitted potentially relevant evidence without a hearing or allowed the defense attorney to use legally inadmissible evidence the victim cannot appeal the acquittal or the judge's decisions. If, on the other hand, the judge followed the law and refused to admit seemingly irrelevant sexual history evidence, the defendant can appeal his conviction. All of the consequences, in other words, would lead judges and prosecutors to err in favor of the defendant (155–6).

Although it is still difficult to judge whether the enforcement of the Canadian sexual assault law is more effective than that of its predecessor (see the chapter by Clark and Hepworth for data relating to this issue), it seems clear that the normative function of sexual aggression trials remains unchanged. They continue to define and legitimate the historical disparity between the sexual rights of men and women.

The practice of law is structurally shaped by the existing power differentials. It also expresses and is moulded by the dominant forms of political discourse and its tacit assumptions and boundaries. Accordingly, 'public' rapes (i.e., in public places, by strangers) are more likely to be prosecuted, because women are still generally construed as relatively unthreatening and powerless in the public area. Unless they grossly violate their gender-role norms, they deserve legal protection. 'Private' rapes, however, are prosecuted with great reluctance. Women, who are socially constructed as the pillars and symbols of the private sphere (matrimony, motherhood, family, intimacy), are also believed to have a potential to threaten its stability and sanctity. Moreover, as Stacey and Price (1981) indicate, 'the political power that women have exercised in the past and in other societies has always derived from their position in a familial or kinship group' (2). This potential female power must be controlled, and patriarchy is a time-honoured way to achieve this. Violence applied against women in the private area (date rape, incest, marital rape, wife battering) erodes this traditional source of limited power for women. Ironically, actions taken by the state – in response to women's pleas – often further restrict this shaky power base: battered women are encouraged to leave their home and go to a shelter, details of women's private habits and domestic arrangements are scrutinized in court, and whatever attempts they might have made to exercise some control over their private lives may be turned against them.

The long struggle over the definition of rape illustrates well the male resistance to any attempt to limit traditional male sexual rights. A law that would effectively expand the scope of prosecution beyond the type of rape that is committed by a small minority of men would challenge the very attributes of the 'maleness' on which its claim to superiority is founded. Since men have acquired certain rights at the expense of women's rights – and nowhere is this more clear than in the area of sexuality – rectifying this situation may not be possible without a deliberate curtailment of those rights perceived as vital and inalienable by many men. Any law that aims at limiting the scope of a right hitherto enjoyed by some group goes against the grain of the liberal society. Backing it with criminal sanctions that apply in individual cases of transgression does not only exalt repression, it also produces bona fide opposition legitimated by fundamental libertarian principles. Faced with the inherent rules and biases of the prevailing legal discourse and narrow limits of the criminal law, women lobbyists eventually concentrated on the defence of women against the legal system rather than against rape. Their partial success in this area was virtually undone, however, when the Supreme Court of Canada recognized (on 22 August 1991) as legitimate a Charter challenge to the Criminal Code section that had curbed the admissibility of evidence on the complainant's sexual history (known as the 'rape shield' provision). A Criminal Code amendment passed in 1992 gave more discretion to judges in deciding whether the advantages of admitting such evidence outweigh the diadvantages (see Chapter 1)

The Project of Redefining Rape

For a long time, women – due to their inferior status and the cultural myths surrounding sexuality – were silent partners in the perpetuation of the inequality of sexual rights. Young girls unready for sexual intercourse agreed to it under a threat of the withdrawal of the man's love or fear of being ridiculed; more mature women did the same to defend themselves against the accusation of being frigid, to secure or save a marriage, to obtain or maintain employment or economic support. The pressure, force, and threats used by men in these situations were normalized by the prevailing belief that they were only exercising their natural rights. Feminists of the 1970s challenged this tacit assumption of the superiority of male sexual rights. Their identification with the victimized (i.e., the weak) gave women's organizations legitimate standing as a lobby or group with a clear constituency. It was unlikely, however, to become a source of power. Just as rape symbolized unequal power relations between genders, the lobbying for a law reform on behalf of rape victims put women automatically in a subordinate, easily trivialized position.

While many aspects of the sexual assault legislation of 1983 coincided with or were based on the relevant demands by major women's groups, the latter were often informed and motivated by considerations other than the internal consistency of the law, formal equality, and gender neutrality that dominated the official legal discourse. Due to the very nature of the law and legal reform, however, women's initial ambition to redefine rape in a way true to its complex sociopolitical context was compromised and had to be reduced to a set of formal demands congruent with the overall legal system, its language and philosophy. Repeatedly, however, when feminist language was translated into legal formulas, the essential opposition and incompatibility between the two became obvious.

The formidable legal machinery adjusted and perfected throughout modern history in the name of protection of individual rights proved incapable of showing sensitivity to women's arguments grounded in their existential experience of living in fear of male violence. It was blind to the fact that the rights assigned to men and women – ostensibly equal and universal – have grown out of the reality of inequality justified by the disparity in the culturally legitimated gender ideals. The obvious advantages of the liberal legal philosophy thus disguise its dangerous potential for entrapping those who have been excluded from the active participation in the law-making process and full citizenship. The philosophical concept of the social contract (or 'the original position' elaborated by John Rawls [1971]) is based on an assumption that rationally minded law-makers (or legal philosophers) are bound to produce fair rules as long as they know that they are not exempt from them no matter what position in life they are destined eventually to occupy. But the law-makers of the past not only knew that they were not going to end up being women, but they also were usually unable to appreciate what women's existence was like and what would matter to them if indeed they were women. Their neutrality and the vision of their 'original position' was therefore compromised. Nevertheless, the rules they passed have been perceived as truly universal as a result of 'the tendency of liberal legalism to dissociate issues from their social, economic, and political context and to utilise a formal model of equality, justice, fairness etc.' (Dawson 1987–8, 314).

The question of whether feminist legal proposals could have been better devised to serve women's interests and philosophy more accurately is a hypothetical one. The changes women's groups asked for were always developed and assessed with the view of the existing practices and biases. They were not necessarily searching for the best legal solutions; rather they were carefully selecting the legal formulae which would cause relatively less damage in the hands of the sexist legal establishment.

However, a test whether certain legal solutions are likely – under the existing circumstances – to contribute to the subordination of women (Boyle 1985, 25) is much more ambiguous than it may appear. For instance, the amendments introduced to mitigate the ordeal of victims testifying in rape trials have apparently brought some improvement in this regard, but by encouraging reporting, they seem to have exposed more women to the humiliation and stigma resulting from the official disqualification of their complaints. This was probably a predictable outcome, but weighing potential gains and losses may not be easily achieved given that most instances of criminal law reform involve choices between different evils rather than potentially positive or negative solutions.

Without doubt, the most active and effective women's groups involved in the rape law reform in Canada had a generally liberal–feminist orientation

(Boyd and Sheehy 1989, 256–7). Their aspirations to achieve formal equality and neutrality in the hitherto heavily gender-biased area of the law were by and large realized. They did not really try to assess a priori the long-term effects of their legal proposals for men and women as 'result equality' feminists would advise (257–8). They were not paralysed by the overwhelming pessimism about piecemeal reforms of any kind, represented by Marxist feminists (258–60) and did not subscribe to any strong essentialist view of women and their unique values, propagated by radical feminists (260–1). They saw women being treated unfairly by the criminal justice system, which put rape victims on trial and let disproportionate numbers of offenders go free. They quickly realized that they had to use the language of the law to achieve legal amendments. They knew that real women's issues had to be left out of the criminal law process, but they also noticed that the law reform and the related publicity creates an opportunity to at least raise some broader aspects of violence against women that had been routinely prevented from entering the public discourse.

Despite the many recent discussions on feminism and the law, no realistic alternative to this early practical, liberal reformism has been articulated. Indeed, the fact that women's activization (or 'liberation') occurs in an already shaped institutional world might have put them at a permanent disadvantage. The whole complex sociotechnological world has evolved to accommodate the male physiology, life cycle, and needs. There are many examples of it, starting from industrial work tools that are designed to fit the average man's hand, strength, and size, to career expectations that are conceived for lives with no pregnancies and child-rearing duties, to social security programs that are adjusted to the man's life expectancy and uninterrupted employment record, to a whole range of social, economic, and political institutional arrangements that have evolved around male ideas of competition, hierarchical organization, and management. It is therefore not surprising that the law has assumed male-constructed sexuality is a natural standard that defines the sexuality of 'the other.'

The feminist question of whether to stress 'equality' or 'difference' in the fight against institutional patriarchy has proved to be yet another insoluble dilemma. What should perhaps be strived for is a world that accommodates equally the obvious physical and physiological differences and assures that they do not become a basis for discrimination and the ascription of inferiority. For example, the recognition of pregnancy as a natural part of the life of many people would force not only a revision of standard career criteria, but also a recognition that child-rearing is a natural part of life for the majority of people and cannot be construed as the exclusive responsibility of the woman. Those numerous arrangements that have evolved from the assumption that women are biologically predestined to be caregivers have stifled male potential in this area just as they have effectively blocked women's opportunities in the marketplace. A task of rectifying these losses calls for a new concept of equality and not a new 'radical' vision of women as uniquely caring, nurturing, 'relational,' altruistic, community-oriented beings.[27]

The traditional dichotomy that has led to a distorted notion of male and female sexualities as opposites should not be replaced by an equally false new dichotomy. As well, the recognition of difference should not lead to demands for legal provisions that construe women as incapable of sexual assertiveness or pleasure-seeking behaviour. It should not be assumed that women are natural victims and men are natural predators. Women should strive for policies that would address their historical vulnerability to sexual violation and recognize how this hampers progress toward equality, but would avoid reinforcing objectification that women have suffered in the male-dominated culture.[28] The latter seems unavoidable, however, if criminal law is used as a vehicle for such policies.

On balance, Canadian rape law reform has neither significantly facilitated the task of dismantling patriarchy nor seriously prejudiced it. Women activists were caught in a dilemma whereby, on the one hand, the harm done by a certain institution can hardly be expected to be corrected by the same, basically unchanged, institution, while, on the other hand, the harm cannot be effectively addressed if this institution continues actively to propagate the harmful pattern. Their cautious approach was to try to restrain the ability of the criminal justice system to continue the damaging pattern without entrusting it with a grander but perhaps unrealistic mission of more profound social change and active involvement in the revamping of its own heritage. It may be argued that at that time, such a mission would only empower men to become agents of change for women, but on their own rather than women's terms. Insofar as women's groups attempted to redefine rape on their own terms, they were unlikely to achieve this through the legal channels structured and dominated by the very group whose control over this issue they wanted to break.

Perhaps the greatest mistakes of the rape law reform movement were not even related to the exact legal demands, but to some broader political aspects of feminist strategies of that period. For women's organizations, rape became a suitable issue to organize around (see Edwards 1987). To make their mark as a political lobby they chose to get involved in the official process of law reform, rather than concentrate on the more fundamental process of consciousness-raising. To mobilize and demonstrate their power and distinct interests as women, they excluded men, the very group whose consciousness needed to change. Men were excluded from many anti-rape marches or rape-crisis organizations. Because of their cultural conditioning and prevalent sexualization of violence, all men were believed to be potential rapists, just as all women were potential victims.

The solidarity within the movement was founded on intense self- identification of women as victims, objects, bodies. This was hardly an 'empowering' approach. In fact, for many women it might have been a deeply threatening and disabling experience. Moreover, identifying all women as victims fully united in their fear and vulnerability led to a false claim[29] that the threat of rape affects equally all women, regardless of age, status, class, or race. This generalization, made by middle-class organizers, glossed over the substantial differences in women's experience of victimization depending on their socio-economic status and in particular their community and ethnic affiliations.

This earlier view of women as undifferentiated victims – just as more recent attempts to identify a universal 'women's voice' – sacrificed concrete experiences of different groups of women for a political display of sisterhood and dismissed as irrelevant both the multitude of dimensions of sexism within each society and different combinations of sexism with other types of discrimination.

In this chapter I have discussed the nature, purpose, and origins of the 1983 legislation. Of course, whether any legal reform achieves its goals or not is an empirical question. The chapters that follow explore the impact of Bill C-127 upon victims of sexual assault as well as the official processing of sexual assault cases. Chapter 3 begins with an examination of reports of sexual assault made to the police over the past few years.

Notes

1 This chapter overlaps to some extent with M. Łoś, 'Feminism and Rape Law Reform,' in L. Gelsthorpe and A. Morris, eds., *Feminist Perspectives in Criminology* (1990). I am grateful to the publisher, Open University Press, for the permission to use here parts of this published text. I would like to acknowledge the help of Ms. Colleen Gildert whose research assistantship was covered by the Sustaining Grants Program of the Ministry of the Solicitor General of Canada.

2 To some extent, even some feminists fall into this trap when they present women as meeting the first description in such pairs of features as: continuity/rupture, empathy/isolation, other-centredness/ self-centredness, experiential/instrumen-

tal, quality/quantity, cooperation/management, equality/ hierarchy, harmony/
conflict, peace/war, life/death, and so forth.

3 Of course, the actual processes of construction of gender roles and stereotypes are
   far more complex, ambiguous, and contradictory than may be suggested by a simple binary model. The latter has been identified, however as a part of the logic that
   has played a significant role in structuring both science and the law (see, for example, Smart 1989, 33–4). It has contributed to the marginalization and often exclusion of women's voices. While both men and women participate in 'social
   contruction' processes, they do not participate as equals.

4 The Criminal Code of Canada, ss. 139–154, of which ss. 143–145 dealt directly
   with rape.

5 Section 143 explicitly states: 'A male person commits rape when he has sexual
   intercourse with a female person who is not his wife.' In 1978, the minister of Justice introduced, albeit unsuccessfully, a bill (C-52) that not only proposed to maintain the spousal exemption – with the exception of separated spouses living apart –
   but recommended its *extension* to all forms of indecent assault.

6 While amendments in 1975 appeared to limit the admissibility of such evidence,
   the 1980 ruling of the Supreme Court of Canada (*Forsythe* v. *The Queen*, 2
   S.C.R.268) interpreted these amendments as permitting evidence of the past sexual
   history of the complainant to be used to attack her credibility.

7 According to these amendments, 'no questions shall be asked as to the sexual conduct of the complainant with a person other than the accused' unless reasonable
   notice in writing has been given to the prosecutor and a hearing in camera concluded that the exclusion would prevent a just determination of an issue of fact,
   including the credibility of the complainant (s. 142).

8 See, for example, numerous psychology handbooks on the unconscious desire of
   women to be raped. To quote *Psychology of Crime* by Abrahamsen (1960, 61):

   The conscious or unconscious biological or psychological attraction between man and woman
   does not exist only on the part of the offender toward the woman but, also, on her part
   toward him, which in many instances may, to some extent, be the impetus for his sexual
   attack. Often a woman unconsciously wishes to be taken by force.

9 Evident both in the minutes of the parliamentary debates and in mass media
   reporting.

10 An earlier bill (C-52), submitted to Parliament in 1978 and strongly criticized by
    CACSW, NAC, WLCA, and the Canadian Association of Sexual Assault Centres, died
    on the order paper (Kinnon 1981, 43–4; Rioux and McFadyen 1978). Bill C-53
    incorporated many suggestions made by the women's lobby and by the Law
    Reform Commission (1978a, b) which had also consulted women to some extent.

11 Two other principles behind Bill C-53 seem to be more directly related to other sec-

tions of the bill. They were: the protection of children and special groups, and the safeguarding of public decency (House of Commons 1981, 11,300).

12 Another legal problem with the requirement to prove penetration (under s. 143 of the Criminal Code) was indicated by the parliamentary secretary to the minister of Justice: 'It has created an anomaly in the law. Some brutal and injurious sexual attacks not involving penetration have been charged, out of necessity, as the lesser offence of indecent assault' (House of Commons, 1981, 11,300).

13 The number of tiers was, however, a contentious issue, with women's groups insisting on three or four levels of severity instead of the two proposed in Bill C-53. They also demanded that the lowest-tier offence be of a hybrid (summary/ indictable) nature. These solutions were adopted in the final version of the law. Interestingly, the main argument put forth initially by NAWL in support of raising the number of tiers from two to three was the desire to conform to the existing assault sections of the Criminal Code and to avoid any reduction in penalties:

> Over the years the law has evolved to develop a sophisticated method of dealing with assault charges ... To tamper unnecessarily with the present assault model will only lead to confusion and costly delays ... [Moreover, the repeal of s. 228 "Assault with Intent to Maim or Endanger Life" and its inclusion in the second level of assault] will have two negative results: (1) the maximum penalty for wounding will be reduced from 14 to 10 years; and (2) the alleged *increase* in the maximum for the second level of regular assault (from 5 years to 10) will be nullified, since only the former wounding offences will merit the maximum penalty (NAWL 1981, 15).

In their later statement to the House of Commons Standing Committee on Justice and Legal Affairs, NAWL representatives gave the following justification for their demand for a three-tiered sexual assault offence:

> Offences are differentiated according to the degree of violence and risk to the victims, with the degree of intimacy taken into account at the sentencing stage only.

> The offences parallel the present assault offences.

> The sexual element makes these crimes more serious than assault: therefore the penalties are correspondingly higher.

> Men and women are equally protected and equally culpable (NAWL, 1982b, 4).

14 Section 246.6 (later changed to 276), which required a written notice and an *in camera* hearing, permitted the inclusion of evidence that rebutted evidence of the complainant's sexual activity (or its absence) that had been adduced by the prosecution. It also permitted evidence on sexual activity that took place on the same occasion as the activity named in the charge, if it related to the identity of the per-

son who had had the sexual contact described in the charge or related to the consent issue. The complainant was not to be a compellable witness at the *in camera* hearing.

These changes were seen by women's representatives as only a partial victory. Nevertheless the Supreme Court of Canada ruled in 1991 that Section 276 violated the accused's right to a full defence.

15 This drawback to the feminist proposals was recognized by many within their ranks. For instance, while NAWL officially promoted the terminological shift, it also circulated a dissenting opinion whose authors claim that:

> Rape victims perceive rape as an act which is qualitatively different from other forms of physical assault. The fear that it engenders can best be likened to the male fear of castration ... There is no need to abolish rape entirely, since women who wish to have their rapes viewed as assault can choose that route now ... It is not necessary to eliminate the crime of rape, especially since there will always be women who define their attack as rape (NAWL n.d., 7, 12; also Cohen and Backhouse 1980).

16 A survey of several hundred sexual assault sentencing reports, conducted in the late 1980s in Toronto by the Metro Action Committee on Public Violence Against Women and Children, has indeed shown that:

> In case after case, the inherent violence involved in sexual violation is not recognized. The absence of overt physical force or weapons is often seen to imply the lack of coercion ... In the majority of sexual assaults, the assailant uses verbal threats, a position of authority, or the fear evoked by his size and strength to establish power over the victim ... Yet, gradation of sexual assault offences in the criminal code reinforces the notion that sexual assault is not of itself violent; violence is seen as an added factor (Marshall 1988, 7; see also Heald 1985, 123, and Schwartz and Clear 1980, 137).

17 The quoted feminist arguments are quite persuasive when applied to the question of classification of the offence. However, as two American authors have claimed, this does not necessarily mean that psychological harm must be ignored in the sexual assault cases; instead, the amount of harm will have to be 'averaged' across the entire population of anticipated victims and written into the law beforehand. Certain crimes will have to be treated as if they did in fact always cause this kind of harm, with the question of actual psychological injury ignored in the instant case (Schwartz and Clear 1980, 140).

Although this was not raised by the women's representatives in their testimonies to the Senate Committee, the difference between the penalties for non-sexual and sexual assault is supposed to express this additional 'average harm' incurred by the victim of sexual attacks. The issue of 'averaged harm' should thus be better publicized and explained not only to the public, but most urgently to the judges in order to make them aware that their 'no harm done' claims actually contradict the law.

18 In this context, it may be appropriate to quote an instructive comment by Smart and Brophy (1985, 17): 'Our analysis ... assumes that women do constitute a specific category in relation to law, and that although legal statutes may refer to spouses, parents, applicants and defendants as if gender was irrelevant, the *effect* of the law is never gender neutral.'

19 'It will be ironic if this is the approach taken by Parliament and accepted by the courts since it will mean that the only impact of the Charter is to require the creation of a new crime that women can theoretically commit without addressing at all the unequal burden of victimization that women bear in this context' (Boyle 1984, 41).

20 'This bill ... gets rid of the outdated notion that rape can only take place if the penis penetrates the vagina and that a man can only rape a woman' (a statement by Svend Robinson, House of Commons 1981, 11,347).

21 For reviews of feminist writings on the issue of formal equality and gender neutrality, see Boyd and Sheehy 1986; Boyle et al. 1985, 13–26; Sheehy 1987.

22 The opposition to this amendment is well illustrated by a statement by Gordon Taylor: 'Many people are charging that this will put another nail in the coffin of the family unit. There are too many things today which make it difficult for family units to operate, and this item will certainly not help' (House of Commons 1981, 14,170).

   The feminist response to these critics is succinctly summarized by Jillian Ridington, a witness before the Senate Legal and Constitutional Affairs Committee: 'To those who fear that the removal of spousal immunity will undermine the institution of marriage, we must point out that, if it were true that marriage has to be maintained through the violation of women's bodies, surely that would be proof that there were fundamental problems with this institution' (Senate of Canada 1982, vol. 27, 8).

23 For an interesting discussion of the role of gender bias in judicial decision-making in the light of the Charter of Rights and Freedoms, see Boyle and Worth Rowley 1987.

24 As shown by Boyle and Worth Rowley (1987) and Dawson (1987–8), the relevance of such evidence is judged by typically male standards that 'look upon women as sexual objects and [do] not reflect a woman's perspective on consensual sex or autonomy' (Dawson 1987–8, 325).

25 For a more detailed discussion of the incompatibility of male beliefs in the sexual domain and women's security and autonomy, see Łoś 1990.

26 A study conducted in Montreal estimates that in 1984–5, 85 per cent of the accused in sexual assault cases were either unemployed or unskilled workers, 13 per cent were skilled workers, and less than 3 per cent were professionals. These data may not be fully accurate, because not all court files gave the occupational status of the

accused, but nonetheless they confirm the tendency to prosecute those at the lower end of the economic spectrum (Baril, Bettez, and Viau 1989, 161).

27 See Alcoff (1988) for a sensitive critique of this 'tendency to offer an essentialist response to misogyny and sexism through adopting a homogeneous, unproblematized, and ahistorical conception of woman' (265). (See also Fraser and Nicholson 1988).

28 Given that in their attempts at legal reforms women can only be effective if they enter into successful coalitions with men who control the legal system, it may be worthwhile to try an alternative strategy, whereby women would enter in coalitions with men active in other areas of social activity (the mass media, education, different types of employment, neighbourhoods) to try to pursue their goals through nonpunitive, nonlegalistic means. For instance, by influencing attitudes of male opinion-formers and current youth leaders in Western, highly fashion-oriented societies, broad male audiences may be reached. Their messages would be far more convincing than those delivered directly by women labelled radical and perceived as threatening, bent on robbing men of their natural rights. If male sexual conquest is presented as an old-fashioned, compromised approach to sex, and respect for sexual autonomy as an attractive alternative, liberating for both sexes, at least a climate may be created whereby male sexual 'scoring' will be met with ridicule and it would be easier for both men and women to ascertain themselves as autonomous individuals.

29 Contradicted by the available research evidence – see, for example, Curtis 1975; Schwendinger and Schwendinger 1983; Smith and Bennett 1985).

References

Abrahamsen, D. 1960. *The Psychology of Crime*. New York: John Wiley

Alcoff, L. 1988. 'Cultural Feminism vs. Poststructuralism. The Identity Crisis in Feminist Theory.' In E. Minnich et al., eds., *Reconstructing the Academy*. Chicago: University of Chicago Press, 257–88

Baines, B. 1988. 'Women and the Law.' In S. Burt, L. Code, and L. Dorney, eds., *Changing Patterns: Women in Canada*. Toronto: McClelland and Stewart, 157–83

Baril, M., M.-J. Bettez, and L. Viau. 1989. *Les agressions sexuelles avant et après la réforme de 1983*, vol. 1. Montréal: Université de Montréal

Bartky, S.L. 1988. 'Foucault, Femininity, and the Modernization of Patriarchal Power.' In I. Diamond and L. Quinby, eds., *Feminism and Foucault*. Boston: Northeastern University Press, 61–86

Bell, V. 1991. 'Beyond the "Thorny Question": Feminism, Foucault and the Desexualisation of Rape.' *International Journal of the Sociology of Law*, 19:83–100

Borgida, E. 1981. 'Legal Reforms and Rape Laws.' In L. Bickman, ed., *Applied Social Psychology Annual*, vol. 2. Beverly Hills, CA: Sage, 211–41

Box, S. 1983. *Power, Crime, and Mystification*. London: Tavistock

Boyd, S.B., and E.A. Sheehy. 1986. 'Feminist Perspectives on Law: Canadian Theory and Practice.' *Canadian Journal of Women and the Law*, 2:1–52

Boyd, S.B., and E.A. Sheehy. 1989. 'Overview.' In T. Caputo, M. Kennedy, C.E. Reasons, and A. Branningan, eds., *Law and Society*. Toronto: Harcourt Brace Jovanovich, 255–70

Boyle, C.L.M. 1984. *Sexual Assault*. Toronto: Carswell

Boyle, C.L.M. 1985. 'Constitutional Implications of Reform.' In C.L.M. Boyle et al., *A Feminist Review of Criminal Law*. Ottawa: Status of Women Canada; Minister of Supply and Services Canada

Boyle, C.L.M., and S. Worth Rowley. 1987. 'Sexual Assault and Family Violence: Reflections on Bias.' In S.L. Martin and K.E. Mohoney, eds., *Equality and Judicial Neutrality*. Toronto: Carswell, 312–25

CACSW (Canadian Advisory Council on the Status of Women). 1975. 'The Web of the Law: A Study of Sexual Offences in the Canadian Criminal Code,' by Marcia H. Rioux

– 1982. 'A New Justice for Women.' Ottawa

Caringella-MacDonald, S. 1985. 'Sexual Assault Prosecution: An Examination of Model Rape Legislation in Michigan.' In C. Scheber and C. Feinman, eds., *Criminal Justice Politics and Women: The Aftermath of Legally Mandated Change*. New York: The Haworth Press, 5–82

Chappell, D., R. Geis, and G. Geis, eds., 1977. *Forcible Rape: The Crime, the Victim, and the Offender*. New York: Columbia University Press

Chase, G. 1983. 'An Analysis of the New Sexual Assault Laws.' *Canadian Women Studies*, 4:53–4

Clark, L., and D. Lewis. 1977. *Rape: The Price of Coercive Sexuality*. Toronto: The Women's Press

Cohen, L., and C. Backhouse. 1980. 'Desexualising Rape: Dissenting View on the Proposed Rape Amendments.' *Canadian Women Studies* 2:99–103

Curtis, L. 1975. *Violence, Rape and Culture*. Lexington, MA: Lexington Books

Dawson, T.B. 1987–8. 'Sexual Assault Law and Past Sexual Conduct of the Primary Witness: The Construction of Relevance.' *Canadian Journal of Women and the Law* 2:310–340

de Jong, K. 1985. 'Sexual Equality: Interpreting Section 28.' In A. Boyefsky and M. Eberts, eds., *Equality Rights and the Charter of Rights and Freedoms*. Toronto: Carswell, 493–528

Edwards, A. 1987. 'Male Violence in Feminist Theory: An Analysis of the Changing Conceptions of Sex/Gender Violence and Male Dominance.' In J. Hanmer and M.

Maynard, eds., *Women, Violence and Social Control*. London: Macmillan Press, 13–29

Estrich, S. 1987. *Real Rape*, Cambridge, MA: Harvard University Press

Foucault, M. 1978. *The History of Sexuality*, vol. 1. New York: Pantheon

Fraser, N., and L. Nicholson. 1988. 'Social Criticism without Philosophy: An Encounter between Feminism and Postmodernism.' *Theory Culture and Society* 5:373–94

Goldsmith Kasinsky, R. 1978. 'Rape: The Social Control of Women.' In W.K. Greenaway and S.L. Brinckey, eds., *Law and Social Control in Canada*. Scarborough, ON: Prentice-Hall, pp 59–69

Griffin, S. 1978. *Women and Nature*, New York: Harper and Row

Heald, S. 1985. 'Social Change and Legal Ideology: A Critique of the New Sexual Assault Legislation.' *Canadian Criminology Forum*, 7:117–27

Hinch, R. 1985. 'Canada's New Sexual Assault Laws: A Step Forward for Women?' *Contemporary Crises* 9:33–44

Hindelang, M.J., and B. Davis. 1977. 'Forcible Rape in the United States: A Statistical Profile.' In D. Chappell, R. Geis, and G. Geis, eds., *Forcible Rape: The Crime, the Victim and the Offender*. New York: Columbia University Press.

Horney, J., and C. Spohn. 1987. 'The Impact of Rape Reform Legislation.' Presented at the Annual Meeting of the American Society of Criminology, Montreal

Hosek, C. 1983. 'Women and the Constitutional Process.' In K. Banting and R. Simeon, eds., *And No One Cheered*. Toronto: Methuen, 280–300

House of Commons Debates. 1980–3. *Minutes of Proceedings*

House of Commons Standing Committee on Justice and Legal Affairs. 1982. *Minutes of Proceedings*

Keet, J.E. 1985. 'Women and the Law: The Charter of Rights and Freedoms.' *Canadian Criminology Forum* 7:103–16

Kelly, L. 1987. 'The Continuum of Sexual Violence.' In J. Hamner and M. Maynard, eds., *Women, Violence and Social Control*. London: Macmillan Press, 46–60

Kinnon, D. 1981. *Report on Sexual Assault in Canada*. Ottawa: Canada Advisory Council on the Status of Women

LaFree, G.D. 1989. *Rape and Criminal Justice. The Social Construction of Sexual Assault*, Belmont, CA: Wadsworth

Law Reform Commission of Canada. 1978a. *Sexual Offences*. Working Paper 22. Ottawa: L.R.C.C.

– 1978b. *Sexual Offences*, Report 10. Ottawa: L.R.C.C.

Loh, W.D. 1980. 'The Impact of Common Law and Reform Rape Statutes on Prosecution: An Empirical Study.' *Washington Law Review* 55:506–43

Łoś, M. 1990. 'Feminism and Rape Law Reform.' In L. Gelsthorpe and A. Morris, eds., *Feminist Perspectives in Criminology*. Buckingham: Open University

Macdonald, D. 1982. 'The Evolution of Bill C-127.' Prepared for the Standing Committee on Legal and Constitutional Affairs. Ottawa: Library of Parliament, 37p.

Marsh, J., A. Geist, and N. Caplan. 1982. *Rape and the Limits of Law Reform*. Boston, MA: Auburn House

Marshall. P. 1988. 'Sexual Assault, The Charter and Sentencing Reform.' Toronto: Metro Action Committee on Public Violence Against Women and Children. A paper presented to a conference of the Society for the Reform of the Criminal Law in Common-Law Jurisdictions, Ottawa, August 1988.

McCann, K. 1985. 'Battered Women and the Law: The Limits of the Legislation.' In J. Brophy and C. Smart, eds., *Women-in Law, Explorations in Law, Family and Sexuality*. London: Routledge and Kegan Paul, 71–96

Minch, C., R. Linden, and S. Johnson. 1987. 'Attrition in the Processing of Rape Cases.' *Canadian Journal of Criminology* 29:389–404

NAWL (National Association of Women and the Law). 1979. 'Recommendations on Sexual Assault Offences.' Ottawa, (August), 2p.

– 1981. 'A New Image for Sexual Offences in the Criminal Code.' A Brief in Response to Bill C-53. Ottawa (October), 40p.

– 1982a. 'Comments on Bill C-157,' Ottawa, 4p.

– 1982b. 'Statement by the NAWL to the House of Commons Standing Committee on Justice and Legal Affairs re Bill C-53' (April), Ottawa, 13p.

– (n.d.) 'Desexualising Rape: A Dissenting View on the Proposed Rape Amendments' (unpublished)

Pitch, T. 1985. 'Critical Criminology, the Construction of Social Problems, and the Question of Rape.' *International Journal of Sociology of Law*, 13:35–46

Polk, K. 1985. 'Rape Reform and Criminal Justice Processing.' *Crime and Delinquency* 31:191–205

Pollak, O. 1961. *The Criminality of Women*, New York: A.S. Barnes

Radford, J. 1987. 'Policing Male Violence – Policing Women.' In J. Hamner and M. Maynard, eds., *Women, Violence and Social Control*. London: Macmillan Press, 30–45

Rawls, J. 1971. *A Theory of Justice* Cambridge, MA: The Belknap Press

Renner, K.E., and S. Sahjpaul. 1986. 'The New Sexual Assault Law: What Has Been Its Effect?' *Canadian Journal of Criminology* 28:407–14

Rioux, M.H., and J. McFayden. 1978. 'Notes documentaires sur les modifications proposées au Code criminel en ce qui à l'attentat à la pudeur (Bill C-52).' Ottawa: Le Conseil consultatif canadien de la situation de la femme

Roberts, J. 1990. *Sexual Assault in Canada: An Analysis of National Statistics*, Report 4. Ottawa: Department of Justice Canada

Schwartz, M.D., and T.R. Clear. 1980. 'Toward a New Law on Rape.' *Crime and Delinquency* 26:129–51

Schwendinger, J.R., and H. Schwendinger. 1982. 'Rape, the Law and Private Property.' *Crime and Delinquency* 28: 171–91
– 1983. *Rape and Inequality*, Beverly Hills, CA: Sage
Sebba, L., and. S. Cahan. 1973. 'Sex Offences: The Genuine and the Doubted Victim.' In I. Drapkin and E. Viano, eds., *Victimology: A New Focus*, vol. 5. Lexington: D.C. Heath, 29–46
Senate of Canada, Legal and Constitutional Affairs Standing Committee. 1982. *Minutes of Proceedings*, Queen's Printer for Canada
Sheehy, E.A. 1987. *Personal Autonomy and the Criminal Law: Emerging Issues for Women*. Ottawa: Canadian Advisory Council on the Status of Women
Smart, C. 1989. *Feminism and the Power of Law*. London: Routledge
Smart, C., and J. Brophy. 1985. 'Locating Law: A Discussion of the Place of Law in Feminist Politics.' In J. Brophy and C. Smart, eds., *Women in Law. Explorations in Law, Family and Sexuality*. London: Routledge and Kegan Paul, 1–20
Smith, M.D., and N. Bennett. 1985. 'Poverty, Inequality, and Theories of Forcible Rape.' *Crime and Delinquency* 31:295–305
Snider, L. 1985. 'Legal Reform and Social Control: The Dangers of Abolishing Rape.' *International Journal of Sociology of Law* 13:337–56
Stacey, M., and M. Price. 1981. *Women, Power and Politics*, London: Tavistock
Temkin, J. 1986. 'Women, Rape and Law Reform.' In S. Tomaselli and R. Porter, eds., *Rape*. Oxford: Basil Blackwell, 16–40
Temkin, J. 1987. *Rape and the Legal Process*. London: Sweet and Maxwell
Toronto Star. 1981. January 24:A14
Woodhull, W. 1988. 'Sexuality, Power and the Question of Rape.' In I. Diamond and L. Quinby, eds., *Feminism and Foucault*. Boston: Northeastern University Press, 167–76

3

JULIAN V. ROBERTS AND
MICHELLE G. GROSSMAN

Changing Definitions of Sexual Assault: An Analysis of Police Statistics[1]

The next few chapters of the volume examine various evaluations of the 1983 rape reform legislation. These researchers have, from differing perspectives, tried to evaluate the impact of Bill C-127 upon the criminal justice response to reports of sexual aggression. Law reform is an iterative process: no single piece of legislation, whether it pertain to young offenders, prostitution, or sexual assault, will alone resolve the problems that gave rise to the legislation in the first place. This is particularly true of a far-reaching piece of legislation such as the rape reform of 1983. The aims of Bill C-127 have been articulated elsewhere (e.g., Begin 1989), but they included all stages of the process that commences with a report of a crime and terminates when the case reaches a judicial determination. Bill C-127 attempted to make the criminal justice system more responsive to sexual assault complainants and more equitable in terms of the processing of sexual assault cases. Did it achieve these goals? The following chapters provide valuable insights into the utility of the law reform process to change the behaviour of criminal justice professionals. In this chapter, Roberts and Grossman examine statistics relating to a complainant's first contact with the system, namely when a report is made to a police officer. These statistics represent but a fraction of all sexual assaults committed, but they shed important light upon the police response to reports of sexual assault. The authors first present an analysis of recent trends in the numbers of reports made to the police. These data show a significant increase since 1983. After evaluating various alternative explanations for this increase, the authors conclude that Bill C-127 has had a positive impact on victims' behaviour in terms of reporting to the criminal justice system. However, other trends in the police statistics offer a less positive interpretation of the police response. For example, there appears to have been a shift in the way that police officers classify reports of sexual assault.

There has been an ever-increasing tendency for the police to classify reports at the lowest level of seriousness. This has consequences for all concerned, but especially for the victim. As well, subsequent chapters will show that there has been no change in terms of the percentage of cases cleared by the laying of a charge. The material discussed in this chapter raises a central theme in this volume, one that will be explored by several other contributors: the critical role of interpretation of the Criminal Code sections dealing with sexual assault. Even if the law changes, this does not necessarily mean that social and professional reaction will also change. Chapters 4 and 5 take up the story at later stages of the system.

Introduction

All victims of sexual assault are confronted with a critical decision: to whom should they turn? Some victims turn to family or friends, others to sexual assault crisis centre workers or medical professionals. Many victims report the crime to the police. In 1990, 32,861 individuals reported an incident that was subsequently classified by the police as a crime of sexual assault (Canadian Centre for Justice Statistics 1991). The number of sexual assaults committed is obviously much greater than this. Victims who report to the police represent just part of the picture. It is nevertheless a vital part. The rape reform legislation of 1983 was not aimed so much at attempting to reduce the incidence of sexual assault (although it was hoped that through increased efficiency on the part of the criminal justice system this would be an ancillary benefit), but rather at increasing the proportion of crime victims who report to the police. In this chapter we are concerned with statistics regarding those victims who turn to the police. More specifically, we are interested in a number of questions, particularly those relating to the effects of the 1983 legislation. Thus we do not attempt to estimate the incidence of sexual assault in Canadian society – although this is a critical question that needs to be addressed (see, for example, DeKeseredy and Hinch 1991). In 1993, the Canadian Centre for Justice Statistics conducted a major national survey of adult females in Canada. The results of that survey (details will be available in 1994) will provide (among other things) data on the incidence of various kinds of abuse, including sexual abuse.[2] For our purposes, the aims of the present chapter are more limited, and focus upon the incidence of sexual assaults recorded by the police. In the first part of the chapter we review recent trends in the police statistics pertaining to sexual assault; in the second part we summarize some experimental simulations that attempted to shed light upon the effects of the legislative changes of 1983.

How many sexual assaults are reported to the criminal justice system annually? Are victims of sexual assault in some provinces more likely to report incidents than are victims in other provinces? Did the 1983 reform legislation have any impact on reporting rates? In this chapter we draw upon national criminal justice statistics to address these and other questions. As will be seen, the statistics of assaults reported to the police tell us more than just how many victims are coming forward. They also offer insight into the police response to reports of sexual assault. Victims do not report crimes in terms of Criminal Code section numbers; they talk about specific incidents. A police officer must then decide which level of sexual assault is appropriate, and, as we shall later see, some interesting patterns emerge from the data.

The decision of whether to report or not is critical to the criminal justice system; unless victims (or friends or relatives of victims) come forward, there is little that the justice system can do to address the problem of sexual assault. In fact, unless victims report to the police, our knowledge of the true incidence of the crime will be very poor. As Clark and Lewis (1977) noted: 'We cannot hope to have anything like a complete picture of rape until all victims are willing to report the crime' (41). They were writing six years before the passage of Bill C-127, but their statement holds true today.

One of the principal goals of all recent rape reform initiatives has been to increase the number of victims of sexual aggression who report to the criminal justice system. This was certainly true in Canada, where as Begin (1989) wrote, 'the sexual assault legislation was intended to have an impact on a host of unique behaviours. These include victims' reporting behaviour' (65). Similar aims were attributed to rape reforms in the United States (see Marsh et al. 1982) and in New Zealand (see Barrington 1984). The reason for this interest in the reporting behaviour of victims is that surveys have shown that, in the past at least, most victims of sexual aggression did not report to the police.

REPORTED AND UNREPORTED CRIMES OF SEXUAL AGGRESSION

Reporting Rates

As noted above, the focus of this chapter is upon officially recorded rates of sexual assault. All too often we tend to assume that crimes reported to and recorded by the police represent the universe of victimization. This is obviously not the case. Before proceeding with our analysis of the 'official' (in this case, police) statistics, we briefly discuss what is known about the unreported rates of sexual aggression. The best estimates of reporting rates come from victimization surveys. Research in several American states (see Legrand

1973) suggested that only about one sexual assault in four is reported to the police. More recently, Adler et al. (1991) cite a reporting rate of 55 per cent for rape in the United States. In Canada, a victimization survey was conducted by the federal Ministry of the Solicitor General in 1982 (known as the Canadian Urban Victimization Survey, hereafter CUVS; Solicitor General 1985). Members of the public in several Canadian cities were asked about a series of offences, including rape and indecent assault. The reporting rate for rape and indecent assault that emerged (38 per cent[3]) was higher than estimates in the United States, but still meant that the majority of incidents were not reported to the criminal justice system (see Table 1 in Solicitor General 1984; see also Gunn and Minch 1988, 13–14). The CUVS data described rape and indecent assault, and are accordingly out of date now. The most recent data on the reporting of sexual assaults comes from the Violence Against Women Survey, the results of which are being reported as this volume goes to press. The findings of that survey suggest that the reporting rate of sexual assault is lower than the reporting rate of rape and indecent assault. Only 6 per cent of sexual assaults recorded in that survey had been reported to the police (Statistics Canada 1993). This is considerably lower than the CUVS estimates, and significantly lower than the reporting rate of non-sexual assaults (28 per cent). These data make it clear that although it is important to study incidents reported to the police, they represent a very small fraction of all incidents committed.

Reasons for Not Reporting to the Police

There are many reasons why victims of sexual assault might not wish to report to the police. Perceived ineffectiveness of the police was cited by 52 per cent of rape/indecent assault victims, and by a comparable percentage of assault victims. However, the most frequently cited reason for failing to report in cases of assault was that the incident was too minor (cited by 56 per cent). This was not the case for crimes of sexual aggression: only 26 per cent of rape/indecent assault victims failed to report because the incident was too minor. As well, the CUVS makes it clear that for a substantial minority (44 per cent) of the non-reporting sexual assault victims, anticipation of a negative reaction from the police was a factor in their decision. And here differences also emerge between the victims of crimes of sexual and non-sexual aggression. Only 12 per cent of assault victims stated that the negative attitudes on the part of the police contributed to their decision not to report the crime. To summarize, victims of sexual aggression in the 1982 Canadian survey cited the ineffectiveness and negative attitudes of the police as reasons for not reporting. By comparison, victims of simple common assault cited police inef-fectiveness and the fact that the assault was minor in nature.

If increasing reporting rates is an aim common to all rape reform legisla-tion, there is less uniformity as to the degree to which reforms have to date succeeded in achieving this goal. At this point we shall briefly review the empirical research on the effects of legislative interventions in the United States.

Effects of Rape Reform on Reporting Trends in the United States

One of the most systematic evaluations was conducted in Michigan (see Marsh 1981; Marsh et al. 1982), where rape reform legislation was intro-duced in 1975. The Michigan experience is of particular interest to Canadians, because that state also adopted a tiered offence structure. Thus the crime of forcible rape was replaced by four levels of the new offence of criminal sexual conduct. The evaluation conducted by Marsh and her colleagues shows that the criminal sexual conduct law had no significant effect on the number of reports made to the police (see Marsh et al. 1982, 28–31). It is important to note, however, two important trends. First, that there was a tendency for the number of reports to increase over the period covering the introduction of the legislation, and second, that three-quarters of the criminal justice profes-sionals interviewed by researchers attributed this increase to 'a change in public attitudes toward rape' (see Marsh 1981, 101). Perhaps the legislation increased public awareness of the crime and contributed, over time, to chang-ing attitudes towards reporting to the police. Thus we cannot discard the pos-sibility that the reform legislation played a role – albeit an indirect one – in changing reporting patterns of crimes of sexual aggression (see also Loh 1980).

In some states the results are somewhat more positive. Lebeau (1988) studied the reporting of rape in California before and after passage of rape reform legislation and found an increase in reporting after the legislation was passed. Largen (1988) reports the results of interviews with criminal justice practitioners in several states. She notes that 'respondents noted that when a victim knows of changes [in the law] ... law reform may serve to encourage reporting' (281). Smith and Chapman (1987) interviewed criminal justice practitioners (including district attorneys, defence counsel, police officers, and judges) from six American cities in three states. A common perception was that rape reforms had in fact encouraged the reporting of crimes of sexual aggression. This view was shared by three-quarters of the entire sample.

Horney and Spohn (1989) report the results of impact analyses in six U.S.

jurisdictions. They found a significant increase in reporting in the jurisdiction that had passed the most radical reform. These researchers conclude that legislation can affect reporting rates, but only if the reforms are sufficiently broad and well-publicized (see also Lebeau 1988, Table 1). Finally, Sawyer and Maney (1981) present the results of an evaluation in another area, child abuse reporting. They summarize their research in this way:

We have offered evidence to suggest that people will respond in designated ways to legal mandates governing the reporting of child abuse. *In each phase of the analysis legislative action was found to result in increased reporting levels.* (780; emphasis added)

The evidence from the United States, then, is mixed, suggesting that rape reform legislation has had an effect upon reporting rates, but that this effect has been neither uniform nor easily achieved. Two final points should be made. First, if a general lesson can be derived from the conflicting evidence in the area of sexual assault reporting, it is that the likelihood of a positive result is correlated with the extent to which the reform changes the criminal justice system and the society. Mild reforms will, in all likelihood, have undetectably weak effects on victims' reporting behaviour. Second, there is a limit to what we can learn about the Canadian experience from rape reform legislation in the United States. While Bill C-127 shares features with several American reforms (e.g., the replacement of rape with an offence that stresses the assaultive nature of the crime, and a tiered offence structure), the Canadian legislation (and the social environment in which it functions) is obviously quite different.

Source of Data

In Canada, a report of a crime is recorded whenever someone notifies the police that an offence has been committed. (The exact Criminal Code section to which a report is assigned may not be determined until later, after an 'on-the-scene' appraisal – see Canadian Centre for Justice Statistics 1988). The data summarized in this chapter are national in scope, deriving from the Uniform Crime Reporting System (UCR). This database was created in 1962 to produce a standardized index of the incidence of crime in Canadian society. Local law enforcement agencies submit information to the Canadian Centre for Justice Statistics (located in Statistics Canada – see Canadian Centre for Justice Statistics 1988 for further description of the UCR system). The exact statistic examined is 'reports made.' There is another, related statistic provided by Statistics Canada – so-called 'actual' offences. This term refers to the number of reports that remain after reports deemed to be 'unfounded' have been deleted. Since the founding of sexual assault reports can be a controversial process (see Bowland 1986), in this chapter we are restricting our attention principally to the first statistic: all reports of sexual aggression that are made to, or that otherwise come to the attention of, the police.

The strength of the UCR database upon which we have drawn is its breadth of coverage. There is an important limitation however upon the depth of the data: they do not speak to the factors influencing victims' decisions to report a crime. Nor can they tell us anything about the victims who reported incidents elsewhere (for example to a sexual assault crisis centre) or who did not report the incidents to any official agency. Nevertheless, these data are important for they convey an indication of the pattern (and volume) of crimes reported to the criminal justice system, and can help to resolve questions such as whether the reform legislation of 1983 has had any impact upon the volume of sexual assault cases processed by the justice system. Finally, although the database employed here also provides information on founding and charging practices, the focus in this chapter is on reports of sexual assault (see the next chapter, Roberts 1990b, and Roberts [forthcoming] for national trends regarding these other critical statistics in the area of sexual assault).

Comparisons between Rape/Indecent Assault and Sexual Assault

Is it appropriate to compare pre-reform offences with post-reform ones? Comparisons between the earlier offences of rape and indecent assault and the new offences of sexual assault (hereafter referred to as sexual assault I, II, and III) are far from straightforward. For example, there is no direct legal correspondence between the old offence of rape and the new crimes of sexual assault. Incidents that prior to 1983 would have been classified as rape may now be classified at any of the three levels of sexual assault. This makes some pre–post legislation comparisons inappropriate. It is hard, for example, to compare sentencing patterns between the old and the new offences without knowing a great deal about details of the individual cases (see Roberts 1990a for a discussion of sentencing issues in the area of sexual assault). However the issue of reporting rates is not undermined by this problem to the same degree. While it may not be appropriate to compare the reporting rates of rape to any particular level of sexual assault, one can compare the *overall* reporting rate of the crimes of sexual aggression prior to 1983 (rape, attempt rape, indecent assault against a male or a female) with their counterparts currently defined in the Criminal Code (sexual assault I, II and III). The comparisons will involve the total volume of reports rather than the distribution of individual offences before and after the 1983 reforms. Thus pre–post comparisons will be made in this chapter, although greater emphasis will be upon trends emerging in the statistics relating to sexual assault since 1983.

Offences Included in the Analysis

The analyses will examine the statistics for the offences of rape (including attempt rape); indecent assault against a male and indecent assault against a female; sexual assault; sexual assault with a weapon or causing bodily harm; and aggravated sexual assault. These offences alone do not define the universe of what might be included in the general definition of sexual offences. While Bill C-127 abolished the offences of rape and indecent assault, it did not touch a number of other sexual offences. These included sexual interference, buggery/bestiality, acts of gross indecency, and incest. There may be overlap between these offences and the Bill C-127 offences. To the extent that this overlap is widespread, inferences about the impact of the reform legislation are going to be problematic. The evidence suggests that the overlap is not widespread,[4] and that there has been no change in police practices in this regard since 1983.

Findings

We first examine police statistics on the reporting of crimes of sexual aggression in Canada, for a 12-year period, beginning in 1977 and ending in 1988. The purpose of the analysis is twofold: to examine trends in the incidence of sexual assault reports, and to make comparisons between the present and the pre-reform period. Renner and Sahjpaul (1986) present sexual assault data for 1983, the year of implementation of the reforms, and they note a significant increase over the previous year in the number of sexual assaults reported to the police. They conclude: 'The new law apparently had one of its intended effects' (409). Hinch (1988) examines data from 1984, and reaches a similar conclusion. While it is hard to draw firm conclusions on the basis of a single year, reporting data since then confirm this interpretation. Table 3.1 presents the incidence of sexual assault reports made to the police from 1977 to 1988, for Canada as a whole, and for each province or territory.

This table aggregates data from the three levels of sexual assault (s. 271, s. 272, s. 273). (For the period 1977–82 the offences aggregated are rape, attempt rape, and indecent assault male and female.) The number of reports of crimes of sexual aggression remained fairly constant over the six years

TABLE 3.1
Number[a] of Reports of Crimes of Sexual Aggression,[b] Canada and Provinces

	1977	1978	1979	1980	1981	1982	1983	1984	1985	1986	1987	1988
Canada	10,285	10,687	11,557	12,077	12,376	12,848	13,851	17,323	21,300	24,114	26,443	29,111
Nfld.	204	212	188	214	220	211	262	276	345	548	688	869
P.E.I.	20	28	18	31	60	33	51	107	107	78	95	118
N.S.	273	312	331	386	348	348	360	511	528	675	837	896
N.B.	147	189	200	243	215	165	232	310	455	630	702	870
Qué.	2,161	1,982	2,520	2,313	2,248	2,130	2,090	2,495	2,807	3,267	3,476	3,778
Ont.	3,887	4,000	4,236	4,334	4,348	4,469	4,773	6,315	8,037	8,374	9,234	9,769
Man.	513	527	599	583	651	646	836	993	1,222	1,310	1,465	1,746
Sask.	345	356	358	397	386	484	565	618	756	938	941	1046
Alta.	1,074	1,237	1,235	1,472	1,622	1,760	1,930	2,192	2,764	3,021	3,069	3,484
B.C.	1,553	1,726	1,753	1,967	2,146	2,473	2,544	3,296	3,970	4,936	5,558	6,140
Y.T.	17	25	25	39	31	28	51	59	75	88	106	86
N.W.T.	91	93	94	98	101	101	157	151	234	209	272	309

[a] Reported or known to police.
[b] Rape, attempted rape, and indecent assault prior to 1983; sexual assault after 1983.
Source: Canadian Centre for Justice Statistics.

that preceded the introduction of Bill C-127. Thus there was a modest 27 per cent increase, from 1976 to 1982, in the total number of reports of crimes of sexual aggression. However, the data reveal a significant increase in reports since 1982. In 1982 there were 12,848 reports of one of the three offences of sexual assault; by 1988 this had risen to 29,111. Statistical analysis (Roberts and Gebotys 1992) confirms (a) that this increase is highly significant and (b) that the increase in sexual assault reports exceeds the increase in reporting of other types of assault (see below). Analysis also shows that the increase in the number of reports of sexual assault made to the police began in 1983, and not before (see Roberts and Gebotys 1992).

Differential Reporting Trends for Sexual Assault I, II, and III

The data presented so far have been aggregated across the three levels of sexual assault. This kind of analysis can be misleading; it suggests that the increase in reporting since 1982 has been uniform across the three levels, and this is far from true. In fact, trends in sexual assault reports across levels I, II and III have been strikingly divergent. Examination of the trend lines for the three individual offences (sexual assault I, II, and III) reveals that the substantial increase in sexual assault reporting occurs *only* for sexual assault I. Remarkably, the number of reports of sexual assault classified at the third level has declined steadily since the offence was created in 1983. Thus there has been a significant reduction in the number of incidents classified as aggravated sexual assault over the period. Thus, in 1983, there were 685 reports classified at this level, declining to 436 in 1990. It seems unlikely that there has been such a substantial decrease in the occurrence of incidents of assaults at this level. It is more likely that recording or classifying patterns by the police have changed in some way, so that incidents that in 1983 would have been classified as level III are now being classified at a lower level of seriousness.

If some form of cascading (in terms of police classifiations of reports) from aggravated sexual assault down to the second level of sexual assault has taken place, it does not appear to have affected statistics for sexual assault II. The reduction in reports of aggravated sexual assault has not been matched by a corresponding increase in reports of sexual assault II. Thus, in 1983, there were 925 reports of sexual assault with a weapon. In 1989 there were 971 reports of this offence (see Table 3.2). This is an increase of 11 per cent at the same time that sexual assault I reports rose by 156 per cent, from 12,241 in 1983 to 31,401 in 1990. This suggests that some incidents previously classified at level III are now classified at level I, and that there is a more general

TABLE 3.2
Frequency Distribution of Three Levels of Sexual Assault Reported in Canada 1983–1990

Year	Sexual Assault I		Sexual Assault II		Sexual Assault III	
	No.	(%)	No.	(%)	No.	(%)
1983	12,241	(88)	925	(7)	685	(5)
1984	15,805	(91)	878	(5)	640	(4)
1985	19,756	(93)	918	(4)	590	(3)
1986	22,623	(93)	1,001	(4)	490	(3)
1987	24,949	(94)	1,034	(4)	460	(2)
1988	27,655	(95)	1,041	(4)	415	(1)
1989	30,340	(96)	971	(3)	445	(1)
1990	31,401	(96)	1,024	(3)	436	(1)

SOURCES: Julian V. Roberts 1990b; Canadian Centre for Justice Statistics 1990, 1991.

cascading at work, with incidents being classified down from both the higher levels of sexual assault. The data are summarized in Table 3.2

Distribution of Sexual Assaults across the Three Levels of Seriousness

Table 3.2 also reveals the breakdown of incidents across the three levels. It shows that, over the six-year period, the vast majority of sexual assault reports were classified as level I. Table 3.2 also shows that the percentage of total reports classified by the police at the first level of sexual assault has been steadily increasing. Thus, in 1983, the first year affected by the new legislation, 88 per cent of all sexual assault reports were classified at the first level of seriousness. This figure has risen steadily to 96 per cent in 1990. One interpretation of this trend is that there has been an increase of reports made of the less serious incidents of sexual assault. This would be consistent with the view that the legislation has had an effect. It seems reasonable to assume that in the past, it was the more serious incidents that were more likely to be reported to the police. It is also possible that the seriousness of the incidents reported has not changed, but that there has been a change in the behaviour of police officers who record complaints. Further research on this question is clearly needed (see Roberts and Pires 1992 for further discussion of this issue).

In 1990, fully 96 per cent of reports of sexual assault were classified by the police as being at the first level of seriousness. Three percent were classified at the second level (sexual assault with a weapon or causing bodily harm); only 1 per cent were classified as aggravated sexual assault. By comparison, the breakdown of cases within the three categories of assault is rather different. In 1988, 80 per cent of all non-sexual assaults were at the first level of seriousness. Unlike non-sexual assault then, the two higher levels of sexual assault account for a very small percentage of cases reported.

It is important to recall that the individuals primarily responsible for these classifications are the police officers to whom victims report. In some cases the classification is not sustained by events taking place in the courtroom. This distribution – of 96 per cent of reported sexual assaults classified at level I – derives from the stage at which the complainant first has contact with the justice system. The distribution of all cases taken from the trial stage would be even more unbalanced, for a proportion of the charges at levels II and III will result, through plea bargaining, in convictions at the first level of sexual assault. For example, data from a study on sexual assault in Toronto (Nuttall 1989) found that two-thirds of aggravated sexual assault charges resulted in convictions for the less serious crime of sexual assault with a weapon. Cascading continued at the second level too: an additional 22 per cent of charges at the second level of sexual assault resulted in convictions for sexual assault I. In addition, individuals other than the police officer may well classify a report of sexual assault at a different level. While it is important, this point cannot be explored further here since we have only statistics reflecting classifications made by the police.

Rate of Sexual Assault Reports: Provincial Variation

Examining sexual assault reporting rates per 100,000 population reveals considerable variability across the country. Thus the police statistics for 1990 range from a national low of 55 in Québec to 801 in the Northwest Territories. It might be argued that the comparisons between the territories and Québec are inappropriate given the size of their populations. But one does not have to look far to see further evidence of variation in provinces of comparable size: the British Columbia rate is almost three times the rate in Québec. Several explanations exist for these highly variable sexual assault reporting rates. It is possible that the actual incidence of sexual assault varies across Canada. Certainly some of the variation in reporting rates must reflect variation in actual crime rates. More likely, however, the variation in reporting rates reflects variable attitudes on the part of victims residing in different parts of the country and differences across Canada in the response of police officers to victims of sexual assault.

Evidence for the former can be found in a 1988 survey of the Canadian public (see Chapter 5 by Clark and Hepworth as well as Roberts and Gebotys 1993). In that survey, adult repondents were asked whether, in the event that they were sexually assaulted, they would report to the police. Respondents

TABLE 3.3
Rank-Ordering of Sexual Assault Reporting Rates[a] (1990)

Rank	Province	Rate
1	Northwest Territories	801
2	Yukon	483
3	British Columbia	160
4	Newfoundland	194
5	Manitoba	137
6	Alberta	134
7	New Brunswick	127
8	Saskatchewan	123
9	Nova Scotia	116
10	Prince Edward Island	101
11	Ontario	97
12	Québec	55

[a]Rate of reports of sexual assault per 100,000 population.
SOURCE: Canadian Centre for Justice Statistics 1991.

from Québec were significantly less likely than respondents from other regions in Canada to state that they would turn to the police. The fact that Québec has the lowest *official* rates of sexual assault in Canada probably reflects in part this differential likelihood of reporting.

A related question in terms of provincial variation is whether the reporting increase – so clear at the national level – is consistently observed across the provinces and territories. Space limitations preclude presentation and discussion of reporting patterns over time in each jurisdiction (see Roberts 1990b for graphs on a province-by-province basis) but two observations can be made. First, increased reporting after 1983 is clear in all jurisdictions. Second, there is manifest variation in the slope of the curve and in the onset of the rise in reporting. In some places the increase is far greater, and is detectable soon after the introduction of Bill C-127. This also warrants further attention from researchers. Table 3.3 presents a rank-ordering of sexual assault reporting rates across Canada.

In discussing the relationship between statistics for sexual and non-sexual assault, it is important to realize that, while they are discrete Criminal Code sections, in practice there may be a degree of impermeability. Incidents initially classified as reports of sexual assault may eventually result in convictions for simple assault. Once again the Toronto study cited earlier is informative. Of all charges of sexual assault I or II, fully one-quarter resulted in convictions for non-sexual assault (Nuttall 1989, 115). There are several causes of transfers of this kind. The most frequent is a decision by the Crown to accept a guilty plea to an assault charge in return for dropping a charge of sexual assault. Such agreements carry benefits for almost all parties except the victim and the public. The state benefits by saving the cost of a trial and obtaining the assurance of a conviction. The defendant gains by obtaining a conviction that carries less stigma and the possibility of a more lenient sentence (the maximum penalty for assault is five years rather than ten for sexual assault). The advantage of such a bargain to the sexual assault victim is far less compelling. And as for the public, they are likely to react with considerable hostility to this kind of plea bargaining (see Cohen and Doob 1989 for results of a recent public survey on this issue). Another possible explanation for this traffic between Criminal Code sections concerns the police. In some cases they may lay a charge of assault, anticipating difficulty in gathering evidence to support a charge of sexual assault. It would appear that this accounts for few cases, however.

Thus the assault statistics mask a certain number of incidents of sexual assault. This is evidence of a more general difficulty in establishing motive in crime statistics: for example, a number of sexual homicides are sometimes misclassified in the same way (see Roberts and Grossman 1991). The transfer phenomenon undoubtedly takes place in the United States and Canada (see Boyle 1984). The magnitude of the problem is hard to estimate. It is an issue for which further research is clearly imperative.

Discussion

National police statistics are clear: there has been a significant increase in the number of reports of sexual assault made to the criminal justice system since 1983. But can the increase be unequivocally attributed to the 1983 legislation rather than some other influence, such as a general change in social attitudes to reporting (as appears to have been the case in Michigan)? In Canada, the co-occurrence of the legislation and the relatively sharp increase in reporting in 1983 would seem to rule out such explanations. However, this does not explain the mechanism by which the legislation changed reporting patterns. This is the problem to which we now turn.

One likely explanation concerns a change in the attitudes of victims of sexual assault, who now see more benefits than costs associated with making a report to the police. But it is only a strong possibility. The weakness of a time-series design (such as the one employed here) is that there are many aspects of the reform legislation that may have had an effect upon sexual assault statistics (see Campbell and Stanley 1963, Cook and Campbell 1979). Thus there may be several alternate explanations for the increase in reporting; four of these will now be evaluated. Periodic reference will be made to the multi-site evaluation studies conducted by the Department of Justice. As part of its evaluation of Bill C-127, the Department of Justice commissioned in-depth studies at several locations across Canada. The results of some of these studies can be of assistance in determining the relative merits of the different explanations for the increase in reporting rates (see Chapter 5 by Clark and Hepworth as well as Department of Justice 1990).

As noted in the introduction, a charge of sexual assault can be laid against husbands who assault their wives. This was one of the reforms introduced by Bill C-127. Is it possible that the increase in reporting statistics simply reflects a wider 'constituency' of potential victims? The UCR data examined in this chapter do not include information on the gender of the victim or the relationship between the victim and the accused (although such data are now available from a limited number of jurisdictions as part of the revised UCR database). However, research carried out by the Department of Justice suggests that the number of cases in which the accused was the husband of the victim is very small (see University of Manitoba Research Ltd. 1988). We would discard this theory as an alternative explanation of the rise in reports of sexual assault.

Another alternate explanation for the increase in reports of sexual assault made to the police relates to recording patterns. According to this explanation, incidents classified as sexual assault now include cases formerly recorded as an offence *other* than rape or indecent assault. The Statistics Canada category 'other sexual offences' includes sexual interference; invitation to sexual touching; sexual exploitation; incest; anal intercourse and bestiality. The incidence of these 'other sexual offences' has increased steadily at a rate unchanged since prior to the 1983 legislation. This is important because it localizes the reporting increase in sexual assault statistics. It shows that the rise in reporting was not associated with all sexual offences, but rather was specific to the sexual assault crimes. Thus there was an 8 per cent increase in reports of 'other sexual offences' between 1978 and 1982, and a similar (5 per cent) increase in the post-reform period (1983 to 1988). Since there has been no decrease in the reports of these other offences, it would seem likely that there has been an increase in sexual assault reporting, independent of the reporting statistics for other sexual offences. There also seems to be no evidence that the police changed their recording practices in 1983. If there had been a shift in recording practices, there would have been changes detectable in the founding rate. In fact the percentage of sexual assault reports deemed by the police to be 'unfounded' has not changed over the period in question (Roberts 1990b).

It might be argued that acts that before 1983 were not brought to the attention of the police are now being reported as sexual assaults. These acts might include some of the less serious forms of sexual assault. Prior to 1983, victims might not have seen them as criminal in nature, not even as indecent assault. After 1983, however, victims see such acts as constituting crimes under the sexual assault legislation. This explanation is hard to sustain or refute; it may explain some of the cases that have come forward since 1983. It is consistent with the increase in numbers of cases classified at the first level of seriousness. However, examination of data uncovered in the course of the evaluation initiative launched by the Department of Justice suggests that the incidents now reported as sexual assault do not differ greatly from the kinds of incidents formerly reported as indecent assault or rape. This explanation of the increase therefore seems unconvincing.

It is harder to eliminate the explanation that the 1983 legislation has had no effect upon the reporting behaviour of adult victims but has had a significant impact upon the reporting of assaults committed against juveniles. Unfortunately, the national data examined in this chapter do not specify the age of the complainant. The evidence on sexual assault reporting from the Department of Justice studies seems to suggest that an increase in young complainants has taken place but that the magnitude of the increase cannot explain the substantial increase in reports of sexual assault. For example, in the Montreal site study, there was only a small shift in the age profile of complainants. In the pre-reform period, young (under 18) complainants accounted for 37 per cent of all cases. This rose slightly to 43 per cent in the post-reform period (Baril et al. 1988). In Winnipeg there was a larger increase in the proportion of young complainants: 43 per cent were under 17 prior to 1983; 66 per cent after (University of Manitoba Research Ltd. 1988). However, it is impossible for this explanation to account for the dramatic increase in sexual assault reports, which have more than doubled since 1983.

Another possible explanation for the increase in reporting relates to sexual abuse of juveniles. In some cases of child sexual abuse, charges of sexual assault are also laid. The Department of Justice research is of use here too: it suggests that while there has been an increase in the proportion of complainants (in cases of sexual assault) under 14, this trend cannot account for the dramatic increase in reports of sexual assault from 1983 to 1988. Moreover, the timing of the increase in sexual assault reporting suggests a direct connection to the reforms introduced in 1983.

Finally, it is possible that there has been a general increase in all crimes of violence over the period in question. Table 3.4 provides comparative report-

TABLE 3.4
Reporting Rates, Canada, Selected Offences (1983–1988)

	1983	1984	1985	1986	1987	1988
Sexual Assault						
II	42	54	67	75	82	91
II	3	3	3	4	4	4
III	2	2	2	2	2	1
Assault						
I	331	366	398	437	483	501
II	98	105	107	113	117	120
III	14	12	10	11	10	11

ing data between sexual and non-sexual assault for the post-reform period (1983–8). The three assault offences used for comparative purposes are: assault (s. 266); assault with a weapon or causing bodily harm (s. 267); aggravated assault (s. 268). These data are provided not because the offences are comparable in terms of seriousness, but rather to see whether there has been a comparable increase for other personal injury offences. In order to compare the two categories of assault, the unit of comparison in this table is the incidence of 'actual offences,'[5] rather than reports made. As this table shows, there has been a rise in the rates of non-sexual assault since 1983, but this increase does not approach the magnitude of the growth in sexual assault reporting rates. Thus, there has been a 51 per cent increase in the reporting rate of assault (s. 266); this compares with the 110 per cent increase in the rate of sexual assault (116 per cent between 1983 and 1988). The hypothesis that the increase in sexual assaults can be wholly attributed to a general increase in crimes against the person can therefore be rejected.

To summarize, none of these alternate explanations can account for the significant increase in reporting rates of sexual assault that is discernible beginning in 1983, the year of the reforms. It would seem that Bill C-127 played a role, directly or indirectly, in encouraging more victims to come forward and report to the police. At this point we describe research that attempted to evaluate the impact upon reporting statistics, of the change in terminology from rape to sexual assault.

FROM RAPE TO SEXUAL ASSAULT: CHANGING THE LANGUAGE
OF THE LAW

In the second part of this chapter, we address the issue of whether the change in language effected by the reform legislation has had an impact on perceptions of crimes of sexual aggression. As already noted, crimes that were previously described as indecent assault, or rape, are now described as sexual assault. This change was made very deliberately, but has it had an effect upon public perceptions? We explore two possibilities: first, that the change in language has had a direct effect upon the probability that victims will report assaults to the police; and second, that the change in terminology has affected public perceptions of the nature of crimes of sexual aggression. One of the authors of this chapter (Grossman) has conducted research on this question, using members of the Canadian public as subjects. We shall conclude this chapter by reviewing this research. First, however, we should be a little more specific about the kinds of positive effects legislators had in mind when they introduced the new term of 'sexual assault.'

Of the offences of sexual aggression that were contained in the Criminal Code prior to 1983, rape clearly carried the greatest degree of stigma for the victim. This stigma probably constrained reporting rates, and, on account of stereotypes held by others, also may well have worked to suppress conviction rates in rape cases. The empirical research literature contains many studies that have demonstrated the differential attributions of responsibility reserved for particular kinds of rape victims. For example, LaFree, Reskin, and Visher (1985) examined data drawn from actual jurors in rape trials. They found that in trials in which the major issue was whether an assault had in fact taken place, evidence of the victim's drinking, drug use, or sexual activity led jurors to harbour doubts about the guilt of the accused. Similar results have been found in experimental studies involving simulated jurors: stereotypical expectations about the appropriate behaviour of rape victims clearly affect attributions of responsibility for the crime. Consequently, the stigma associated with rape inhibited reporting to the police, and placed rape complainants at a disadvantage from the outset of the criminal justice process. Thus a primary reason behind the redefinition and relabelling of these offences was a desire to address problems relating to the perception (and self-perception) of victims of sexual assault.

A second reason for redefining and renaming the offences of sexual aggression concerns the nature of the offences themselves. The crimes of rape and indecent assault were located in the pre-1983 Criminal Code in the section of sexual offences. Several writers have argued that they belong instead in the section of the Code dealing with crime against the person. Creating new offences of sexual assault (and relocating them in the Code) was an explicit recognition of the true nature of the crimes, which until 1983 had been effectively misclassified by drafters of the Criminal Code.

A number of aspects of the 1983 legislation attempted to reform the perception and hence treatment of sexual assault. The aspect of the legislative change we are concerned with is the linguistic transformation from rape to sexual assault. Is there evidence that, in moving from the familiar language of rape to the unknown terminology of sexual assault, the law has changed perceptions of crimes of sexual aggression? As Chappell (1984) noted, proponents of Canada's new law hope to eliminate 'some of the myth and stigma' surrounding rape by substituting new offences, and new labels for the conduct formerly categorized as rape in common law (74–5). Chase (1982) elaborated on this theme:

Advocates of Bill C-127 regard the terms *rape* and *indecent assault* as archaic and inflammatory. Doing away with these terms will also tend to alleviate some of the sex discrimination inherent in sexual assault laws. Stressing the assaultive rather than the sexual nature of sex offences will remove some of the stigma attached to such charges and serve to correct public misperceptions about the nature of such acts (53).

We are not aware of any research that has examined the effect of the legal terminology on public perceptions of offences of sexual aggression. The aim of this research (conducted by Grossman and Anthony N. Doob from the Centre of Criminology at the University of Toronto) was to see if public views of the same crime would change if the incident was described as a sexual assault rather than a rape. After several years, the time has come to see if this aspect of the reform legislation has been successful in achieving the goal of changing perceptions. Has there been a substantial shift in perceptions of sexual assault, or have the legislative changes simply been a semantic exercise?

The method chosen to examine this question was an experimental simulation[6] conducted at the Ontario Science Centre, a science museum in Toronto. Members of the public (all women) were asked to read an account of a sexual attack, one that fit the description of either sexual assault or rape. The description was accompanied by one of two crime definitions: the attack was described as a rape or as a sexual assault. As well, definitions of the offence were provided. Subjects in the study were randomly assigned to one of the two experimental conditions. This guarantees that there were no differences between the two groups *before* the experiment began. Any differences in the two groups' reactions to the cases can therefore be attributed to the manipulation, which was the label describing the offence. If the terminology used to describe an offence of sexual aggression is important, the reactions of the subjects to the crime should be different, depending upon whether the incident was described as a rape or a sexual assault. Although the participants in this study were not victims per se, but members of the public responding to a hypothetical scenario, a number of studies (e.,g., Feldman-Summers and Norris 1984) have shown the utility of such research of this nature.[7] As well, experimental simulations are the principal means by which researchers have explored public reactions to legislative changes. While not perfect they can provide important information about the impact of legislation.

After reading the description of the incident, subjects were asked a series of questions. For example, they were asked whether *they* would report an attack of this kind if they had been the victim. The reasoning behind this question was that if there is less stigma associated with the term 'sexual assault' rather than 'rape,' then subjects might indicate a greater willingness to report the same attack when described as a sexual assault rather than a rape. Other questions dealt with the amount of stigma that subjects thought might be attached to the victim, the seriousness of the offence, and so on.

The primary hypothesis tested in the study was that subjects who had read the description of the attack described as sexual assault would state that they would be more willing to report the crime (than other subjects who had read of the same assault described as rape). The results indicated that the label had few significant effects upon subjects' reactions to the case. What was important was the nature of the assault, rather than the legal label describing the attack. Respondents stated that they would be more likely to report an assault if it had been committed by a stranger than if it had been committed by an acquaintance. In addition, ratings of the seriousness of the crime were also unaffected by whether it was defined as a sexual assault or a rape. This pattern of findings was repeated in a second study using another group of subjects, this time including males as well. Once again, whether the attack was described as a sexual assault or as a rape had no significant effect upon subjects' reactions. These findings suggest that it is not so much the semantic aspects of the criminal justice legislation that counts, but rather the perceived social consequences of the assault. There are important lessons here for law reform in the area of sexual assault. These findings suggest that what needs to be considered when examining issues such as the likelihood of sexual assaults being reported is not so much the semantics of the legislation, but the practical realities and consequences for the victim.

To summarize, while the reform legislation of 1983 appears to have had a positive effect upon the numbers of victims turning to the police, the change in terminology has not been effective in altering public perceptions about the nature of crimes of sexual aggression. We conclude that the increase in reports of sexual assault made to the police did not come about on account of the change in terminology. Other aspects of the 1983 legislation must have been responsible.

Conclusions

In this chapter we have reviewed the trends in sexual assault statistics recorded by the police in Canada over the past decade. As well, we have summarized the findings from experimental research upon the effects of the 1983 reform legislation. Taken together, these sources of data reveal both the limited success, and the limitations of, the sexual assault reforms introduced over ten years ago. Many aspects of the reporting of sexual assaults to the police remain to be explored. The new, revised UCR data, which provide information about the characteristics of the victim and the accused (including the nature of the relationship between the two) will be of use in this regard. For the present, we can draw some conclusions about the impact of Bill C-127 on the behaviour of victims of sexual assault.

The data on sexual assaults reported to the criminal justice system in Canada since 1983 suggest that the reform legislation has had a significant impact on the behaviour of sexual assault victims. Although the influx of additional victims and the presence of a greater number of younger complainants explains part of the increase, in all probability the legislation (although not the change in terminology – see above) has also had an indirect effect upon the attitudes, and hence the behaviour, of victims in general. If more victims are reporting to the police, this implies that the percentage of *un*reported crimes has declined. This hypothesis can be confirmed only by a victimization survey. The Canadian Urban Victimization Survey was conducted in 1982, prior to the rape reform legislation. Unfortunately it has not been fully replicated; it is impossible to know if attitudes toward reporting have changed since the advent of Bill C-127.[8]

There is some evidence however, to support the view that attitudes (and behaviour) have changed. It comes from two sources. First, the Canadian Urban Victimization Survey was replicated in one city (Edmonton) after the sexual assault law was passed. The results showed that the percentage of sexual assault victims reporting to the police – in that jurisdiction at least – had risen from 15 to 39 per cent.[9] This replication was conducted in 1985. If similar changes were taking place across the country, it would support the view that a greater percentage of victims saw a benefit in reporting to the police. And this in turn would explain the rise in the numbers of sexual assaults reported to the police.

To return to the public opinion survey cited earlier (Department of Justice 1990),[10] respondents were asked a series of questions about the issue of sex-

ual assault. The results showed that the public had more positive than negative attitudes toward the criminal justice system's response to victims of
sexual assault. For example, only one-third of the respondents felt the police
treated victims unfairly. Over half felt that Crown prosecutors treated victims fairly (21 per cent felt they treated victims unfairly; 24 per cent had no
opinion). On the critical question of reporting, respondents were asked the
following: 'Imagine that you yourself were the victim of sexual assault.
Would you definitely, probably, probably not or definitely not contact the
following people or institutions?' They were then provided with the following list: the police; a friend or family member; a sexual assault crisis centre; a
telephone distress centre; a family doctor or hospital.

Respondents indicated that they would be most likely to report to the
police. For example, over two-thirds (68 per cent) stated that they would definitely report to the police. This is double the percentage who stated they
would contact a sexual assault crisis centre. In fact, only 3 per cent of respondents stated they would definitely *not* report a sexual assault to the police.
Results were similar when the question concerned a sexual assault involving
a friend: an even higher percentage (90 per cent) stated they would report to
the police if a friend had been sexually assaulted. If these findings can be generalized to the actual victims of sexual assault – and the trends are broad
enough to make this likely – then it suggests a plausible explanation for the
increase in reporting since 1983: victims of sexual assault now have more
confidence in the criminal justice system.

Finally, a survey of sexual assault victims in Toronto (Nuttall 1989) found
fairly positive attitudes toward criminal justice professionals on the part of
sexual assault victims. Fully 90 per cent of the victims said that they felt the
police treated them with a 'a moderate amount' to 'a great deal of understanding.' Only 11 per cent stated that they were not at all satisfied with the
police response. Similar findings emerged for the Crown. Nuttall (1989)
describes victims' reactions to the Crown in the following way:

On the whole, the women interviewed expressed a high level of satisfaction with the
Crown Attorney. The women reported that they were treated with some understanding by the Crown and felt the Crown had fulfilled some fundamental expectations
such as advising women about what to expect in court, explaining the charges that had
been laid, and answering all questions (121).

While they are not directly comparable, these statistics are instructive
when compared with pre-reform victimization surveys. The CUVS found that
the victim reported to the police in only a quarter of cases (see endnote 2).

Another survey also conducted prior to the reform legislation was passed (but published after – see Brillon, Louis-Guérin, and Lamarche 1984) found that only 15 per cent of victims of sexual aggression reported to the police. The results of the poll conducted after 1983 strongly support the interpretation that victims have more positive attitudes toward reporting, and that this transformation took place close to, if not at the same time as, the passage of Bill C-127. One of the principal aims of the 1983 legislation was to encourage the victims of sexual assault to report incidents to the criminal justice system. The data indicate that in this respect the law, or the publicity surrounding its passage, has had some impact. Reporting issues have been addressed, not resolved, by Bill C-127. While evidence suggests that the reform has had a positive impact upon victims – more are coming forward, particularly young complainants – continued monitoring of the law's impact will be necessary before the needs of all sexual aggression victims are adequately met.

Once a report has been reported by the police, criminal justice processing begins. The police will conduct an investigation to determine whether the report (in their view at least) is with foundation. A certain percentage of reports will be discarded as 'unfounded.' Of those that remain, charges will be laid in a certain percentage. This chapter has reviewed recent research pertaining to the processing of sexual assault cases in this country. However, as noted in Chapter 1, sexual assault is not restricted to adult victims: child sexual abuse has also become a major issue of concern to Canadians. This concern resulted, at the legislative level, in the passage of Bill C-15. In the next chapter, Rita Gunn and Rick Linden present the results of a Manitoba study that examined the processing of child sexual abuse cases.

Notes

1 Some material in this chapter draws upon a report written for the Department of Justice (Roberts 1990b) and an article published in *Law and Human Behavior* (Roberts and Gebotys 1992). We thank both the Department and the Journal for permission to use this material. In addition the authors would like to acknowledge the assistance of personnel from the Canadian Centre for Justice Statistics..

2 The 1993 Violence Against Women Survey is part of the overall package of initiatives of the federal government on the issue of family violence. For further details about the survey, the reader is advised to contact Ms. Holly Johnson at the Canadian Centre for Justice Statistics, located within Statistics Canada.

3 The figure of 38 per cent (or sometimes 39 per cent - both figures are cited in different CUVS publications, see Solicitor General 1984, 1985) is usually cited. It suggests that 62 per cent of victims of sexual assault did not report to the police. In fact,

the percentage of non-reporters is higher. Of all the incidents reported, 14 per cent were reported by someone other than the victim. For comparability with other databases (and for consistency) it would be more accurate to say that 76 per cent of sexual assault victims did not report to the police (and not 62 per cent). This correction makes the pre-to-post–reform differences in attitudes even more striking.

4 Interviews with officials responsible for data collection reveal a high degree of confidence that a close correspondence exists between the earlier offences and the new sexual assault offences that have replaced them. That is, all incidents that would previously have been classified as rape, attempt rape, or indecent assault (male or female) are now classified as one of the three levels of sexual assault.

5 The term 'actual offences' is used by Statistics Canada to refer to reports of sexual assault that remain after 'unfounded' reports are dropped – see introduction to chapter. It does not refer, as some have mistakenly believed, to all offences taking place, reported and unreported.

6 A complete account of this study can be found in Grossman (1990).

7 It might be argued that since these subjects were not actual victims, but rather individuals giving their reactions to hypothetical situations, one cannot draw valid inferences from a simulation study of this kind. In fact, previous research has shown a remarkable concordance between the responses of real victims and the responses of women reacting to hypothetical situations. Feldman-Summers and Norris (1984) conducted such comparisons and concluded that 'factors considered by women who were faced with the actual choice of reporting or not appear to be virtually the same as factors that are considered by women who are faced with a hypothetical rape situation' (571).

8 The recent international victimization survey (see van Dijk et al. 1989) has not been discussed here because it used a question that is incompatible with the CUVS surveys.

9 It should be pointed out that since this study was conducted in only one city (unlike the complete CUVS survey), these percentages are based upon small numbers of incidents and are accordingly somewhat unstable. This instability affects both periods, however, and therefore cannot explain the increase from 1981 to 1985.

10 It is important to note, however, that in light of the prevalence of sexual assault, a large-scale survey of the public is likely to include a number of victims of sexual assault. The distinction between a survey of victims and a survey of the public is not that clear-cut.

References

Adler, F., G. Mueller, and W. Laufer. 1991. *Criminology*. New York: McGraw-Hill
Baril, M., M.J. Bettez, and L. Viau. 1988. *Sexual Assault Before and After the 1983*

Reform: An Evaluation of Practices in the Judicial District of Montreal, Quebec.
Ottawa: Department of Justice

Barrington, R. 1984. 'The Rape Law Reform Process in New Zealand.' *Criminal Law Journal* 8:307–25

Begin, P. 1989. 'Rape Law Reform in Canada: Evaluating Impact.' In *Crime and Its Victims: International Research and Public Policy Issues.* Proceedings of the Fourth International Institute on Victimology (NATO Advanced Research Workshop). New York: Hemisphere Publishing Company

Bowland, A. 1986. *Rape, The Family and the State: Controlling Female Deviance.* Manuscript. Toronto: Osgoode Hall Law School

Boyle, C. 1984. *Sexual Assault.* Toronto: Carswell

Brillon, Y., C. Louis-Guérin, and M. Lamarche. 1984. *Attitudes of the Canadian Public Toward Crime Policies.* Montreal: International Centre for Comparative Criminology

Campbell, D., and J. Stanley. 1963. *Experimental and Quasi-experimental Designs for Research.* Chicago: Rand McNally

Canadian Centre for Justice Statistics. 1988. *Excerpts from the Uniform Crime Reporting Manual.* Ottawa: Statistics Canada

– 1990. *Canadian Crime Statistics 1989.* Ottawa: Statistics Canada

– 1991. *Canadian Crime Statistics 1990.* Ottawa: Statistics Canada

Chappell, D. 1984. 'The Impact of Rape Legislation Reform: Some Comparative Trends.' *International Journal of Women's Studies* 7:70–80

Chase, G. 1982. 'An Analysis of the New Sexual Assault Laws.' *Canadian Women's Studies* 4:53–4

Clark, L., and D. Lewis. 1977. *Rape: The Price of Coercive Sexuality.* Toronto: Women's Press

Cohen, S., and A. Doob. 1989. 'Public Attitudes to Plea Bargaining.' *Criminal Law Quarterly* 32:85–109

Cook, T., and D. Campbell. 1979. 'Quasi-experiments: Interrupted Time Series Designs.' In: *Quasi-experimentation.* Chicago: Rand McNally, ch. 5

DeKeseredy, W., and R. Hinch. 1991. *Woman Abuse: Sociological Perspectives.* Toronto: Thompson Educational Publishing

Department of Justice. 1990. *Overview, Sexual Assault Legislation in Canada: An Evaluation, Report No. 5.* Ottawa: Department of Justice, Research Section

Environics Research Group. 1987. *Survey of Public Attitudes Toward Justice Issues in Canada.* Toronto: Environics Research Group Limited

Feldman-Summers, S., and C. Ashworth. 1981. "Factors Related to Intentions to Report a Rape." *Journal of Social Issues* 37:53–70

Feldman-Summers, S., and J. Norris. 1984. 'Differences between Rape Victims Who Report and Those Who Do Not Report to a Public Agency.' *Journal of Applied Social Psychology,* 14:562–73

Grossman, M.G. 1990. *Canadian Legislative Changes in the Area of Sexual Aggression: An Experimental Survey of Female Respondents*. Toronto: Centre of Criminology, University of Toronto

Gunn, R., and C. Minch. 1988. *Sexual Assault: The Dilemma of Disclosure, The Question of Conviction*. Winnipeg: University of Manitoba Press

Horney, J., and C. Spohn. 1989. *The Impact of Rape Reform Legislation*. Washington, DC: National Institute of Justice

LaFree, G., B. Reskin, and C. Visher. 1985. 'Jurors' Responses to Victims' Behavior and Legal Issues in Sexual Assault Trials.' *Social Problems* 32:389–407

Largen, M. 1988. 'Rape-Law Reform. An Analysis.' In A. Burgess, ed., *Rape and Sexual Assault II*. New York: Garland Publishing

LeBeau, J. 1988. 'Statute Revision and the Reporting of Rape.' *Sociology and Social Research* 72:201–7

Legrand, C. 1973. 'Rape and Rape Laws: Sexism in Society and Law.' *California Law Review* 61:919–41

Loh, W.D. 1980. 'The Impact of Common Law and Reform Rape Statutes on Prosecution: An Empirical Study.' *Washington Law Review* 55:542–652

– 1981. 'Q: What Has Reform of Rape Legislation Wrought? A: Truth in Criminal Labelling.' *Journal of Social Issues* 37:28–52

Marsh, J. 1981. 'Combining Time Series with Interviews: Evaluating the Effects of a Sexual Assault Law.' In R. Conner, ed., *Methodological Advances in Evaluation Research*. Sage Research Progress Series in Evaluation. vol. 10. Beverly Hills, CA: Sage

Marsh, J., A. Geist, and N. Caplan. 1982. *Rape and the Limits of Law Reform*. Boston, MA: Auburn House

Marsh, J. 1983. *Policy Research on Sexual Assault in the 80's*. Denver, CO: Annual Convention of the American Society of Criminology

Nuttall, S. 1989. *Toronto Sexual Assault Research Study*. Ottawa: Ministry of the Solicitor General

Renner, K., and S. Sahjpaul. 1986. 'The New Sexual Assault Law: What Has Been Its Effect?' *Canadian Journal of Criminology* 28:407–13

Roberts, J.V. 1990a. *Sentencing Patterns in Cases of Sexual Assault. Sexual Assault Legislation in Canada: An Evaluation, report No.3*. Ottawa: Department of Justice

– 1990b. *An Analysis of National Statistics. Sexual Assault Legislation in Canada: An Evaluation, Report No. 4*. Ottawa: Department of Justice

– 1994 (forthcoming). 'Criminal Justice Processing of Sexual Assault Costs.' *Juristat Service Bulletin*.

Roberts, J.V., and M.G. Grossman. 1991. *Homicide and Sexual Assault. Sexual Assault Legislation in Canada: An Evaluation, Report No. 7*. Ottawa: Department of Justice

Roberts, J.V., and R.G. Gebotys. 1992. 'Reforming Rape Laws: Effects of Legislative Reform in Canada.' *Law and Human Behavior* 16:555–73
– 1993. *Public Attitudes towards Sexual Assault.* Unpublished ms. University of Ottawa: Department of Psychology
Roberts, J.V., and A.P. Pires. 1992. 'Le renvoi et la classification des infractions d'agression sexuelle.' *Criminologie* 25:27–63
Sawyer, D., and A. Maney. 1981. 'Legal Reform in Child Abuse Reporting.' *Evaluation Review.* 5:758–87
Smith, B., and J. Chapman. 1987. 'Rape Law Reform Legislation: Practitioners' Perceptions of the Effectiveness of Specific Provisions.' *Response to the Victimization of Women and Children* 10:3–8
Solicitor General. 1984. *Canadian Urban Victimization Survey: Reported and Unreported Offences.* Ottawa: Supply and Services Canada
– 1985. *Female Victims of Crime. Canadian Urban Victimization Survey Number 4.* Ottawa: Supply and Services Canada
Statistics Canada (1993) The Violence Against Women Survey. *The Daily,* Thursday, 18 November.
University of Manitoba Research Limited. 1988. *Report on the Impact of the 1983 Sexual Assault Legislation in Winnipeg, Manitoba.* Ottawa: Department of Justice
Van Dijk, J., P. Mayhew, and M. Killias. 1989. *Experiences of Crime across the World: Key Findings of the 1989 International Survey.* The Hague: Research and Documentation Centre, Ministry of Justice

4

RITA GUNN AND RICK LINDEN

The Processing of Child
Sexual Abuse Cases

One of the emerging realities of crimes of sexual aggression in Canada (and elsewhere) is that a significant proportion of assaults are committed against children. Until fairly recently, this form of sexual aggression has remained hidden, for many reasons, including fear or a perception of powerlessness on the part of young victims. The after-effects of sexual assault in childhood can last for years, and disrupt a person's life. More recently, as noted in Chapter 1, a number of cases have come to light that will inevitably lead to more victims coming forward. Accordingly, a volume about sexual assault that did not include a chapter on sexual assaults involving children would fail to reflect reality as experienced by victims. In this chapter, Rita Gunn and Rick Linden explore data describing sexual assaults of this nature. As will be seen from their presentation and discussion, several of the themes emerging from other chapters involving adult offenders are also relevant here. For example, the authors explore the origin of child sexual abuse in terms of the inequitable power relations that exist within the contemporary family. Strong parallels exist between adult and child sexual abuse: both women and children are the victims of inequitable distribution of power within an essentially patriarchal society. This chapter also raises an empirical issue of relevance to all forms of criminal sexual aggression: attrition of cases as they are processed by the criminal justice system. Gunn and Linden show that almost three-quarters of the cases in their sample are filtered out at various stages. A similar phenomenon is observed at the adult level. The challenge to researchers now is to understand why this is the case, and to identify the extent to which the attrition rate is higher for sexual offences.

While the other chapters in this volume examine sexual assault primarily as it relates to adult victims, here we address those cases in which the complainant is a minor. As noted in Chapter 1, child sexual abuse has recently received a great deal of attention in the news media. The Canadian public have been made aware of the fact that a substantial proportion of sexual assaults involve children. Child sexual abuse refers to any act involving the sexual exploitation of a child by either an adult or a significantly older child (Giles 1983).[1] Child sexual abuse typically occurs over a fairly long period of time (Gebhard et al. 1965, Maisch 1972), often does not involve physical violence (Gebhard et al. 1965), but is experienced by the child as coercive and assaultive (Berliner, 1980, Breines and Gordon 1983). In this chapter we will explore the processing of child sexual abuse cases in Manitoba.

The sexual abuse of children is widespread (De Francis 1969, Finkelhor 1979, Russell 1983, Badgley 1984). It is difficult to determine the extent of the problem because of the secretive nature of child sexual abuse, so most victims will never be identified (Finkelhor 1984). General population surveys are not helpful because of variations in research definitions and methodology. However, it appears that anywhere from 12 to 38 per cent of all women and 3 to 15 per cent of all men have been subjected to some form of sexual abuse in their childhood (Whitcomb et al. 1985, 3).

Although there are many differing theories on the etiology of child sexual abuse, there is general agreement that offenders are almost always male and are usually related to, or close friends of, the victim (Rush 1980). The largest group of offenders are fathers (Ward 1984) and an estimated 92 per cent of sexually abused children are believed to be female (Herman and Hirschman 1977). Like sexual assaults involving adults, child sexual abuse is commonly an offence against females, perpetrated by men. The abuse usually begins by the time the child is nine or ten (Giles 1983; Jaffe et al. 1975), but, it may begin as young as two or three (Gagnon 1965, Gebhard et al. 1965), or earlier (Sgroi 1975).

The prevalence of child sexual abuse in the family must be seen in the context of broader power relations within society. From this perspective, child sexual abuse is reflective of gender and generational inequalities embedded in our society. Children are vulnerable targets for adults because they are regarded as parental property (Armstrong 1978, Bagley 1986, Chisholm 1978). Their needs and rights are considered secondary to those of adults (Berliner 1980), and they are assumed to be less credible and reliable than adults (Berliner 1980). Further, girls are especially vulnerable because male dominance within our society legitimizes the view that females are suitable objects for male control and pleasure (Finkelhor 1979, Rush 1980, Breines and Gordon 1983, Ward 1984, Bagley 1986, Brock and Kinsman 1986, Clark 1986). Consequently, most children have been afraid to tell anyone about the abuse, and are often not believed when they do come forward.

In 1980 a federal committee was appointed 'to enquire into the incidence and prevalence in Canada of sexual offences against children and youths and to recommend improvements in laws for the protection of young persons from sexual abuse and exploitation' (Badgley 1984). The committee found extensive sexual exploitation and abuse of children combined with inadequate protection and vastly deficient services (39).

SOCIAL SERVICES

Each of Canada's 12 jurisdictions (provinces and territories) has its own child welfare statutes and service programs. The Badgley Report (1984) found that the jurisdictions had no common definition of child sexual abuse, little documentation of the services provided, and no information as to whether these services were effective (541). Furthermore, only four jurisdictions even included 'sexual abuse' as part of the definition of 'children in need of protection' in their child protection statutes (548). In general, child protection workers are responsible for services such as counselling and crisis intervention for the children and their families, as well as coordinating referrals to other agencies. The report found that in the first instance, assessment of cases and follow-up were inadequate. In the second, coordination and contact between services was insufficient (614).

The intervention strategies of child protection agencies were found to revolve around two different models: child-centred and family-centred. In Canada, two provinces follow the child-centred approach, while two follow the family-centred approach. The rest adopt elements from both approaches and, in some instances, appear 'to have no consistent operational approach in serving sexually abused children' (628).

In the child-centred approach, the victim is the focus of service, the abuse is treated as a 'crime' that is also morally wrong and damaging to the child, and the adult is considered responsible for the abuse (620). This approach uses interdisciplinary teamwork involving coordination between legal, medical, and child protection services of which the criminal justice system is an essential element. In contrast, the family-centred approach assumes that the family should be the primary focus of service, that the needs of the child are best served in that context, that children have a right not to be assaulted but also have a right to live in their 'natural' homes, and that intervention is more effective and ethical when it is voluntary (624). The utilization of this model leads to a decreased involvement with the criminal justice system.

The emphasis is on the promotion of voluntary therapy for the entire family.

The Badgley Report found that while the long-term benefits of both models are unknown, the child-centred model clearly offered the most short-term benefits. The documented benefits include: more promptly undertaken initial assessments; more victims receiving medical examinations; broader and more extensive consultation with other disciplines in relation to assessing the child's needs; a slightly higher proportion of victims, their mothers and their siblings being interviewed; a substantially higher proportion of victims being counselled; and, overall, the more frequent provision of a broader range of counselling and treatment services for victims and members of their families. In almost two out of three cases, after notification to an agency, the resident offender was removed from the home (636).

THE MANITOBA CONTEXT

Manitoba was one of the earliest provinces in Canada to become involved in an organized attempt to deal with problems of child sexual abuse. In 1984, specific guidelines were instituted in the province to respond to reported cases of child abuse. The approach is multidisciplinary, and is intended to provide 'a procedural and legal framework for the investigation, detection and management of child abuse cases' (Manitoba Guidelines on Identifying and Reporting Child Abuse 1984). The guidelines were developed to enable professionals and laypersons to work more effectively as a team, and to encourage sharing of information and responsibility. However, despite this intention, those handling child sexual abuse are still confronted with numerous obstacles in processing cases. Most important has been a sharp increase in caseload as a result of growing awareness among professionals and parents.

As a result of the sudden demand on limited services and resources in social and legal agencies, caseloads are exceptionally high. There was almost a 100 per cent increase in reported cases of children being sexually abused by adults in Manitoba between 1981 and 1985, and a 200 per cent increase between 1979 and 1985 (Child and Family Support Branch, Department of Community and Social Services 1986). A study by three physicians from the Winnipeg Children's Hospital Child Protection Centre stated, 'The return of children to unchanged abusive environments continues to be a significant problem, as is the need for treatment resources' (Longstaffe et al. 1986). Even these limited data indicate that the sexual abuse of children is a significant social problem, and that existing programs and services are not sufficient to deal with it.

In the study described in this chapter, we followed the paths of reported cases of child sexual abuse in Winnipeg, Manitoba, as the cases proceeded through the criminal justice, child welfare, and medical systems. This was one of several studies commissioned by the federal Department of Justice as part of its Child Sexual Abuse research initiative. Only by understanding how cases are processed can resources be properly allocated and improvements be made in the way child sexual abuse is dealt with by these systems.

Date Sources

In this study we measure the numbers and kinds of cases reported at each level of intervention; describe the referral system; enumerate which cases lead to police investigation and describe their characteristics; review which cases proceed to court; and, finally, determine the dispositions of these cases in court. At each stage in the process a certain number of cases proceed, while others are deferred or dropped. Comparison of the attributes of the cases (i.e., victim, perpetrator, relationship, injuries sustained, etc.) was a primary focus of the study. Information was gathered from a broad array of sources including administrative files and key informants. The data collection depended heavily on existing arrangements among the social/medical/legal services that deal with sexual abuse of children. Studying the attitudes and behaviours of key individuals and institutions through records, interviewing, and court monitoring provided the insight for a detailed look at the handling of child sexual abuse cases that were known to the system.

FILE DATA

Information was extracted from social services (Winnipeg Child and Family Services) files, police records, Crown files, court documents, and hospital (Child Protection Centre) files.

Child and Family Services Files

Data for the child welfare component of the study were obtained from Winnipeg Child and Family Services. The sample consisted of 50 per cent of all suspected and confirmed cases of child sexual abuse for the years 1984 and 1985, which were taken from the Child Abuse Registry.[2] This generated a sample of 160 cases, which were then linked to each of the six regional agencies in Winnipeg to gain access to the files for review.

Police Files

The Winnipeg police department has a child abuse unit that deals mainly with intrafamilial cases of sexual abuse. The unit has a coordinator and six police officers (three teams) who handle most complaints from children under 18 years of age. Any overload is handled by youth division of the Winnipeg police. The sample consisted of 50 per cent of the child abuse cases for files opened in 1984 and 1985 selected randomly from a log in which the child abuse unit records all suspected cases of child abuse. As well, all cases in the Child and Family Services component of the research were matched to the police sample. Finally, relevant cases from a parallel evaluation of Bill C-127 (1983 amendments to the rape law) were also included and consisted of complainants 17 and under, who were more than two years younger than the accused. This provided several additional cases that were in the criminal justice system but were missed either because they were not within the mandate of child welfare, or because they were not identified by the child abuse unit. These sampling procedures resulted in a total sample of 384 cases from police files.

Crown Files

Data pertaining to the Crown's involvement provided details on charging, evidence, witnesses, plea bargaining, preliminary hearings, and preparation of complainants for court. Information regarding the termination of charges at this level was collected, including details concerning whether this decision was initiated by the Crown, prior to a preliminary hearing, by a judge at a preliminary hearing, or by the complainant, and why this decision was made. At the time, there was a prosecutor assigned to Provincial Court and another to Court of Queen's Bench who handled mainly sexual abuse prosecutions. Although other prosecutors were assigned some of these cases as well, the two 'specialists' dealt with the bulk of the caseload.[3]

One hundred and seventy cases that were still in the system (i.e., those resulting in charges being laid) were tracked at the Crown level. Juvenile offenders, who made up 14.2 per cent of accused, were not tracked beyond the Crown level. These cases are handled by Youth Court and we did not have access to these records.

Court Files

Cases were tracked to this level if a case proceeded to a sentencing appearance, preliminary hearing, and/or trial. Court documents provided information on the nature of final charges, dispositions, sentencing, and appeals. One hundred and twenty-seven cases were tracked at the court level.

Child Protection Centre Files

The Child Protection Centre unit at the Children's Hospital in Winnipeg is the primary resource in Manitoba for recognizing and dealing with child sexual abuse cases as well as providing evidence in court on behalf of the children. The unit is staffed with physicians, nurses, social workers, and a psychologist. The hospital's protocol includes a referral to police and/or Child and Family Services if there is any indication or suspicion of abuse.

Data for the Child Protection Centre were gathered from files of the Winnipeg Children's Hospital. In obtaining the sample, we selected all cases that were studied in the Child and Family Services component of the research and referred to the Child Protection Centre. This provided a group of cases that could be tracked from one agency to the next. After these cases were obtained, 25 per cent of the remaining files were randomly sampled from a log kept by the Child Protection Centre, containing all cases of suspected and confirmed child sexual abuse. This method provided a separate sample of cases whose paths could be traced independently. These two procedures produced a total sample size of 251 cases from the Child Protection Centre.

INTERVIEWS

Interviews were carried out with those involved in caregiving and treatment of child sexual abuse victims, as well as those investigating, prosecuting, defending, and adjudicating such cases. Respondents included members of the police, judges, Crown attorneys, defence attorneys, Child and Family Services personnel, and Child Protection Centre personnel.

Initial interviews and file reviews identified the various professionals most frequently assigned to child abuse cases. These individuals were selected for interviewing and included: six police officers (three teams) who were assigned to the child abuse unit of the Winnipeg police department, three Crown attorneys, two of whom had been designated as specialists in the prosecution of child sexual abuse cases; four defence lawyers, who defended significant numbers of accused in sexual abuse cases; fourteen judges (eight Provincial, five Queen's Bench, and one from the Manitoba Court of Appeal); sixteen representatives from Child and Family Services including social workers from each of the six regional agencies, executive directors and/or a

TABLE 4.1
Victim's Age at Time of Report

Age	Child and Family Services		Police		Child Protection Centre	
	Frequency	Per cent	Frequency	Per cent	Frequency	Per cent
1–3	10	6.3	27	7.3	30	12.0
4–6	14	8.8	69	18.4	53	21.2
7–9	20	12.5	72	19.2	43	17.2
10–12	29	18.2	27	24.1	46	18.4
13–15	52	32.7	90	21.8	59	23.6
16–18	34	21.4	35	9.4	20	8.0
No info.	1	–	–	–	1	–
Total	160	100.0	383	100.0	251	100.0

supervisor from all agencies, and the two child abuse coordinators who work in the agencies with the highest volume of child abuse; and four members of the child abuse team at the Child Protection Centre at Children's Hospital.

Profile of Victims, Accused, and Offences

There were 160 cases in the Child and Family Services sample, 383 cases in the police sample (328 accused), and 251 cases in the Child Protection Centre sample.

VICTIMS

Approximately 90 per cent of the victims in all three samples were female. The age of the victims ranged from 1 to 17 years, although the ages among the children in the hospital sample tended to be younger than those from social services and police (see Table 4.1).

Most complainants knew their assailants. In only 14 per cent (n=53) of the police cases was the accused a stranger to the complainant. In 49 per cent of the cases, the accused was an acquaintance (i.e., persons known to the victim, but not considered an intimate or close friend, including boyfriend's uncle, girlfriend's father, brother, or cousin, friend's mother's common-law husband, landlord, caretaker, foster parents' son-in-law, babysitter's boyfriend, neighbour, relative, or family friend), while 37 per cent of the cases involved abuse by a natural or step/common-law/foster parent. For the Child and Family Services cases, 58 per cent of the accused were parents and 42 per cent were known others. In all but one of the cases where the offence was commit-

TABLE 4.2
Accused–Victim Relationship

	Child Protection Centre		Child and Family Services		Police	
	Frequency	Per cent	Frequency	Per cent	Frequency	Per cent
Stranger	1	0.6	53	14.2	7	2.9
Parent/						
surrogate	90	57.7	137	36.7	111	47.2
Known other	65	41.7	183	49.0	117	49.9
No info.	4	–	10	–	16	–
Total	160	100.0	383	100.0	251	100.0

ted by a stranger the case was reported to the police rather than to Child and Family Services. Only 3 per cent of Child Protection Centre cases involved strangers, while parents and known others were 47 per cent and 50 per cent respectively (see Table 4.2).

Because many of those in the 'known other' category were relatives, over 85 per cent of the victims in the Child and Family Services files, almost 75 per cent of the victims in the Child Protection Centre files, and 58 per cent of the victims in the police files were related to their assailant. This pattern of a family relationship between the abused child and his or her abuser is consistent with the literature. It is also a factor that helps explain why there is often a gap between the age of the victim when the abuse began and the age when first disclosed. The existence of a relationship of trust and dependence between the child and abuser creates barriers to disclosure by the child. There are also other obvious barriers to a child, particularly a young child, reporting parental behaviour to authorities.

Most of the victims were taken to the hospital to determine the nature of abuse and to provide medical evidence for legal proceedings. Attendance at hospital was seldom for treatment of acute injuries. The most common form of abuse was fondling/digital penetration.

ACCUSED

The pattern of gender for accused is the reverse of that for victims. Over 90 per cent of the accused in all three samples were male, and they ranged in age from 8 to 72 years (see Table 4.3).

Well over half the accused were either married or in a common-law relationship, and there were no significant differences on this variable between

TABLE 4.3
Age of Accused

	Child and Family Services		Police		Child Protection Centre	
	Frequency	Per cent	Frequency	Per cent	Frequency	Per cent
Juveniles	26	26.5	53	14.2	7	2.9
18–24	11	11.2	33	12.6	18	16.2
25–29	14	14.3	47	18.0	12	10.8
30–39	29	29.6	75	28.7	11	9.9
40–49	15	15.3	42	16.1	18	16.2
50–59	1	1.0	17	6.5	6	5.4
60 and over	2	2.0	10	3.8	9	8.1
No info.	62	–	67	–	143	–
Total	160	100.0	328	100.0	241	100

the Child and Family Services sample and the police sample. This is consistent with the finding that most abusers are the victims' parents or parental surrogates. Most accused were employed in unskilled (24 per cent) or semiskilled (24 per cent) occupations, and 35 per cent were unemployed. Many had previous juvenile or criminal records (51 per cent), although this information was available in the files for only 230 of the 328 accused. Of those persons with prior records recorded, 12 per cent were for sexual offences (see Table 4.4).

OFFENCES

About three-quarters of the cases were classified by police as sexual assault. Over half the cases were ongoing, rather than single incidents. The type of sexual contact most often described in police files was a combination of: touching, fellatio, cunnilingus, attempted intercourse, masturbation, or digital penetration (37 per cent). Touching/grabbing/fondling was involved in 36 per cent of the cases, and genital–anal intercourse was involved in 27 per cent of the cases. The pattern was similar in the Child and Family Services sample.

Physical force and resistance by the victim were common, but the number of injuries was low. Just over one-half of complainants received medical attention but visible injuries were present in only 16 per cent of the cases. Offences most commonly took place at the shared residence of the complainant and accused (37 per cent). This was followed by the residence of the accused (23 per cent). Only 18 per cent of the offences were witnessed by a third party.

TABLE 4.4
Criminal Record of the Accused

Previous Conviction	Frequency	Per cent
Theft	51	20.9
Robbery	13	5.3
Physical assault	27	11.1
Sexual assault	28	11.2
Weapon	11	4.5
Posses. drugs, fraud	15	6.1
Prop. offence, B & E	31	12.7
Driving intoxicated	26	10.7
Attempted murder	3	1.2
Other	39	16.0
Total Responses	244	100.0

NOTE: The table pertains to 106 valid cases, for which there were 244 responses. Prior record involves more than one offence for many offenders.

Child and Family Services Processing of Child Sexual Abuse

ENTRANCE TO THE SYSTEM

Because child abuse usually occurs in private, the only way it can come to the attention of the public is if the abused child tells someone and that person takes action. However, it is generally believed that many children fail to tell at all, or tell only long after the abuse begins because the abuser occupies a position of trust and exerts pressure on the child to remain silent. Children also may not be aware that sexual abuse should be reported. The Winnipeg data are consistent with this picture, as cases typically involved abuse that had been going on for more than one month. The majority of abusers were either a parent or another relative.

Cases typically entered the system in two ways. Some were reported directly to the police, while others were reported to Child and Family Services. The pattern of disclosure was similar for cases reported to both agencies. Offences were most commonly reported to mothers, followed by social workers, friends, and police.

The similarity of disclosure patterns is to be expected, as 90 per cent of Child and Family Services cases are reported to police. This high rate reflects the mandatory duty of child care workers to report suspected cases of sexual abuse. The majority (85 per cent) of the cases were reported to police by a Child and Family Services worker. While it would seem from these data that most child sexual abuse cases are first reported to Child and Family Services, then to the police, the data collected from police files do not support this conclusion. While the Child and Family Services files indicate that the police were contacted in 143 of 160 cases, the police data show that the police were the first agency contacted in all but 28 of the 82 cases. These differences are likely due to the failure of the police to record the fact that a case was referred from Child and Family Services. In some cases, the police were unaware of prior involvement of Child and Family Services.

REPORTING TO POLICE

Child and Family Services cases were promptly reported to the police. In 80 per cent of the cases where information was available, police were notified the same week the disclosure was made. The majority of cases (85 per cent) were reported to the police by a Child and Family Services worker, social worker, or counsellor. Only 7 cases (6 per cent) took more than one month to be brought to police attention. There were 16 cases (10 per cent) in which the police were not contacted at all. Discretion used by Child and Family Services personnel in choosing not to report a case to the police appears to be based on whether the child is in immediate (or future) danger from the abuser or whether there is evidence to sustain a criminal charge. The mandate of the agency is to protect the child, but the opinion that a child is not in danger does not preclude the possibility that a criminal offence has occurred. However, these decisions are likely based on variation in attitudes and perceptions of individuals. One worker may report a case, another might not, despite identical circumstances.

INTERVENTION PERTAINING TO THE VICTIM

Almost half (69) of the 160 cases handled by Child and Family Services involved removal of the child from the home. In terms of treatment for the child, Child and Family Services made referrals for therapy to other services/ agencies in 50 per cent of the cases. Information was also gathered on the types of long-term intervention that were provided for the abuse victims. The most common form of intervention was temporary placement, which occurred in 43 per cent of the cases. This is an interim measure taken to allow time for the situation to stabilize. For example, the child may be placed in a foster home until the abuser can be removed from the family home. In 16 per cent of the cases a permanent guardianship was provided for the child. Permanent guardianship was most often used in cases involving intercourse, while the majority of temporary placements involved 'other' sexual abuses. Intervention was least likely in cases involving touching.

TABLE 4.5
Offender–Victim Relationship
in Terms of Charges Laid and Nature of Abuse

	Charges Laid (per cent)		
	(n=39)	(n=62)	(n=40)
Relationship	Intercourse	Other	Touching
Parents	70.0	52.9	19.2
Relatives	41.7	40.9	83.3
Other	71.4	16.7	25.0

INTERVENTION PERTAINING TO THE ABUSER

Where the victim and the abuser shared a residence, the abuser was removed from the home in 40 per cent of the cases. This figure may understate the situation because the abuser may also have left the household voluntarily or removed himself at the insistence of the victim's mother. Criminal charges of sexual abuse were laid in 43 per cent of the Child and Family Services cases. The most common long-term intervention for the abuser was criminal court proceedings, followed by counselling/therapy. In many cases there was more than one type of intervention.

CRIMINAL CHARGES

Criminal charges were laid most often when the abuse involved intercourse (in 62 per cent of the cases). Charges were laid in 44 per cent of the cases of 'other' sexual abuse and in 30 per cent of cases involving touching. Where there was proof of penetration, and where the offence was perceived to be more serious, there was a greater likelihood of criminal charges.

An examination of victim–abuser relationship in terms of charges laid and the nature of abuse (Table 4.5) indicates that parents and other accused were most often charged when the abuse involved intercourse, and least likely when the offence was touching. For cases of other abuse, parents and relatives were most likely to be charged.

An examination of the victim–abuser relationship and the laying of charges reveals an interesting pattern with regard to parents. A greater proportion (58 per cent) of step- or common-law parents were charged than natural parents (37 per cent). Step- or common-law parents were more likely to be charged at all levels of offence seriousness (i.e., for genital intercourse, other, and touching and grabbing). This may reflect an historical reluctance to interfere with the parent–child relationship or it may reflect the stability of a family situation that may offer greater potential for treatment. As one would expect, the step- or common-law parent was also more likely to be removed from the residence than a natural parent.

Charges were also more likely where the victim sustained injuries as a result of the abuse. Charges were laid in 56 per cent of cases where injuries occurred, compared with 35 per cent where there were none. One explanation of this is that the presence of injury not only indicates the seriousness of the abuse, it also provides medical evidence that strengthens the legal case against the abuser. Such corroborating evidence is crucial in the case of young children who may not be able to give sworn testimony in court. An examination of the type of injury that victims suffer bears this out: the most common type of injury was a stretched or torn hymen, occurring in 20 of the 32 cases for which the type of injury was recorded. Such injuries indicate the occurrence of sexual intercourse or other penetration, and provide permanent evidence of the abuse. The importance of this type of corroboration is supported by the fact that the relationship between injury and charges being laid is present only for the category of genital intercourse. Charges were laid in six of the eight (75 per cent) cases of intercourse involving injury, and only two of six (33 per cent) of the cases where no injury was reported. There was no relationship between the extent of injuries to the victim and whether the offender was removed from the home. However, a high percentage of injured children were apprehended by Child and Family Services. There were no consistent relationships between either the age of the abuser or his occupation and the laying of charges or removal from the residence.

MacMurray (1987) suggested that child sexual abuse cases that are not dealt with officially within the criminal justice system may be handled through alternative, non-criminal means. There is little support for this view in the Child and Social Services data. Cases where the child was apprehended, where the offender was removed from a shared residence, and where there was long-term intervention for the offender were more likely to be reported to the police and to result in charges being laid. Thus social services were more likely to be involved in the most serious cases, and these usually remained in the criminal justice system.

Neither race nor the age of the victim were related to whether he/she was removed from the home. However, apprehension was more likely if the victim suffered injuries. Approximately two-thirds (65 per cent) of injured victims were apprehended as opposed to approximately 37 per cent of those who were not. This relationship held for all categories of seriousness of abuse. Victims whose families have been in the child welfare system were less likely to be apprehended by Child and Family Services than those who were new cases. New cases are the only category where apprehension is more likely than not. This relationship is difficult to explain, though it held for all categories of seriousness of abuse.

Earlier we saw that charges were more likely to be laid if the abuser was a step- or common-law parent than a natural parent. When we look at whether the child was apprehended, we find apprehension was more likely if the abuser was an adoptive parent than a natural or step-/common-law parent. Step- or common-law abusers may be more likely to be removed from the home, so there is no need for Child and Family Services to apprehend the child. However, this does not explain why the child was apprehended less often when the offender was a natural parent, though it could reflect a bias in the system to preserve the family. This remains a research question.

TRACKING OF CHILD AND FAMILY SERVICES SAMPLE

In Winnipeg, child sexual abuse cases are dealt with through a multidisciplinary approach that involves a process of consultation between the police, the Child Protection Centre, and Child and Family Services. Each of the agencies involved has a protocol defining their respective responsibilities and their relationship to each other. The files that were tracked from Child and Family Services were used to study the processing of child sexual abuse from one component of the system to the next. To examine the effectiveness of the multidisciplinary team, it is useful to proceed using Child and Family Services as a starting point because a child abuse case that is handled by the police is not necessarily a case that falls within the mandate of child welfare.[4] Consequently, the team approach is not required in all instances of child sexual abuse.

Of the 144 cases, Child and Family Services was the first agency of contact in 98, or 68 per cent of cases. The hospital was contacted first in 22, or 15 per cent of cases, while 16, or 11 per cent of cases entered the system through the police. Six (4 per cent) began at an 'other' agency, and in two cases (1 per cent) the first contact was with the Sexual Assault Centre (see Table 4.6).

Seventy-six cases (53 per cent) had contact with all three of the primary agencies – Child and Family Services, Child Protection Centre, and the police. Offenders were convicted in 16 of these cases. Of the 68 cases that did not have contact with all of the three primary agencies, convictions were obtained in 8 cases. However, information on conviction was not available for 48 or 36 per cent of the valid cases. Although Child and Family Services or hospital files stated that there was police contact, the Winnipeg police had no record

TABLE 4.6
Order of Agency Contact

	1st	2nd	3rd	4th	5th
Police	16	82	34	3	–
Child Protection Centre	22	13	42	3	–
Sexual Assault Centre	2	–	9	9	1
Child and Family Services	98	44	2	–	–
Other	6	–	15	22	6
Attrition	–	5	42	107	137

for these. More than half these cases (26 or 54 per cent) came from Child and Family Services East, which includes Eastern Manitoba in its catchment. Because this area is beyond the city limits, it is under the jurisdiction of the RCMP rather than the Winnipeg Police. The RCMP did not participate in the study. The remaining 22 cases indicate a discrepancy in administrative records and may be explained in the following ways: a police report was not made, though records state there was; a report was received, but not filed by the police; or, the case was not from Child and Family Services East, but was handled by the RCMP.

Of the nine cases that did not go to the police, seven files had no reason stated as to why police were not called. In one case the worker felt that the allegations were unfounded and in another the offender was convicted and jailed for a sexual assault on another child.

Of the 47 cases where the child did not attend the hospital, 30 files had no information on medical contact. In the remaining cases, the child did not receive medical treatment because: there was a lengthy delay between the incident and reporting (n = 9), the offence was touching and grabbing (n = 6), the victim refused contact (n = 1), and the victim denied the assault (n = 1).

Criminal Justice Processing of Child Sexual Abuse Cases

This section describes the processing of child sexual abuse cases through the criminal justice system. As previously indicated, the police sample involves 384 separate occurrences. Incidents that were one-time events and that involved more than one victim or more than one offender were classified as a single case of abuse. There were six such occurrences that applied to the child abuse study, and in all but one case, the similarities in the "multiples' were sufficient so that no information was lost by using only the first interaction in every case.[5] Ongoing sexual abuse cases that pertained to multiple victims and involved one offender, or alternately multiple offenders and one victim, were classified as separate incidents. Because in some cases multiple offenders or multiple victims were involved, these totals differ somewhat from the incidents. There were 383 victims and 328 accused.

INITIAL CLASSIFICATION OF COMPLAINTS

When the police first receive a report of a sexual assault, they apply an initial classification to the report and these classifications often do not reflect the official charges. The overwhelming number of complaints were first classified by police as sexual assault (72 per cent) followed by other sexual offences[6] (22 per cent). There was also one each of buggery and rape, five each of sexual assault with threats/bodily harm, and aggravated sexual assault, ten complaints classified as indecent assault, three as gross indecency, and two as sexual intercourse with a female under 14. The complaint that was designated as rape and one indecent assault were misclassified by the police. Under the 1983 amendments to the legislation, rape and indecent assault are no longer proper designations (see Chapter 1 of this volume). The remaining complaints of indecent assault refer to offences committed prior to the law reform although they were not reported to police until the 1984–5 study period. Police regarded more than three-quarters of the complaints received as 'founded' (76 per cent).

CRIMINAL CHARGES LAID BY POLICE

Police laid charges in more than half the cases. We looked at the type of abuse and whether a charge was laid (see Table 4.7). When the offence involved genital/anal intercourse, a charge was laid in 74 per cent of the cases. Touching and grabbing led to charges 60 per cent of the time, while other, or a combination of other, offences led to charges 74 per cent of the time. There was a lower proportion of charges in the Child and Family Services data. For Child and Family Services cases charges were laid in 62 per cent of intercourse cases, in 44 per cent of 'other,' and in 30 per cent of touching and grabbing cases.

We also looked at the nature of relationship between the victim and accused and its impact on charging. Parents and parental surrogates (i.e., adoptive, step-, common-law, foster parents) accounted for 28 per cent of the abuse cases, 16 per cent involved strangers, and the largest category (55 per

TABLE 4.7
Charges Laid by Type of Abuse

| | Child and Family Services | | Police | |
	Frequency	Per cent	Frequency	Per cent
Genital/anal intercourse	24	61.5	51	73.9
Touching/grabbing/fondling	12	30.0	55	59.8
Other	28	44.4	68	73.9

cent) was known others, which comprised of family friends, acquaintances, relatives, and so on.

Charges were laid in 72 per cent of the cases in which a parent was the abuser. This was much higher than what was found in the Child and Family Services component of the study (45 per cent). Known others were charged 78 per cent of the time, while strangers were charged only 30 per cent of the time. This difference was due to the fact that strangers were much less likely to be apprehended than parents or known others. Parents were also more likely to admit guilt, which also contributed to the higher likelihood of charges.

There are several additional factors that might be expected to have an impact on classifying a case as founded and on charges being laid. MacMurray (1984) found that age was related to a decision to forward a case for prosecution in that cases involving older victims were more likely to be retained in the system. This might be because older victims would be seen as being more likely to testify convincingly in court. The Winnipeg data showed no such relationship – cases involving younger victims were about as likely as those with older victims to be classified as founded and to result in charges being laid.

Cases that were ongoing were slightly less likely to be classified as founded and more likely to result in charges as single events. Cases with female victims were more likely to be founded and to result in the laying of charges than cases in which the victims were male, though the differences were minimal and the sample too small to draw any meaningful conclusion.

Relationships between founding cases and laying charges and several variables relating to the strength of corroboration were examined. Injury to the victim did not appear to influence whether the case was classified as founded (80 per cent of cases with injuries were founded compared with 75 per cent of cases where there were no injuries reported) and negatively related to the laying of charges (64 per cent of injury cases resulted in charges compared with 70 per cent of non-injury cases). There was no relationship between either found-

TABLE 4.8
Nature of Bad Character

	Frequency	Per cent
Not virgin/chaste	25	35.2
Prostitute	6	8.5
Prev. sex w/offender	1	1.4
Ulterior motive	6	8.5
Inconst. accts/lied	29	40.8
Willing participant	2	2.8
Alcohol/drug problems	2	2.8
Total	71	100.0

ing or charging and whether or not the victim received medical attention.

Cases where there was a witness were more likely to be classed as founded than those without (91 per cent compared with 74 per cent). However, charges were less likely to be laid when there was a witness (64 per cent with a witness and 70 per cent without). There was no relationship between the length of time taken to disclose the abuse and classifying the case as founded. Charges were more likely to be laid in cases where reporting was not immediate.

The only corroborating variable that was related in the expected fashion to founding and charging was evidence of the victim's 'bad character.' In 19 per cent of the cases there was a notation in police files implying that there was evidence of 'bad character.' This term was used to refer to comments written in files pertaining to the complainant having a bad reputation, being promiscuous, not being a virgin, working as a prostitute, having had sex with the accused in the past, having alcohol problems, giving inconsistent accounts, or being a willing participant in the incident. Table 4.8 shows the distribution of the 71 cases that contained any such reference. These cases were less likely to be founded (60 per cent compared with 80 per cent) and less likely to result in charges (60 per cent compared with 70 per cent).

The initial charge most often laid by police was sexual assault (s. 246.1). There were 266 counts of sexual assault, consisting of 42 per cent of initial charges laid. Almost half the charges (44 per cent) were laid within 48 hours of the complaint (n = 72). In 54 per cent of the cases, the police were the first agency contacted by the complainants.

INTERVIEWS WITH COMPLAINANTS

The majority of the complainants (74 per cent) had one interview with the police. In 163 cases (61 per cent) a family member or surrogate was present during the interview. The victim was able to identify the suspect in 88 per cent of the cases, and in 78 per cent a suspect was questioned and/or apprehended.

Of the 261 cases where information was available, 82 or 31 per cent of the accused admitted their guilt to the police. About a third (44 per cent, n = 170) of the cases were terminated at the police level. The police decided to end the investigation in 41 per cent (n = 158) of these cases, and 13 per cent (n = 21) were discontinued because the suspect was not apprehended or questioned. In 3 per cent of the cases (n = 12), the victims or the victims' parent/guardian requested that the investigation be terminated. A slightly low bias is reflected in the 3 per cent because cases that were classified by police as unfounded were coded as police- terminated. However, some were unfounded because the victim wanted the investigation terminated and would not cooperate. Therefore, only cases that were founded *and* classified as victim-terminated are indicated in the 3 per cent.

In approximately 20 per cent of the police files (n = 80) there was a reference to difficulties with investigating the case. In 63 per cent of these, the young age of the victim made the prospect of obtaining evidence extremely onerous. A polygraph test was used on an accused in 14 of the cases (4 per cent), and a complainant was tested once.

CROWN LEVEL

Forty-four of the 214 cases retained by the police involved juveniles, 38 of which were processed by the Youth Court (six were unfounded). In 68 per cent of the 170 remaining cases, the charges proceeded with by the Crown were consistent with those initially laid by police. Forty-seven of the cases (28 per cent) were eventually stayed, 26 before the preliminary hearing, 17 before the trial, and 4 at trial.

COURT LEVEL

Sixty-one cases were committed to trial. Forty (70 per cent) of those committed to trial were tried by a Court of Queen's Bench judge, 13 (23 per cent) were tried by a Provincial Court judge, and 4 (7 per cent) of the cases were heard by a judge and jury.

A guilty verdict was delivered in 23 of the cases (see Table 4.9). In 19 cases there was a guilty plea at trial. Four had their charges stayed by the Crown,

TABLE 4.9
Outcome at Trial

	Frequency	Per cent
Guilty	23	37.7
Not guilty	15	24.6
Pleaded guilty at trial	19	31.1
Charges stayed at trial	4	6.6
No formal trial	109	–
Juvenile offender	44	–
No formal charges	83	–
Unfounded by police	87	–
Total	384	100.0

and 15 were found not guilty. A total of 110 offenders were convicted. Of these, 66 pleaded guilty before trial, 19 pleaded guilty at trial, 23 were found guilty at trial, and in two cases sexual charges were stayed at the trial but they were convicted of non-sexual charges.

There were 110 convictions on the following: 89 sexual assault, 25 gross indecency, 29 indecent assault, 4 buggery, 2 sexual intercourse with a female under 14, 1 sexual intercourse with a female 14–16, 6 incest and 2 other offences (see Table 4.10).

Dispositions imposed were: incarceration 61 per cent, suspended sentence 23 per cent, probation 7 per cent, discharge 7 per cent, and fine 2 per cent. The average sentence length was 24.3 months. Other than cases originally classified as 'other sexual offences,' almost all the cases that received a disposition of guilty were initially classified as sexual assault (s. 246.1). Of the five cases classified as sexual assault with threats (s. 246.2), three resulted in a conviction. The average sentence for those convicted of sexual assault with threats was 64 months. Two of the five cases initially recorded as aggravated sexual assault (s. 246.3) resulted in convictions for sexual assault (s. 246.1). Both offenders received 36-month sentences.

Offenders whose offence involved 'other' sexual offences were more likely to be convicted than those whose offences involved intercourse or touching and grabbing. Where an offender was convicted, incarceration was more likely for intercourse and 'other' offences than for touching and grabbing. Case attrition accounted for the termination of 71 per cent of the cases (Table 4.11).

OTHER VARIABLES

Cases where the victim received medical attention were more likely to result

TABLE 4.10
Offence of Conviction

Offence	Frequency	Percent
Sexual assault guilty	89	59.3
Indecent assault	29	18.4
Gross indecency	25	15.8
Buggery	4	2.5
Sexual intercourse with a female under 14	2	1.3
Sexual intercourse with a female 14–16	1	0.6
Incest	6	3.8
Other	2	1.3
Total	158	100.0

TABLE 4.11
Filtering Out of Charges at the Police/Crown/Court Levels

	ATTRITION Number	Per cent remaining
Police Level	384	100.0
Unfounded	87 (22.7)	77.3
No suspect apprehended	21 (5.5)	71.8
Victim initiated	12 (3.1)	68.7
Charges not laid	50 (13.0)	55.7
Crown Level		
Youth court	44 (11.5)	44.2
Stayed	43 (11.2)	33.0
Court Level		
Stayed at trial/acquitted	17 (4.4)	28.6
Guilty plea	85 (22.1)	6.5
Founded guilty at trial	25 (6.5)	–
Total attrition	274	71.4

in conviction (61 per cent vs. 56 per cent) than when medical attention was not obtained. Of those convicted in cases where the victim received medical attention, 48 per cent were incarcerated, compared with 26 per cent of the rest. Cases where the victim was injured were no more likely than others to result in conviction, but where there was a conviction it was more likely to result in incarceration (94 per cent vs. 61 per cent).

A higher proportion of cases involving male victims resulted in conviction (67 per cent vs. 58 per cent for females), but a higher proportion of those convicted of abusing females were incarcerated compared with those convicted of abusing males. Cases that were disclosed immediately after the offence took place were about as likely as others to result in conviction and incarceration. The presence of a witness resulted in a lower rate of conviction (46 per cent vs. 62 per cent) and higher rates of incarceration to those where there was no witness (80 per cent vs. 63 per cent). If physical force was used by the offender, the chances of conviction were no higher than if no force was used (56 per cent vs. 61 per cent), but incarceration was more likely (73 per cent vs. 60 per cent). There was no pattern in either conviction or incarceration for victim's age. Charges were less likely to be laid in cases where there was some evidence of 'bad character' (38 per cent vs. 62 per cent). These cases were also less likely to result in the offender being incarcerated (56 per cent vs. 67 per cent).

APPEALS

Seventeen decisions were appealed: ten by the defence and seven by the Crown. In two cases decisions were overturned; six appeals were dismissed; three sentences were reduced; and five sentences were increased. There was no information for one case.

SUMMARY

To summarize, of 384 reports to the police, a total of 170 were terminated prior to any formal charges being laid – 87 reports were declared unfounded by the police; of the 71 founded cases, charges were not laid in 50 cases, while in 21 cases the suspect was not arrested. The remaining 12 were terminated at the request of the victim or the victim's parent/guardian. Charges were laid in 214 cases; 44 of these involved juveniles and 170 proceeded to the adult system. The Crown stayed 43 of the 170 cases, retaining 127, which proceeded to Court. Of the 127, 66 pleaded guilty before trial and 19 pleaded guilty at trial. Fifteen accused were acquitted, 4 cases were stayed, and 23 were convicted. The filtering out of reports at the police/Crown/court levels accounted for the termination of 71 per cent of the cases.

Discussion

Many of the findings substantiate much of what is reported in the child sexual abuse literature. The victims of child sexual abuse in Winnipeg were predominantly female. The distribution of ages ranged quite broadly from 1 to 18. The large majority of complainants knew their assailants and most were relatives.

Many cases involved families who had multiple social problems. Offences usually occurred at the victim's home and she is as likely as not to be removed from the home after disclosure. Virtually all offenders were males and their age range was very broad. Over half the offenders were married or living in common-law relationships, and most were employed in unskilled or semi-skilled occupations. Many had previous criminal records. About three-quarters of the cases were classified by police as sexual assault and over half were ongoing, rather than single incidents. Charges were most likely to be laid in cases involving intercourse that provides physical evidence of assault.

When they were interviewed, the police reported that the investigating officer decided to charge in consultation with the Crown. Most said that it was preferable to lay the maximum charges that can be sustained by the facts of the case. According to the police, the most important considerations in charging decisions are physical evidence and the credibility of the complainant. When asked about specific factors, the police indicated that among the most important evidentiary factors were the presence of witnesses and other corroborating evidence, the age of the complainant (young children are seen as making less credible victims), and the ability of the child to testify under oath. Factors seen as important by some of the respondents included the time delay between offence and reporting, type of abuse, and the presence of injuries. The complainant's knowledge of the offender, the location of the offence, alcohol and drug use, and the criminal record of the assailant were not seen as important.

The Crown attorneys who were interviewed all felt that prosecuting cases of child sexual abuse is very difficult. One reason for the difficulty is the typical pattern these cases take. The abuse usually occurs within the family context and has gone on for some period of time. The child has a great deal of difficulty disclosing the abuse, and so prompt complaint is highly unlikely. In addition, the abuse takes place in private, and hence there is unlikely to be a witness or corroborating evidence. As a result, the ability of the Crown to prove the defendant's guilt beyond a reasonable doubt is an arduous task.

It was also felt that the credibility of child victims is always an issue for the court. The age of the victim makes the court very cautious about convicting without corroborating evidence, and such evidence rarely exists in these cases. The combination of long delays in complaint, lack of corroboration, and the Court's suspicion of children's evidence, all reduce the chances of successful prosecution.

In making the decision whether or not to proceed with a prosecution of a case of child sexual abuse, the two Crown attorneys specializing in these types of cases believed that they exercised their discretion not to proceed more frequently in child sexual abuse compared with other crimes against the person. This is because they recognize the court process is traumatic for sexually abused children and it is irresponsible for the Crown to proceed in really weak cases. The typical nature of these cases (i.e., complaints that are several years old and without corroboration) makes conviction less likely, and so only the stronger cases proceed to trial. None of the Crown attorneys felt the criteria used to determine whether to proceed with a case had changed over time, but they noted that because more cases now come to light due to increased public awareness, there had been an increase in the number of prosecutions.

The Crown attorneys all regarded recency of complaint as extremely impor- tant. Corroboration is a legal requirement when the child gives unsworn tes- timony, but they felt it was important in other cases as well. They also saw physical force and evidence of injury as extremely important. A final factor they felt was important in the decision to prosecute was the previous record of the accused. Elements they felt did not enter into their decision to prosecute were the complainant's previous sexual activity and juvenile record and the resistance by the complainant.

A somewhat different perspective was obtained from defence counsel who viewed a number of other factors as also being important in sexual abuse cases. They felt that the Crown's case was enhanced if there was corrobora- tion, resistance by the victim, a more serious type of sexual contact, relation- ship between victim and accused, and if the child's testimony was sworn. Factors the defence lawyers considered unimportant were the complainant's juvenile record and previous sexual history, the offender's 'honest belief' in the victim's consent, and the recency of complaint.

In general, representatives of the medical, social services, and criminal jus- tice systems were reasonably satisfied with the way in which child sexual abuse cases were handled in Winnipeg. The main system-wide problem iden- tified was a lack of resources to obtain sufficient personnel for victim assis- tance and counselling.

This chapter concludes the empirical research on sexual assault in Canada that adopts a sociological perspective. It is important to realize the limitations of social science data, and to attempt to get 'behind' the quantitative data. In the next chapter, the authors discuss criminal justice processing of sexual assault reports. They draw upon national statistics provided by Statistics Canada, as well as in-depth studies recently conducted by the federal Depart- ment of Justice. As we shall see, while the 1983 legislation appears to have had positive effects on reporting trends, it has so far had a limited impact upon the way the system deals with sexual assault cases.

Notes

1 'Significantly older' varies in definition from three years (Giles 1983) to five years (Finkelhor 1979).

2 Manitoba's first Child Abuse Registry was established in 1971. This registry, which was struck down in the courts on 19 June 1987, required notification of both suspected and confirmed cases of sexual abuse. These names were retained in the registry, whether or not a case was confirmed. With the passing of Bill 72 on 1 September 1987, a new Child Abuse Registry came into effect. The new registry is both an abused child registry and an abuser registry. The guidelines stipulate that agencies are required to report to the director for entry in the abused child registry and submit a reporting form in cases where:

   a. a person has been convicted by a court of abusing the child;

   b. there is a finding by the court that the child is in need of protection on the basis of abuse; or,

   c. the agency has received an opinion of a duly qualified medical practitioner or psychologist consistent with the child being a victim of abuse and, in the opinion of the agency child abuse committee, the child has been a victim of abuse.

   Agencies must also report to the director for entry into the abuser registry and submit a reporting form if the following conditions are met:

   a. the person has been convicted by a court of abusing a child;

   b. the person has been found by a court in a proceeding under this Act to have abused a child; or,

   c. the agency child abuse committee is of the opinion that the person has abused a child (Manitoba Community Services 1988, 2,3).

3 Most child sexual abuse cases are now handled by a Family Violence Court in Winnipeg which was established in 1990.

4 For example, a child may be sexually abused by a stranger. This type of offence need not be dealt with by Child and Family Services since it does not involve a family problem.

5 For example, a stranger exposed himself and attempted to remove clothing from two girls, ages 7 and 8; a caretaker at a school 'tickled and rubbed the backs' of three students, 12–13 years old; two sisters were fondled in their beds by their father's cousin while he was babysitting.

6 Other sexual offences was used as a catch-all category by the police and includes a variety of offences, many of which did not involve official charges. This category was also used by the coders to include initial classifications of non-sexual offences.

References

Appleford, B. 1986. 'Response of the Canadian Psychological Association to the Badgley and Fraser Reports.' In J. Lowman et al., eds., *Regulating Sex*. Burnaby, BC: Simon Fraser University, 55–73

Armstrong, L. 1978. *Kiss Daddy Goodnight*. New York: Pocket Books

Badgley, R., et al. 1984. *Sexual Offences Against Children: Report of the Committee on Sexual Offences Against Children and Youths*. Canada: The Minister of Justice and Attorney General, and the Minister of National Health and Welfare, 1984

Bagley, C. 'Mental Health and the In-Family Sexual Abuse of Children and Adolescents.' In B. Schlesinger, ed., *Sexual Abuse of Children in the 1980s*. Toronto: University of Toronto Press, 30–50

Berliner, L. 1980. 'Seattle Sexual Assault Centre.' *Sexual Abuse of Children within the Family*: Conference Proceedings. Vancouver: n.p.

Berliner, L., and M. Barbieri. 1984. 'The Testimony of the Child Victim of Sexual Assault.' *Journal of Social Issues* 40(2):125–7

Bernstein, A., and P. Cowan. 1975. 'Children's Concepts of How People Get Babies.' *Child Development* 46:77–91

Breines, W., and L. Gordon. 1983. 'The New Scholarship on Family Violence.' *Signs* 8(3):490–531

Brock, D., and G. Kinsman. 'Patriarchal Relations Ignored: An Analysis and Critique of the Badgley Report on Sexual Offenses Against Children and Youths.' In J. Lowman et al., eds., *Regulating Sex*. Burnaby, BC: Simon Fraser University, 107–25

Bulkley, J. 'Evidentiary Theories for Admitting a Child's Out-of-Court Statement of Sexual Abuse at Trial.' In J. Bulkley, ed., *Child Sexual Abuse and the Law*. Washington, DC: American Bar Association

Chisholm, Barbara. 1978. 'Questions of Social Policy – A Canadian Perspective.' In J. Eckelaar and S. Katz, eds., *Family Violence*. Toronto: Butterworths, 367–76

Clark, L. 1986. 'Boys Will Be Boys: Beyond the Badgley Report, A Critical Review.' In J. Lowman et al., eds., *Regulating Sex*. Burnaby, BC: Simon Fraser University, 93–106

Conte, J., and L. Berliner. 1981. 'Sexual Abuse of Children: Implications for Practice.' *Social Casework* 62(10): 601–7

De Francis, V. 1969. *Protecting the Child Victim from Sex Crimes Committed by Adults*. Denver: American Humane Society

de Young, M. 1982. The *Sexual Victimization of Children*. Jefferson, NC: McFarland and Company

Farrell, M., M. Billmore, J. Shamroy, and J. Hammond. 1981. 'Pubertal Gonorrhea: A Multidisciplinary Approach.' *Pediatrics* 67(1):151–3

Finkelhor, D. 1979. *Sexually Victimized Children*. New York: Free Press

– 1984. *Child Sexual. Abuse: Theory and Research*. New York: Free Press

Fritz, G., K. Stoll, and N. Wagner. 1981. 'A Comparison of Males and Females Who Were Sexually Molested as Children.' *Journal of Sex and Marital Therapy* 7(1):549

Gagnon, J. 1965. 'Female Child Victims of Sex Offenses.' *Social Problems* 13:176–92

Gebhard, P., et al. 1965. *Sex Offenders: An Analysis of Types*. New York: Harper and Row

Gibbins, T., and J. Prince. 1963. *Child Victims of Sex Offences*. London: Institute for the Study and Treatment of Delinquency

Giles, L. 1983. 'Sexually Abused Children.' *Sexual Offences – Bill C-127: Proceedings*. Vancouver: The Continuing Legal Education Society of British Columbia

Goodman, G. 1984. 'Children's Testimony in Historical Perspective.' *Journal of Social Issues* 40(2):9–31

Goodman, G., and V. Helgeson. 1985. 'Child Sexual Assault: Children's Memory and the Law.' *University of Miami Law Review* 40:181–208

Herman, J., and L. Hirschman. 1981. *Father–Daughter Incest*. Cambridge, MA: Harvard University Press

Jaffe, A., L. Dynneson, and R. ten Bensel. 1975. 'Sexual Abuse of Children: An Epidemiologic Study.' *American Journal of Diseases of Children* 129(1):689–92

Johnson, M., and M. Foley. 'Differentiating Fact from Fantasy: The Reliability of Children's Memories.' *Journal of Social Issues* 40(2):33–50

Jones, D., and M. McQuiston. 1985. *Interviewing the Sexually Abused Child*. Colorado: University of Colorado School of Medicine

Longstaffe, Sally E., Kenneth N. McRae, and Charles A. Ferguson. 1986. 'Child Sexual Abuse in Manitoba.' *Contemporary Pediatrics* (March/April)

MacMurray, Bruce K. 1987. 'Criminal Decision Making for Child Sexual Abuse: Important Factors in Initial Screening Judgements by Prosecutors.' Paper presented at the annual meeting of the American Society of Criminology, November

Maisch, H. 1972. *Incest*. New York: Stein and Day

Marin, B., D. Holmes, M. Guth, and P. Kovac. 1979. 'The Potential of Children as Eyewitnesses: A Comparison of Children and Adults on Eyewitness Tasks.' *Law and Human Behavior* 3:295–306

Meiselman, K. 1978. Incest: *A Psychological Study of Causes and Effects with Treatment Recommendations*. San Francisco, CA: Jossey-Bass

Melton, G. 'Child Witnesses and the First Amendment: A Psycholegal Dilemma.' *Journal of Social Issues* 40(2):109–23

Minch, Candice, Rick Linden, and Stuart Johnson. 1987. 'Attrition in the Processing of Rape Cases.' *Canadian Journal of Criminology* (October):389–404

Reifen, D. 1975. 'Court Procedures in Israel to Protect Child Victims of Sexual Assault.' In I. Drapkin and E. Viano, eds., *Victimology: A New Focus*, vol. 3. Lexington: Lexington Books

Rush, F. 1980. *The Best Kept Secret: Sexual Abuse of Children*. New York: McGraw Hill

Russell, D. 'The Incidence and Prevalence of Intrafamilial and Extrafamilial Sexual Abuse of Female Children.' *Child Abuse and Neglect: The International Journal* 7:133–46

Sgroi, S. 'Sexual Molestation of Children: The Last Frontier of Child Abuse.' *Children Today* 18(21):44

Ward, E. 1984. *Father–Daughter Rape*. London: The Women's Press

Whitcomb, D., E. Shapiro, and L. Stellwagen. 1985. *When the Victim Is a Child: Issues for Judges and Prosecutors*. U.S. Department of Justice

Yuille, J., M. King, and D. MacDougall. 1987. 'Child Victims and Witnesses: A Research Evaluation and Annotated Bibliography.' Unpublished report. University of British Columbia

5

SCOTT CLARK AND
DOROTHY HEPWORTH

Effects of Reform Legislation on the Processing of Sexual Assault Cases[1]

The authors of this chapter take up the story after a report of sexual assault has been classified (by the police) at one of the three levels of seriousness. Scott Clark and Dorothy Hepworth provide a broad overview of the findings from the evaluation initiative launched by the federal Department of Justice. The aim of this research was to examine every aspect of the criminal justice system to ascertain where Bill C-127 may have had an impact, and to document those areas that remained problematic after the legislative reforms of 1983. Although rape reform evaluations have been conducted elsewhere (notably in the United States), the research program reported here is broader than any other rape reform evaluation conducted to date. Accordingly, there are lessons to be learned here not just for rape reform in Canada, but in other jurisdictions that have implemented comparable reforms. Clark and Hepworth present data on many aspects of the criminal justice system, and address many impact questions such as whether the conviction rate has changed as a result of the 1983 reforms. The data reviewed in this chapter reveal the limitations of law reform to achieve radical change in terms of the processing of sexual assault cases by the criminal justice system. They also underline the fact that changing the way we respond to sexual assault is not a goal that can be achieved overnight. It requires continual examination of the legislation, and of the interpretation placed upon that legislation by criminal justice actors.

As noted in Chapter 1 of this volume, the sexual assault provisions of Bill C-127, which became law in 1983, made fundamental changes to the Criminal Code. These affected the substantive, procedural, and evidentiary aspects of Canada's laws regarding crimes of sexual aggression. Shortly after the legislation was passed, the Department of Justice launched an evaluation initiative to understand the impact of Bill C-127 upon the criminal justice system. In this chapter we summarize some of the more important findings from that initiative. We attempt to answer the general question: What effect did the reform legislation have upon the processing of cases of sexual aggression reported to the criminal justice system? An earlier chapter by Julian Roberts and Michelle Grossman examined trends in the numbers of assaults reported to the police. In this chapter we take up the story once a police report has been completed. We examine the response of the criminal justice system from this point through to the sentencing decision.

The objectives of the evaluation included the following: to describe how the new legislation has been implemented and how it works in the various segments of the criminal justice system as well as to determine how the legislation has effected changes in justice system practices, attitudes, and procedures. All components of the study were coordinated from within the Department of Justice and all phases of the research were reviewed by a national advisory committee. In planning for the evaluation research, we determined that, at a minimum, a three-year hiatus from the law's proclamation to the start of the evaluation was desirable. It takes time for legal reform to be implemented and become incorporated into public knowledge and behaviour. As well, attempts to assess the impact of policy innovations require the passage of sufficient time to allow one to make sense of the complex interaction of motives and behaviour that implementation encompasses (Casper and Brereton 1984 143). Further, it was necessary for the courts to have decided and interpreted a sufficient number of cases. Case law is an important indicator of the effects of legislative change.

The Research Components

The evaluation research program undertaken by the Department of Justice began in 1985 (two years after the law reform) and was completed in 1991. It is clear now that, in comparison with other evaluations of sexual assault reform, the Canadian initiative was extensive. This is owing, in part, to its national scope. The research program included seven major components: baseline studies; multi-site field research; a survey of front-line agencies; a second review of sexual assault case law (May 1985 to April 1988); an analysis of police statistics across the country; an analysis of homicide committed in the course of sexual assault; and an analysis of sentencing patterns in cases of sexual assault. Each component is described in more detail below. (See the References for this chapter for Department of Justice publications.)

In preparation for the full-scale evaluation, two baseline studies were conducted. On the basis of published and unpublished studies, the first study documents rape victims' experiences with the Canadian criminal justice system prior to the amendment of the rape laws (Stanley 1985). The second study documents reported court decisions from the passage of the new sexual assault legislation in January 1983 to April 1985 (Ruebsaat 1985).

The field research component of the evaluation was the most extensive aspect of the program of research and a key source of data for the evaluation. Six site studies were conducted in Vancouver, British Columbia; Lethbridge, Alberta; Winnipeg, Manitoba; Hamilton-Wentworth, Ontario; Montréal, Québec; and Fredericton–Saint John, New Brunswick. These sites were selected to reflect the country's regional character. The individual site researchers analysed sexual offences reported to the police both before and after the 1983 legislation came into force. The field studies permitted the collection of detailed information on criminal justice system practices, on victims' experiences, and on key actors' opinions.

A survey of front-line agency personnel was carried out to ascertain how victims were treated before and after the legal changes. Included in this analysis were respondents from police-based victim/witness assistance programs, rape or sexual assault centres, and hospital-based treatment forensic units. These data are essentially qualitative due to the small number of agencies surveyed. From May 1985 to April 1988, a second review of selected sexual assault case law was analysed. The report provides insight into how judges have interpreted the new law and how lawyers have built their own legal arguments (see Department of Justice 1991).

Using national Uniform Crime Reports,[2] we undertook an analysis of national reporting, founding, and charging data for sexual assault and other serious crimes to identify trends and patterns associated with rape and sexual assault over an 11-year period (1977 to 1988; see Roberts 1990b as well as the chapter by Roberts and Grossman in this volume). Similar numbers and rates of reporting, founding and charging for the three levels of assault and manslaughter were also analysed as a basis for comparison.

A tragic minority of sexual assaults end in death for the victim. A study of homicide in the course of sexual assault examined the available statistical data on all homicides that have occurred during the commission of a rape or a sexual assault (since 1974). A statistical profile of the victims of rape/sexual assault homicides, the suspects, and the offence itself (including situational contingencies) is provided (see Roberts and Grossman 1991).

In the absence of national data on sentencing in Canada, an analysis of sentencing patterns in cases of sexual assault was conducted. This report draws upon secondary data sources, including a computerized sentencing information system in British Columbia.[3] It addresses selected issues with respect to sentencing in cases of sexual assault. To the extent possible and where data permit, it deals with sentences imposed across the country both before and after the 1983 law reform, and the variation in current sentences imposed from region to region.

Some General Issues in Assessing Legislative Impact

Two methodological considerations have emerged from a review of research intended to assess legal impact. One concerns the difficulty of measuring the impact that the law itself has had on observed changes in behaviour and attitudes. The other concerns the limit of law reform on motivating or modifying behaviour or attitudes.

First, impact implies, inter alia, 'effect' or 'influence.' Therefore, to refer to the *impact* of legal policy-making is to take an instrumental view of law – that is, one that sees law as an instrument to influence or order individual or group behaviour to achieve particular ends or goals. In this formulation, law is regarded as what researchers term 'an independent variable.' The pivotal question in legal impact studies is: What has been the impact of the law on behaviours, practices, experiences, attitudes, that the law was designed to affect or influence? An ideal research design would involve a control group design in which two jurisdictions, identical in every respect, would be randomly chosen. In one location the law reform would be introduced, in the other it would be withheld. The strategic issue in the impact assessment would be how to obtain estimates of the differences between legal behaviour and practices in two jurisdictions. In this way, practices and behaviour motivated by the law reform could be distinguished from other behaviours or practices occurring independently or in spite of the law reform.

In Canada, however, the authority to enact criminal legislation is within the mandate of the federal government, while the administration of justice is a provincial responsibility. Therefore, criminal legislation in Canada is national in scope as soon as it is proclaimed in force. For research purposes, this precludes a control population for the purposes of drawing comparisons. In addition, implementation of legislative initiatives is influenced by a number of extra-legal factors including available resources, time, emphasis placed on training of the various practitioners in the field, and pressures that emanate from within and outside the criminal justice system either to maintain the status quo or to make changes. These factors can affect how evenly criminal legislation is implemented across the country and will affect our ability to generalize across sites.

The second methodological consideration concerns the limit of laws, once implemented, on motivating or modifying behaviour and attitudes. Research has not borne out the notion that once a law has been enacted and made public, it becomes part of the stock of knowledge of society, and that behaviour is automatically adjusted accordingly. Kutchinsky's (1973) review of studies related to 'knowledge and opinion about law' found no empirical evidence to support this direct linkage between law and legal attitudes or behaviour. This fact led Kutchinsky to conclude that 'knowledge about law is neither a necessary nor a sufficient condition for conformity to the law' (104). On the other hand, certain changes in behaviour will probably result only with an increased public awareness of a new law; if so, there may be some degree of direct linkage between legislation and public behaviour. For example, the evaluation research identified a significant increase in the rate of reporting of sexual assaults after the 1983 legislation – a change that may (or may not) be attributable to widespread public awareness of the legislative changes.

Historical factors and self-motivation make it possible for behaviour consistent with the goals of the sexual assault legislation to have occurred in any event, irrespective of the law reform. As Lempert (1966) noted:

Any research design purporting to deal with the impact of a particular law on the behaviour of a populace will have to make certain that the law is indeed more than an expression of the popular will of the people and that the people would be acting differently without the law (121).

In Canada, certain historical factors that might affect the behaviour of victims, offenders and people working in the criminal justice system include:

1 The changing status of and advances made by women in the social, economic and political domains, and the potentially empowering effect of these developments;
2 An international movement striving for gender equality in the courts, aiming to eradicate attitudes and behaviours in the legal system based on sex stereotypes, and resulting in the establishment of task forces in 23 American states by 1988. This movement has focused current media scrutiny and reporting on judicial comments made during trials and sentencing decisions, particularly in cases of sexual assault and child sexual abuse;
3 The visibly heightened awareness and focus on victims of crime in general

and female victims in particular, accompanied by government initiatives and services;

4 The establishment of sexual offence investigation divisions in police forces where continuity and expertise have developed regarding the investigation of complaints and the gathering of evidence;
5 An increased sensitivity to complainants of sexual offences evident by the appointment of female officers to sexual assault squads;
6 The expansion of sexual assault support centres (originally, rape crisis centres) providing counselling and, in some centres, encouraging victims to report victimizations to police;
7 The addition of specialized forensic teams to hospital intake services, ensuring the preservation of evidence and, in some cases, providing psychosocial care and follow-up;
8 The women's lobby that long preceded the passage of Bill C-127; and
9 The ongoing movement toward rape law reform in other countries.

The proclamation in 1983 of the sexual assault legislation coincided with a heightened community awareness of the problem of child sexual abuse. (By January 1988, Bill C-15, designed to deal with specific offences pertaining to sexual offences against children, had been proclaimed in force; see Chapter 1 of this volume.) Possibly this new level of awareness led to increasing the general public's sensitivity to victims of sexual abuse, whether the victims are children or adults.

All of these factors and others serve as intervening variables that can easily interfere with the ability of researchers to attribute perceived changes to the law reform. Thus, while research results are extremely important in helping us understand the effectiveness of the new sexual assault legislation, we must also recognize that coincidental changes in public attitudes will inevitably confound the identification of simple causal relationships between law reform and behaviour.

Findings

THE OFFENCE AND THE INDIVIDUALS INVOLVED

Types of Sexual Offences

Researchers in each of the site studies collected information comparing the repealed offences (rape, indecent assault male and female) with the three levels of sexual assault. In the pre-reform period indecent assault against a female person and rape and attempted rape (which was the more serious infraction in the pre-reform period) had generally similar levels of police occurrence reports – that is, between 45 and 55 per cent (with the exception of Hamilton-Wentworth).

In the post-reform period, in which rape and attempted rape accounted for only 24 per cent of the reported cases, sexual assault level I (the least serious level of sexual assault) accounted for the largest number of cases – that is, between 55 and 85 per cent of all police occurrence reports of sexual offences in the study sites.

Severity of the Offences

There is no consistent pattern indicating that more or less infractions involving penetration have been committed in the post-reform period than in the pre-reform period. With two exceptions (Lethbridge in the pre-reform period and Fredericton-Saint John in the post-reform period), in each study site and in both time periods the incidence of sexual touching recorded in police files is greater than the incidence of penetration. Furthermore, there is no noticeable change over the two time periods.[4]

Information on the use of force by offenders and on physical injuries sustained by victims was obtained from police records and from files kept by sexual assault centres. As with findings for the type of sexual contact, there is no indication that offences are becoming more serious in terms of either the degree of force exerted on victims or the extent of injuries to victims. Vancouver is the only exception, showing increases in both indicators between pre-reform and post-reform periods according to police data. Although most respondents to the front-line agency survey (CS/RESORS Consulting Ltd. 1988) perceived little change in incident characteristics over time, it is important to note that 8 respondents from the 33 sexual assault centres had observed an increase in the level of violence associated with sexual assault incidents coming to their attention, as did 2 out of 25 respondents from police-based victim/witness programs.

Other Offence Characteristics

With respect to the location of the offence, no significant pattern emerges either within or between time periods (see Table 5.1). Insofar as the use of intoxicants is concerned, generally fewer than 30 per cent of either offenders or victims had been consuming intoxicants before the offence was committed.

TABLE 5.1
Location of Assault by Time Periods and Study Sites – Police Records

	Pre-reform			
	Victim's Home	Offender's Home[a]	Outside[b]	Other[c]
Vancouver	25 (13%)	59 (30%)	77 (40%)	34 (17%)
Lethbridge	10 (21%)	8 (17%)	9 (19%)	21 (44%)
Winnipeg	55 (18%)	37 (12%)	83 (27%)	131 (43%)
Hamilton	41 (21%)	29 (15%)	71 (36%)	55 (28%)
Montreal	111 (25%)	72 (16%)	164 (37%)	102 (22%)
Fredericton[d]	–	–	–	–

	Post-reform			
	Victim's Home	Offender's Home	Outside	Other
Vancouver	39 (18%)	70 (33%)	42 (20%)	34 (17%)
Lethbridge	23 (20%)	29 (26%)	43 (38%)	21 (44%)
Winnipeg	67 (13%)	97 (19%)	251 (49%)	131 (43%)
Hamilton	56 (26%)	38 (17%)	79 (36%)	55 (28%)
Montreal	52 (18%)	56 (20%)	72 (25%)	102 (22%)
Fredericton[d]	49 (24%)	25 (12%)	80 (39%)	–

[a] Includes offender's car in the case of Vancouver only.
[b] Includes 'other public place' in Montréal.
[c] Other locations include a common residence, the offender's car, or other public places such as buses, hotels, etc.
[d] Data for Fredericton–Saint John are not recorded by time period.

The role played by intoxicants or by the location of the offence is unclear in explaining either the seriousness of the offence or its classification by police.

Complainant Characteristics

What kinds of victims report to the police? Obviously, the vast majority are women. But what are their ages? Have the modifications to the sexual assault legislation tended to increase or reduce the average age of sexual assault victims? If one agrees that an objective of the new legislation was to encourage non-stereotypical victims to report (e.g., women who are sexually abused by their partners; prostitutes; younger victims), how has the situation changed between the two time periods measured? What is the relationship between victims and offenders? Are more cases of spousal sexual aggression reported to police or sexual assault centres? These are some of the questions to which we now turn.

Table 5.2 provides the age and gender distribution of sexual assault victims

TABLE 5.2
Age and Gender of Victims by Time Periods and Study Sites – Police Records

| | Pre-reform | | | | |
| | Age | | | Gender | |
	<18	18–30	>30	M	F
Vancouver	–	133 (76%)	43 (24%)	7 (4%)	184 (96%)
Lethbridge	25 (50%)	14 (28%)	11 (22%)	3 (6%)	47 (94%)
Winnipeg	135 (43%)	132 (42%)	47 (15%)	22 (7%)	295 (93%)
Hamilton	95 (51%)	68 (36%)	24 (13%)	19 (10%)	180 (90%)
Montréal	167 (37%)	210 (46%)	77 (17%)	39 (9%)	414 (91%)
Fredericton	25 (56%)	16 (36%)	4 (9%)	–	–
	Post-reform				
	Age			Gender	
	<18	18–30	>30	M	F
Vancouver	–	148 (71%)	60 (29%)	11 (5%)	205 (95%)
Lethbridge	82 (68%)	15 (13%)	23 (19%)	20 (17%)	100 (83%)
Winnipeg	347 (67%)	140 (27%)	31 (6%)	26 (5%)	502 (95%)
Hamilton	145 (65%)	64 (29%)	13 (6%)	36 (15%)	204 (85%)
Montréal	123 (43%)	113 (40%)	49 (18%)	19 (7%)	266 (93%)
Fredericton	45 (42%)	39 (36%)	23 (22%)	12 (9%)	116 (91%)

by study sites and time periods. This table shows a variable pattern of findings in different sites across the country.

Police data from Lethbridge, Winnipeg, Hamilton-Wentworth, and Montréal show an increase in the proportion of victims who were 18 years of age or younger, whereas the reverse trend occurred in Fredericton-Saint John. (Data relating to victims under 18 years of age were not collected in the Vancouver site study.)

Conversely, there were proportionately fewer reports of adult sexual assaults after the new law. In Lethbridge, the decline in victims' ages seems to be confirmed by data from the sexual assault centres, the proportion of victims aged 14 and younger rising from 44 to 60 per cent (University of Manitoba Research Ltd. 1988b, 49). In Winnipeg, according to data from sexual assault centres, the proportion of victims 18 years and older declined dramatically from 32 per cent to 5 per cent between the pre-reform and post-reform periods. The authors of the Winnipeg site report explain this decline by the fact that child victims of sexual abuse are now referred to child welfare agencies in Winnipeg and that a protocol now exists whereby child sexual abuse cases must be reported to police (University of Manitoba Research Ltd. 1988b, 78).

The Hamilton-Wentworth, Montréal, and Winnipeg site reports provide information on victims' ages from sexual assault centre files only for the post-reform period. In these cases, it is apparent that the sexual assault centres' services are oriented to an adult population, with generally fewer than 35 per cent of their clientele being juveniles (17 per cent under age 18 in Montréal, 33 per cent under age 16 in Hamilton-Wentworth, and 5 per cent under age 14 in Winnipeg).

On the basis of other Department of Justice studies currently underway, there is strong evidence that an increasing proportion of child sexual abuse cases are being reported to police. This is in all probability due to increased awareness of child sexual abuse as a problem in Canadian society, particularly since the publication in 1984 of the Report of the Committee on Sexual Offences Against Children and Youths. This was followed in 1988 by a series of profound modifications of the Criminal Code and Canada Evidence Act that were intended to deal with perpetrators of child sexual abuse and to facilitate processing these cases in the criminal justice system. The Committee's findings and conclusions – as well as the extensive media coverage the report received – may partly explain why more cases of child sexual abuse have been reported to, and recorded by, the police since 1984.

Victims' Relationships to Offenders

It is apparent from Table 5.3 that the proportion of reported sexual assaults committed by strangers diminished significantly between the two time periods. A greater proportion of post-reform infractions involved persons known to the victim, particularly parents and other members of the family and friends who make up a significant proportion of the 'other' category in police reports. Thus, in Lethbridge, the proportion of offenders who were parents, surrogates, and other relatives increased between 1981–2 and 1984–5 from 52 per cent (n=26) to 75 per cent (n=88); from 37 per cent (n=114) to 54 per cent (n=279) in Winnipeg; and from 32 per cent (n=63) to 52 per cent (n=117) in Hamilton-Wentworth.

Table 5.3 also reveals a modest increase in the proportion of sexual assaults involving spouses or partners. Unfortunately, this information was not separated out from the 'other' offender category in three of the six sites. Finally, data from Vancouver reveal that a significant number of sexual assault complainants were prostitutes in both time periods: 24 per cent and 31 per cent, respectively. No other site reports contain information on this

TABLE 5.3
Relationship Between Victim and Offender – Police Records

	Pre-reform			Post-reform		
	Stranger	Spouse/ Partner	Other[a]	Stranger	Spouse/ Partner	Other
Vancouver	156 (81%)	4 (2%)	34 (17%)	138 (67%)	15 (7%)	52 (26%)
Lethbridge	24 (48%)	–	26 (52%)	29 (25%)	–	88 (75%)
Winnipeg[b]	195 (63%)	–	114 (37%)	237 (46%)	–	279 (54%)
Hamilton	126 (64%)	6 (3%)	63 (32%)	94 (42%)	12 (5%)	117 (52%)
Montréal	362 (81%)	11 (2%)	64 (14%)	196 (71%)	12 (4%)	61 (22%)
Fredericton	31 (62%)	–	19 (38%)	50 (42%)	–	70 (59%)

[a] 'Other' includes relative, friend, associate, other family member.
[b] In Winnipeg, data were collapsed into two categories: stranger and unknown.

issue, so we must refrain, for the moment, from generalizing to Canada as a whole.

Characteristics of the Accused

Three types of reliable information are generally available on accused persons: age, gender, and past criminal records. Data on offenders are not usually available unless charges are laid. This means that the data must be interpreted cautiously since there are no guarantees that unknown offenders would have comparable characteristics. Predictably, the site studies confirm that the vast majority of sexual assault cases were perpetrated by males in both the pre-reform and post-reform periods.

As for victims' ages, a pattern of decreasing age was established. Conversely, offenders' ages appear to have increased between the two time periods, as revealed in Table 5.4.

The proportion of accused persons less than 18 years old remained fairly constant between the two time periods. However, the proportion of accused between ages 18 and 30 diminished in all sites,[5] while the proportion of offenders who were older than 30 years of age increased. Finally, many sexual assault offenders known to police were repeat offenders, although not necessarily for sex crimes. Table 5.5 shows that in four out of six study sites (Vancouver, Lethbridge, Winnipeg, and Fredericton-Saint John) well over 60 per cent of offenders had criminal records. In the cases of Montréal and Hamilton, the proportion appeared to be over 40 per cent. No pattern was identifiable over time.

TABLE 5.4
Age and Gender of Accused by Time Periods and Study Sites – Police Records

| | Pre-reform | | | | |
| | Age | | | Gender | |
	<18	18–30	>30	M	F
Vancouver	2 (6%)	16 (47%)	16 (47%)	46 (98%)	1 (2%)
Lethbridge	2 (4%)	28 (56%)	20 (40%)	195 (99%)	2 (1%)
Winnipeg	29 (18%)	68 (43%)	64 (40%)	304 (99%)	3 (1%)
Hamilton[a]	24 (25%)	70 (75%)	–	196 (99%)	1 (1%)
Montréal	32 (7%)	270 (62%)	130 (30%)	449 (99%)	5 (1%)
Fredericton[b]	2 (8%)	12 (46%)	12 (46%)	–	–
	Post-reform				
	Age			Gender	
	<18	18–30	>30	M	F
Vancouver	4 (5%)	30 (36%)	49 (59%)	99 (99%)	1 (1%)
Lethbridge	2 (3%)	37 (51%)	34 (46%)	216 (99%)	2 (1%)
Winnipeg	61 (18%)	119 (35%)	160 (47%)	464 (99%)	4 (1%)
Hamilton[a]	27 (18%)	120 (86%)	–	228 (99%)	3 (1%)
Montréal	29 (10%)	152 (55%)	94 (34%)	272 (99%)	3 (1%)
Fredericton[b]	6 (10%)	18 (30%)	37 (61%)	–	–

[a] Age of offender is classified as <18 and >18 only.
[b] Categories are 16–19, 20–29, and >30. Gender is not provided although we may legitimately suspect that 99 per cent are males.

TABLE 5.5
Past Criminal Records of Offenders by Time Periods and Study Sites – Police Records

| | Pre-reform | | Post-reform | |
	Yes	No	Yes	No
Vancouver	19 (69%)	8 (30%)	39 (72%)	15 (28%)
Lethbridge	12 (60%)	8 (40%)	25 (78%)	7 (22%)
Winnipeg	121 (82%)	26 (18%)	184 (61%)	117 (39%)
Hamilton	38 (36%)	66 (64%)	73 (42%)	101 (58%)
Montréal[a]	–	–	–	–
Fredericton[b]	–	–	–	–

[a] Only available information is that 46 per cent of offenders apprehended by police (n=127) have a past criminal record.
[b] Only available information is that 71 per cent of offenders apprehended by police (n=101) have a past criminal record.

THE RESPONSE OF THE CRIMINAL JUSTICE SYSTEM TO REPORTS OF
SEXUAL ASSAULT

Attrition in Cases of Sexual Assault

Research prior to the legislative reforms in 1983 indicated that most incidents
of rape were not reported to the police. Of those cases reported to the police,
not all resulted in laying a charge against a suspect, and only a small percentage of reported sexual assault incidents resulted in a conviction. This filtering
of incidents is known as 'case attrition,' and while it is not unique to sexual
assault (the number of cases of any criminal offence declines at each stage of
the criminal justice process), earlier research has suggested that the attrition
rate is higher for sexual assault than for other crimes against the person. Several reasons were advanced to explain this difference in attrition rates, including the nature of the earlier legislation, as well as the negative attitudes of
criminal justice personnel toward victims of sexual assault. More recent
research suggests that the attrition rate for sexual assault does not differ
greatly from the attrition rate for other crimes. The latest data from the
Canadian Centre for Justice Statistics and from the site studies commissioned
by the Department of Justice provide insights into the treatment of sexual
assault cases.

Cases designated as unfounded
Of the 29,111 reports of sexual assault made to the police in 1988 (the most
recent year for which data are available), 15 per cent were declared
'unfounded.' A report is classified as unfounded when, after a preliminary
investigation, police officers determine that a report is without foundation
because of insufficient evidence. The unfounded rate for crimes of sexual
aggression has not changed appreciably since 1983, when it was 14 per cent.
The legislation has therefore not resulted in an increase in the proportion of
reported sexual offences being designated as founded cases.

Cases cleared by charge
The cases that remain once unfounded reports have been screened out are
termed by Statistics Canada 'actual offences.' Cases in which a charge is laid
against a suspect are designated as 'cleared by charge.' The clearance rate is a
critical statistic in the treatment of sexual assault cases. The clearance rate as
a percentage of founded cases for sexual assault was 48 per cent in 1988. The
overall clearance rate for all crimes of violence was 46 per cent. Thus, the
clearance rate for sexual assault is comparable to the clearance rate for other

crimes involving violence. As with the statistics on founding rates, the 1983 legislation does not appear to have had any significant impact on the likelihood that a charge will be laid in cases of sexual assault.

Finally, there is considerable variation in the clearance rate for sexual assault from one province to another. Data from 1988 show that in New Brunswick 38 per cent of offences were cleared by charge; in the Northwest Territories, the rate was 72 per cent.[6] In order to know why clearance rates vary across the country, it will be necessary to undertake more detailed research into charging practices of police officers and crown attorneys.[7]

Conviction rates

The evidentiary difficulties in prosecuting sexual crimes were well known prior to the introduction of Bill C-127. It was no surprise, therefore, that the rate of attrition was high for these offences. The 1983 legislation aimed to address this concern in various ways. If successful, the legislation might produce an increase in the conviction rate, as well as an increase in the reporting rate. Table 5.6 shows pre- and post-1983 conviction rates expressed as a percentage of cases committed for trial in each of the study sites. Data from the site studies suggest that conviction rates have not increased significantly since the introduction of the new legislation, except in Fredericton-Saint John. In some sites the conviction rate even decreased. This variation might be explained by the number of convictions recorded at the study sites. In most cases, they were small enough that a fluctuation of two or three convictions or acquittals could make a significant difference in the overall rates. At this point it is difficult, therefore, to say with any certainty that conviction rates are changing and, if they are, in which direction. The problem could be addressed, in part, by establishing a national database that could be used for this purpose.

Qualitative information collected as part of the site studies provided generally similar views regarding conviction rates. Most of the defence counsel interviewed in Vancouver responded that sexual assault cases have become more difficult to defend with the new legislation. On the other hand, half the Crown attorneys interviewed said that their chances of winning sexual assault cases have remained the same since the legislative change; the other half suggested their chances of winning have improved.

In Hamilton-Wentworth, while legal practitioners indicated that the 1983 amendments have enhanced the chances of successful prosecution, few have actually seen this belief translate into a higher rate of conviction. Lawyers in Winnipeg responded that the likelihood of conviction has increased simply because the Crown attorney now has to meet a less stringent standard of

TABLE 5.6
Pre- and Post-reform Conviction Rates (as a per cent of cases committed for trial)

	Pre-reform		Post-reform	
	(%)	No.	(%)	No.
Vancouver	53	(17)	56	(36)
Hamilton	80	(30)	75	(57)
Winnipeg	64	(25)	47	(66)
Fredericton	64	(14)	79	(24)
Lethbridge	40	(5)	46.7	(15)
Montréal	74	(n.k.)	57	(nk)

NOTE: n.k. indicates 'not known.'

proof. As well, most defence counsel interviewed said the new evidentiary provisions have made it more difficult to defend the accused. Again, however, the conviction rate does not appear to bear this out, at least on the basis of the data collected in Winnipeg as part of the evaluation. Crown attorneys in Lethbridge viewed the new legislation as improving the chances of conviction but not necessarily as facilitating their jobs, since they perceived that more difficult cases are now being pursued.

In summary, the perceptions of practitioners in the sites were similar. In all sites where qualitative data were available, the perceived improvement in the Crown attorney's position was generally thought to relate to the abrogation of the recent complaint rules, the inadmissibility of evidence pertaining to prior sexual history of the complainant, and the relaxation of the corroboration requirement. Police officers in the individual sites noted that issues of credibility constitute the major obstacle in obtaining convictions in cases of sexual assault. Included in these issues are such factors as the conduct of the complainant immediately following the assault, and the existence of corroborative evidence. Future research will have to determine whether these views can be corroborated by the actual conviction rates.

Case Facts and Plea Bargaining

Perhaps nowhere else in the criminal justice system is the exercise of discretion subject to so little scrutiny as in the area of plea bargaining. Information is disclosed that may not be admissible in a court hearing,and commitments may be made regarding sentence submissions that have little bearing on the final outcome. The potential impact on the victim, particularly in a case of sexual assault, can be substantial. She may be angered that she was deprived of the chance to tell her story in court, or she may be relieved that a plea was entered without having to endure testifying in court. For these kinds of reasons, and because plea bargaining does not take place in open court, it invites a strong degree of public criticism.

Descriptive information about plea bargaining was collected from key informants in each of the site studies. The aim was to gain some understanding as to whether the plea bargaining process had changed with the new sexual assault legislation. While there was variation in opinion within and among sites, the possibility of plea bargaining was generally perceived to be greater since the new law. The different views expressed by informants suggested, however, that the increase in plea bargaining may not have been very significant in practice.

Sentencing

Sentencing was not a major focus of Bill C-127; accordingly, neither was it a major focus of the legislative evaluation research. In this respect, the individual site reports are of limited use in any discussion of sentencing in cases of sexual assault. The limited role of sentencing in the site studies was due, in large part, to the difficulty in obtaining relevant data from police and Crown attorney files, and to the time lag between the time of reporting and sentencing. Roberts' (1990a) report on sentencing, commissioned as part of the overall evaluation of the legislation, is not drawn from a nation-wide survey of sentencing patterns since truly national data are not presently available. Instead, it drew on a computerized sentencing information system in British Columbia, other earlier sources of data, and the limited data on sentencing contained in the site reports. These data sets covered different time periods encompassed within the years 1985 to 1988.

It is relevant to a discussion of sentencing that almost all sexual assaults (95 per cent) reported to the police are classified at the first (lowest) level of seriousness. For the databases included in Roberts' study, most convictions for sexual assault level I (between 60 and 80 per cent) resulted in imprisonment. Incarceration was imposed in over 90 per cent of convictions for sexual assault with a weapon (level II). For convictions for aggravated sexual assault (Level III), almost every offender convicted was incarcerated. More recent research has sustained this view: Pasquali (1991) reports a 100 per cent incarceration rate in her analysis of sexual assault sentences imposed over an 18-month period in the Yukon.

There is a great deal of concern, both public and professional, about the sentencing of offenders convicted of sexual assault. Paradoxically, sentencing is one of the areas in which statistical information is most lacking since, as noted earlier, sentencing statistics are not at present published on a routine basis at the national level.[8] In light of the widespread public and professional concern about sentencing in cases of sexual assault, it is clear that establishing a national sentencing database is a priority in this area. One of the important issues to be addressed concerns the kinds of mitigating and aggravating factors being considered by judges (see Mohr, Chapter 7 of the present volume, and Marshall 1986). As well, we need to know the extent to which sentences vary from province to province across the country.[9]

VICTIMS AND VICTIMS' SERVICES

Treatment of Victims – Practitioners' Views

One goal of the sexual assault legislation was to reduce what has been referred to as the 'secondary victimization' of complainants as they approach and move through the criminal justice system. The site researchers dealt with this issue, some more comprehensively than others. Most described in some amount of detail the victims's current treatment by both criminal justice practitioners and support services (medical and sexual assault centres), noting whether there were special police units to deal with sexual assault; whether female officers were assigned to this duty; and whether the Crown attorney offices now have personnel specialized in prosecuting sexual offences. The front-line agency study focused primarily on the treatment of the complainant and whether there has been any improvement over time. Data from all study sites on this issue are largely qualitative. Again, there was some variation in key informant opinion among the sites; however, it was generally agreed that while the judicial process remains traumatic for the victim, the new law has made it somewhat more humane and thus has tended to reduce stress.

Awareness and Perceptions of the Law

Public views and knowledge of the law
A nation-wide opinion poll taken in 1987 indicated that 80 per cent of Canadian adults did not know that rape is now known legally as sexual assault.

However, 84 per cent knew that sexual assault may be charged even if there is no lasting physical injury or use of weapon; and 83 per cent knew that sexual assault may be committed by a man or woman against his or her spouse (Department of Justice 1988, 65).

It is clear from the site report findings that many justice system workers believed that eliminating questioning on the victim's past sexual history had greatly eased the trauma of the court experience, and one could presume that this factor contributed to the willingness of victims to report. However, the survey cited above also indicated that one-half of the public still believed (incorrectly) that it is acceptable to question victims about past sexual behaviour in court. Changes in the way sexual assault victims are treated are so recent that it will take time for adjustments requiring knowledge of the law to take effect.[10]

Victims' views

To what extent were victims themselves aware of the 1983 sexual assault legislation? From the limited data collected as part of the site studies, it appears that among victims of sexual assault, familiarity with the law at the time of the assault was no greater than that of the general public. The few references to the legislation simply confirm that it was not taken into account in the victims' actions or later evaluation of their experiences.

Front-line agency study findings

A number of changes in the treatment of the sexual assault victims preceded the legislative amendments. Among these, the emergence of sexual assault centres and police-based victim/witness assistance programs were accompanied by hospital forensic units and a careful concern with the introduction of material evidence into court. These three types of service-providing agencies were included in the front-line agency study. In this study questionnaires were administered in person, by telephone, and by mail, yielding usable responses from 39 sexual assault centres, 27 victim/witness assistance programs, and 7 hospital forensic units. However, response rates to the individual questions were quite low, thus making the sample size for each response very small. An additional caveat is that few of the agencies existed prior to 1983, making a pre- and post-reform comparison difficult.

Notwithstanding its limitations, the front-line agency study provided an account of the agencies' assessment of changes in the victim's treatment by the criminal justice system, as well as an examination of the agencies' accounts of how their own treatment of the victim meshes with the personnel, policies, and procedures of the criminal justice system. The overall improvements noted by the sexual assault centres and the police-based victim/witness assistance programs were manifest in terms of practitioners' attitudes and procedures being followed during the study. Most of these agencies attributed improvements to the legislative amendments.

When asked what further improvements could be made in victims' treatment by police, Crown attorneys, and defence counsel, agency personnel suggested increased education for each about the nature and impact of sexual assault and training for police and Crown attorneys about how to deal with victims. The agencies also suggested that there should be procedures for ensuring more accountability by police, Crown attorneys, and defence counsel.

The degree of inter-agency cooperation occurring under the new law is separate from, but related to, the question of improved victim treatment by persons in the criminal justice system. The overall view of the agencies about relationships among themselves and between the agencies and the criminal justice system is cautiously positive. Eighty-five per cent of sexual assault centres and all of the police-based victim/witness programs found their relationships with police and Crown attorneys to be neutral or better. The sexual assault centres and the victim/witness assistance programs rated their relationships with hospitals and each other positively as well. Again, suggestions for improvement included more education and training in dealing with victims of sexual assault and more police and Crown attorneys specialized in the area, with a larger complement of women in both fields.

Conclusion

A survey of the literature conducted by the Department of Justice revealed that while sexual assault laws had been studied elsewhere, no evaluation had approached the scope and level of detail planned for the evaluation of Bill C-127. In particular, the coordination of national level analyses and more detailed site studies is new to legislative evaluation. The comparison of pre-reform and post-reform conditions also contributed to the comprehensive nature of the research. In all, the project was unique in its approach and goals.

The evaluation of Bill C-127 has provided needed information on a number of topics ranging from the experiences and needs of sexual assault victims to the factors that influence the handling of sexual assault cases by the criminal justice system and the limits and possibilities of criminal law reforms to prevent or mitigate personal offences. The research has also raised new and important questions about how to deal with sexual assault and ideas about directions in which the criminal justice system might look for improvements.

The study has shown that the reform legislation achieved some, but by no means all of its objectives. It would be naïve to think that a single piece of legislation could address the many problems associated with a complex socio-legal phenomenon such as sexual assault. The knowledge gained from the first systematic evaluation initiative will nevertheless be of use to policy-makers as they strive to improve the criminal justice response to incidents of sexual assault in Canada.

In the next chapter, Christine Boyle explores the issue of sexual assault from a legal perspective. Judges have a great deal of law-making power through their role as interpreters of legislation. This is particularly true for sexual assault, which was left undefined by the reform legislation of 1983. Boyle examines the judicial creation of the boundaries of sexual assault. The fundamental question that she addresses in the following chapter is whether the law is confronting the use of power, or simply siding with those who currently exercise that power.

Notes

1 This paper draws upon a report written by Patricia Begin while she was a research officer in the Department of Justice. Her complete paper was subsequently published as 'Rape Law Reform in Canada: Evaluating Impact' in *Crime and Its Victims: International and Public Policy Issues,* ed. Emilio Viano, New York: Hemisphere Publishing

2 Uniform Crime Reports are collected from police forces across Canada by the Canadian Centre for Justice Statistics, an arm of Statistics Canada.

3 The Sentencing Database System produced by the Legal Information Systems and Technologies (L.I.S.T.) Foundation, British Columbia.

4 Files maintained by sexual assault centres consistently record more incidents involving penetration than do police files. Whether this is a characteristic of the incidents reported to sexual assault centres as compared with police (a possibility supporting the hypothesis that cases reported to centres differ from cases reported to police), or whether this results from different recording practices, remains unknown on the basis of this information alone. Based on other quantitative and

qualitative information contained in the site reports, it is probably fair to state that this divergence can be explained by a combination of the two factors. Nevertheless, there remains an absence of significant change between the two time periods in terms of the frequency of offences involving intercourse for the sexual assault centres, as well as for the police.

5 With the possible exception of Hamilton-Wentworth, which provides only two age categories, placing all offenders over age 18 in one category

6 Because of the relatively low population of the Northwest Territories, as well as its low absolute numbers of sexual assault cases, percentage figures must be treated cautiously.

7 In most jurisdictions the police are responsible for laying charges; in others, cases are referred by the police to Crown attorneys, who then decide whether or not to lay charges. In some jurisdictions police are responsible for laying charges but must first consult with Crown attorneys as to the grounds for laying a charge and the type of charge to be laid.

8 This is changing. The Canadian Centre for Justice Statistics hopes to be able to release sentencing data from the Adult Criminal Court Survey in the near future.

9 The Research Section, Department of Justice, is planning research to further examine sentencing in cases of sexual assault.

10 This paper was written prior to the *Seaboyer* decision of the Supreme Court of Canada, which struck down the law restricting the admissibility of evidence concerning prior sexual history.

References

Baril, M., M.J. Bettez, and L. Viau. 1988. *Sexual Assault Before and After the 1983 Reform: An Evaluation of Practices in the Judicial District of Montreal, Quebec.* Ottawa: Department of Justice (November) WD1991-2a

Begin, Patricia. 1989. 'Rape Law Reform in Canada: Evaluating Impact.' In Emilio Viano, ed., *Crime and Its Victims: International and Public Policy Issues.* New York: Hemisphere Publishing

Bienen, Leigh. 1980. 'Rape III – National Developments in Rape Reform Legislation.' *Women's Rights Law Reporter* 6:3

Casper, Jonathan, and David Brereton. 1984. 'Evaluating Criminal Justice Reforms.' *Law and Society Review* 18:1

CS/RESORS Consulting Ltd. 1988. *The Impact of Legislative Change on Survivors of Sexual Assault: A Survey of Front Line Agencies.* Ottawa: Department of Justice (November) WD1991-8a

Department of Justice, Research Section. 1988. An Analysis of Public Attitudes Toward Justice Related Issues 1986-1987. Working Document. Ottawa: Department of Justice
– 1990. 'A Review of the Sexual Assault Case Law, 1985–1988.' Sexual Assault Legislation in Canada: An Evaluation, Report No. 6. Ottawa: Department of Justice
– 1990a. 'Overview.' Sexaul Assault Legislation in Canada: An Evaluation, Report No. 5. Ottawa: Department of Justice
– 1991. 'A Review of the Sexual Assault Case Law, 1985–1988.' Sexual Assault Legislation in Canada: An Evaluation, Report No. 6. Ottawa: Department of Justice
Ekos Research Associates Inc. 1988a. Report on the Treatment of Sexual Assault Cases in Vancouver. Ottawa: Department of Justice (September) WD1991-3a
– 1988b. Report on the Impacts of the 1983 Sexual Assault Legislation in Hamilton-Wentworth. Ottawa: Department of Justice (July) WD1991-4a
J. and J. Research Associates Ltd. 1988. An Evaluation of the Sexual Assault Provisions of Bill C-127, Fredericton and Saint John, New Brunswick. Ottawa: Department of Justice (November) WD1991-5a
Kutchinsky, Berl. 1973. 'The Legal Consciousness: A Survey of Research on Knowledge and Opinion about Law.' In C.M. Campbell, et. al., eds., Knowledge and Opinion about Law. Great Britain: Barleyman Press, 101–38
Lempert, Richard. 1966. 'Strategies of Research Design in the Legal Impact Study. The Control of Plausible Hypotheses.' Law and Society Review 1:1
Marshall, P. 1986. 'Sexual Assault, The Charter and Sentencing Reform.' Criminal Report 63:216–35
Pasquali, P. 1991. Sexual Assault Sentencing in the Yukon. The Yukon: Association for the Prevention of Community and Family Violence (Yukon Law Foundation)
Roberts, Julian V., 1990a. Sentencing Patterns in Cases of Sexual Assault. Sexual Assault Legislation in Canada: An Evaluation, Report No. 3. Ottawa. Department of Justice
– 1990b. An Analysis of National Statistics. Sexual Assault Legislation in Canada: An Evaluation, Report No. 4. Ottawa: Department of Justice
Roberts, J.V., and M. Grossman. 1992. 'Homicide and Sexual Assault.' Sexual Assault Legislation in Canada: An Evaluation, Report No. 7. Ottawa: Department of Justice
Ruebsaat, Gisela. 1985. 'The New Sexual Assault Offences: Emerging Legal Issues.' Sexual Assault Legislation in Canada: An Evaluation, Report No. 2. Ottawa: Department of Justice

Stanley, Marilyn G. 1985. 'The Experience of the Rape Victim with the Criminal Justice System Prior to Bill C-127.' *Sexual Assault Legislation in Canada: An Evaluation, Report No. 1.* Ottawa: Department of Justice

University of Manitoba Research Ltd. 1988a. *Report on the Impact of the 1983 Sexual Assault Legislation in Lethbridge, Alberta.* Ottawa: Department of Justice (August) WD1991-6a

– 1988b. *Report on the Impact of the 1983 Sexual Assault Legislation in Winnipeg, Manitoba.* Ottawa: Department of Justice (August) WD1991-7a

6

CHRISTINE BOYLE[1]

The Judicial Construction of Sexual Assault Offences

To this point in the volume we have addressed the origin of the 1983 reform legislation, and have explored some of the empirical consequences in terms of the criminal justice response to sexual assault. Now we turn to a legal perspective. As noted earlier in Chapter 1, this volume attempts to synthesize the sociological and legal perspectives on the phenomenon of criminal sexual aggression. In the first of the legally oriented chapters, Christine Boyle examines the nature of the substantive offences created by Bill C-127. Maria Łoś, in Chapter 2, referred to the fact that the reform legislation failed to provide a definition of exactly what constitutes a sexual assault. In this respect sexual assault is different from many other offences in the Code that do carry a definition to guide police officers, Crown counsel, and of course also judges. The observation by Maria Łoś is the point of departure for Boyle, who explores the ways in which the judiciary in Canada has grappled with, and come to define the nature of the sexual assault offences. The findings of the analysis contained in this chapter are critical to the debate over sexual assault, and should be borne in mind as the reader proceeds to the subsequent legal chapters by the other contributors to this volume.

The focus of this chapter is on the substantive criminal law of sexual assault, that is, the offences that became a part of Canadian law in 1983. The relevant sections of the Criminal Code provided a framework for the development of a whole new body of jurisprudence about the actual behaviours that had been criminalized. Difficult decisions about meaning and detail were left by Parliament to be made by the judiciary. Shortly after the new offences were introduced I wrote a short book, called *Sexual Assault*, on the changes and the issues that were likely to be judicially considered. At that point there was no case law to use for the purpose of analysis. In the years that have passed, the courts have had to grapple with a range of challenging issues, although a number of uncertainties remain. Since this chapter was written, Parliament has made some further changes to the substantive criminal law of sexual assault, in Bill C-49, An Act to amend the Criminal Code (sexual assault), 1992. A comprehensive analysis of these changes is beyond the scope of a paper focusing on judicial law-making, but some reference to them is included where appropriate. My chief objective in this chapter is to revisit some of the substantive issues I addressed in *Sexual Assault*, and to comment on the judicial responses.

The Material Elements of Sexual Assault

What is it that an accused person has to have done in order to be found guilty of sexual assault? There are three elements the Crown must prove under this heading. First, the accused must have done something that can be legally labelled as *sexual*. Second, there must have been an *application of force*. Last, the force must have been applied *without consent*. These three material elements will be discussed in turn.

THE MEANING OF 'SEXUAL'

What distinguishes a sexual assault from an ordinary assault? 'Sexual' was undefined in section 271 of the Criminal Code, for understandable reasons, since a non-circular definition is still elusive. In *Sexual Assault* I suggested a test of resemblance to what we would identify as sexual if it were non-coercive. Certainly this does not satisfy any standard of non-circularity. Perhaps a tautology is inevitable (Usprich 1987, 202), as the Supreme Court of Canada did not escape circularity in the leading case on the subject (*Chase*, 1987). The test adopted, using the standpoint of the reasonable observer, is that an assault is sexual if it is committed in circumstances of a sexual nature such that the sexual integrity of the victim is violated. Various factors are relevant: the part of the body touched, the nature of the contact, the situation in which it occurred, accompanying words or gestures, a motive of self-gratification. It was made clear that while such factors were relevant the test did not turn on the part of the body touched or the motive of the assaulter. This approach has since been used in a number of cases.[2] There are interconnected questions that the Supreme Court of Canada decision in *Chase* does not confront. If dominance and submission are eroticized[3] and if dominance is linked in some way to the cultural construction of maleness while submission is linked to femaleness,[4] does the distinction between assault and sexual assault disappear where a man assaults a woman (Boyle 1985, 106)? Furthermore, can 'masculine' and 'feminine' qualities be separated from biological men and women, so that an assault on anyone in a position culturally constructed as female (for instance a vulnerable man in a prison or possibly a male child) could be seen as sexual even without such usual indices of sexuality as the touching of genitalia?

Does 'sexual' connote sexuality, or gender as in sex discrimination, or both? If 'sexual' had connotations of gender, then this would be another route to the conclusion that gender assaults could include hate-motivated attacks on women, irrespective of whether they are sexually arousing. In other words, the law could define sexual assault as assault on the basis of sex. The Women's Legal Education and Action Fund (LEAF) has argued in its intervention in *Norberg* v. *Wynrib* (1992), a case involving a civil action for sexual assault:

> Just as women are sexually harassed based on their sex, women are sexually assaulted based on their sex. [The Supreme Court of Canada] has recognised that sexual harassment is used to 'underscore women's difference from, and by implication, inferiority with respect to the dominant male group' and to 'remind women of their inferior ascribed status.' The same is true of sexual assault.[5]

LEAF does not go so far as to suggest that any assault of a woman because she is a woman is a sexual assault,[6] but does make a link between sexual assault and sex inequality that might inform interpretations of the word 'sexual.'

As the law stands, at the moment, people who perceive themselves to be victims of sexual assault are dependent on a decision-maker's intuitive understanding of when an assault is a violation of sexual integrity. Since a concept of gender integrity is not at all developed in law, it is likely that the courts will continue to focus on sexuality rather than expand the inquiry to ask whether the abuse of power in and of itself can be sexual and whether a misogynistic assault should fall within the 'sexual' category.

THE APPLICATION OF FORCE

Section 265(1)(a) of the Criminal Code says that a person commits an assault if 'he applies force.' Such words may conjure up an image of a violent attack, but in fact *any* touching may be legally classified as the application of force, and thus an assault. The practical significance lies in whether sexual harassment – type touchings have been criminalized. A classic example could be a case where a male employee touches a co-worker on her bottom or breasts. While the word 'force' does suggest more than touching, the cases on assault in general, at the time the law came into force, tended to favour the view that any unconsented-to touching was an assault (*Burden* 1981). A little attention has been paid to this question since. *Cook* (1985) has reinforced the *Burden* approach, and made clear that it applied to sexual assault.[7]

In my view, this *Burden* and *Cook* line of authority should be strengthened when the opportunity presents itself. If sexual touchings occur in the workplace, or even in the home, then at least they can be oppressive reminders of sexual status. If the toucher is a stranger then any unconsensual sexual touching can be very frightening indeed, especially since the limits of the experience will not be obvious at the time. Indeed, in any situation, where one person makes it clear that he does not respect the physical integrity of another, the person touched cannot be confident where such disrespect will end. Such touchings should be seen as a form of sexual aggression.

THE ABSENCE OF CONSENT

With respect to any form of assault, including sexual assault, section 265(3) of the Criminal Code provided some assistance with the difficult line between consent and submission:

For the purposes of this section, no consent is obtained where the complainant submits or does not resist by reason of
(a)   the application of force to the complainant or to a person other than the complainant;
(b)   threats or fear of the application of force to the complainant or to a person other than the complainant;
(c)   fraud; or
(d)   the exercise of authority.

Is this list exhaustive? I suggested in *Sexual Assault* that there was nothing in this section to indicate that this is an exclusive list of the situations in which no consent is obtained. The Ontario Court of Appeal took a different view in *Guerrero* (1988) and decided the list was exhaustive.[8] Parliament has now added flexibility in Bill C-49. After adding to the list of situations where no consent is obtained in section 1 (now section 273.1(2)),[9] the bill states:

Nothing in subsection (2) shall be construed as limiting the circumstances in which no consent is obtained.

This is a positive development since, if the judicial interpretation in *Guerrero* had become settled law, it would have had significant implications for the boundaries of sexual assault. With respect to the consent/submission boundary, the present law seems to make clear that there is no consent where the victim had a gun to her head (force or threat of force). On the other hand, it is also clear that there is consent where the only motive for engaging in sexual activity is self-gratification. There are many other motives falling on a spectrum between these two extremes: a desire to reproduce, to avoid hurt feelings, to get a job, to avoid losing a job, to avoid the circulation of embarrassing photographs, to avoid an undeserved 'F' in a course, to avoid a deserved F in a course, to make money, to make enough money to feed one's children, to get medical treatment, to avoid rejection by one's therapist or spiritual adviser. Which of these situations should be legally stamped consent and which submission?

There are at least two possible approaches to consent in law. First, attention could be focused on the individual complainant. Taking all the facts into account in deciding whether she consented or submitted, the courts could ask the following question: 'Was this person's will overborne?' Such an approach could be adopted to discourage any attempt to influence a person's decision, and could be appropriate for a legal system that valued equality of initiative in sexual contact. An isolated example of such an approach can be found in the English Court of Appeal decision in *Olugboja* (1981), where a young girl was found not to have consented even though there was no force or threat of force.[10]

Such an approach has advantages in that it *might* render suspect any sexual contact absent clear indications of willingness. This is because the focus would be on the complainant's willingness rather than on whether the accused's conduct could be labelled as force or fraud or whatever is on the list of vitiating factors at any point in time. However, that is not necessarily the case, since 'facts' about willingness and communication of willingness are not analysed in a cultural vacuum. This approach thus presents as factual, difficult normative issues of when we have a responsibility to avoid sexual contact with others for fear of taking advantage of their vulnerability.[11] The question of an appropriate standard, and in particular a standard consistent with equality between women and men, remains.

For example, the issue of whether silence can be construed as consent clearly requires a normative rather than a factual response. The authors of one leading text (Keeton et al. 1984) state that the 'girl who makes no protest at a proposal to kiss her in the moonlight may have mental reservations that it is without her consent, but the man who does it is none the less privileged' (113).

This expresses a rule that it is permissible to have sexual contact with passive persons. Lucinda Vandervort (1990) has argued that 'more effective legal protection for individual control over outcomes chosen can be achieved by interpreting the law of consent so as to restrict legal legitimacy to those interventions with the person that the individual expressly and affirmatively permits'[12] (500).

Irrespective of which approach to the meaning of silence one prefers, the difference of opinion makes clear that the determination of consent cannot be simply factual.

Thus the factual approach, while having the potential to be respectful of the perspective of the individual, risks presenting rule-creation as fact-finding. If a conclusion is presented as factual, then it is a lot more difficult to challenge as, for instance, being inconsistent with equality rights for women. An example can be found in a British Columbia case (*Letendre* 1991). The judge based his decision to acquit on a finding that lack of consent had not been proved beyond a reasonable doubt. Part of his reasoning was that the 'mating practice, if I may call it that, is a less than precise relationship. At times no may mean maybe, or wait awhile.' Such a decision would be difficult to appeal, as it seems to be a factual decision that when the complainant said no she may still have been consenting. This is so, even though the judge was asserting a legal conclusion, that it is not against the law to have sexual contact with a person who has just said no to you. The Crown announced a decision not to appeal as there was no error of law.

The other, more traditional, approach to consent, revealed in section 265 of the Criminal Code and section 1 of Bill C-49 (now section 273.1(2)), is to list unacceptable pressures and influences. This has advantages in the relative visibility of the standard set. Thus, as the list now stands, one submits, rather than consents, where force is present. One probably[13] consents, rather than submits, where one fears male disapproval, removal of economic support, the withdrawal of companionship in a world where heterosexual couples are the social norm, and so on. A visible standard is susceptible to a critique that it reflects male interests,[14] in terms of the classification of listed, illegitimate pressures, and unlisted, thus possibly legitimate, pressures. The standard is a statement of male expectations of women's accessibility (Dawson 1985).[15]

It is clear, however, that this approach places the obligation on people subjected to 'legitimate' pressure to have sexual contact to withstand that pressure, rather than on others to avoid exerting that pressure. This might not be troublesome with respect to social, economic, physical, and psychological equals. The situation is different where a vulnerable person (such as a person in need of medical treatment) is expected to display fortitude and a more powerful person (such as a doctor, in a position to abuse confidential information and to write prescriptions) is expected to display none.[16] The gender implications are obvious with respect to sexual assault, where the vulnerable persons are likely to be women and children and the more powerful persons are likely to be men (Solicitor General 1985, 2).

If this approach is continued, the question therefore is whether the list adequately recognizes situations where power can be exploited. It would not be surprising were the law to take account of imbalances of power in setting the consent standard, since there is some precedent for this. For instance, the offences of sexual interference (s. 151), invitation to touching (s. 152), and sexual exploitation (s. 153(1)) are all offences directed at protecting children and young persons. Consent is not a defence. It is clear that the responsibility for avoiding sexual contact is placed on older persons. While women should not be legally categorized as, or as analogous to, children, these offences reflect an understanding of how age can be a factor in classifying sexual contact as exploitative and/or a breach of trust rather than as an exchange between equals. A further example can be found in section 265 itself, in its reference to the exercise of authority, discussed below.[17]

In my opinion, the courts should approach consent as a concept requiring the setting of legal standards in addition to fact-finding[18] and expand the present list of vitiating factors to offer increased protection to vulnerable people. However, to an extent, the need for judicial understanding of the potential for sexual coercion inherent in various forms of inequality has been lessened by the changes in Bill C-49. For instance, section 1 (now section 273.1(2)(c)) states that no consent is obtained where 'the accused induces the complainant to engage in the activity by abusing a position of trust, power or authority.' It is noteworthy, nonetheless, that while Bill C-49 was being passed by Parliament, the Supreme Court of Canada was deciding, in *Norberg* v. *Wynrib* (1992), that unequal distributions of power are relevant to the determination of consent.

Space does not permit an examination of each factor that points to submission rather than consent. It is probably reasonable to assume that force or the threat of force is alleged in most cases that are actually prosecuted. Attention will be focused here on the other factors that were listed in the Code prior to the passage of Bill C-49.

FEAR OF THE APPLICATION OF FORCE

The Code makes it clear that a person may submit, rather than consent, where they fear the use of force. This is so even though the accused was not responsible for that fear (although he may still be acquitted because of a lack of a guilty intent, discussed below).

The question is how the courts will apply this provision. It will be important to adopt a different approach from that in the Ontario Court of Appeal case of *Bursey* (1957). The incident occurred in an isolated area. The complainant testified that she engaged in sexual activity because she feared the accused would attack her and leave her in a ditch. In overturning the conviction, Laidlaw J.A. referred to the absence of signs of struggle or injury and the minimum of evidence of threats or fear of bodily harm exerted to extort consent.

Letendre (1991, 21) provides an example of the difficulty in applying this provision in practice. The complainant, who was having a drink with the accused in her home, testified that she was 'scared for her life.' The judge was very frank about his inability to understand why she would be afraid. 'She acknowledged that the accused never threatened her in anyway at any time, and there is really no evidence of his having used force or hurt her. It is therefore difficult to understand the basis for her statements that she was afraid, that she was scared for her life.' It is not enough for the law to make clear that a person may be afraid in the absence of threats. To use this case as an example, such legal recognition would have to be translated into judicial understanding that a woman alone with a strange man who had already ignored her 'no' would be very sensible to be afraid. An approach more consistent with what we know of women's vulnerability to sexual assault would be to ask why would any woman *not* be afraid.

FRAUD

This issue will be discussed at some length because it is largely neglected in the literature and in prosecutions. In my view it raises some interesting questions about judicial creation of the boundaries of sexual assault. Section 265(3) states that assault is committed where a person 'submits or does not resist by reason of ... fraud.' In other words, it is possible to commit a form of sexual assault by deceiving the victim rather than forcing her or taking advantage of her fear.[19] These words, 'submits or does not resist by reason of fraud' were a change from the old rape law. The offence of rape referred to situations in which consent was obtained by personation of a woman's husband or by false and fraudulent representations as to the nature and quality of the act. An example of the operation of these limiting rules in practice can be found in the Supreme Court of Canada decision in *Bolduc* (1967). This was an indecent-assault case, but the law on fraud was the same. A doctor had misrepresented a friend to be a doctor so that he was permitted by the patient to be present at a vaginal examination. The reason for quashing the conviction was that this was not fraud as to the nature and quality of the act. In other words, the group of women and girls protected by the old law was very small indeed – those rather absent-minded women who could be mistaken about their husbands and those young girls who, in all probability, had absolutely no knowledge of sex, and could be deceived, for instance, by unscrupulous doctors into thinking that sexual intercourse was treatment, or by singing teachers into thinking that intercourse would improve the voice. In 1983, the old narrow wording disappeared, and sexual assault was brought into line with assault generally. The Criminal Code now simply refers to fraud. The question was therefore bound to arise about what was the meaning of fraud. Should the old narrow meaning be retained, or a brand new meaning be adopted?

In *Sexual Assault*, I discussed the range of possible choices about the meaning of fraud, and suggested that since the wording of the law had been changed, the courts should take a fresh look at the types of fraud that ought to attract criminal penalties. Today I would add that the issues are complicated by the fact that heterosexual, and some homosexual, activity takes place between social and economic unequals, so that lying might have significance in terms of gender.[20]

Since then the British Columbia Court of Appeal has examined the meaning of fraud in the case of *Petrozzi* (1987). The case involved a charge of sexual assault of a prostitute. Petrozzi agreed to pay her $100 in exchange for sex. However, at his trial he testified that he only had $10 left from an evening's drinking and never intended to pay $100. She testified that he refused to pay in advance and instead attacked and raped her. He denied forcing her to have sex. At trial the judge wanted to leave fraud to the jury as well as the issue of whether he had forced her to have sex. In other words, the trial judge seemed to feel that whoever the jury thought was telling the truth about forced sex, the accused could be found, on his own admission, to have committed sexual assault by fraud. Both counsel objected – they wanted the jury to decide on the issue of forced sex alone. When the jury convicted, the defence appealed.

There was a different Crown counsel at the appeal, but again the same pattern emerged. Both sides argued that fraud had nothing to do with this case, since it was not fraud as to identity or the nature and quality of the act. The Crown argued against conviction on this ground.

To adopt an expansive interpretation would lead to a whole series of socially unacceptable results. One example would be that an adult who lied to another adult and thereby had consensual intercourse with that individual would render themselves liable to a charge of sexual assault.

Well, exactly. But why is that socially unacceptable, especially in the context of examples used in the case itself of people lying to others about the fact that they have an infectious disease and of people lying to prostitutes about willingness to pay them? The case raises a disturbing question about who was supposed to be the advocate for those vulnerable to sexual assault.

In any event, the adversary system was not being adversarial, so the court appointed an *amicus curiae*, a lawyer who would address the issue as a friend of the court, to provide arguments on whether fraud should be given a broader meaning, as I and other commentators had suggested. In the end, the majority came to a rather mixed conclusion. They did not see why, as a matter of policy, fraud should be given the old restricted meaning. However, the court was unanimous in deciding that Parliament had not intended to broaden the meaning of fraud, so they sent the case back for a new trial. The court opened the door to a new approach and then closed it again.[21]

The issue is complex for several reasons. First, it can be difficult to distinguish a lie from, say, a perspective. What is truth? As well there are many forms that lies can take in the context of sexual and sexually assaultive activity. What forms of fraudulent sexual assault *should* be treated as criminal by future courts? How should we distinguish between lies and criminal lies? It might be useful to think of a range of lies and ask which should fall within the criminal definition of fraud. It is important to remember that the law does not only have to be relevant to the first sexual contact, but also to ongoing sexual relationships, since there must be fresh consent every time one person wants to have sexual contact with another, no matter how old the relationship is.

There are the very scary lies: I will not kill you – I do not have any infectious disease. But there are lots of others. I think some of them are men's lies, some are women's lies, and some are gender-neutral lies. In other words gender might have something to do with how we deceive each other. Some of the ones I can think of are probably heterosexual lies (or white lies?) and may be youthful lies: I love you – I like you – I will respect you in the morning – I will marry you – I have lots of money – I am in favour of equality for women – You are beautiful – I prefer small breasts – What an enormous penis – I like hockey – I am interested in art – I am not married – I will pay you for sex – I will never leave you – I don't normally sleep with students – I am not interested in marriage – I have had a vasectomy – I am on the pill – Everybody does this – Your mother is charming – I am not interested in one-night-stands. And of course the old favourites: You would if you really loved me – My wife doesn't understand me – Come up and see my etchings. My guess is that the most commonplace lie is simply embellishing our everyday characters to be more attractive.[22]

It is clear that the spectrum of lies runs from the commonplace, trivial deceits of sexual relations, through lies that trample on the morality or exploit the ignoble ambitions of others, to life-endangering lies. None of the lies mentioned above would presently qualify as fraud within the Court of Appeal's definition in *Petrozzi*.

A different approach would be to use the wording of the Code itself, as did the trial judge in *Petrozzi*. The wording is broad enough to cover any untrue statement that had a causative connection with the fact that the complainant did not resist sexual contact. Given that the Crown has the burden of proof, the courts could treat as criminal all untrue statements where the fact-finder was persuaded that sexual contact would not have taken place had the truth been known. A possible objection is that this could include somewhat trivial lies, but the victim's perpective on importance would be embodied in the law, the accused being adequately protected by the requirement of proof of a causative link beyond reasonable doubt. After all, the more common form of sexual assault covers a broad range of activities, from the relatively trivial to the life-threatening.

At least the law of sexual assault should cover lies such as denials of infectious disease or defrauding a prostitute into providing sexual services. This would be respectful of physical and economic autonomy. A broader approach, such as the one suggested above, however, has the merit of showing most support for other, more intangible forms of autonomy, such as moral and psychological autonomy. In future, the courts may consider taking a broader approach than one that simply covers fraud as to identity or the nature and quality of the act.[23]

THE EXERCISE OF AUTHORITY

This is the provision that has considerable potential to allow the courts to take imbalances of power into account in deciding whether there was consent.

The term 'authority' has been applied to predictable persons – a teacher (*Schofield* 1986), a stepfather (*S.(C.E.)*1988), a man who purported to have authority over the complainant at work (*Tremblay* 1988), a foster father (*F (A)* 1989), and a corrections worker with respect to inmates (*White* 1990). It should be noted that authority is a somewhat limited concept in itself – a broader provision would include power and trust.

The requirement that the authority be exercised further limits this provision. As recognized in Bill C-49 in its reference to 'trust' and 'power,' mentioned above, some people may occupy positions of power such that there is no need for any overt use of authority.[24] For both the above reasons, the section therefore might not be helpful with respect to doctor–patient sexual assault for example. Thus legislative reform, in response to growing concern about sexual exploitation by such persons as physicians and priests, was more likely to address this boundary on the offence of sexual assault, than judicial interpretation.

The Mental Elements of Sexual Assault

It is not enough for the Crown to prove that the material elements of sexual assault are present. A guilty intent on the part of the accused must also be established.

A MISTAKEN BELIEF IN CONSENT

A mistaken belief in consent, even if rarely raised, is the most politically significant aspect of the law relating to the mental elements of sexual assault, and perhaps more than any other, is the issue that epitomizes the debate over the sexual politics of judicial decisions in this area. The law was settled, prior to the introduction of the present structure of sexual assault offences, by the famous case of *Pappajohn* (1980). The Supreme Court of Canada decided that, in accordance with general principles of criminal law, a person accused of sexual assault may claim as a defence that even if the complainant did not consent, he honestly (though unreasonably) thought that she did. The *Pappajohn* approach was put in legislative form in section 265(4) of the Criminal Code.[25] The question whether it should be changed occupied an important place in discussions of reform of sexual assault law, and no doubt the controversy will continue after the change introduced in Bill C-49.

In its choice of the perspective of the accused over the perspective of the victim, the case has given rise to considerable criticism (Pickard 1980a). The benefit of the *Pappajohn* rule is that it avoids the danger of punishing someone who is incapable of taking reasonable care to ascertain consent and who thus does not deserve to be punished. There are at least two problems with this. First, individuals who are capable of taking care may escape conviction or prosecution.[26] Second, those who are incapable of taking care may pose a grave danger to others. For instance, some men may have been socialized to have significant and self-interested misconceptions about the behaviour of women (Abbey 1982). Males have been found to be less likely than females to believe that females really meant no when they said no (Abbey 1982). There may be men who are capable of believing that a passive, weeping woman (*Plummer and Brown* 1975) or a passive, sick woman (*Weaver* 1990) is consenting to sex. Weaver was acquitted on the basis of an honest belief in consent after he had had intercourse with a drunk woman who was lying on a bed recovering from severe bouts of vomiting.[27] It can work both ways, however. Passivity may be perceived as consent, as may resistance. To some men, a woman's resistance may present a challenge, an invitation to 'rough sex,' or a sign that she must yet be shown what she really wants.[28] This is part of a mythology of male sexual conquest, the mendaciousness of women, and the sexual double standard. In addition, there is a type of rapist who uses violence to excite himself and believes that the victim welcomes the violence even when she is literally fighting for her life. (Cohen et al. 1977). The danger that such people pose to women was not addressed in *Pappajohn*.

However, there have been signs that the courts are not prepared to apply the rule literally. The clearest example of an attempt to find a way around *Pappajohn* can be found in *Sansregret* (1985). In this case, the accused, who used to live with the victim, broke into her house and terrorized her into submission to intercourse. In fear for her life, she had pretended a willingness to renew their relationship and to have sex. The trial judge found that the accused was totally deceived and that, while no rational person would have believed she was consenting, Sansregret did. Following *Pappajohn*, as she was bound to do, the trial judge acquitted. The case went to the Supreme Court, where a new form of the old doctrine of wilful blindness was developed in order to convict. Even though the trial judge had found an honest belief in consent, thus leaving no room for a finding of recklessness, Sansregret was convicted. What this means, in effect, although this was not acknowledged by the Court, was that he was being punished for having a belief that no reasonable person would have had in the circumstances. A functional willingness to punish for negligent sexual assault, disguised by the term wilful blindness, has resulted in a lack of clarity in the law. For example, in a recent decision of the British Columbia Court of Appeal (*Paré* 1990), the Court states unanimously:

The judge unfortunately couples the two concepts of being reckless and being wilfully blind. If the latter concept applies there can be no defence of honest but mistaken belief in the consent of the complainant. Such a defence may however be available, if the evidence supports it, even if the jury finds the conduct of the accused reckless.

In my view, the courts have revealed ambivalence about *Pappajohn* in the new extension of the concept of wilful blindness.[29] They have not, however, utilized one possible limit on the *Pappajohn* rule that is consistent with general principle. An accused who argued that he thought a woman who was inert, weeping, sick, or saying no was consenting could be told that he made a mistake of law (Vandervort 1987–8). Judges could say that it is against the law to have sexual contact with people who have not indicated consent or who have said no and that thinking otherwise is a normative, rather than factual, mistake. Reconsideration of this issue, by Parliament or the Supreme Court of Canada, even if only on the ground of unpredictability in the law alone, was long overdue.

In the event, it was Parliament that took the plunge, in section 1 of Bill C-49 (now section 273.2(b)):

It is not a defence to a charge [of sexual assault] that the accused believed that the complainant consented to the activity that forms the subject-matter of the charge, where

...

(b) the accused did not take reasonable steps, in the circumstances known to the accused at the time, to ascertain that the complainant was consenting.

The judicial power over this provision is, of course, extensive. It will be challenged as inconsistent with principles of fundamental justice under section 7 of the Charter. I hope I have shown above that the provision does not make a stark break with the values implicit in the pre–Bill C-49 case law. If it survives, then it will have to be given meaning. What are reasonable steps? Is straightforward inquiry one? Is honesty another? Are reasonable steps the same between social and economic equals as they are between unequals? This is perhaps the most significant challenge for judges as they draw the boundaries of sexual assault in the future.

Conclusion

The sexual use of more vulnerable people is one form that power takes in our cultures. The fundamental question underlying the discussion in this chapter is whether the law is confronting that use of power or siding with those who have it.

The picture I have painted is not a clear one. On the one hand, there is authority that any unconsented-to touching is an assault, an acknowledgment of the importance of physical autonomy; there is recognition, in *Chase*, that sexual assaults can be motivated by something other than sexual gratification; while not discussed above, the excuse of intoxication has been denied, at the cost of some departure from principle (seen as too high a price in *Pappajohn*).

On the other hand, until *Norberg*, the courts had really not examined the meaning of sexuality or the meaning of consent in a world where heterosexual activity between social and economic unequals is the norm. They have said that people do not have to take reasonable care to ensure consent to sexual activity; that a man who deceives a prostitute into providing sexual services for nothing is not guilty of sexual assault; and, in at least one case, that it is not against the law to touch a woman sexually after she has said no.

This picture causes me concern about the role of the judiciary in striking the right balance between the interests of people who subject other people to unconsented-to sexual activity (mostly males) and the interests of people who are thus subjected (mostly women and children). The law could place a higher value on the security of the person of women and children without imposing unreasonable demands on individuals, and I believe that Parliament, in 1992, has taken steps in that direction in Bill C-49. Judicial acceptance of the values underlying this bill, as well as further judicial initiative, for instance in giving meaning to reasonable steps, would be a significant indicator of equal respect and dignity and an acknowledgment of the distinctive harms of sexual assault.

This chapter has not explored the role of the judiciary in terms of the sentencing of offenders convicted of sexual assault. That is the critical area addressed in the following chapter by Renate Mohr. The paradox unveiled in the following chapter is that although the public and the news media often look to individual sentences to judge the efficacy of our sexual assault laws, the sentences often reflect the conceptions of individual judges rather than a common perception of the seriousness of the offence. Since the Supreme Court of Canada does not hear appeals that challenge the 'fitness' of sentence, each of the ten Courts of Appeal sets its own standard of what is 'fit.' As Mohr reveals in the next chapter, these standards also vary considerably, reflecting the variable sentencing philosphies of the individual judge.

Notes

1 The author would like to thank the Faculty of Law for its support as well as Melody Schalm and Catherine Laurie for their research assistance.

2 See, for example, *R. v. L.(F)* (1988), *R. v. Chen* (1990), *R. v. Ali* (1990), and *R.v.Brenton* (1990).

3 See generally MacKinnon (1985).

4 Gillespie (1989, 106–9) discusses the research on sex-role characteristics. For instance, stereotypical 'feminine' characteristics include being submissive rather than aggressive or independent. 'Masculine' characteristics include assertiveness, forcefulness, and willingness to take risks.

5 LEAF factum (1991), quoting *Janzen v. Platy Enterprises* (1989)

6 For a discussion of U.S. law on crimes variously referred to under headings such as hate crimes or bias-related violence, see Boyle (1991).

7 See also *R. v. L. (F)* (1988) where a youth was convicted of sexual assault for touching and grabbing girls at his school.

8 In this case the accused, who was a sort of father figure to the victim, threatened to reveal nude photographs if she did not have sex with him. The trial judge convicted on the basis that her consent was vitiated by the accused's exercise of authority. On appeal, the Crown conceded that the authority exercised by the accused had nothing to do with the consent in issue. However, it was argued that section 265(3) was not exhaustive of the means by which consent may be vitiated. The conviction was overturned on the basis that the vitiation of consent must occur by reason of one of the enumerated sorts of behaviour, listed in the text. Other academic analysis supported a more expansive view. Bryant (1989, 131–40) suggests that common sense favoured the recognition of other vitiating factors. He discusses the common law factors of unconsciousness, mental impairment, and immaturity.

9 For instance, section 1(2)(d) states that no consent is obtained, for the purposes of the sexual assault offences, where 'the complainant expresses, by words or conduct, a lack of agreement to engage in the activity' – the 'no means no' amendment.

10 See Boyle (1981). *R. v. Cadden*, August 16/1989, Vancouver Registry: 006595, (B.C.C.A.) could be seen as a functionally similar case, although the court seemed to find implied threats. A Grade 4 teacher had his students perform fellatio on him on several occasions. His conviction was upheld on appeal even though defence counsel argued that he had not committed an assault because he never applied or threatened force.

11 It has traditionally been assumed that consent is a factual matter in the context of

the mistaken belief in consent defence. For a powerful argument that at least some mistakes are mistakes as to law not fact, see Vandervort (1987–8).

12 Bill C-49 contains a definition of consent in section 1 (now section 273.1(2)) – 'the voluntary agreement of the complainant to engage in the activity in question.' However, this leaves the question of whether a silent person is voluntarily agreeing to the judiciary. If a person is unable to communicate because of a disability or is paralysed by fear even though no overt threats were used, the courts will have to decide whether silence means consent or the absence of consent. The definition has at least transformative potential since 'voluntary agreement' can be interpreted as requiring more than passivity.

13 Since Bill C-49 makes it clear that the list is not exhaustive, this is of course speculation.

14 It was interesting that Bill C-49 was subjected to public criticism on the basis that it tilted the law too much toward the protection of female interests. For example, in its presentation to the legislative committee studying the bill, REAL Women said the bill was 'unfair to men.'

15 In my view it is fair to say that those expectations, to the extent that they are expressed through legislation, have now been significantly limited by Bill C-49.

16 This has been recognized in the context of the doctor–patient relationship by the Supreme Court of Canada in *Norberg* v. *Wynrib* (1992). This involved a torts action and is discussed by Elizabeth Sheehy in her chapter entitled 'Compensation for Women Who Have Been Raped.'

17 One can range further afield in an attempt to show that the law is not impervious to imbalances of power. Duress, undue influence, and unconscionability are contract law doctrines that provide relief against unfair contracts. Unconscionability in particular is directed at situations where there has been an 'unfair advantage gained by an unconscientious use of power by a stronger party against a weaker.' One of the elements is 'inequality in the position of the parties arising out of ignorance, need or distress of the weaker, which left him in the power of the stronger' (*Morrison* v. *Coast Finance Ltd.*, 1965).

18 It should be helpful that Bill C-49 contains *some* definition of consent, even if vague. This ought to make it clearer that consent is a legal construct and that some claims of mistaken belief in consent may indeed involve mistakes as to the legal meaning of consent rather than facts. See generally Vandervort (1987–8).

19 Those readers who know the movie *Cyrano de Bergerac* will remember that Cyrano helps another man court Roxanne by writing poetic letters on his behalf and masquerading as him under her balcony. Roxanne falls in love first with the physical beauty of the other man but then more permanently with the poetic soul she has been deceived into thinking he has. No sexual contact takes place after the deception, but if it had I wonder if both men would have been guilty of sexual

assault. The movie has a sad ending so perhaps the author did intend to portray divine retribution for the deceit.

20 You might think that is a relatively modern insight, but in fact the old law reflected some kind of understanding of this. Until just a few years ago, there was a set of seduction offences designed to protect young women and girls. One of them was seduction under promise of marriage, which reflected some insight into the social and economic vulnerability of some women, and may well have criminalized a form of fraud.

21 The courts do not always refuse to take creative approaches to applying old offences to new fact situations. See, for example, *R. v. Thornton* (1991) involving a conviction for common nuisance of a man who had tested positive for HIV antibodies.

22 In the Al Pacino movie, *Sea of Love*, one of the clues to the murderer in that film was that an old 45 record was playing at the murder scene. The detective deduced that a new relationship must have been involved. Is it only when someone is trying to attract another person that he or she gets out such a thing as their old record collection? Once a relationship is established then the hidden depths that have come to the surface can go back to being hidden.

23 If such an approach were to be adopted, we might develop a considerable interest in erring on the side of honesty, rather than erring on the side of embellishing our own virtues as some of us may do now. What would total honesty require in sexual relations, especially heterosexual relations, that is, between people who have sex with each other in a context of sex inequality? The truth for Petrozzi would have been: I just want to use you for sexual purposes and then not pay you, even though that is the way you earn your living. What might other people say? I really didn't feel interested in you at all until I had that sixth beer – I like to think I believe in equality for women, but fundamentally my career is more important than yours – I do join in the sexist jokes after the hockey game, well actually I think this whole thing about sexism is way overdone – I have no intention of calling you tomorrow – I am pretending to be interested in your boring stories about your work – I really don't want to sleep with you at all, but I can't figure out how to say no without hurting your feelings – I only pretend to have orgasms – You really are a pretty mediocre lover.

24 However, it should be noted that Bill C-49 requires that the accused 'induce' the complainant to engage in the activity 'by abusing a position of trust, power or authority.'

25 See *Robertson* (1987) and *Laybourn* (1987).

26 For instance, in *Plummer and Brown* (1975), the accused came across the complainant crying after she had been raped by another man. The accused had intercourse without seeking consent. She was still in a state of fear. A new trial was

ordered. There was no suggestion in the appeal that the accused was incapable of understanding that a passive, weeping person was not consenting.
27 The Alberta Court of Appeal thought it was significant that the victim was not actually vomiting at the time. But why?
28 The legal reflection of such views can be found in *Letendre* (1991). The acquittal of a man who went on touching a woman after she had said no, presumably on the basis that it was legitimate to continue touching her sexually to see if she meant no or if she would change her mind, is disturbing in that it gives support to such opinions about women.
29 Evidence of ambivalence might also be found in the cases that show a reluctance to find an 'air of reality' to the defence so that it must be left to the jury. *Pappajohn* itself might be an example of that. See also *Guthrie* (1985) and *White* (1986), and *Reddick* (1988), conviction upheld [1991] 1 S.C.R. 1086. A further example of ambivalence could be that intoxication has not been held to be a defence to sexual assault. See, for example, *Moreau* (1986), *Murray* (1986), and *Bernard* (1988).

References

Abbey, A. 1982. 'Sex Differences in Attributions for Friendly Behaviour: Do Males Misperceive Females' Friendliness?' *Journal of Personality and Social Psychology* 42:830-8.
Boyle, C. 1981. 'Married Women: Beyond the Pale of the Law of Rape.' *Windsor Yearbook of Access to Justice* 1:192–213
– 1984. *Sexual Assault.* Toronto: Carswell
– 1985. 'Sexual Assault and the Feminist Judge.' *Canadian Journal of Women and the Law* 1:93–107
– 1991. 'Hate, Hierarchy, and Homicide.' Unpublished Walter S. Owen lecture. University of British Columbia
Bryant, A.W. 1989. 'The Issue of Consent in the Crime of Sexual Assault.' *Canadian Bar Review* 68:94–154
Cohen, M.L., et al. 1977. 'The Psychology of Rapists.' In D. Chappell et al., eds., *Forcible Rape.* New York: Columbia University Press, 291–314
Criminal Code, R.S.C. 1985, c. C-46
Criminal Law Amendment Act, S.C. 1980–81–82, c.125
Dawson, T.B. 1985. 'Legal Structures: A Feminist Critique of Sexual Assault Reform.' *Resources for Feminist Research* 14:40–3
Gillespie, C.K. 1989. *Justifiable Homicide.* Columbus: Ohio State University Press
Heald, S. 1985. 'Social Change and Legal Ideology: A Critique of the New Sexual Assault Legislation.' *Canadian Criminology Forum* 7:117–27

Keeton, W.P., et al. eds. 1984. *Prosser and Keeton on the Law of Torts*. St. Paul, MN: West Publishing Co.

LEAF factum in *Norberg* v. *Wynrib* (1991)

MacKinnon, C.A. 1984. 'Not a Moral Issue.' *Yale Law and Policy Review* 2:321–45

Osborne, J. 1984. 'Rape Law Reform: The New Cosmetic for Canadian Women.' *Women and Politics* 4:49–64

Pickard, T. 1980a. 'Culpable Mistakes and Rape: Harsh Words on *Pappajohn*.' *University of Toronto Law Journal* 30:415–20

– 1980b. 'Culpable Mistakes and Rape: Relating *Mens Rea* to the Crime.' *University of Toronto Law Journal* 30:75–98

Solicitor General. 1985. 'Female Victims of Crime.' *Canadian Urban Victimization Survey Bulletin* 4

Usprich, S.J. 1987. 'A New Crime in Old Battles: Definitional Problems with Sexual Assault.' *The Criminal Law Quarterly* 29:200–21

Vandervort, L. 1987–8. 'Mistake of Law and Sexual Assault: Consent and Mens Rea.' *Canadian Journal of Women and Law* 2:233–309

– 1990. 'Consent and the Criminal Law.' *Osgoode Hall Law Journal* 28:485–500

Cases Cited

Bolduc v. *R.*, [1967] S.C.R. 677

Janzen v. *Platy Enterprises*, [1989] 1 S.C.R. 1252

Morrison v. *Coast Finance Ltd.* (1965), 55 D.L.R.(2d) 710 (B.C.C.A.)

Norberg v. *Wynrib* [1992], 4 W.W.R. 577 (S.C.C.)

Pappajohn v. *R.*, [1980] 2 S.C.R. 120

R. v. *Tremblay*, [1988] O.J. No. 2436

R. v. *F (A)*, [1989] N.J. No. 279

R. v. *Guerrero* (1988), 64 C.R. (3d) 65 (Ont. C.A.)

R. v. *Guthrie* (1985), 20 C.C.C. (3d) 73 (Ont. C.A.)

R. v. *Weaver* (1990), 80 C.R. (3d) 396

R. v. *Petrozzi* (1987), 35 C.C.C. (3d) 528 (B.C.C.A.)

R. v. *Plummer and Brown* (1975), 31 C.R.N.S. 220

R. v. *S. (C.E.)*, (1988) 63 C.R. (3d) 194 (N.S. County Court)

R. v. *Robertson*, [1987] 1 S.C.R. 918

R. v. *Reddick* (1988), 31 O.A.C. 246, [1991] 1 S.C.R. 1086

R. v. *Schofield*, [1986] B.C.J. No. 121

R. v. *Ali* (1990), 79 C.R. (3d) 382 (Ont. Prov. Ct.)

R. v. *White*, (1990), 88 Sask. R. 54, affirmed (1991), 91 Sask. R. 225 (C.A.)

R. v. *White* (1986), 24 C.C.C. (3d) 1 (B.C.C.A.)

R. v. Thornton, [1991] 1 O.R. (3d) 480 (C.A.) affirmed [1993] 2 S.C.R. 445

R. v. Paré, [1990] B.C.J. No. 774 (B.C.C.A.)

R. v. Murray (1986), 31 C.C.C. (3d) 323 (N.S.C.A.)

R. v. Chase (1987), 37 C.C.C. (3d) 97 (S.C.C.)

R. v. Chen (1990), 63 Man.R. (2d) 79 (Man. Q.B.)

R. v. Bursey (1957), 26 C.R. 167 (Ont. C.A.)

R. v. Burden (1981), 25 C.R. (3d) 283 (B.C.C.A.)

R. v. Brenton (1990), 80 Nfld. & P.E.I.R. 247

R. v. Cook (1985), 46 C.R. (3d) 129 (B.C.C.A.)

R. v. Canadian Newspapers (1988), 43 C.C.C. (3d) 24 (S.C.C.)

R. v. Moreau (1986), 26 C.C.C. (3d) 359 (Ont. C.A.)

R. v. Bernard (1988), 67 C.R. (3d) 113 (S.C.C.)

R. v. Olugboja, [1981] 3 W.L.R. 585, petition for leave to appeal to the House of Lords dismissed, [1981] 1 W.L.R. 1382.

R. v. Letendre (1991), 5 C.R. (4th) 159 (B.C.S.C.)

R. v. Laybourn, [1987] 1 S.C.R. 782

R. v. L (F), [1988] M.J. No. 607

Sansregret v. R., [1985] 1 S.C.R. 570

7

RENATE M. MOHR

Sexual Assault Sentencing:
Leaving Justice to Individual Conscience

At this point in our volume we turn to one of the most critical issues in the area: the sentencing of offenders convicted of sexual assault. Although only a minority of the total offender population is ever sentenced (on account of the process of attrition – see the preceding Chapters 3, 4, and 5) the sentencing stage has enormous symbolic significance, for the victim, for the offender, and for society in general. The public expect the sentencing judge to address the problem of sexual assault. It is an unrealistic expectation, at least in terms of affecting crime rates: the sentencing process has only a limited role to play in this regard (see, for example, Ashworth 1992). Renate Mohr places sentencing in the context set by previous contributors, particularly the chapter by Christine Boyle. She also discusses sentencing issues and relates them to the substantive area of sexual assault. One of the central themes of this book, identified in Chapter 1 and echoed in several chapters thereafter, is that by leaving the interpretation of broad statutory provisions to individual decision-makers, the criminal justice system creates a host of new problems, including ones of inequity of treatment. Nowhere is this more evident than in the area of sentencing. Truly national sentencing statistics are not yet publicly available in Canada; accordingly, Mohr's analysis is based upon a sample of Court of Appeal decisions. These decisions are critical to the practice of sentencing at the trial court level, and therefore they reveal a great deal about judicial conceptions of what constitutes a sexual assault, and what constitutes an appropriate punishment for these crimes.

In the preceding chapter Christine Boyle explored the judicial role in interpreting what constitutes a sexual assault. The role of the judiciary is of course critical in the area of sentencing. Sentencing has long been called the pinnacle of the criminal justice process. It is both ignored and sensationalized. It is rarely mentioned in legal texts and articles on criminal law and yet remains a preoccupation of the media (Roberts 1990). It is the stage in the criminal process where judges may exercise their discretion, almost completely unencumbered by rules (Canadian Sentencing Commission 1987). It is at the sentencing hearing that pain and suffering become facts that must be weighed. In short, it is an important vantage point from which to evaluate law reform efforts. The question I seek to address in this chapter is 'What can we learn about the 1983 sexual assault legislation through an examination of sentencing judgments?'

The importance of the sentencing hearing, and the ultimate sentence imposed on the defendant is recognized by all. However, legal research and writing on sentencing is usually relegated to a short end-chapter of a criminal law text dealing almost exclusively with substantive criminal law and the criminal trial. The explanation for this dissonance can best be understood through an examination of law as a gendered arena where the more 'abstract,' 'rational,' rule-governed trial is privileged (in terms of research, analysis, and legislation) and the more 'contextual,' 'emotional,' policy-oriented sentencing hearing is trivialized or virtually ignored (Mohr 1990b). As a result, the sentencing hearing, which is the only experience of the criminal justice system for that vast majority of accused persons who plead guilty, is loosely governed by maximum penalties and strongly driven by the individual concerns of the presiding judge (Hogarth 1971).

When faced with a guilty plea or conviction for a sexual assault offence, judges in Canada have very few sources of guidance to assist them in the determination of the sentence. There is no single pronouncement, either in the Criminal Code or in a Supreme Court of Canada (S.C.C.) judgment, as to the principle(s) that should govern sentencing in Canada (Canadian Sentencing Commission 1987). In a 1982 decision (*Gardiner*), the S.C.C. announced that it would not entertain sentencing appeals. Consequently, ten distinct courts of appeal have the final word(s) on the principle(s) of sentencing, appropriate range(s) and appropriate factors for consideration. The only two existing sources of guidance for trial courts and appeal courts, with few exceptions, are first, reported sentencing decisions and second, legal texts on sentencing in Canada. The two texts that are most often quoted in judgments are Ruby (1987) and Nadin-Davis (1982). Both texts are primarily descriptive of current practices and offer little or no analysis of the problem of unwarranted disparity resulting from different approaches to sentencing taken by the different courts of appeal. In fact, Nadin-Davis begins his treatise by asserting that 'we have, indeed, a logical sentencing process in Canada' (3).

This influential text trivializes the importance of studying regional disparities and dismisses the significance of the admitted 'personal whim and inclination of the individual judge' (3).

The sentencing judgments that I examine in this chapter were selected through a computer search that sought to identify all Canadian Appeal Court judgments on sexual assault that were reported in the provincial law reports between 1983 and 1991. Of the 336 judgments that were selected, 196 were 'pure' sentencing appeals involving adult defendants. The full texts of these judgments were analysed and organized by province to allow for a clear analysis of provincial variation in the approaches to the sentencing of sexual assault cases. Judgments were then sorted according to the victim's status as either an adult (over 14 years) or a child (under 14 years). Almost all of the victims were female, and all but one of the 196 defendants were male. Slightly over half (54 per cent) involved child victims; in 4 per cent of cases there was no information on the victim's age, and the remainder (42 per cent) involved adult victims.

In *Sexual Assault* (1984), Christine Boyle predicted that 'sentencing decisions will reveal the most about the reality of the law on sexual assault' (171). Indeed, as I hope to illustrate through an analysis of the cases, sentencing decisions reveal a great deal about the different 'realities' of the law on sexual assault. As feminist scholars have long maintained, 'realities' are not gender-neutral, nor are they neutral regarding class, race, sexual identity, or physical or mental disability. The sentencing process itself is gendered, the act of exercising of discretion is gendered, and clearly sexual assault is a gender-specific crime. To speak of 'one reality' is to ignore gender, class, colour, sexual identity, and disabilities (see, for example, Fudge 1991, Lahey 1985, Monture 1991, Thornhill 1985). To ask questions about the success or failure of this law reform effort without asking 'according to whom or what criteria' is an empty exercise. The conclusion to this chapter offers one answer to the question 'What can we learn about the 1983 sexual assault legislation through an examination of sentencing?' The answer is that no law reform effort will ever achieve anything of any importance so long as there is so little shared understanding of the offence, of its impact, of the purpose of sentencing, and of the role of the law in the achieving the ultimate goal of a society without sexual assault. We can no longer afford to assume that even this ultimate goal is shared (Brownmiller 1975, Clark and Lewis 1977, MacKinnon 1984).

In order to reveal the complexities of the sentencing process and the approaches taken by the different courts of appeal, this chapter will be divided into five main parts. In the first part, the kinds of information available to courts of appeal will be explored. In the second part, the significance of the three-tiered maximum penalty structure will be examined to reveal the difficulties in simply comparing sentence lengths in determining whether sentences are too lenient or too harsh. The third and fourth parts survey the difference in articulated purposes of sentencing and the development of tariffs in certain courts of appeal. In the final part, the evidence available to the court in assessing the 'harm to the victim' and the 'blameworthiness of the offender' will be examined, and the different approaches to the determination of whether a particular factor is aggravating or mitigating will be set out. In conclusion, the analysis of the reported sentencing decisions reveals not only that there is no single approach to sentencing in Canada (as asserted by Ruby and Nadin-Davis) but that the approaches to sentencing sexual assault cases vary widely across the ten jurisdictions.

Information Available to the Court: The Determination of Fitness of Sentence

GUILTY PLEAS

Approximately 80 per cent of reported cases in the sample were cases in which the defendant pleaded guilty in the first instance. This figure is significant because it reveals that Appeal Court judges are most often reviewing decisions made by trial court judges on the basis of the information presented at sentencing hearings. Sentencing hearings are typically very short and often consist of a reading of the facts by the Crown and submissions by defence counsel regarding any mitigating factors she or he wishes to present. In those rare cases where a sentencing hearing follows a trial, a judge may decide on a fuller presentation of the evidence proved according to the rather strict rules of the trial. As I shall later discuss, the kinds of information admissible at a sentencing hearing are potentially much broader in scope, but in practice the sentencing hearing is brief and the facts presented in aggravation or mitigation are usually uncontested.

CROWN- OR DEFENCE-INITIATED APPEALS

The majority of reported appeals were sentence appeals brought by the defendant, claiming that the sentence was too severe. Although the success rate of defence-initiated appeals varied from province to province, in most provinces well over 50 per cent of the defendants who appealed were successful at having their sentences reduced. Fewer reported appeals are initiated by the Crown, and the success rate in having the sentence increased was even higher than defence success rates.

INFORMATION VALUE OF COURT OF APPEAL SENTENCING JUDGMENTS

There is great disparity in the length and detail of the information set out in sentencing judgments from one province to the next. For example, while Ontario and Nova Scotia court of appeal judgments provide adequate information on both the facts of the case and the factors that the court considered in mitigation or aggravation, judgments from Saskatchewan, Alberta, and Manitoba courts of appeal were generally either very brief or extremely weak on the facts. Examples from Alberta include: *L* (1986), where a father sexually assaulted his ten-year-old daughter, and where the assault is described as 'fondling not penetration' and virtually no other facts or factors are cited; *D. (B.)* (1988), where a father sexually assaulted his daughter and her two friends over a two-year period and the court states that it 'will not set out detailed facts.' *Sandercock* (1985), perhaps the most widely cited sexual assault sentencing decision is unusual in both its length (approximately eight and a half pages) and in the detailed facts and factors. The Saskatchewan Court of Appeal, although sometimes quite helpful in setting out detailed information, has shown a reluctance to provide any detail regarding the nature of the sexual assault. For example, in *B. (M.)* (1988), which involved the sexual assault of a nine-year-old stepdaughter, the court stated that it 'was not necessary to review' the facts surrounding the 'revolting behaviour' and the only indication of the nature of the assault was that there was 'no intercourse' but 'forced sexual activity'; in *W. (V.M.)* (1989), involving the sexual assault of two stepdaughters and one niece, the court again stated that it was not necessary 'to describe unpleasant and revolting details.' The court added, however, that 'the degree of sexual abuse was not as pronounced as in some cases' (digital manipulation was mentioned); in *Poll* (1987), which involved the sexual assault of a 4-year-old boy by a 64-year-old man, the court stated that it did 'not need to set out details,' and the only information regarding the sexual assault was that it involved 'no violent conduct.' Manitoba Court of Appeal judgments, with some exceptions, are extremely terse, and in many cases the only information presented to shed light on the nature of the sexual assault is the charging section of the Code and the age of the victim.

There is an obvious need for all courts of appeal to set out the facts of each case and the factors they considered in their evaluation of the sentence. Although sometimes the facts that the trial level court is presented with are incomplete, especially where the sentencing hearing follows a guilty plea, courts of appeal must at a minimum set out all the facts that are available to them. Judgments that attempt to spare the readers the 'unpleasant and revolting details' offer little guidance to lower courts and make it difficult for anyone to assess the 'fitness' of the Appeal Court decision.

POWERS OF COURT ON APPEAL AGAINST SENTENCE

Section 687 of the Criminal Code directs courts of appeal to 'consider the fitness of the sentence appealed against' and to vary the sentence 'within the limits prescribed by law' or dismiss the appeal. The limits prescribed by law simply refer, in most cases, to the maximum penalty prescribed for the offence in the Code. The ten provincial courts of appeal are the final courts to decide on the fitness of sentence (the final Court of Appeal for the Yukon and the Northwest Territories is the British Columbia Court of Appeal and the Alberta Court of Appeal respectively). There is no legislative guidance regarding what principles or factors courts should consider in determining 'fitness.' Some courts of appeal have made pronouncements to help define when a sentence should be interfered with, but the majority of cases are silent regarding the role of the court in determining 'fitness.' Even in those rare cases where courts try to offer some guidance it is often so vague that it is entirely unhelpful. In three cases in which the Newfoundland Court of Appeal was unwilling to interfere with the original sentence, some basic rules were articulated. In *Onalik* (1987) the court stated that it would not interfere with a sentence imposed by a trial judge except where she or he 'erred in considering basic principles of sentencing' or where the sentence was 'excessive or unduly low given the particular offence and antecedents of the accused.' In *J.J.E.* (1986), the court held that a trial judge was in 'a better position to weigh factors' and hence the Court of Appeal was 'loath' to interfere and 'should not interfere unless the trial judge is manifestly in error either in the principles applied or the sentences imposed.' In *Hoskins* (1987) the Court of Appeal stated the 'basic rule' that it would only interfere where a trial judge: considered the 'wrong principles'; was 'influenced by improper considerations"; 'failed to consider all relevant circumstances, or imposed a sentence inordinately too high or too low.' Upon a close examination, these criteria or rules are so subject to interpretation that it is not surprising that in fact the Newfoundland Court of Appeal did interfere with the original sentence in well over one-half of the cases heard.

In New Brunswick, in only two cases where the court did not wish to interfere with the original sentence did it justify non-intervention by stating a threshold that the sentence did not appear 'manifestly wrong' *(S.(W.T.)* 1987) and the trial judge did not fail 'to consider appropriate principles of sentence or [make] some error' *(Harmon* 1985). In Nova Scotia in only one of the reported cases did the Court of Appeal articulate a test for interference. In *MacDonald* (1985), the court stated it would not change the sentence unless it was 'manifestly inadequate or excessive as to be clearly erroneous.' A Quebec Court of Appeal judge used similar language in *Pronovost* (1987), where the court found a sentence severe but 'not manifestly excessive or unreasonable.' In only two Ontario cases did the court attempt to express any principle for when it would interfere with the decision of the trial judge. In both cases the court explained its decision not to interfere by stating there was 'no error in principle made by the trial judge' *(J. (F.E.)* 1989, *Tuckey* 1985). In Manitoba the language of 'fitness of sentence' was used. In three cases, (*Chartrand, Bush,* and *Horvat*) all heard in 1986, the court stated it would not interfere since the sentence was not 'excessive' or 'unfit.' Finally, in only one Saskatchewan Court of Appeal decision was any mention made of the basis for interference. In *Marks* (1985), the court stated that although it would have imposed a more severe sentence (incarceration) in the first instance, it would not interfere where there was no error on the part of the trial judge.

In the vast majority of reported decisions in all of the courts of appeal there was a conspicuous silence regarding the stated rationale for interference. Although the ten courts of appeal play the role of the Supreme Court of Canada in determining 'fitness' of sentence, there is little legislative or common law guidance as to what this means. In most cases no reference was made to the concept of how 'fitness' is determined, and in those few cases where the court does comment on its rationale for interference, it seems to be in circumstances where they are in fact justifying their non-interference. These pronouncements are at best broad and fail to provide any context for an evaluation of how courts determine what a 'fit' sentence for sexual assault is. In a few provinces there is an established 'range of sentence' that is used as a yardstick, but this is by no means true for all provinces. There is not, needless to say, any national standard regarding 'fitness of sentence' for sexual assault or any other crimes.

The Charge: Significance of Three Tiers

Although all the reported sentencing decisions in this study involved behav-

TABLE 7.1
Sexual Assault Offences: Levels of Seriousness

Offence	Section	Description	Maximum	# Decisions
Level I	271	sexual assault	10 years[a]	130
Level II	272	weapon, threaten bodily harm to 3rd party, causes bodily harm to complainant, party to the offence	14 years	26
Level III	273	aggravated: wounds, maims, disfigures, dangers life of complainant	life	5
Other				35

[a] This is a hybrid offence. If the Crown proceeds by way of summary conviction, the maximum penalty is six months or a $2000 fine.

iour clearly identified as 'sexual assaults' by the courts, not all charges were laid under one of the three sexual assault provisions in the Code (see Table 7.1).[1] However, the vast majority of cases (161 of 196) were sentence appeals following conviction for sexual assault.

SEXUAL ASSAULT LEVEL I (s. 271)

Again, this sample of reported sentencing judgments seems to mirror results of other studies which indicate that almost all charging for sexual assaults takes place at level I, the least serious sexual assault offence category. In 1989, 96 per cent of reports of sexual assault were classified as level I (see Chapter 5 in this volume). There are a number of explanations for this.

The first has to do with the reality of the circumstances in which the sexual assault of children takes place. A clear pattern in this sample of cases was that the sexual assault of children almost always occurs within a context of abuse of trust. An authority figure (e.g., natural father, stepfather, uncle, brother, minister, teacher) who sexually assaults a child does not need a level II weapon, or threats to a third party, nor does the assault result in 'bodily harm' that is unrelated to the harm caused by digital manipulation or penetration (Marshall 1990). An authority figure who sexually assaults a child does not cause the 'extra' level III wounding, maiming, and disfiguring that results from a struggle or the use of weapons, because the child 'submits.' Not even in those cases where the sexual assault of the child involved a rape (including a case where a three-year-old girl suffered vaginal abrasions (*Beyonnie* 1988) was there ever a conviction for level II or level III sexual assault, nor was any mention made of the 'bodily harm' that resulted.[2]

There were cases where the facts, as set out in the appeal court sentencing judgments, clearly indicated the presence of a weapon or a bodily injury (other than that which would result from penetration), and yet the convictions were for level I sexual assaults. Fewer than half of these cases involved a guilty plea, which suggests that plea bargaining is a partial explanation. There are clear data to support the conclusion that undercharging at the police and Crown level may be the rationale for the remaining cases. Police are almost exclusively laying level I charges; one explanation for this is that they hold the perception that a conviction will more easily follow a simple sexual assault charge.

Examples of the level I sexual assaults that clearly involved level II weapons or bodily harm and level III endangering life include: *Cormier* (N.B.), where the victim suffered contusions to her neck and throat as the result of a struggle to resist a rape; *Ogden* (N.B.), where the victim was choked with a pillow and threatened with death if she looked at her assailant's face while he raped her; *Lafford* (N.S.), where the victim was beaten, threatened with a knife, and raped; *Blackburn* (N.S.), where an 86-year-old woman who was asthmatic was gagged and hospitalized after the rape; *Newman* (Ont.) where a five-year-old girl was struck on the head and suffered facial bruising as a result of her struggle during a rape; *L. (J.L.)* (Sask.), where the victim was threatened with death and forced at knifepoint to perform fellatio on her assailant; and *Gleason* (Yukon), where the husband of the estranged wife banged her head on the fridge, beat her with his fists, and raped her.

Although these 'factual' level II and III cases resulted in level I convictions, they did generally result in more severe sentences than other level I cases (generally in the range of three years to eight years). Exceptions to this included the three-year-old child who was raped (sentence: 11 months and three years' probation) and the estranged wife (one year reduced to time served in custody prior to conviction). On the whole these sentences are higher than most of the sentences for simple sexual assault, revealing that threats of power are underestimated, bodily harm resulting from rape is underestimated, and violence is often considered as an 'added' consequence of sexual assault.

SEXUAL ASSAULT LEVEL II (s. 272) USE OF A WEAPON, THREATENS BODILY HARM TO 3RD PARTY, CAUSES BODILY HARM ETC.

Of the only 25 sentencing decisions that followed a conviction for a level II charge, only 2 of those cases involved children. In one Ontario case (*Jondreau*, 1986), a seven-year-old girl was taken to a secluded area by a stranger and, after being subjected to anal intercourse and attempted vaginal intercourse, was ordered to swallow feces after the defendant defecated on her face. What appeared to ground this case in a level II charge was that the defendant threatened that he would kill the child's mother if she did not comply. The other case was a Saskatchewan Court of Appeal decision (*Meesto* 1988) in which the police found the defendant, a stranger who had broken into the home, with a three-year-old girl under him; 'sexual parts on both' were naked, he had an erection and made motions of intercourse. The 'minor facial bruising' suffered by the child elevated this sexual assault to level II.

The remaining 23 cases involved either bodily harm and/or the presence of a weapon. In some cases it was unclear why the injury was not considered a 'wounding' (level III) or why the attacks were not considered 'endangering life' (level III). In *Wadden* (1986), a 16-year-old girl was brutally attacked at night by a stranger with a machete. She suffered cuts on her hand and neck from the struggle which ensued from the attempted intercourse. In *Graves* (1988), the defendant entered a pizza establishment after it was closed, cut the phone lines, bound and gagged the two 18-year-old woman employees, held a hunting knife with a 2–3 inch blade to their throats, raped them, and forced them to perform fellatio a number of times over a two-hour period.

SEXUAL ASSAULT LEVEL III (s. 273) WOUNDS, MAIMS, DISFIGURES, ENDANGERS LIFE

Only six reported decisions fell into the category of aggravated sexual assault. Three of those cases were from the province of Quebec. In *Champagne* (1987), a 12-year-old girl contracted 'serious venereal diseases' after her father raped her in front of her two brothers. In *Plourde* (1985), which involved the only female defendant in the whole sample of 196 cases, the defendant was a party to forced vaginal and anal intercourse, threatened use of a weapon, and she herself forced a wine bottle in the vagina of the woman victim. Of the remaining three cases, two cases took place in Nova Scotia and one in Saskatchewan. In *Connors* (1983), a seven-year-old girl was abducted and forced to commit 'different sexual acts' for 12 hours. Although the Novia Socia Court of Appeal commented that there was 'negligible wounding,' the accused did have a prior record for indecent assault of an 11-year-old girl. In *Challis* (1990), a motel chambermaid was held at knifepoint, threatened with death, bound and gagged, subjected to 'indecent acts and intercourse,' and had a knife held to her vagina. Finally, in *Morrison* (1989), the defendant broke into a house, used a 'long knife' to inflict stab wounds in the 25-year-old victim's neck and shoulders, punctured her lung, removed her clothes, and raped her. The defendant later returned, apologized to the victim and shot himself in the stomach.

Approach: The Articulated Purpose or Aims of Sentencing Sexual Assaulters

It is fairly well accepted now that Canadian courts do not share a single approach to sentencing. What is not accepted is whether a uniform approach to sentencing is either necessary or desirable. The conflicting purposes of sentencing articulated by Canadian judges in the sexual assault judgments reveal yet another difficulty in evaluating whether a sentence is too lenient or too harsh. When faced with sentencing a man convicted of a level I sexual assault, a judge may choose from a variety of non-carceral and carceral dispositions. Sentences for level I sexual assaults generally range from a suspended sentence and probation to a number of years of imprisonment. The only legislative direction judges receive is the maximum penalty prescribed in the Code; for level I sexual assaults that is 10 years (six months if summary conviction). With the exception of those courts of appeal that articulate a 'tariff,' range or starting-point sentence, there does not exist any accepted sentence for sexual assault that criticisms of 'leniency' or 'severity' relate to. If 'disparity' in sentences is understood to mean difference, then few would argue that sentences for sexual assault should all be the same. However, if unwarranted disparity is understood to refer to those differences that cannot be justified with reference to a stated principle or purpose, then most would argue that unwarranted disparity is a bad thing. Under current conditions, almost all disparity can be justified by judges according to the purpose(s) of sentencing they have selected. This is by no means to suggest that all sentences imposed are fair, but rather, as the examples will show, it is to suggest that until the statement of purpose is taken seriously, the concept of 'fairness' will continue to shift along with the winds that move the decision-makers.

It follows that where there is no stated purpose of sentencing, there are no articulated factors that courts must consider in aggravation or mitigation of the sentence. Consequently, the factors that judges consider relevant to their sentencing decisions are to a great extent dictated by their particular approach to sentencing. For example, the prevalence of sexual assaults in a community may cause a judge concerned with general deterrence to impose a more severe sentence than she or he otherwise might have. If, on the other hand, the judge is primarily concerned with the rehabilitation of the defendant, then the fact that crimes of sexual assault appear to be on the rise in a particular community is irrelevant – primary consideration will be given to evidence regarding the prospects of successful treatment or rehabilitation of the offender. In over half of the sentencing judgments in this sample, the appeal courts made no mention of any sentencing purpose or principles. Of those that articulated a purpose, deterrence was the most popular approach.[3] When judgments cited the need for considering rehabilitation, it was almost always in support of an accused's appeal to decrease the sentence. The courts that adopted the purpose of deterrence almost always did so in support of the Crown's appeal to increase the sentence. Only in rare cases where deterrence was cited as the aim was the sentence reduced in severity.[4]

DETERRENCE

Although the Nova Scotia Court of Appeal adopted a rehabilitation approach in two earlier cases (*Williams* 1983, *Fadelle* 1985), almost all of the following cases in which a sentencing purpose was articulated adopted an approach of general and specific deterrence. This Court of Appeal, more than any other, considered the factor of prevalence of the crime in the community (only Northwest Territories, Prince Edward Island, and Newfoundland courts mentioned prevalence as a factor). In every case but one, the 'alarming frequency' of crimes of sexual assault was cited in support of a more severe sentence to satisfy the aim of general deterrence (in those cases where the accused brought the appeal the sentences were not reduced).[5]

   Ontario courts of appeal have also adopted a deterrence approach, but the above 'aggravating factor' of prevalence of the crime in the community was never cited in support of any judgment. Although in two early cases the court still supported a rationale of rehabilitation (*Dickinson* 1984, *Clubb* 1984), since 1984 the court has fairly consistently followed a deterrence rationale and increased the severity of sentences where trial judges indicated that their sentence was based on a philosophy of rehabilitation. The court does appear, however, to have made an exception in cases where the defendant was diagnosed as a paedophile.[6]

REHABILITATION

The Newfoundland Court of Appeal, although supporting the need for deterrence, more often interfered with sentences using a rationale of rehabilitation. With the exception of an early case (*Sacrey* 1984) where the court increased the sentence and stated that the trial judge was wrong in giving primary consideration to rehabilitation, the court has fairly consistently interfered with sentences to reduce their severity, citing the need to 'balance' deterrence with rehabilitation.[7] The Newfoundland Court of Appeal is one of the few remaining courts that appear to have retained an approach that attempts to 'balance' rehabilitation with deterrence. In reality this appears to mean that it will cite the need to consider rehabilitation when it wants to reduce the severity of the sentence.

OTHER RATIONALES

Although 'retribution' or 'punishment' were cited in a few judgments, none of the courts of appeal appeared to have adopted an approach known as 'just deserts' or proportionality. Many writers have recently promoted this as the most important purpose of sentencing and one that should be adopted by Canadian courts (see for example von Hirsch 1990, Canadian Sentencing Commission 1987). The just desert approach says that although the punishment imposed may hopefully deter or rehabilitate the defendant, neither deterrence nor rehabilitation are valid purposes of sentencing. The just desert approach dictates that 'the punishment should fit the crime.' The seriousness of the crime is determined by the 'blameworthiness of the accused' and the 'harm caused' or threatened. Factors such as prevalence of the crime in the community would hence be irrelevant according to a just deserts approach. As I have argued elsewhere (Mohr 1990b), this approach leaves many questions unanswered, however, if an attempt is made to answer those questions (e.g., is a diagnosed paedophile more or less blameworthy? does the harm caused to the victim have to be proved in each case or should long-lasting effects be a matter of 'common sense'?) there may be some progress in the direction of developing a more uniform and informed approach to the sentencing of sexual assault.

Tariffs: The Development of 'Going Rates'

Although Canadian writers on sentencing have not agreed as to the existence of a system of 'tariffs' created by appeal courts to guide the sentencing of specific offences, there is little to be learned from this debate. Although the term 'tariff' is rarely applied, certain courts (most notably the Alberta Court of Appeal) have articulated clear 'going rates' or starting points for crimes such as sexual assault and robbery. The judgment in *Sandercock* (1985) is one of the most often cited by courts (primarily in Alberta but also in other provinces), as setting a three-year starting point for the sentencing of level I sexual assault cases. It is not unusual, therefore, for three years to be cited as the reference point in Alberta Court of Appeal judgments.[8] Using *Sandercock* as setting the starting point of three years, the judgments generally go on to justify a greater or reduced sentence in light of the aggravating or mitigating factors. Hence, although the three-year sentence is a guide, the court still has enormous flexibility as to which factors it will consider to be relevant and whether those factors are aggravating or mitigating.

In Newfoundland, the Court of Appeal made reference to a 'range' of sentence normally imposed, but rarely did it articulate what that range was and what types of sexual assault it applied to. Only in the case of *J.J.E.* (1986) was a specific range articulated. In that case (involving the rape of the woman jogger), the court stated that 'the sentencing range for rape is from 3–7 years.' As mentioned above, although the court suggested that this was a case that would normally support a five-year sentence, the mitigating factors supported the original sentence of three years of imprisonment. In the other cases, the sentences would be referred to as falling 'in the higher range,' in the 'low to mid part of the range,' or as 'not outside the range,' but the judgment would not set out which range it was referring to.[9]

Ontario Court of Appeal judgments cited a sentencing range in two cases. In *B.* (1990), the court confirmed a sentence of eight years in a case in which the defendant had anal and vaginal intercourse twice weekly with his stepdaughter from ages 6 to 14 years. The court cited 10 precedents that supported sentences from three to five years for cases involving the sexual assault by someone 'in loco parentis.' The court exceeded the five-year limit because of the factors it found in aggravation, including: the duration and frequency of the rapes; the effects on the victim; the defendant's criminal record for attempted rape and his constant use of threats for non-compliance with his demands. In *Wellington* (1985), the court cited a number of cases in support of an eight-year sentence for level II sexual assaults (with a weapon). Although other court of appeal judgments included some reference to a 'range,' only the above cases revealed an attempt by the court to offer guidance in the form of a stated numerical starting point or range.

Evidence: Factors Considered in Determining the Seriousness of the Sexual Assault

HARM TO VICTIM: NO VICTIM-BASED FACTORS MENTIONED

For almost every Criminal Code offence, whether it be a robbery or a common assault, the sentencing judge considers at least three major factors in determining seriousness: the presence of a criminal record, the blameworthiness of the accused (whether there had been planning, premeditation etc.), and the harm caused by the offence. The harm caused by a property crime may be assessed by the size of the take (in a robbery for example), or in the case of a crime against the person, the extent of the physical/bodily injury (in a common assault for example). Sexual assault is an exception. In well over one-half of the entire sample of appeal court judgments, aside from a brief description of the facts of the offence, no mention was made of harm to the victim.

Although some appeal court judgments omitted reference to the victim more than others, there was a great deal of variation of approach within a single appeal court bench. In Nova Scotia, for example, the judgment in *Fillis* (1986) made no reference to the effects of the sexual assaults suffered by a ten-year-old girl over a period of several years. In this case, the sexual assaults committed by the father consisted of the touching of her breasts, digital vaginal penetration, and fellatio. Although typically there were a number of accused-based factors cited in the judgment (including the father's problem with alcohol since his wife started 'seeing other men' and a long letter from a medical practitioner regarding the father's sexual behaviour), there was no mention made of the 10-year-old victim after the brief facts were set out. In the same provincial appeal court, in the same year, the 'traumatic effect' of the sexual assault on the victim was considered by the Court in *Blackburn* (1986). This case involved the attempted rape of an 83-year-old widow. The court spoke of the 'stark horror' of the crime and stated that although the elderly victim 'suffered no permanent physical injury,' that as a consequence of the traumatic effect of the assault, she 'apparently cannot or will not live alone' because of her fear of intruders. Although in a few cases the Nova Scotia Court of Appeal considered the effect of the assault on the victim, in some of these few, the court found that the sexual assault had no effect on the victim, and hence 'harm to the victim was not an aggravating factor' (those cases will be discussed below).

This difference in approach can be found in almost every province. In some judgments there is no reference to the victim and only passing reference to 'other circumstances' which the court may have considered.[10]

Although, as mentioned above, there was variation within the 10 appeal courts, some courts (e.g., Ontario and Saskatchewan) mentioned victim-based factors more than other courts (Alberta, Manitoba, and Newfoundland judgments rarely included any reference to the victim).

VICTIM-BASED FACTORS MENTIONED

In the surprisingly few judgments that included reference to harm caused to

172 Confronting Sexual Assault

the victims (less than half of the entire sample), very different approaches were taken in assessing whether the effects of the offence were aggravating factors to be considered by the court in determining the seriousness of the assault. There appear to be three different approaches taken by appeal court judges in assessing victim-related evidence: 'strict evidence' approach; 'judicial notice' approach; and 'other or unknown sources of evidence' approach. Before defining each approach, a brief description of the sentencing hearing is necessary.

Unlike at trial, where strict rules of evidence govern the kinds of information that may be used by the court in adjudicating guilt or innocence, at the sentencing stage there are very few rules to govern the admissibility of evidence. In *Gardiner* (1982), the Supreme Court of Canada articulated one of the only rules that governs sentencing hearings. That rule is that where the Crown introduces evidence of aggravating factors, and the veracity of those factors is challenged by the defendant, the Crown must prove that evidence beyond a reasonable doubt. Whereas the trial has strict rules surrounding the admissibility of hearsay evidence (whether challenged or not), at the sentencing hearing both Crown and defence counsel have unlimited scope to introduce any information about the accused, the victim, or other circumstances that surround the offence. At the sentencing hearing, virtually all information put before the court by Crown or defence counsel is admissible. All that *Gardiner* establishes is that where the defendant or his counsel wish to challenge the veracity of any evidence that may increase the severity of the sentence, they may require the Crown to prove that evidence beyond a reasonable doubt.

Strict Evidence Approach

The strict evidence approach refers to those cases where the appeal court states that because there was no evidence before it regarding the effects of the sexual assault on the victim, the court cannot find that 'adverse effects' should increase the severity of the sentence. It is unclear whether 'no evidence' in these cases means that the Crown counsel did not make any submissions to the court regarding the victim, or whether the Crown had failed to prove these submissions beyond a reasonable doubt and they were successfully challenged by the defence. It is most likely, however, that most of these cases reveal the inadequate nature of Crown's submissions. In most of the cases where the court found no evidence of harmful effects on the victim, the sentence was reduced. For example, in *Rafuse* (1985), the court reduced a sentence of 18 months to 4 months and along with other mitigating factors stated that not only was there no evidence of force, but there was no 'indication that the actions of the appellant had any psychological effect on the children.' In this case the victims were nieces of the defendant. The sexual assault of the seven-year-old involved him 'placing his penis on her legs from behind' and touching 'her genitals,' and the sexual assault of the four-year-old involved 'fingers on her genitals.'[11]

In addition, there is the problem of the definition of 'force.' In assessing the effect on the victim, courts are likely to say there was no 'force' if the behaviour fell short of forced sexual intercourse. For example, in *Sharpe* (1988) the court reduced sentences adding up to three years to a total of one year (with three years' probation) and found that there was 'no force' and 'no evidence of any adverse effects on the three children.' This case involved the sexual assault of three six- to seven-year-old girls. In two of those cases the defendant placed his hand on the girls' vagina, and in the third case he removed his clothes, began to remove her clothes, and placed his penis on her leg.

Although it is difficult to ascertain the kinds of evidence heard at the sentencing hearing and the appeal court review, there are some cases where Crown counsel is clearly responsible for making submissions that the sexual assault caused 'no harm to the victim,' and hence concluding there were no aggravating features to the assault. In the 1990 British Columbia Court of Appeal case (*L. (D.)*) which was widely reported in the news media, the trial judge commented that the three-year-old girl was 'sexually aggressive.' The B.C. Court of Appeal rejected the Crown's attempt to have the sentence increased from a suspended sentence and probation, stating that although the victim did 'not like the experience, Crown counsel also very fairly mentioned that there is no indication of any impact this [sexual assault] has had on the victim.' In this case a 32-year-old man rubbed his penis on the vagina of a three-year-old girl.

One of the few cases that actually cited *Gardiner* as the authority for excluding evidence was a 1986 decision of the Ontario Court of Appeal (*Owens*). That case involved a grade two teacher who touched the genitals of three eight-year-old boys. In reducing the sentence of nine months with three years' probation to three months with two years' probation, the Court held that the trial judge had put undue reliance on the evidence of an expert regarding the potential long-term effects of sexual abuse on young children. The appeal court found that the trial judge had placed too much reliance on the testimony of a 'pediatrician professor' who 'was not a psychologist or a psychiatrist [and whose] conclusions are based largely on sociology literature, personal experience and statistics.' In rejecting this evidence the Court cited *Gardiner*, stating that 'the onus is on the Crown to prove aggravating factors beyond a reasonable doubt, not through hypothetical theorising as was done here.'

Judicial Notice Approach

Fundamental to the adversary process is that all information considered by the judge must be introduced into evidence by either of the two parties. As described above, the strict evidence approach dictates that unless the court is presented with information by the Crown (e.g., that there were long-term or other adverse effects of the sexual assault), the court will not use its 'common sense' to make that inference but will rather feel constrained to find that no formal evidence means no adverse effects. There is a kind of exception to this rule which states that for certain matters regarded as shared knowledge by all, the court needs no formal evidence in order to take notice of those facts. As defined in *Black's Law Dictionary*, 'judicial notice' refers to those circumstances where 'a court ... without the production of evidence, recognises the existence and truth of certain facts ... which are universally regarded as established by common notoriety' (761).

Clearly the strict evidence approach is in direct conflict with the judicial notice approach. Whereas courts that adopt a strict evidence approach require the Crown to lead evidence of the effect of the sexual assault on the victim before they will consider effects on the victim as a factor in sentencing, those courts that take judicial notice of the effects of the sexual assault on the victim do so in the absence of any evidence produced by the Crown. Whether a judge takes judicial notice or requires a Crown's submissions on the effects of the assault on the victim has a clear impact on the sentence. Almost all cases in which a strict evidence approach was taken, the sentence was either reduced or not varied. In almost all cases in which the judicial notice approach was taken, the sentence was increased. Although there is no indication of the judicial notice approach being taken by most courts of appeal, some judges in Ontario and Saskatchewan have clearly adopted this approach. For example, in a 1987 decision of the Ontario Court of Appeal (*Fraser*), in increasing a suspended sentence and probation to 14 months and probation, the court stated that although there was no evidence of the effects of the assaults on the victims, 'courts can take judicial notice of the serious psychological effect this type of conduct can have on adolescent girls.' In this case a 36-year-old man had forced sexual intercourse with his 11-year-old stepdaughter twice a week over an unspecified period of time. In two 1989 decisions of the Saskatchewan Court of Appeal, the sentences were increased where the court took judicial notice of harm to the victim.[12]

Other or Unknown Sources of Evidence

There appears to be an approach that falls somewhere between the strict evidence approach and the judicial notice approach. Unlike 'judicial notice,' the approach I call 'inferential evidence' is applied to those cases where it is unclear whether there has been any evidence before the court but where the judges do not acknowledge that they are taking judicial notice of the harm done to victims. For example, in *Morrison* (1989), in one of the few cases where the charge was aggravated sexual assault, the court increased a sentence from two years less a day (with two years' probation) to four-and-one-half years and commented that although the victim was released from the hospital after two weeks, 'the psychological and emotional scars remain.' This case involved the stranger-rape of a 25-year-old victim who was stabbed in the neck and shoulder and suffered a punctured lung. It is difficult to tell whether the court was taking judicial notice of the long-term effects or whether some evidence had been presented to that effect.

In some judgments, case law is referred to in order to support a finding that the assault had a detrimental effect on the victim. In *G.L.* (1985), the court increased a sentence of 18 months to three years where the father had forced intercourse with three daughters – one over a period of months, the second over a period of two years, and the third over a period of three years. Although the court made no mention of any evidence before it regarding the effects of the assaults on the victims, they cited a case that stated that although incest 'may be performed without violence, it may well leave lasting scars.'

In *Childs* (1987), the court appeared to infer from the evidence that the victim suffered some anxiety, but certainly did not take judicial notice of long-term effects of the sexual assault. In reducing the father's sentence from two years less a day to 10 months for touching his daughter's vagina on two occasions, the court stated that there was 'nothing in the record to indicate that the child suffered any psychological harm beyond the obvious, but, hopefully transitory phases of anxiety and feelings of guilt.'

Interestingly, in a recent judgment of the Saskatchewan Court of Appeal, *(K. (P.L.)* (1989), the court increased a sentence of 90 days intermittent to two-and-one-half years and referred to some 'current literature' in response to the defence's suggestion that long sentences in cases where family members were involved would produce guilt in the child.[13]

RELEVANCE OF THE VICTIM'S CONDUCT

In the fewer than 50 per cent of the cases that mentioned any victim-related considerations, only a few mentioned the victim's conduct as a factor in their determination of sentence. In *Sparks* (1986), the Nova Scotia Court of Appeal reduced a sentence for a level II sexual assault from seven years to four years and appeared to consider the victim's conduct as a factor in reducing the severity of the sentence. In that case the victim had gone drinking to an after-hours club until 3 A.M., at which time she accepted the doorman's offer to drive her home. The victim invited the doorman in for a drink and when she resisted his advances he struck her in the face and raped her. At 6:40 A.M. police found the victim barefoot on the sidewalk in a state of emotional distress and took her to the hospital. As to the victim's conduct, the court stated 'although we question the wisdom of the victim in inviting the appellant ... such invitation did not give the appellant license to partake of sexual intercourse without consent.' The court then qualified this statement by saying, however 'that course of conduct does distinguish this case from others' and reduced the sentence accordingly. In an Ontario Court of Appeal decision, *Stefanidis* (1988), where the court increased a 30-day sentence to six months' imprisonment, it stated that the conduct of the victim was in no way a factor that lessened the seriousness of the rape. In this case the 35-year-old victim was hitchhiking home and, prior to accepting a ride from men in a van, 'relieved herself' in the parking lot. The victim was later raped in the van. The court explicitly stated that the victim's conduct was not a mitigating factor and that 'the inebriated condition of the victim and the plight in which she found herself that is, her inability to find her way home unassisted, were simply matters that made her especially vulnerable and cannot be considered mitigating factors.'

There were only two cases in which it was clearly stated that the victim was a prostitute. These two cases were both Ontario Court of Appeal judgments. In *Sullivan* (1987), the court found that a 'prostitute is as much entitled to the protection of the law as any other woman,' and clearly stated that the fact that the victim is a prostitute is not a mitigating factor. In *Resendes* (1988), the court backs up a bit and says the 'most that can be said is that because of her occupation, any lasting psychological trauma of this experience might be less to the victim than it would be to someone else whose life was more sheltered.'

Perhaps the most striking feature of the approaches taken by courts of appeal to evaluating the 'seriousness' of the sexual assault with reference to the victim is that almost all courts appear, more often than not, to fail to mention *any* victim-based factors. This makes it difficult, and sometimes impossible, to assess how factors like the class or race of the victim are considered by judges. In the words of the Toronto Rape Crisis Centre (1985), these silent factors may in fact play a role in decision-making at all levels:

Another factor in [the vulnerability of working-class and immigrant women and women of colour] is the classism and racism inherent in the goddess/whore dichotomy still operative in our society. The women who are characterised as goddesses will always be white and middle class (74).

RELATIONSHIPS OF TRUST: ADULT DEFENDANTS AND CHILD VICTIMS

Over half of the cases in this sample (53 per cent) involved an adult defendant and child victim(s). Of those cases, almost all involved relationships of trust (e.g., father, stepfather, adoptive father, uncle, teacher, minister, priest, etc.). Although most sentences in these cases involved a period of incarceration (from three months to 10 years), in those cases where a suspended sentence and a period of probation were imposed, the 'good character' of the defendant was invariably the strongest mitigating factor. Unlike at the trial where evidence of character is generally inadmissible (so that findings of guilt will not be influenced by a person's 'bad' character), at the sentencing hearing all manner and forms of character evidence may be introduced.

In the Ontario Court of Appeal judgment in *Lysack* (1988), an elderly teacher was sentenced to six months concurrent (with an unspecified length of probation) on four counts of sexual assault and one count of indecent assault. In reducing the sentence to a suspended sentence with probation (unspecified length), the judgment included lengthy descriptions of the teacher's successful career, his community work, and how overall his life before the offences was 'not only blameless but exemplary.' Although the sexual assaults were relatively minor (touching eight-to-nine-year-old girls over their clothing around their pubic areas), the court stated that 'a term of imprisonment should be the almost invariable result of a sexual assault by a teacher on a student.' The factors surrounding the defendant's age and good character were cited in support of a suspended sentence.[14]

In the vast majority of cases involving some relationship of trust, a sentence of incarceration was ordered. In fewer than half of these cases was the factor of 'breach of trust' articulated by the court. In almost all cases where breach of trust was mentioned by the court, the sentence was increased on appeal. The most severe sentence imposed in a breach of trust situation was in a Quebec Court of Appeal judgment, *Champagne* (1987). In this case the court doubled a sentence of five years where a mother entrusted the care of her 12-year-old daughter and two sons to their father for the summer; the day after the children arrived the father raped his daughter in front of the two boys. The court cited the importance of deterring those who abuse parental authority and the additional aggravating factor that 'besides physical and emotional trauma which the child suffered, she also contracted serious venereal diseases' as a result of the rape.

The nature of the sexual assault committed is clearly used by the court as an aggravating or mitigating circumstance. Since simple or level I, sexual assaults can consist of a range of behaviour from touching to forced vaginal or anal penetration, the courts sometimes see the absence of penetration as a mitigating factor that results in a reduction of the sentence. In *McGibbon* (1989), for example, the Ontario Court of Appeal reduced a sentence of three years to two years less a day where a babysitter attempted vaginal and anal penetration of an eight-year-old girl. The court reduced the sentence having regard to the mitigating factors that the offence was of short duration, there was no proof of penetration, and the defendant had no criminal record.[15]

Once again, the value of guidance offered by court of appeal judgments is greatly diminished by the fact that only in a minority of cases are aggravating and/or mitigating circumstances clearly stated. In most reported cases the judges list a number of factors, and leave it to the reader to ascertain whether, for example, alcoholism or an employment record served as aggravating or mitigating factors or whether they were just defendant-based factors that the court cited as a matter of course.

ADULT DEFENDANTS AND ADULT VICTIMS

Sexual Assaults Involving Acquaintances

This heading includes all cases where the defendant and the victim were known to each other before the sexual assault (almost all were rapes) took place. The sentences for these rapes ranged from 90 days to 6 years. Most sentences fell between one and two years. As will become apparent, this range of sentence is much less severe than in cases where the rape victim was unknown to the defendant.

Surprisingly, violence was rarely cited by the court as a factor in any of these cases that involved a forcible rape. In the Ontario Court of Appeal judgments, violence was mentioned in one case and bodily injury was mentioned in another. Interestingly, the two cases in which the courts expressly recognized the violence of the sexual assaults were the same two cases where the court did not increase the sentence on appeal. In the first case the mitigating factors centred around the defendant's 'good background,' and in the second case, a short judgment, the only factors that the court mentioned in reducing the sentence was that 'the several individuals involved [including the victim] are Native Canadians and can fairly be characterised as street people.' In that case, *McPherson* (1989), after 'quantities of beer had been consumed,' the appellant and another man 'had sexual intercourse with a native woman.' The men took their turn holding the woman's legs while the other raped her. The court stated that 'bodily harm appears to have resulted from the sexual intercourse' but allowed the defendant's appeal (for a level I sexual assault) and reduced the sentence to time served. Unfortunately the original sentence was not specified and the court only indicated that 'time served' added up to less than one year.[16]

In Nova Scotia Court of Appeal judgments, the factors considered in cases of acquaintance rape are rarely set out. Aside from age, employment record and criminal record, factors in support of the court's judgment are rarely articulated.[17]

Two of the cases that involved the sexual assault of an estranged wife were appeals taken from the Yukon Territorial Court. In *Atlin* (1986), the Crown unsuccessfully appealed a sentence of two years less a day with probation. The victim was the former common-law wife of the accused and had separated four years previously after a 'serious beating' that resulted in a conviction for assault causing bodily harm. On this occasion, after a day and an evening of heavy alcohol consumption in the company of her brothers and others, the victim passed out, while fully clothed, on a couch in the living room of a residence. She awoke in the morning when the defendant was raping her, demanded that he stop, but he refused and continued the rape. In its decision, the British Columbia Court of Appeal cited the defendant's lengthy record and his conviction for assault causing bodily harm to the same victim, and stated that the sentence was not outside the range of what was 'fitting.'

In *Gleason* (1987), the defendant and victim had been separated for one month (living in separate rooms in the same house) when the defendant pulled her out of bed, threw her down the hallway, smashed her head on a fridge, sat on her and beat her with his fists, and then raped her. Between the time of conviction at trial and the sentence, the appellant received medical testing and learned that he suffered from hypoglycaemia. The evidence of a psychiatrist linking the violence with hypoglycaemia was accepted by the court. The Court of Appeal reduced the sentence of one year with two years' probation to time served (two-and-one-half months) plus two years' probation. The factors that the court cited in reducing the original sentence were that: the 50-year-old defendant was 'a well-known respected business man in Whitehorse'; he was now divorced with access to his two children; he was fighting to overcome an alcohol problem; and there was no reason to expect a repetition of attacks.

Although courts rarely mentioned violence as an aggravating circumstance in sexual assaults between acquaintances, the lack of any violence other than the sexual assault itself is never explicitly used by the appeal courts in mitigation of the sentence, although it appears it may sometimes be used at the trial court level. For example, in *Desbiens* (1985), the Saskatchewan Court of Appeal increased a sentence of two years to four years where a trial judge had cited lack of violence, apart from the level II sexual assault itself, to be a mitigating factor. In that case a neighbour who had told the 16-year-old who was babysitting for a friend to send her friends home, returned to the house at 2 A.M., locked her in the house and holding a knife, forced fellatio, raped her, and threatened to kill her if she told anyone. The assaults took place over the course of one-and-one-half hours. In the words of the trial judge, 'leaving your victim in sexual assault cases unharmed apart from the assault is something that deserves more than a little attention.' In increasing the sentence, the Court of Appeal held that the judge was wrong in stating that the fact that the knife was 'not used' was a mitigating factor, and cited other factors for increasing the sentence (a history of violence including a manslaughter conviction four years earlier 'for killing his girlfriend').

Sexual Assaults Involving Strangers

When comparing the appeal courts' treatment of sexual assaults involving acquaintances with those perpetrated by men who are strangers to the victim, the most striking difference seems to be linked primarily to charging practices. Although the range of sexual assaults in this category was as wide as in the other categories canvassed, fully one-third of these sentencing judgments followed a conviction for a level II sexual assault. As discussed at the beginning of the chapter, even the most serious rapes involving threats of death or weapons are often charged as level I sexual assaults, and the only significant difference in level I or level II assaults appears to be that Level II assaults appear to attract a significantly higher sentence. So it is in the case of sexual assaults where the defendant is a stranger to the victim. Although the range of sentence was extremely wide (six months to 14 years), the average sentence was between four years and eight years. Although the behaviours resulting in the convictions appeared no more serious on the whole in this category of 'stranger' sexual assaults, most of the level II and level III charges were in this category.

Although the increase in the severity of sentences imposed in 'acquaintance rape' cases and 'stranger rape' cases can be explained by charging practices and multiple convictions, the other cases also carried more severe sentences for behaviours that, in respect of circumstances other than the relationship between victim and offender, appeared to involve similar levels of threats and violence. Although judges rarely cited the fact that the defendant was a stranger to the victim as an aggravating factor, the sentences on the whole were more severe. Very few of these cases involved the sexual abuse of children, and so, unlike the cases involving teachers and ministers, the 'antecedents' of the defendants were rarely cited by courts to support a more lenient sentence.

Most of these appeals were initiated by the Crown, and, in most cases, the sentences were increased. The increase in the severity of sentences was often quite marked. In two of the three cases that originated in the Northwest Territories, for example, the Alberta Court of Appeal doubled the original sentence imposed. In *Petaulassie* (1986), the court increased a 5-year sentence to a 10-year sentence where a masked man broke into a family dwelling and threatened to kill the family if the woman did not comply with his demands, which included submitting to a rape. In *Beaulieu* (1988) the court doubled the four-year sentence where a woman was wrestled to the floor, choked, blindfolded, had her hands tied behind her back, and was raped. Both cases involved convictions for level II assaults.

Conclusion

The consequences of a discretionary process that has virtually no legislative restrictions and ten distinct judicially constructed approaches to the sentencing of sexual assault cases are particularly significant since criminal law in Canada is a matter of federal jurisdiction. Criminal law initiatives, like rape law reform, are meant to have uniform federal application. One clear finding from an examination of reported sentencing appeals is that there is no uniform interpretation of this legislation. Different judges in different courts across the country continue to use different yardsticks to measure the 'seriousness' of sexual assaults for the purposes of sentencing. Given the absence of clear direction, the different approaches of these different courts can all be 'justified' according to their different aims or purposes of sentencing.

To examine only the trial decisions and the judicial constructions of the substantive offences of sexual assault is to focus on one part of a process that is, given the high percentage of guilty pleas, the exception rather than the rule. An examination of the appeal court sentencing judgments reveals the consequences of law reform efforts that ignore the sociolegal context in which decision-making takes place (see, for example, Brickey and Comack 1987). The 1983 legislation sought to address the admittedly serious problems of how rape laws had served to further entrench a sexualization and hence trivialization, of an act of violence against women. The language of the substantive offence was changed to highlight the violence through the word 'assault,' and three levels of seriousness were legislated in recognition of the increasing levels of violence. Apart from its symbolic significance, this legislative change did nothing to address the reality of a sentencing process that gives all the legally trained participants enormous scope in defining a sexual assault and no meaningful guidance as to the purpose of or approach to punishment. Law reform efforts fail to address the individual attitudes and perceptions that drive such decision-making. As the discussion of the cases illustrates, the impact of gender, race, and class on judicial decision-making can no longer be ignored (see generally Martin and Mahoney 1987). As feminist scholars have long proclaimed, 'every decision maker who walks into the courtroom to hear a case is armed not only with relevant legal texts, but with a set of values, experiences and assumptions that are thoroughly embedded' (Abella-Silberman 1987, 8).

These values, experiences, and assumptions must be articulated. Law reform efforts usually drive them underground. The effectiveness or success of legislative reforms cannot be evaluated until there is an articulated and shared understanding of what 'success' is. There can be no measurement until there is a yardstick. There can be no real accountability until there is a yardstick. There can be no shared sense of justice unless and until there is a yardstick. Currently, virtually any sentence that does not exceed the legislative maximum penalty can be justified according to the individual decision-maker's yardstick.

In order to develop a shared notion of success, difficult questions must be asked and answered. According to what purpose or principles do we wish to sanction state intervention and/or state violence? In other words, why do we punish?

And the simple question, 'What are we doing this for?' cannot be answered by: 'The fundamental purpose of sentencing is to preserve the authority of and to promote respect for the law through the imposition of just sanctions.' If this is what the law depends on for authority and respect, it deserves neither (Mohr 1990a, 531).

Only when this question is addressed can we begin to assess how this stated aim may best be achieved. Only then can one construct a new basis of measurement that takes seriously the questions that are central to evaluating the legal response to sexual assault. How do gender, race, and class influence our understanding of this 'crime' and the response to it? Should 'social standing' ever be a factor in the sentencing of sexual assaults? Is the perceived 'prevalence' of a crime ever a valid consideration? Should the fact that the victim was unknown to the sexual assaulter ever be an aggravating factor? Should racially motivated sexual assaults receive explicit legislative recognition? Just as the list of factors currently cited by judges reveals, the list of considerations is a long one. As I have attempted to show in this chapter, it is a list that women and men can no longer afford to ignore.

A legal response to a social problem will always be limited in its ability to eradicate the problem. In the words of the Toronto Rape Crisis Centre (1985):

The reforms are ... problematic in that women can be persuaded to believe that, because the government is spending money and changing laws and doing research, and because the police and hospitals are creating special programs that will make us safe, that this will stop rape. The truth is that it will not. Institutions cannot stop rape, though they can make it easier for individual women who are raped (80).

A criminal law response to a social problem is even more limited. Its symbolic significance, however, cannot be ignored. The criminal law will never stop men from sexually assaulting women and children. That does not mean that we should not demand a sense of justice in our response to sexual assault. And therein lies the importance of the construction of a new yardstick. It may well be that women and men have a different understanding of 'justice.' Feminist literature has begun to explore these differences and to articulate understandings of justice rooted in a different theoretical grounding (MacKinnon 1984, Boyle 1991). Until legislative reform is explicitly rooted in a theoretical grounding, then 'justice' will remain in the eyes of the beholder.

To suggest that any legislative criminal law reform can provide a meaningful solution to a social problem as serious as sexual assault is naïve. The 1983 legislative changes had an important purpose. They revealed that any legislative change that does not question the very basis of our criminal law system will ultimately serve the purposes of the existing system. To ignore the power of the state to intervene and to punish is dangerous. If there is to be justice, there must be accountability. For there to be accountability, there must be a clear statement of responsibilities. Sentencing judges are given no clear guidance as to their responsibilities, nor are Crown or defence counsel, and all are accountable only to his/her own conscience. Sexual assault is a serious crime. Punishment is a serious response. Justice cannot be left to an individual sense of conscience.

In the next chapter, Teressa Nahanee examines sentencing judgments in northern communities. She specifically addresses the perception that judges

in the North are more lenient when sentencing men who have been convicted
of sexually assaultiing Inuit women.

Notes

1 For example, indecent assault charges were laid in cases involving parent/child
   sexual assault where the assault occurred prior to 1983 but the charge was laid
   after 1983.
2 As mentioned in the introduction to this volume, judicial constructions of what
   constitutes 'bodily harm' has been one of the most controversial aspects of the
   new legislation. See, for example, *Ottawa Law Review* 21:199, in which a number
   of authors discuss the issue of 'bodily harm' (as raised by the *McCraw* case).
3 Alberta, Ontario, Nova Scotia, Saskatchewan, and Quebec Court of Appeal judgments clearly were most likely to increase a trial judge's sentence if it was based on
   a rehabilitation rationale. The Newfoundland Court of Appeal, on the other hand,
   appears to retain rehabilitation as an important sentencing purpose, and judgments often articulate the need to balance deterrence with rehabilitation.
4 The Manitoba Court of Appeal rarely articulated a purpose and when it did it
   chose either deterrence or rehabilitation. In the New Brunswick judgments, the
   court also vacillated between deterrence (in some judgments) and rehabilitation
   (in others).
5 In *Murray* (1986), in denying the defendant's appeal to reduce the sentence of
   four years and nine months for a level II sexual assault, the judge wrote that the
   sentence was severe, but 'this particular crime, however, appears to be occurring
   with alarming frequency.' In *Bryson* (1987), which involved a level I sexual assault
   where a woman was forced to masturbate a stranger in her car, the court increased
   the sentence of one day to nine months' imprisonment stating that 'charges of
   sexual assaults are before the courts with increasing frequency' and that a more
   severe sentence was necessary to convey the message to 'those who commit it or
   contemplate it,' that the court will not tolerate that behaviour. In *Langille* (1987),
   in support of denying the defendant's appeal, the judge wrote, 'Crimes of this
   nature are not uncommon in our society today and strong sentences are called for
   to deter adults from sexual assault and abusing helpless children who are under
   their care, custody and control.'
6 In *Nye* (1988), the court increased a suspended sentence and three years' probation to a sentence of six months and three years' probation for a sexual assault that
   involved forcing a 13-year-old girl to the ground and digitally penetrating her
   vagina. Nye was a 41-year-old, diagnosed as a paedophile, and although the court
   stressed that it had established an approach of general deterrence, it recognized

paedophilia as a disease that may in some cases be better dealt with through rehabilitation.

7 In *J.J.E.* (1986), the court denied a Crown appeal to increase the three-year sentence imposed on a 17-year-old man who dragged a 38-year-old woman jogger
into the woods and raped her. The court stated that although this case would normally attract a sentence of five years, the youthful age of the defendant and his
'rehabilitation potential' justified the original three-year sentence. In *Atkins*
(1988), the court examined the smorgasbord of factors that it must consider in
sexual assault cases. The court stated that sexual assault involved a 'wide range of
behaviours' and the following factors had to be considered in determining a sentence: degree of violence or force; impact on victim's family and offender's family;
degree of trust; public abhorrence of this type of crime; attitude of offender
regarding his act; plea; biological and psychological factors; need for special or general deterrence; prospect of successful rehabilitation; antecedents and age of
offender; time spent in pre-trial custody; and sentences imposed in other courts in
Newfoundland and Canada. This list of factors is so open to interpretation that it
in fact does little to offer any guidance (for example, 'prospect of successful rehabilitation' is important only to courts adopting a rehabilitation approach).

8 In *Johnston* (1988), for example, the court increased a sentence of 29 1/2 months
to 4 years with little discussion except to comment that, with reference to *Sandercock,* 'a sentence below the normal range was not justified.'

9 In *Janes*(1987), a 30-month sentence was reduced to 18 months with three years'
probation where a 52-year-old man touched the vaginas and breasts of three 9–10-
year-old girls and forced one girl to masturbate him. The court stated that
although sexual assaults involving children were serious, this case 'was not in the
higher range.' Sometimes it is in fact difficult to determine if the court is referring
to a numerical range or a range of behaviours. In *Atkins* (1988), the court reduced
a sentence of three years to two years citing that the original sentence 'was well
out of line with the range of sentences imposed in Canadian courts for offences of
this kind.' No references were made to any Canadian cases to support this assertion. This case involved four counts of indecent assaults and four counts of sexual
assaults against 9–12-year-old girls. The sexual assaults consisted of the 60-year-
old defendant touching the girls' breasts and vaginas, showing them pictures of
naked women, inviting one girl to 'watch him copulate with a woman,' and exposing his penis to be touched.

10 For example, in an Ontario Court of Appeal judgment, *D. (J.F.)* (1988), the court
reduced a two-and-one-half-year sentence to two years less a day for sexual
assault with a weapon of a 20-year-old woman. In the very brief judgment the
only factors the court cites are the age of the defendant (16 years), the fact that it
was a first offence, and 'circumstances surrounding the offence.' What those cir-

cumstances are and how they are weighted is never stated. There are, however, many more detailed judgments where offender-based factors are given full consideration, but there is absolutely no mention made of harm to the victim. In *Onalik* (1987), the Newfoundland Court of Appeal refused to increase a sentence of nine months with three years' probation that was imposed on the father for raping his 13-year-old daughter. The court considered a number of factors in determining the seriousness of the offence (including his record for having assaulted the same daughter two years previous), but never mentioned the harm to the daughter as a relevant factor.

Interestingly, the victim and offender in this case were Inuit and the court took time to justify the lenient sentence through the explanation that 'prison terms may be modified to reflect different impacts and difficulties of incarceration for a person from a remote settlement.' The court failed to consider the 'different,' or in fact any, impact on the child victim of such an assault.

11 In *Dehann* (1986), a 15-year-old stepdaughter was subjected to daily sexual touching over a three-year period. The behaviour involved 'continually touching' her breasts, buttocks, and genitals, exacting 'sexual favours by withholding privileges,' and once knocking her on the floor and sucking her breasts. The court reduced the one-year sentence to six months and stated that although the victim was 'understandably upset' there was 'no evidence of psychological damage.'

12 In *W. (V.M.)*, where a 31-year-old man sexually assaulted his seven- and eight-year-old nieces, the court stated that 'we cannot assess the long term effects except to say that we are prepared to take judicial notice of the serious psychological effect that this type of conduct has on young girls.' Unfortunately the nature of the sexual assault was unspecified as this was a case where the court found it was 'not necessary to describe the unpleasant and revolting details.' In this case the court increased the suspended sentence and probation to a nine-month term of imprisonment plus probation. In *L. (J.L.)* (1989), the court increased a two-and-one-half-year sentence to four years where evidence indicated that the victim continued to suffer emotional damage, and the court stated that although it could not predict long-term effects, it was 'prepared to take judicial notice of the serious effect such conduct would have on young female victims.' This was a level I sexual assault in spite of the level II facts. In this case a 14-year-old girl was threatened by her uncle, who had a knife, blocked a doorway with a freezer, demanded that she strip, took off his pants and rubbed his penis on her, ordered fellatio, placed his penis in her anal area, and threatened her with death if she told anyone about the assault. The 31-year-old uncle had a criminal record including one rape and one attempt rape.

13 In this case a church missionary sexually assaulted his adopted daughter from the time she was 6 years old to 11 years old. In this five-year period the child told a

psychologist about her father's assaults and the father was warned. The assaults continued and included placing his penis on her 'vaginal area' and ejaculating on top of her. In responding to the defence's submission for a lenient sentence for the sake of the child, the court stated 'we note that some current literature in this field accepts now that victims find an adjudication of guilt by a court and the imposition of a severe sentence as an external objective affirmation that the abusive adult is wholly to blame.'

14 In a Nova Scotia Court of Appeal judgment, *Baker* (1988), the sexual assault consisted of an uncle digitally rubbing his 11-year-old niece's vagina at his cottage. In reducing the sentence from 18 months to a suspended sentence with one year probation, the court twice mentioned the 62-year-old defendant's 'outstanding service in the Canadian army and airforce.' In another N.S.C.A. judgment, *Ross* (1989), a Crown appeal to increase a suspended sentence with probation (unspecified length) was denied. This case involved the sexual assault of a 10-year-old girl by her grandfather over a period of five years. The assaults consisted of touching her 'inside her clothes,' feeling her vagina, and making her 'touch him inside his clothes.' The 56-year-old grandfather had no memory of the events and had entered a detoxication program to stop drinking. The court held that concerns for general deterrence in this case had to be overridden by the apparent 'disease of alcoholism.' The defendant was married with three children and his family was 'well-known in the community.'

15 In *Corbière* (1987), the court reduced a sentence of two years less a day to nine months where a father sexually assaulted his seven-year-old daughter over a period of nine months. As well as finding that 'the girl suffered no apparent trauma,' the court repeated that the trial judge had a reasonable doubt that the accused's actions fell short of intercourse. The child had testified that she was not sure if sexual intercourse had occurred since she had her eyes closed; however she testified that she thought she had been penetrated by a penis.

16 In *Boss* (1988), the court denied the Crown appeal to increase the sentence of two years and nine months where the defendant raped, attempted to suffocate, and confined the victim. The court recognized that the actions of the defendant were 'violent demeaning and terrifying' but found the mitigating factors supported the original sentence. Those factors included: no criminal record; good background; had led a blameless life since release; and the offence was 'out of character.' The facts of this case revealed that the 22-year-old victim had recently moved to Georgetown to teach and knew the defendant (although not well) through church. He arrived at her door on the pretext of wanting to see her apartment and in the course of raping her, stuffed a shirt in her mouth, burned her skin with matches, put his penis in her mouth, kicked her, and threatened to kill her. After the sexual assault the defendant sent the victim approximately 30 notes as well as flowers.

Two months after reporting the offence to the police, the victim voluntarily admitted herself to a psychiatric hospital for a period of two months.

17 Interestingly, almost all of the charges involving an accused and a victim known to each other were for a level II sexual assault causing bodily harm. In one case, *Brun* (1987), a simple sexual assault charge was combined with a charge of assault causing bodily harm. The sentences accordingly fell into a slightly higher range than in other provinces (one year with two years' probation to four years and nine months' imprisonment). In only one case was the sentence increased on appeal, and that too was the only case in which any factors were explicitly mentioned. In *Brun*, the victim had known the appellant for one year. On a visit to his apartment he hit her in the chest, and when she fell he gave her mouth-to-mouth resuscitation. When she became conscious, he hit her (causing facial bleeding and a broken nose) and then sexually assaulted her. The court increased the sentence from six months and nine months concurrent (nine-month total) to 12 months and two years concurrent (12-month total), stating that it would 'normally' impose a three-year sentence but for the mitigating factors that it was his first offence and the offence was 'out of character' given the one-and-one-half-year friendship.

References

Abella-Silberman, Rosalie. 1987. 'The Dynamic Nature of Equality.' In S. Martin and K. Mahoney, eds., *Equality and Judicial Neutrality*. Toronto: Carswell

Ashworth, Andrew. 1992. *Sentencing and Criminal Justice*. London: Weidenfeld and Nicholson

Boyle, Christine. 1984. *Sexual Assault*. Toronto: Carswell

– 1991. 'A Feminist Approach to Criminal Defences.' In R. Devlin, ed., *Canadian Perspectives on Legal Theory*. Toronto: Emond Montgomery

Brickey, Stephen and Elizabeth Comack. 1987. 'The Role of Law in Social Transformation: Is a Jurisprudence of Insurgency Possible?' *Canadian Journal of Law and Society* 2:97

Brownmiller, Susan. 1975. *Against Our Will: Men, Women and Rape*. New York: Bantam

Canadian Sentencing Commission. 1987. *Sentencing Reform: A Canadian Approach*. Ottawa: Supply and Services Canada

Clark, Lorenne, and Debra Lewis. 1977. *Rape: The Price of Coercive Sexuality*. Toronto: The Women's Press

Fudge, Judy. 1991. 'Marx's Theory of History and a Marxist Analysis of Law.' In Richard Devlin, ed., *Canadian Perspectives on Legal Theory*. Toronto: Emond Montgomery

Hogarth, John. 1971. *Sentencing as a Human Process*. Toronto: University of Toronto Press

Lahey, Kathleen. 1985. '... Until Women Themselves Have Told All That They Have To Tell ...' *Osgoode Hall Law Journal* 23:519

MacKinnon, Catherine. 1982. 'Feminism, Marxism, Method and the State: An Agenda for Theory.' *Signs* 7:518

– 1984. 'Not a Moral Issue.' *Yale Law and Policy Review* 2:321

Martin, Sheila, and Kathleen. 1987. *Equality and Judicial Neutrality* Toronto: Carswell

Marshall, Patricia. 1990. 'Understanding of Sexual Abuse Involving Breach of Trust: A Barrier to Equality in the Administration of Justice.' Paper presented at Society for the Reform of Criminal Law, Conference

Mohr, Johann. 1990a. 'Sentencing Revisited.' *Canadian Journal of Criminology* 32:531

Mohr, Renate. 1990b. 'Sentencing as a Gendered Process: Results of a Consultation.' *Canadian Journal of Criminology* 32:479

Monture, Patricia. 1991. 'Reflecting on Flint Women.' In R. Devlin, ed., *Canadian Perspectives on Legal Theory*. Toronto: Emond Montgomery

Nadin-Davis, Paul. 1982. *Sentencing in Canada*. Toronto: Carswell

Roberts, Julian. 1990. *Sentencing Patterns in Cases of Sexual Assault*. Ottawa: Department of Justice

Ruby, Clayton. 1987. *Sentencing*. Toronto: Butterworths

Thornhill, Esmerelda. 1985. 'Focus on Black Women.' *Canadian Journal of Women and the Law* 1:153

Toronto Rape Crisis Centre. 1985. 'Rape.' In C. Guberman and M. Wolfe, eds., *No Safe Place: Violence Against Women and Children*. Toronto: The Women's Press

von Hirsch, Andrew. 1990. 'The Politics of Just Desert.' *Canadian Journal of Criminology* 32:397

Cases Cited

Atkins, R. v. (1988), 69 Nfld. & P.E.I.R. and 211 A.P.R. 99 (Nfld. C.A.)

Atlin, R. v. (1986), I.Y.R. 21 (B.C.C.A.)

B. (M.), R. v. (1988), 62 Sask. R. 79 (Sask.C.A.)

Baker, R. v. (1988), 85 N.S.R. (2) and 216 A.P.R. 96 (N.S.C.A.)

Beaulieu, R. v. [1988] N.W.T.R. 1 (Alta.C.A.)

Beyonnie, R. v. [1988] N.W.T.R. 390 (N.W.T.C.A.)

Blackburn, R. v. (1986), 75 N.S.R. (2d) 30 (N.S.C.A.)

Boss, R. v. (1988), 46 C.C.C. (3d) 523 (Ont.C.A.)

Brun, R. v. (1987), 81 N.S.R. (2d) and 203 A.P.R. 384 (N.S.C.A.)
Bryson, R. v. (1987), 80 N.S.R. (2d) and 200 A.P.R. 334 (N.S.C.A.)
Bush, R. v. (1986), 40 Man.R. (2d) 78 (Man.C.A.)
Challis, R. v. (1990), 95 N.S.R. (2d) and 251 A.P.R. 57 (N.S.C.A.)
Champagne, R. v. (1987), 7 Q.A.C. 129 (Que.C.A.)
Chartrand, R. v. (1986), 43 Man.R. (2d) 79 (Man.C.A.)
Childs, R. v. (1987), 81 N.S.R. (2d) and 203 A.P.R. 380 (N.S.C.A.)
Clubb, R. v. (1984), 20 O.A.C. 157 (Ont.C.A.)
Connors, R. v. (1983), 62 N.S.R. (2d) 251 (N.S.C.A.)
Corbière, R. v. (1987), 79 A.R. 179 (Alta.C.A.)
Cormier et al., R. v. (1985), 64 N.B.R. (2d) 188 (N.B.C.A.)
D. (B.), R. v. (1988), 90 A.R. 373 (Alta.C.A.)
D. (J.F.), R. v. (1988), 25 O.A.C. 78 (Ont.C.A.)
Dehann, R. v. (1986), 60 Nfld. & P.E.I. 267 (Nfld.C.A.)
Desbiens, R. v. (1985), 43 Sask.R. 169 (Sask.C.A.)
Dickinson, R. v. (1984), 4.O.A.C. 45 (Ont.C.A.)
Fadelle, R. v. (1985), 69 N.S.R. (2d) 102 (N.S.C.A.)
Fillis, R. v. (1986), 94 N.S.R. (2d) and 247 A.P.R. 356 (N.S.C.A.)
Fraser, R. v. (1987), 20 O.A.C. 78 (Ont.C.A.)
G.L., R. v. (1985), 64 N.B.R. (2d) 116 (N.B.C.A.)
Gardiner, R. v. [1982] 2. S.C.R. 368 (S.C.C.)
Gleason, R. v. (1987), 3 Y.R.2 (B.C.C.A.)
Graves, R. v. (1988), 84 N.S.R. (2d) and 213 A.P.R. 321 (N.S.C.A.)
Horvat, R. v. (1986), 43 Man.R. (2d) 158 (Man.C.A.)
Hoskins, R. v. (1987), 63 Nfld. & P.E.I.R. 111 (Nfld.C.A.)
J. (F.E.), R. v. (1989), 53 C.C.C. (3d) 64 (Ont.C.A.)
J.J.E., R. v. (1986), 57 Nfld. & P.E.I.R. 204 (Nfld.C.A.)
Janes, R. v. (1987), 63 Nfld. and P.E.I.R. and 194 A.P.R. 288 (Nfld.C.A.)
Johnston, R. v. (1988), 86 A.R. 295 (Alta.C.A.)
Jondreau, R. v. (1986), 18 O.A.C. 120 (Ont.C.A.)
K. (P.L.), R. v. (1989), 72 Sask.R. 156 (Sask.C.A.)
L., R. v. (1986), 50 C.R. (3d) 398 (Alta.C.A.)
L. (D.), R. v. (1990), 53 C.C.C. (3d) 365 (B.C.C.A.)
L. (J.L.), R. v. (1989), 76 Sask.R. 305 (Sask.C.A.)
Lafford, R. v. (1983), 61 N.S.R. (2d) 130 (N.S.C.A.)
Langille, R. v. (1987), 77 N.S.R. (2d) 224 (N.S.C.A.)
Lysack, R. v. (1988), 26 O.A.C. 338 (Ont.C.A.)
McGibbon, R. v. (1989), 23 O.A.C. 363 (Ont.C.A.)
McPherson, R. v. (1989), 34 O.A.C. 76 (Ont.C.A.)
MacDonald, R. v. (1985), 72 N.S.R. (2d) 245 (N.S.C.A.)

Marks, R. v. (1985), 38 Sask.R. 70 (Sask.Q.B.)
Meesto, R. v. (1988), 66 Sask.R. 122 (Sask.C.A.)
Morrison, R. v. (1989), 77 Sask.R. 315 (Sask.C.A.)
Murray, R. v. (1986), 75 N.S.R. (2d) 361 (N.S.C.A.)
Newman, R. v. (1988), 27 O.A.C. 141 (Ont.C.A.)
Nye, R. v. (1988), 27 O.A.C. 136 (Ont.C.A.)
Ogden, R. v. (1986), 68 N.B.R. (2d) 180 (N.B.C.A.)
Onalik, R. v. (1987), 65 Nfld. & P.E.I.R. and 199 A.P.R. 74 (Nfld.C.A.)
Owens, R. v. (1986), 55 C.R. (3d) 386 (Ont.C.A.)
Petaulassie, R. v. [1986] N.W.T.R. 294 (Alta.C.A.)
Plourde, R. v. (1985), 23 C.C.C. (3d) 463 (Que.C.A.)
Poll, R. v. (1987), 61 Sask.R. 168 (Sask.C.A.)
Pronovost, R. v. (1987), 7 Q.A.C. 309 (Que.C.A.)
Rafuse, R. v. (1985), 54 Nfld. & P.E.I.R. 59 (P.E.I.C.A.)
Resendes, R. v. (1988), 29 O.A.C. 335 (Ont.C.A.)
Ross, R. v. (1989), 90 N.S.R. (2d) and 230 A.P.R. 439 (N.S.C.A.)
S. (W.T.), R. v. (1987), 82 N.B.R. (2d) and 208 A.P.R. 304 (N.B.C.A.)
Sacrey, R. v. (1984), 54 Nfld. & P.E.I.R. 249 (Nfld.C.A.)
Sandercock, R. v. (1985), 62 A.R. 382 (Alta.C.A.)
Sharpe, R. v. (1988), 70 Nfld. & P.E.I.R. and 215 A.P.R. 60 (Nfld.C.A.)
Sparks, R. v. (1986), 75 N.S.R. (2d) 91 (N.S.C.A.)
Stefanidis, R. v. (1988), 28 O.A.C. 317 (Ont.C.A.)
Sullivan, R. v. (1987), 20 O.A.C. 323 (Ont.C.A.)
Tuckey, R. v. (1985), 9 O.A.C. 218 (Ont.C.A.)
W. (V.M.), R. v. (1989), 76 Sask.R. 299 (Sask.C.A.)
Wadden, R. v. (1986), 71 N.S.R. (2d) 253 (N.S.C.A.)
Wellington, R. v. (1985), 24 C.C.C. (3d) 252 (Ont.C.A.)
Williams, R. v. (1983), 60 N.S.R. (2d) 29 (N.S.C.A.)

8

TERESSA NAHANEE[1]

Sexual Assault of Inuit Females:
A Comment on 'Cultural Bias'

In the previous chapter, Renate Mohr examined reported sentencing deci-
sions in order to reveal judicial conceptions of sexual assault and to highlight
the ways in which the broad discretion afforded to judges leaves the determi-
nation of sentence up to the conscience of individual decision-makers. Hence,
the seriousness of the particular offence before the court is a matter of indi-
vidual assessment. In this chapter, Teressa Nahanee comments upon the
ways in which men who sexually assault Inuit women benefit from this kind
of individual assessment. The Inuit are the largest group of Aboriginal peo-
ple who comprise the majority of the population of the Northwest Territo-
ries. Today, the Inuit are subject to Canadian criminal laws and a judicial
system dominated by non-Inuit judges, Crown attorneys, and lawyers. The
sentences she discusses were all imposed by non-Inuit male judges, and all
suggest the existence of a 'cultural bias' that works to the disadvantage of
Inuit women. As an Aboriginal woman, Teressa Nahanee struggles with the
implications of her call for harsher sentences. Her conclusion, however, is
that until other solutions can be found, Inuit women want sexual abuse
treated as a serious crime and lenient sentences cannot and should not be
masked behind a 'cultural defence' invented by some northern judges. As
Nahanee observes, if the criminal justice system remains the same, Inuit
females will continue to be the victims of race and gender bias as reflected in
the sentencing decisions she examines.

Previous chapters of this volume have been concerned with the problem of
sexual assault as it pertains to victims in general. In this chapter I shall discuss the impact of sexual assault upon a specific group of victims: Inuit
females. My introduction to sexual assault of Inuit females occurred in my
first year Criminal Law and Procedure class at the University of Ottawa. The

class was asked to comment on the case of a 21-year-old Inuit male who bound and raped his 14-year-old cousin. He received a 90-day sentence from Judge Michel Bourassa. The Court of Appeal of the Northwest Territories increased the sentence to four months. As Inuit women struggle with the notion of harsher sentences for their men convicted of sexual assault, and their desire to live in harmony as communities of men and women, they are forced by circumstance to sacrifice some of their values. I think their story is worth telling. As you read this comment, you will see that there are still many areas that require research and documentation. It is not easy to write in an area where few, if any, Aboriginal women have written before. It is difficult to validate what we feel as Aboriginal women if we have not had a voice. If anything, I hope this chapter will act as an important first step in stimulating discussion on what I view as a critical area of Aboriginal life.

As Aboriginal people we have not admitted to the high level of sexual abuse within our communities. Sexual abuse of our children, our teenagers, our adult women, and, at times, our elders has been accepted as a way of life. It is only in our very recent past that we have admitted this abuse, and certainly among the Inuit women it is only recently that they have placed more emphasis on publicizing and correcting abuse within their communities. In my discussions with Pauktuutit, an organization representing Canada's Inuit women, they indicated that they had two major concerns respecting the administration of criminal justice in the Northwest Territories: lenient sentencing, and use by some northern judges of a 'cultural defence' for Inuit males accused in sexual assault cases. I am writing this chapter in the hope that, in future, sexual abuse in Inuit communities will be deterred, and changes brought about within the criminal justice system.

The Inuit[2] are the largest group of Aboriginal people who comprise the majority of the population of the Northwest Territories.[3] For the past decade they have been negotiating with the government of Canada to establish a separate territory north of the 60th parallel to be called 'Nunavut.' Although it is hard to predict how this will affect the administration of criminal justice there are three possible implications for the creation of a Native justice system. First, it may mean the creation of an almost totally Inuit-administered justice system. Second, it may mean the continuation of a judicial system dominated by non-Inuit judges, Crown attorneys, and lawyers until sufficient numbers of Inuit people are trained for these positions. Third, it may mean the continued application of Canadian criminal laws as is the case in all provinces and territories. If the criminal justice system remains the same, Inuit females will continue to be the victims of race and gender bias as reflected in sentencing decisions in sexual assault cases in the Northwest Territories.

One of the events that brought these issues to the attention of the Canadian public was the media attention given to the controversial comments made by Judge Michel Bourassa in the course of a sexual assault sentencing. The comments, as reported in the *Edmonton Journal* in December 1989, included the following remarks:

'The majority of rapes in the Northwest Territories occur when the woman is drunk and passed out. A man comes along and sees a pair of hips and helps himself,' a Quebec-born territorial court judge said in a recent interview with The Journal. 'That contrasts sharply to the cases I dealt with before (in southern Canada) of the dainty co-ed who gets jumped from behind.'[4]

Judge Bourassa also noted that 'southern Canadian victims of major sexual assault often suffer "vaginal tears" and psychological trauma related to sexual intercourse for several years afterward.'[5] These comments are based on underlying assumptions about differences in the impact of sexual assaults on women in the North as compared with women in the rest of Canada. Implicit in this assumption is that the experience of sexual assault for Inuit women (and girls) is different. The difference, as suggested by Judge Bourassa is that for Inuit females in the North, sexual assault is less physically and psychologically traumatic.

For a woman to suffer vaginal tears, the level of violence in the sexual assault must be massive. It generally means the victim was very young, or an assaultive instrument was used.[6] Vaginal tears are not common in sexual assaults in the North, but as a study of reported sentencing judgments from across Canada revealed (see Chapter 7), evidence of vaginal tears appears to be equally uncommon in the South. Judge Bourassa's assertions about psychological trauma are also problematic for a number of reasons. The psychological measurement of rape trauma syndrome is not known to have been cross-culturally tested for validity. One reality that might exacerbate the experience of rape trauma for Inuit women and children in the North is that no counselling services are provided in the Northwest Territories to victims of sexual assault.

Given the reality that most residents of the Northwest Territories are Aboriginal, Judge Bourassa's comments can be said to contain a reasonable apprehension of cultural bias. 'Cultural bias' means displaying an opinion regarding another culture 'which is stereotypic and insensitive to the cultural attributes of the people involved.'[7] As a consequence of the widely reported nature of his comments, Madame Justice Conrad of Alberta was appointed to investigate Judge Michel Bourassa for the remarks he made to the *Edmonton Journal*.

Madame Justice Conrad's mandate was to determine whether Judge Bourassa's comments amounted to 'misbehaviour' or made him 'unable to perform his judicial duties properly.' If Judge Bourassa's comments were found to be evidence of misbehaviour, or behaviour not appropriate to a judge, a recommendation could be made for his removal from the bench. On 28 September 1990, Madame Justice Conrad found Judge Bourassa's comments did not constitute misbehaviour, and she did not find he was unable to perform his judicial duties. She found that Judge Bourassa did not refer to 'Native' women in his remarks on sexual assault, but he admitted he referred to all northern women. These comments, in her view, did not constitute misbehaviour. She also found that the Montréal massacre of 16 female engineering students, as well as heated debates in the legislature on lenient sentencing in sexual assault cases contributed to the adverse reactions to Judge Bourassa's remarks in the *Edmonton Journal*.

On 29 October 1990, Pauktuutit asked all Canadians who believe in justice and sexual equality to condemn the decision of Madame Justice Conrad. Pauktuutit, representing Inuit women, asked for a full review of that decision. The organization felt that Madame Justice Conrad had not fully explored the issue of lenient sentencing in cases of sexual assault in the Northwest Territories, nor addressed the possibility that Judge Bourassa's attitudes and behaviour reflected those of other members of the northern judiciary. Pauktuutit demanded that the judiciary recognize that sexual assault is a crime that must be deterred and denounced regardless of the race or culture of the victim.[8] The organization announced that it was applying to the Court Challenges Program for funding to bring a Charter case against the Attorney-General of Canada and the Minister of Justice of the Government of the Northwest Territories. The organization is currently pursuing that case and is exploring whether the Charter applies to the exercise of judicial discretion in the determination of sentences. What this means is that the judiciary should be held accountable for sentencing decisions when the judgments reveal bias or a reasonable apprehension of bias with respect to prohibited grounds of discrimination (particularly sex and race) under the Charter.[9]

Pauktuutit has been critical of some northern judges because the judges have no evidence of traditional or current Inuit sexual mores and practices that would justify a 'cultural defence' or a mitigation of sentence for perpetrators of sexual assault of Inuit women and children. The so-called 'cultural defence' that has been used in these sexual assault cases is a judicial fiction according to Pauktuutit. The organization said there is no foundation to judicial belief that according to Inuit culture girls are ready for sex at 13 years of age.

Instead of following the guidelines for sentencing sexual assault cases as set by the Alberta Court of Appeal in *Sandercock*, (a minimum sentence of three years for a major sexual assault), judges in the North have adopted a particular sentencing strategy in cases where the defendant is Inuit. Regardless of individual circumstances (criminal record, employment, premeditation, etc.), sexual assaulters who are Inuit do not seem to receive more than two years' imprisonment. Unless there is severe violence or if the victim is not Inuit, sexual assaults by Inuit men do not appear to meet the *Sandercock* threshold of three years' imprisonment. In my view, this skewed cultural consideration assures Inuit females that they will not enjoy equal protection and benefit of the law as guaranteed by section 15 of the Charter. This supports the argument made by both Pauktuutik and the N.W.T. Status of Women Council that these 'cultural considerations' do indeed reflect a 'reasonable apprehension' of judicial bias. What is seen in the judgments in sexual assault cases involving Inuit are Eurocentric cultural biases against the Inuit people. These judicial remarks in no way resemble or reflect the northern community.

The use of the 'cultural defence' is also evident upon examination of cases decided in the Northwest Territories. For purposes of this chapter I reviewed all reported decisions on major sexual assault involving Inuit people, whether as accused or victims.[10] By 'cultural defence' I mean the judiciary has suggested sexual exploitation of young females is an Inuit cultural practice and, therefore, acceptable. For example, in *W.U.* (1984), Judge Bourassa gave a six-month sentence to a father who indecently assaulted his daughter with violence over a period of years. While condemning incest, Judge Bourassa noted the accused had no previous criminal record. He held, 'I have nothing before me to indicate that he is anything but a good hunter and a competent provider for his family' (136). In another case (*Curley et al.* 1984) the trial judge held that:

the morality or values of the people here are that when a girl begins to menstruate she is considered ready to engage in sexual relations. That is the way life was and continues in the small settlements ... These men were living their lives in a normal acceptable fashion in the way life is lived in the High Arctic.

These judgments reveal a perception on the part of some northern judges that, unlike in Canadian Eurocentric society, child sexual assault among the Inuit is acceptable. What Pauktuutit has said is that this kind of sexual exploitation of the young must stop because it is not 'culturally' acceptable, and it is not part of Inuit sexual mores and practices. Professor Mary Ellen Turpel in her writings asks judges to examine their own value-systems 'to eliminate as much as possible racial or cultural biases.' Turpel asks, 'If choices are personal (and therefore cultural): can the judge weigh a value system which is culturally different? Can a judge *know* a value which is part of an aboriginal culture and not her own?'[11]

In its submission to the Bourassa Inquiry, the N.W.T. Status of Women Council cautioned against the use of sexist or deceptive language in sentencing decisions. Objection was taken to Judge Bourassa's use of the pejorative term, 'a pair of hips' in the *Edmonton Journal* article because it was clearly sexist. The Council referred as well to the use of the words 'fondling' and 'cuddle' in sexual assault judgments because these words suggest affection rather than exploitation for sexual gratification.[12] In *Issuqanqituk* (1989), Judge Richard handed down a suspended one year sentence to an accused convicted of sexually 'fondling' girls aged 9 and 12. Both accused and victims were Inuit. He noted in sentencing that 'the accused has told the author of the pre-sentence report that in the home in which he grew up this kind of sexual touching of young girls was common and that it is one reason he did it.' The judge noted there was no violence in this kind of crime. In staying the charges against a white male taxi driver who had sexual intercourse with a 12-year-old Inuit virgin, Judge de Weerdt noted that the accused thought he had found some 'Lolita' (*Perkins* 1987). The Council said in its brief the use of this kind of language 'might well give rise to an apprehension of bias.'[13] Because the judiciary has focused on the blameworthiness of the accused, and has failed to implement the guidelines set out in *Sandercock*, little or no consideration has been given to the lifelong impact of the offence upon the young victim.

Other sentencing decisions, such as *Naqitarvik* (1986), illustrate why Inuit women are concerned about their failure to receive equal benefit and protection of the law. In this case the Inuit male accused, 21, was given a 90-day sentence for a major sexual assault of his 14-year-old cousin. *Curley et al.* (1984), in which three adult Inuit males were convicted of major sexual assault against a 13-year-old mentally impaired Inuit girl, was cited as the authority for this lenient sentence. The offences took place on different occasions, but within a short period of time. Each accused was sentenced to one week imprisonment based on their cultural defence discussed earlier.[14]

Comments on intoxication and its relation to major sexual assault are frequently mentioned in Northern case law. In *Apawkok* (1986), Judge Davis noted the accused, a former RCMP constable, was intoxicated at the time of two violent sexual assaults. He held that intoxication 'had reduced the intent to commit the offence, and therefore, there was probably no premeditation.'

He gave a sentence of 14 months protective custody. In another case, *Avadluk* (1989), Judge Richard sentenced an 18-year-old Inuit male convicted of major sexual assault of a 29-year-old female to one year imprisonment, two years' probation, and 150 hours of community service. He noted:

She remembers nothing about this sexual assault. She did not suffer any injuries, physical or psychological ... Other than the violence against the person which is inherent in a non-consensual act of intercourse with a woman, there were no further or additional acts of violence or threats of violence in this case (236–7).

In *McPherson* (1984), Judge de Weerdt, as he then was, said of one victim of a sexual assault that she was 'unaware of what was happening.' He sentenced the accused to 21 months, and two years less a day for pointing a firearm. He told the accused, 'Perhaps you should look at this as your last chance to stay out of the penitentiary, and to make a good life for yourself.' In *Ekalun* (1986), Judge de Weerdt sentenced an accused to two years less a day for an attempted sexual assault. The woman was attacked while asleep. Both had been drinking, but the judge noted the accused had a psychotic reaction to intoxication. In *Qavavau* (1988), Judge Bourassa gave a one-month sentence to an accused, aged 36, convicted of attacking a sleeping female, aged 22. Although Judge Bourassa's comments suggest that intoxication should not be a mitigating factor, the leniency of the sentence suggests otherwise.

You might think of that the next time you've had a few drinks and you see a woman lying around, asleep. First of all, you have no right to force yourself on a woman, asleep or any other way ... They're not there just to keep you happy ... [no man] can simply go along helping himself to whatever he thinks is available.

In cases where there is no intoxication, sentences that are clearly more lenient than the *Sandercock* guideline are imposed (e.g., two years less a day down to a suspended sentence). Where an employer had non-consensual sexual intercourse with his 19-year-old live-in female babysitter (*Nitsiza* 1989), the Crown attorney and defence counsel agreed this was not major sexual assault as described in *Sandercock*. Judge Richard agreed with them and gave a 20-month jail sentence. He noted:

· No blows were struck. There were no resulting physical injuries, and he did not threaten her in any way ... [he] was the employer of his victim, and in a sense breached a trust relationship between himself and the baby-sitter.

In a 1987 case, *Tartuk*, Judge de Weerdt gave a sentence of two years less a day to an accused convicted of having non-consensual sexual intercourse with a sleeping victim who had not been drinking. He noted:

Our courts have been conscious for many years of the undesirability of sending Inuit or other aboriginal residents of the N.W.T. to penitentiaries in southern Canada ... The infection of those communities by the culture of the penitentiary population is something which should be avoided, if at all possible.

It is commendable that some judges in the North seem to have agreed that it is undesirable to send Inuit males to southern penitentiaries. This discretion has resulted in sentences of two years less a day to Inuit male sexual offenders because under s. 40 of the Northwest Territories Act the sentence can be served within the territory. Section 731.(1) of the Criminal Code requires offenders sentenced to more than two years less a day to serve their time in a federal penitentiary. In its original application to the Court Challenges Program, which was funded, Pauktuutit sought to challenge the constitutionality of sections 40 and 731.(1) on the basis that sections 7 and 15 Charter rights of Inuit females are infringed by the imposition of lenient sentences designed to keep Inuit sexual offenders in northern prisons.

The victim may also be blamed for exposing herself to major sexual assault, and this results in a lenient sentence for the accused. If a woman falls asleep in the company of men [or a man], passes out, or is otherwise unconscious, there appears to be a blurring of consent as far as the northern judiciary is concerned. In *Gargan* (1988), Judge de Weerdt sentenced an accused who admitted to sexually assaulting women who were apparently asleep. The judge noted this was not a "sexual deviance" according to a psychologist. He held this type of activity was distasteful, abhorrent, and morally wrong 'no matter how much such victims may regrettably and foolishly expose themselves to attack.' In a Yukon case, *Atlin* (1986), not involving an Inuit victim, McLachlin J.A. held the woman had exposed herself to unnecessary risk by passing out. She woke up to find her former common-law partner having sexual intercourse with her.

The concerns surrounding the judicial responses to the sexual assaults of Inuit women and children are many, and efforts to address these concerns must be accelerated. Unless the government of the Northwest Territories makes significant changes in the administration of criminal law, Inuit females will continue to be victimized in their communities. Not only will they continue as victims of sexual assault, but also as victims of the administration of justice. They will continue to be denied equal protection and benefit of the law. The minister of Justice should heed a call from the Inuit women for a review of the entire justice system in the Northwest Territories as it affects Inuit and all Aboriginal people. I would recommend a program to ensure that Inuit men and women (particularly women) are trained as lawyers, Crown attorneys, and judges so that they can assume their rightful administrative positions when Nunavut is created. The minister of Justice should commence a study of sentencing practices in sexual assault cases in the Northwest Territories for the period 1984 to the present. Finally, the minister should convene an Aboriginal/feminist conference on the criminal justice system to seek recommendations on changes to the administration of justice in the territory.

The state should ensure greater access to the justice system for youthful victims of sexual crimes because so many northern victims are so young. A child advocate's office should be established by the minister of Justice of the Northwest Territories, whose staff should be readily available and easily accessible to all Inuit communities. An education program for all communities should be instituted through the Inuit Broadcasting Corporation to help expose and eradicate child sexual abuse. Print, radio, and video information should be made available as quickly as possible to promote cultural practices for child-rearing and respect for women. Removal of children and women from their homes and communities is not an acceptable alternative. Pauktuutit has called upon the government of the Northwest Territories to conduct a public inquiry into the treatment of women and children as victims of violence.[15]

Finally, I wish to repeat the recommendations of Pauktuutit on Inuit child sexual abuse. The organization has stated:

Governments must view the elimination of child sexual abuse as an urgent matter and place it on the forefront of their agenda. They must show a commitment to its resolution by developing long-term strategies and programs, in consultation with Inuit, even during times of tight economic restraint. The courts have a responsibility to ensure that the public understands that child sexual abuse is the most atrocious crime – crimes which will result in the highest penalty under the law. Mandatory counselling must be given to offenders so that when they return to our communities, which they will, our children will not be endangered. Treatment facilities with trained personnel must be created in the north to help the victims, families and offenders of child sexual abuse.[16]

In conclusion, I want to stress the importance of understanding sexual assault in its social context and of recognizing that it is a long and difficult path between the secrecy of sexual abuse in homes and communities, and

public disclosure. Often this disclosure takes place in the courts before lawyers, Crown attorneys, experts, and judges who do not belong to the community. The solutions that emerge from that forum have little connection to the
Native community.[17] While sexual abuse is a crime, it is also now sadly a fact
of life within the Inuit and other Native communities. Part of the solution is
harsher jail sentences. It is unfortunate that we, as Aboriginal women, must
advocate stiffer jail sentences for our own people because we will be criticized
for adopting the 'foreign' justice system. Nevertheless, until other solutions
can be found, Aboriginal women want sexual abuse treated as a serious crime,
detrimental to females, and undesirable as a practice within Native communities. What Inuit women have said is that lenient sentences cannot and should
not be masked behind a 'cultural defence' invented by some northern judges.
The Inuit women want some dialogue with the minister of Justice to make
improvements to the northern criminal justice system. I hope this will take
place.

The criminal law response to sexual assault has punishment of the
offender as its principal aim and does little or nothing to address the needs of
victims. In the next chapter, Elizabeth Sheehy examines other responses to
sexual assault that result in compensation for the victim.

Notes

1 I gratefully acknowledge the editorial assistance, guidance, and encouragement
   from Professors Elizabeth A. Sheehy and Darlene Johnston of the University of
   Ottawa Law School, and Professor Mary Ellen Turpel of Dalhousie Law School. I
   also want to thank Pauktuutit: Inuit Women's Association of Canada for reviewing
   drafts and discussing this issue with me, and for providing materials. Finally, I
   wish to sincerely thank Professor Renate Mohr for her editorial assistance,
   patience, and kindness.
2 Inuit were formerly known by the pejorative term no longer in use, 'Eskimos.'
3 Statistics based on the June 1989 population estimates indicate that 38 per cent of
   the population of the Northwest Territories is non-Native and the remaining 62
   per cent are Inuit (38 per cent) Dene (17 per cent) or Métis (7 per cent). *In the
   Matter of An Inquiry Pursuant to Section 13(2) of the Territorial Court Act,
   S.N.W.T. 1978(2), c. 16* and *In the Matter of An Inquiry Into the Conduct of Judge
   R.M. Bourassa*, 28 September 1990, Carole Conrad J. (Commissioner), 29.
4 The *Edmonton Journal*, 20 December 1989
5 Ibid.
6 In the sentencing cases involving sexual assault in the Northwest Territories that I
   reviewed, only one case involving a vicious sexual assault of a 9-year-old Inuit girl

received a lengthy sentence of imprisonment. The presiding judge Marshall noted, 'the assault was physically traumatic, [with] extensive internal injuries [perineum torn into her rectum].' *R. v. Emikotailuk* (1988), N.W.T.J. No. 76.

7 N.W.T. Status of Women Council, *Brief to the Judicial Inquiry into the Conduct of Territorial Court Judge R.M. Bourassa* (Yellowknife: N.W.T. Status of Women Council, 18 June 1990),10

8 Pauktuutit: Inuit Women's Association of Canada, *Pauktuutit Condemns Madam Justice Conrad's Decision on Judge Bourassa* (Ottawa: Pauktuutit, 29 October 1990)

9 I would contend that one of the major reasons why the Charter has not resulted in reducing the already high numbers of Natives going to prison is the lack of accountability of many of the actors in the criminal justice system. Native justice inquiries in Nova Scotia, Alberta, Manitoba, and current studies by the Law Reform Commission of Canada.

10 A number of unreported decisions were also analysed as available from Quicklaw, copies of which were provided to the author by Margo Nightingale who has also written on Natives and sexual assault ("Natives and Sexual Assault," *The Ottawa Law Review* 24(1991), 2). The cases analysed were reported for the period 1984 to 1989.

11 Mary Ellen Turpel, 'Aboriginal Peoples and the Canadian Charter: Interpretive Monopolies, Cultural Differences,' *Canadian Human Rights Yearbook* (1989–90):4, 24

12 N.W.T. Status of Women Council, 8, 9

13 Ibid.

14 *Naqitarvik*, 205, citing *R. v. Amauyak* (unreported). In the dissent in *Naqitarvik*, Belzill J.A. noted that in another case 'Justice de Weerdt of the Supreme Court of the Northwest Territories imposed a suspended sentence for rape.' Although the Court of Appeal raised the sentence to 18 months it still appears lenient when compared with the three-year standard set in *Sandercock*. The Chief Justice noted that the accused apologized to the girl right after the assault and later in public. This was a mitigating factor.

15 Annie Banksland and Edith Haogak moved and seconded a Motion at the 1990 Annual General Meeting of Pauktuutit in Iqaluit, Northwest Territories, on 13–16 March 1990. The Commission of Inquiry should be mandated to consider the following:

- the recruitment and appointment process for the judiciary and Crown attorneys;
- sentencing practices;
- victims' services;
- the roles and relationships of social agencies, law enforcement agencies, and various parts of the judicial system in dealing with victims;

– the knowledge base and attitudes of mandated agencies and the public toward women, and toward the values and practices of different cultures.

Pauktuutit asked that the Commission of Inquiry be headed by a chairwoman, and that the Commission be comprised of 50 per cent women. It should include representation from Inuit, Inuvialuit, Dene, and Métis communities. Suggestions for such members should be sought from NWT aboriginal and women's organizations. It should be adequately funded, travel throughout the NW, and undertake independent research.

The recent study completed by Katherine Peterson entitled *The Justice House: Report of the Special Advisor on Gender Equality* submitted to the minister of Justice of the Northwest Territories, May 1992, does not satisfy the mandate put forward by Inuit women. The methodology of the study did not require the special adviser to review sentencing of Inuit male offenders for sexual assault of Inuit females. There is still a need for the NWT minister of Justice to examine this whole question of cultural defences and sentencing practices of the northern judiciary.

16 Rosemarie Kuptana, *No More Secrets: Acknowledging the Problem of Child Sexual Abuse in Inuit Communities: The First Step Towards Healing* (Ottawa: Pauktuutit, 1991), 18

17 In August 1991 the Minister Responsible for the Status of Women appointed a Canadian Panel on Violence Against Women, and after some pressure from Aboriginal women, she appointed the Aboriginal Women's Circle on Violence. The representatives of Aboriginal women include Martha Flaherty, now president, Pauktuutit (Inuit Women's Association of Canada). Also, in 1991, the federal government appointed the Royal Commission on Aboriginal Peoples, which included former President of Pauktuutit, Mary Sillet.

The Aboriginal Women's Circle has travelled across Canada with the Canadian Panel and has heard testimony on violence against aboriginal women and children. Their report was published July 1993 along with that of the Canadian Panel of Violence Against Women. The Panel Report included a discussion of violence against Aboriginal women and a specific section on Inuit women. The Royal Commission on Aboriginal Peoples, which includes four Aboriginal commissioners, has held hearings throughout Canada and in July–August 1992, they drafted an initial report. This report will be sent to Aboriginal peoples in advance of further hearings to be held in late 1992 and early 1993. Both forums have heard from Aboriginal women on violence within aboriginal communities.

The *Report of the Aboriginal Justice Inquiry of Manitoba*, released in 1991, reported on violence against women and children within the aboriginal communities. It said such violence has reached epidemic proportions, and Aboriginal leaders are doing nothing to protect these victims of crime. In 1991, the Law Reform

Commission of Canada released its *Report 34*, having examined the question of Natives and criminal justice administration for the federal minister of Justice. It did not deal in any significant way with sexual violence against Aboriginal women and children.

Cases Cited

R. v. *Avadluk,* (1989) N.W.T.R. 235

R. v. *Apawkok* (1986), N.W.T.J. No. 72

R. v. *Atlin,* 23 April 1986 (Unreported) (Y.C.A.)

R. v. *Curley, Nagmalik, and Issigaitok,* [1984] N.W.T.R. 263 (T.C.);

R. v. *Ekalun,* [1986] N.W.T.J. No. 40

R. v. *Gargan* (1988), N.W.T.J. No. 56

R. v. *Issuqanqituk,* [1989] N.W.T.R. 259.

R. v. *McPherson,* [1984] N.W.T.R. 225.

R. v. *Naqitarvik* (1986), 26 C.C.C. (3d) 193.

R. v. *Nitsiza,* (1989) N.W.T.R. 231

R. v. *Perkins,* [1987] N.W.T.R. 308.

R. v. *Qavavau* (1988), N.W.T.J. No. 83

R. v. *Sandercock* (1985), 62 A.R. 382 (Alta. C.A.)

R. v. *Tartuk* (1987), N.W.T.J. No. 22

R. v. *W.U.,* [1984] N.W.T.R. 135.

9

ELIZABETH A. SHEEHY

Compensation for Women Who Have Been Raped[1]

In the last chapter, Teressa Nahanee concluded that lenient sentences imposed on men who are convicted of sexually assaulting Inuit women can no longer be tolerated. Implicit in this conclusion is her concern for a recognition on the part of judges that sexual assault is one of the most serious harms that any woman could ever suffer. The sentence imposed in a criminal court is an important symbolic recognition on the part of the state of the serious nature of the harm suffered by the individual victim. However, as earlier chapters in this book illustrated, the criminal trial and sentencing hearing is the exception rather than the rule in cases of sexual assault. As reporting statistics reveal, few sexual assault victims choose to initiate the criminal process. In this chapter, Elizabeth Sheehy describes two other routes of redress for women who are raped. Unlike the outcome of the criminal trial process where the focus is on the punishment of the offender rather than compensation for the victim, these two routes offer individual rape victims financial redress. For these women, tort and criminal injuries compensation offer the possibility of the recovery of financial losses and of some degree of recognition of the seriousness of the wrong that has been done. After describing the trends in the awards and the specific barriers to claims, the author addresses the challenging question of whether these forms of compensation can be conceptualized as progressive for all women.[2]

A woman who has been raped may have many reasons to pursue compensation. It may be the most empowering action available to her, especially if the criminal process has derailed, as it so often does.[3] Compensation may be the only process which *she* gets to drive, instead of respond to; it may be the only time when the legal system focuses on *her* needs; and it may be the only state acknowledgment of a wrong against her that she will receive.

Compensation symbolizes recognition of the high costs of sexual assault to women.[4] More practically, it may replace the financial losses a woman sustains through missed time at work, moving expenses, and counselling fees, among the many costs of rape. It may be therapeutic and empowering for a woman to recount her story, although unfortunately women's voices have not yet been heard on this very important question.[5] It has also been suggested that women may choose compensation over prosecution because they do not, for different reasons, want to send their assailant to jail (West 1992, 113). Activists who have been raped may view the compensation process as a chance to somehow turn their own rape into something positive for other women by making plain the personal, social, and economic costs of sexual assault, by educating those who administer compensation and perhaps the wider public in issues about rape, and by challenging the structures in Canada that support and reproduce violence against women.[6]

In this chapter I will examine the two major avenues for compensation for women who have been raped: tort actions and claims under provincial criminal injuries compensation schemes. For each avenue I will describe the trends in the awards and the specific barriers to women's claims. I will conclude with an assessment of these forms of compensation from a feminist standpoint.

Tort Compensation

Feminist authors have called upon the tort action as a strategy in aid of the individual woman's processing of her rape and in aid of educating judges, the woman's family and friends, and the public about rape: 'A rape victim can refuse to be isolated by "going public" with a civil suit ... Like a funeral, the victim's civil action may provide a ceremonial context that brings her private grief into the open and helps her dispense with it' (Batt 1984, 62; see also Freedman 1985).

Tort litigation has been compared with the 'procès-spectacle' – suits by women who have been raped – litigated by the feminist group Choisir in France. Because the woman and her lawyers are in charge of the civil suit, it can be used as a political trial around which women can be mobilized, press coverage garnered, and demands articulated. In fact, when Choisir litigates a rape claim, it requests and accepts only one franc in damages, as part of its political strategy.[7]

These concepts of the tort suit – as 'public funeral' and as 'political weapon' – are severely limited in reality by the structure of the tort system in Canada. For many women it will not be safe to grieve publicly, and particularly not in front of the rapist and his friends and family in open court. In terms of the tort suit as political strategy, our law is focused on proof and quantification of damages, so that a tort suit without a huge damage tag would almost be an oxymoron. Further, the personal costs of presenting oneself publicly in the role of 'victim' are very high (Bumiller 1987): which women are going to bear the burden of this label for the benefit of other women? In the remainder of this section, therefore, I will try to identify what other advantages and disadvantages women might find in pursuing a tort action.

A woman who has been sexually abused or raped may sue the attacker for the intentional torts of assault and battery; she may also be able to sue in negligence another individual, corporate entity, or representative of the state who failed in some duty that would allegedly have protected her from the assault. To prove assault and battery the plaintiff must show, on the balance of probabilities, that the defendant intentionally applied force to her person. 'Consent' is a defence to this tort (Wright et al. 1985). Some amount of damages will be presumed (and therefore the need for strict proof will be obviated) given that the tort is assaultive, but the plaintiff will usually want to adduce evidence to prove further losses. In a negligence suit against a third party, the plaintiff must prove that the defendant third party owed her an obligation by virtue of their relationship, that the defendant failed to meet that obligation, and that the plaintiff suffered a legally recognizable injury as a consequence of the failure on the part of the defendant.

Both types of civil action present initial barriers of access to legal services and limitation periods that are unrealistically short. Pursuit of a civil suit requires legal services that few women can afford. Even if a lawyer were willing and legally able to pursue a woman's claim on a contingent fee basis, meaning that fees to the lawyer would be payable only in the event of recovery, many lawyers might still be unwilling to litigate these cases given that the average award for sexual assault remains quite low.[8] Legal aid is available for tort actions of this nature, but not all lawyers are willing to accept the scales of payment that legal aid provides. The Women's Legal Education and Action Fund (LEAF) offers an alternative for some women. This organization will litigate a tort suit if it can be framed as a Charter[9] test case implicating women's section 15 rights to equality, and, in fact, it has pursued at least two such cases to date (*Jane Doe* v. *Metropolitan Toronto Police, Norberg* v. *Wynrib*). However, given the enormous demands on LEAF, it is obvious that it cannot fund more than the occasional tort suit.

More pragmatically, the chances of the woman actually collecting any damages awarded in a tort victory are remote. The individual defendants are likely to be impecunious or incarcerated, as many of the cases discussed later demonstrate. Defendants cannot self-insure for intentional conduct such as sexual abuse or assault, and thus women will also be denied recovery against insurance companies. For example, in *Storrie* v. *Newman and Insurance Corporation of British Columbia*, the plaintiff sued the defendant and was awarded $13,400 in damages for his assault upon her and for injuries she sustained when she managed to escape from the moving vehicle he was driving. The defendant's third-party claim against the insurer was unsuccessful because his assaultive conduct was held to be separate and apart from the operation of a motor vehicle.

On the other hand, women may be able to recoup their awards against the insurance policies of non-individual defendants such as the Children's Aid Society for negligence in failing to prevent sexual assault or abuse. Insurance coverage is just now being developed for organizations like the Catholic Church.[10]

Limitation periods for commencement of suits in assault and battery are usually short, i.e., two years,[11] thus posing another barrier to compensation. These limitation periods ordinarily begin to run when the assault occurs, or, if the person is a child, when she reaches the age of majority (*Murphy* v. *Welsh; Rothwell* v. *Raes*). The limitation period for actions framed in negligence is also two years in most provinces, although several legislatures have extended it to six years (Newfoundland, s. 2; Ontario, s. 45; Nova Scotia, s. 2(1)(e)).

These time limits will pose a problem for women who were assaulted as children and who survive by repressing their own knowledge of the assault(s) well into adulthood. Even those women who have identified and disclosed abuse as children are unlikely to be in a position to recognize and litigate the wrong once they have reached 18 years of age. The legal doctrine that holds that the limitation period should not begin to run until the injury is 'reasonably discoverable' (*Central Trust* v. *Rafuse*) could theoretically be given a generous interpretation in a suit for sexual assault, but it will require more than a mere extension of doctrine to benefit many women. It is almost impossible for adults to identify precisely when they became aware of abuse in their own backgrounds: often the information comes in bits and pieces in the form of flashbacks, leaving the woman frightened, confused, and uncertain about the validity of these memories and experiences. The concept of 'reasonable discoverability' has its roots in the standard of the 'reasonable man' and, given that the judges who implement the test understand the concept from the point of view of men's experience, the standard may in fact be quite 'gendered' (Finley 1987, Dawson 1984). Thus a male judge applying 'neutral' tools of judicial reasoning may have no ability to understand the woman's experience or to label her delayed 'discovery' as 'reasonable.'

Even if abuse has been unequivocally 'discovered' by the woman, it can take years of arduous work and therapy before she recognizes the losses she has sustained as a result of the assaults. If the assaults were committed by some member of her family, as is often the case, she must also struggle with issues of loyalty, the safety of other vulnerable members of her family, and the implications for future relations between herself, her own children if she is a mother, and her family members, before she is capable of making a decision about the matter of a law suit.

It is impossible to know how many women have been discouraged or prevented from pursuing a tort claim because of the limitation periods. We do have the example of the 1989 case of *Marciano* v. *Metzger* from the Ontario Court of Appeal. The jury found in the plaintiff's favour and assessed damages at $50,000, but the claim, filed in 1985, was dismissed on a motion by the defendant because it was filed past the four-year limitation period for assault actions in Ontario. The woman had become aware of the abuse by the time she was 16; she had reached the age of majority (18 years) in March 1975; she therefore lost her right to sue as of March 1979, six years earlier. The Court of Appeal decision is a one-page document that simply upholds the trial judge's dismissal of the claim without further reasoning, and expressly refrains from considering the effect of the 'reasonable discoverability' principle on cases involving childhood sexual abuse.[12]

Marciano was not followed by the British Columbia Supreme Court in *Gray* v. *Reeves*, decided in February 1992. In *Gray*, the court heard expert testimony from the plaintiff's psychologist, and concluded that although the parents of the plaintiff had several times discovered the assaults by the uncle, thereby ensuring that the plaintiff was made aware that she had been sexually abused, the limitation period should not be taken to have commenced as of her age of majority because it was not until years later that she became aware, through a second course of therapy (in her first course of therapy a relationship of trust did not develop, and the therapy did not focus on the impact of the abuse), of the connection between her problems and the childhood abuse. The court held that at the earliest, the limitation period began to run once she commenced that second course of therapy and was in a position to assess the impact of the abuse, which occurred six years after the limitation period would have expired under the age of majority rule (312).

Unfortunately, the *Gray* case is of limited use to other women who have been sexually assaulted as children. First, the court distinguished *Marciano* on the basis that the British Columbia legislation contains a provision that expressly contemplates the possibility of extending the limitation period.[13] Second, the court also distinguished a contrary authority from the United

States because the woman in that case had endured 'serious' and 'violent' sexual abuse as a child, whereas the abuse inflicted on Ms. Gray was in the nature of sexual touching: 'If evidence were to disclose serious assaults such as were alleged in [the case being distinguished], then the court may find that a reasonable plaintiff did possess sufficient knowledge of the relevant facts and ought in his or her own interest to have proceeded with a suit very soon after attaining the age of majority' (313). The distinction drawn in this case diminishes the seriousness of the abuse inflicted on Ms. Gray, ignores the possibility that her current memories may not accurately reflect what her uncle did to her, and minimizes the impact of 'serious' abuse in terms of the destruction of self-confidence in one's perceptions of 'reality' and one's ability to act powerfully in the world. Third, the court rejected Ms. Gray's s. 15 equality rights Charter argument to the effect that the statutory limitation periods have an unequal impact upon women who have been sexually assaulted, on the technical ground that the period had expired before the coming into force of s. 15 of the Charter and that Ms. Gray's argument was therefore precluded (314). Thus a broader argument, which would have benefited many more women, was not even considered by the court.

Ontario has responded to the lobbying of women's groups in the wake of *Marciano* with a reform bill. The proposed legislation runs a 20-year limitation period from the point at which the person discovers her abuse,[14] giving sufficient time thereafter for the person to go through whatever she needs to by way of healing before deciding whether to sue. Unfortunately, this bill appears to have died on the order table.[15]

If a woman who has been raped wishes to sue a government representative in a negligence suit, the limitation periods may be even more fleeting – six months![16] Such a short limitation period is a problem even for adult women who need time to absorb the losses that follow upon a rape before they can be expected to make legal decisions; it is obviously completely unrealistic to expect children to make such decisions within six months of turning 18 years old.

If we assume that these two barriers of money and time can be crossed, what then are the dimensions of tort suits for sexual abuse and assault? One author's research (Batt 1984) for the period 1900-80 found only eight reported cases involving claims for either rape or seduction (see also Backhouse 1986). The plaintiffs won in four of the cases, lost in two cases, and no final decision was rendered in the remaining two cases.[17] In the successful cases, the highest damage award was for $2400 in 1976, and the lowest award was for $1500 in 1969 (*Pie* v. *Thibert, S.* v. *Mundy*).

Since 1980, another thirteen cases have been reported[18] and there are at least seven unreported tort suits against rapists and third parties whose actions facilitated the attacks.[19] In these recent suits against abusers, all but one plaintiff (*Marciano* v. *Metzger*) were successful. In addition, when compared to the pre-1980 grouping of cases, these later judgments display considerably more respect for the veracity of the plaintiff, and more sympathy for her injuries. The highest award is a 1991 award of $170,000;[20] the lowest was $5000 in 1988 (*Lyth* v. *Dagg*). Of the cases against third parties in negligence, one against a private corporation has succeeded (against Minto and the rapist) (*Q. et al.* v. *Minto Management Ltd. et al.*), two against public officials have failed (although the same suits against the individual rapists succeeded) (*Lyth* v. *Dagg, M. (M.)* v. *K. (K.)*), one against public officials was settled (*Jane Doe* v. *Awasis Agency of Northern Manitoba et al.*), and one case against the Metro Toronto police (*Jane Doe* v. *Metropolitan Toronto Police*) has not yet been litigated on the merits.

The successful cases highlight advantages to pursuing a tort claim. First, the woman may stand a better chance of having her claim upheld in this forum than in the criminal courts. For example, in three of the cases, police had failed to press charges (*Myers* v. *Haroldson, Harder* v. *Brown, S.* v. *Mundy*); in a fourth, the accused had been acquitted of sexual assault at trial (*C. (M.)* v. *M. (F.)*); and in a fifth, the defendant had died before the commencement of his criminal trial (*Kunz* v. *Kunz*). In spite of the fact that proof of non-consent must have been considered problematic for the purposes of criminal prosecution in four of these cases, all five defendants were found liable in tort. Furthermore, in those cases where defendants have been found liable in negligence for failing to prevent sexual assaults upon women and girls, it is unlikely that prosecution could even have been attempted given that our criminal laws have not yet identified these wrongs as 'crimes.'

Second, it appears that in the torts cases, judges have a relatively sophisticated understanding of sexual assault. Many seem prepared to accept what I would call a feminist analysis – the idea that 'consent' to sexual relations is contextually related to power and to authority (Boyle 1981, MacKinnon 1983). For instance, consent was advanced as a defence in *Harder* v. *Brown*, a case in which the defendant, 60 years of age and in a wheelchair, was found liable in assault and battery in the amount of $50,000. He had abused the plaintiff beginning at the age of ten, and continuing intermittently over the years until she was 17. The trial judge was able to understand the dynamics of such long-term abuse and to make a distinction between consent and acquiescence:

As time went by, he [the defendant] gradually expanded the scope of his assaults and increased his influence over her self-respect to the point where there was no will left to resist that which others would too easily characterize as preventable. When she needed sympathy, understanding, an opportunity to unburden herself of her troubled thoughts and even money, he was always there. But there was a terrible price attached to his friendship and she paid that price so often that she gradually lost the ability to question it (39).

In a decision from the British Columbia Court of Appeal, (M. (M.) v. K.(K.)), the defendant was a foster father who had had intercourse with his 15-year-old foster daughter. He asserted that she offered him 'comfort' upon his marital breakdown and thus was the 'aggressor,' that they fully discussed the dangers and implications before embarking upon a sexual relationship, and that therefore she 'consented' to the acts. While the court below had accepted this defence and ruled in favour of the defendant, the Court of Appeal unequivocally rejected 'consent' on policy grounds:

In order to raise the defence of consent it became necessary for the defendant to rely on his own unlawful acts and breach of duty. The defendant should have rejected any advances made by the plaintiff and, by accepting her consent to sexual intercourse, he caused harm to the very person he was bound to protect ... In our view, the conduct of the defendant was analogous to incest and it is unthinkable that the courts of justice would permit such a defence to be put forward in a case involving incest (288–9).

In another case, *Lyth* v. *Dagg*, the defendant high-school teacher argued 'consent' based on lack of resistance by the plaintiff, his 15-year-old male student. This trial judge was also able to put 'consent' in perspective and thereby to reject the defence:

In those circumstances, Dagg became much more than the teacher in a student-teacher relationship. He dominated and influenced the 15-year old Lyth, who did not want to offend Dagg or do anything which would disrupt their relationship. It was into that kind of relationship, after an evening of beer and marijuana in a foreign country, that Dagg made the sexual advances (32–3).

The three cases described above all involved assaults on children that were further 'substantiated' by criminal convictions. It might thus be said that while the judicial language was progressive, any other result would have been perverse. With one exception, described below (*Norberg* v. *Wynrib*), the defence of consent did not arise as a serious issue for the judges in the eighteen recent cases even with respect to adult women. This judicial stance seems to hold true in cases where the plaintiff was intoxicated (*Myers* v. *Haroldson, S.* v. *Mundy*) and where she had a prior relationship with the defendant (*C. (M.)* v. *M. (F.)*) – situations where criminal convictions are often difficult to secure.

My assertion that the judges in the reported torts cases seem to deal with consent in a more 'feminist' manner is not, of course, wholly supportable. In fact, the same judge in *Lyth* showed an uneven understanding of the reality of 'consent' between a teacher and a student. He was willing to label the first advance by Dagg as an assault, but thereafter the judge held that the boy should have been able to express his non-consent. The sex acts that occurred on later dates were therefore held not to be assaultive, as if this boy had real-istic options to extricate himself from the power relationship in which he found himself! The damages were also set at the low sum of $5000.

More shocking, perhaps, is that the same court that articulated a policy decision on the applicability of 'consent' in situations of breach of trust in *M. (M.)* v. *K. (K.)*, the British Columbia Court of Appeal, also utilized a 'victim-blaming' approach in a case involving sexual abuse by a doctor of a patient. In *Norberg* v. *Wynrib* the British Columbia Court of Appeal rejected the claims in assault and in negligence by a woman who, at age 18, became an addict to painkillers through medical misdiagnosis, and who confided her addiction when she was 24 years of age to the defendant doctor, then 78 years of age. He refused to prescribe any further drugs unless she complied with his sexual demands, which she finally did. Both the B.C. Supreme Court[21] and the Court of Appeal accepted the doctor's defence of 'consent':

She went voluntarily in order to get drugs with a clear understanding of the sordid arrangement to which she had agreed. (B.C.C.A., 51).

The plaintiff also lost her claim in negligence for breach of professional duty, with different reasons being given by the different judges. At the lower court level, her action was barred by the doctrine of *ex turpi causa*, which precludes redress for illegal or immoral actions: she herself was said to be guilty of involvement in illicit sexual relations and 'she was receiving drugs not for medicinal but for illicit purposes' (B.C.S.C., 313). The judge stated fur-ther that the plaintiff could not prove physical damage and that emotional distress standing alone was insufficient to support a claim in negligence.

At the appellate level, two of the justices affirmed the application of the *ex turpi causa* bar to Ms. Norberg's negligence claim (she was a party to a 'crim-inal enterprise to traffic unlawfully in a prohibited drug'), but would have found that the plaintiff's prolonged addiction amounted to physical damage sufficient to support the claim (B.C.C.A., 52–4). The dissenting judge would not have applied *ex turpi causa* because the woman's drug *use* was not illegal and because 'immorality' should not be invoked to bar her claim (B.C.C.A., 64).

Ms. Norberg has finally been vindicated in her tort suit upon appeal to the Supreme Court of Canada, where she received a unanimous judgment in her favour, albeit on different grounds. One justice insisted that she had 'consented' to the sexual assault, stating that 'community standards of sexual conduct have no bearing on the question of whether or not there was consent to sexual contact in a particular case' (per Sopinka J., 636), but instead upheld her claim in negligence for failure to meet professional standards of medical treatment. Three justices found in Ms. Norberg's favour using the tort of battery and holding that there can be no genuine consent in circumstances of a 'power dependency' relationship, where a defendant has exploited the plaintiff's particular vulnerability (per La Forest, Gonthier, and Cory JJ.). Two justices held that Ms. Norberg should receive a remedy in equity for breach of fiduciary duty through sexual exploitation (per McLachlin and L'Heureux-Dubé, JJ.). In spite of this legal victory, like the plaintiff Dagg (*Lyth* v. *Dagg*), Ms. Norberg appears to have been judged at fault, ultimately, in that her damages were assessed at $20,000 – the lowest tort award for sexual assault since *Lyth* v. *Dagg*.

The generally positive reception given to women's torts claims – through discounting of the response by the criminal justice system and a contextual understanding of consent – may be accounted for in several ways. While both criminal and civil suits require proof of an intentional assault, the standard of proof in criminal law is proof beyond a reasonable doubt whereas the civil standard is proof on the balance of probabilities: the lower burden of proof in tort may facilitate a finding that an assault in fact occurred. The tort requirement that the defendant prove consent, rather than requiring that the Crown demonstrate non-consent as part of proof of a criminal offence, may also assist the tort claimant.

The judges and lawyers who are involved in tort litigation may bring to their work a different attitude: they may be less incredulous or hostile[22] toward a plaintiff who is suing for damages than they would if an accused's liberty were at stake in a criminal trial. In a tort suit the woman also has an attorney representing *her* interests, and not simply the Crown as overworked and sometimes ambivalent advocate for the state.[23]

The greater latitude in civil suits regarding the type of evidence that can be heard may also influence the outcome. For instance, while evidence of the trauma associated with a sexual attack is ordinarily not brought forward in a criminal trial,[24] the plaintiff in a tort suit may be able to introduce 'rape trauma' as part of her proof of damages.[25] This evidence may in fact influence the judge or jury in finding non-consent to the assault even though technically this might be an improper use of such evidence.[26] At the least, evidence about rape trauma most certainly helps the judge in a civil action to appreciate the impact that sexual abuse and rape has on the lives of women.

Third, tort litigation may provide the advantage of a relatively amenable environment for recognition of the harm that rape causes to women. The cases suggest that perhaps judges have begun to comprehend the impact of rape, although some judges are quite uncomfortable with the notion of quantifying the harm. An example that illustrates the discomfort of the judiciary can be found in C. (M.) v. M. (F.) where the judge stated:

There is no scale upon which one can weigh the severity of the injuries to a person who suffers permanent physical injury because of the unintentional negligence of a stranger against the severity of the emotional injuries suffered by a victim of a brutal violation of her private person against her will by a person who had been a trusted friend. The injuries are so different in their nature and effect that it seems inappropriate to attempt to compare them (9).

...

A similar sort of dilemma exists in attempting to determine whether a rape victim suffers more or less if the rapist is a total stranger than if he is a former lover (11).

The judge in this case awarded the plaintiff, who had been assaulted by her former boyfriend, $40,000 in damages, giving recognition to the fact that the resulting emotional trauma may be with her for life.[27] While the award itself may be within the average range of sexual assault damages, the judge in fact articulated no principles for assessing damages and seemed to select the figures from the air.[28]

In other cases the judges have calculated damages by focusing on the losses resulting from rape. In *Myers* v. *Haroldson* the judge took great care to list and describe all of the plaintiff's losses, including her lack of trust in strangers, particularly men; her lost enjoyment of sexuality; nightmares; feelings of loss of control; lower self-esteem; basic insecurity in social situations; the question of the parentage of her child; and the fact 'that the suffering has been of significant duration, and may therefore last indefinitely' (611–12). This plaintiff's general damages were assessed at $10,000 in addition to $40,000 in punitive damages awarded for reasons that will be described below.

In *Harder* v. *Brown* the plaintiff was awarded $40,000 general damages and $10,000 in punitive damages. The judge emphasized that the plaintiff's resulting feelings of worthlessness 'affect her life in many ways, including her outlook towards others, her choice of friends and jobs, and her confidence in her ability to overcome life's problems' (95). The judge also noted that the woman lived in 'constant fear' that her own children would be sexually abused, that she suffered from flashbacks, and that she was 'constantly apprehensive' that someone would confront her with what she viewed as her 'sordid past.'

In *Q. et al. v. Minto Management Ltd. et al.* the judge considered, in assessing damages, the fact that the plaintiff's 'pattern of life has changed with emphasis being placed on security since she now owns a large dog and has additional locks' (545); in *B. (A.) v. J. (I.)* the judge noted that 'for years after the abuse stopped, A.B. slept with a butcher's knife under her pillow to "protect herself"' (753). In several of the cases, judges have acknowledged that sexual assault brings with it alienation from one's closest family members (*Myers v. Haroldson*, 612; *Q. et al. v. Minto Management Ltd. et al.*, 545). Heightened vulnerability to future sexual abuse and to self-destructive behaviour has been recognized by judges as well in their calculation of damages.[29]

Specific sums have been awarded for long-term counselling, particularly where the plaintiff was subjected to repeated abuse during childhood. Some judges recognize that the memories of abuse may be hidden or dormant for years, and that the human psyche can only absorb and process so much pain at a time.[30] In several recent cases, a sum of $20,000 has emerged as the award for counselling fees on the assumption that a woman abused as a child will require weekly counselling over a period of approximately five years.[31] Of course the adequacy of these sums must be questioned in light of the frequent judicial acknowledgment that the recovery process for sexual abuse is lifelong.

The judges in these cases express strong condemnation of the behaviour of the defendants with virtually no blaming of the women for the assaults. In five cases where the defendant was not convicted in the criminal courts, judges have imposed punitive damages as high as $40,000.[32] One judge justified this award as follows:

(b) It is conduct needing deterrence as the predominance of sexual assaults primarily by adult males upon females in our society is real and unabating. This court is aware of the many studies and reports as will evidence the number of sexual assaults upon women in Canada which go unreported, and others reported but where requisite evidence is lacking, allowing the offender to escape without penalty of law;

(c) The defendant has done more than offend the ordinary standards of morality and decency. He has done so in a cold and calculating way, uncaring as to the consequences;

(d) The defendant, in carrying out the sexual attack, has acted arrogantly and callously. He simply did not care what harm or consequences would flow from his act; and

(e) Specifically, the court must consider that in the assault, her life was threatened and the defendant brutally raped her. (*Myers* v. *Haroldson*, 614).

In cases where punitive damages are not awarded because the defendant has already been punished by the criminal justice system, judges have upped the general damage award by adding aggravated damages in recognition of the impact of the extremity of the insult to the plaintiff's physical and psychological integrity. For instance, in one such case aggravated damages were set at $50,000.[33] Finally, in another recent case, the court imposed punitive damages upon a man who had been convicted of the abuse on the basis that his charges had resulted from a one-year period when, in fact, he had abused the three children over a much longer period.[34]

However, my praise for these judicial acknowledgments of the harm caused by rape must be tempered. First, the monies awarded in many of these cases will, in all likelihood, never be collected. As illustration, I note that the defendant failed to appear in at least six of the recent cases, which is usually a good indication that he has no assets worth protecting.

Second, one of the problems with damage assessments that has yet to be recognized by the judges is that in complying with limitation periods, women may well have incomplete knowledge about what has happened to them and the long-term repercussions of that abuse. For example, although the court in *Gray* v. *Reeves* gave the plaintiff the benefit of an extended limitation period, it was clear from the evidence that she was still in the process of uncovering her own feelings about the assaults, which poses a risk that she will also uncover further details of which she was unaware at the time of trial. The difficulty is that the trial judge compared and emphasized the more 'minor' nature of the assaults upon Ms. Gray with those suffered by other plaintiffs in assessing her general damages,[35] without recognizing that her course of therapy may lead her to more information about the 'seriousness' of the assaults.

Third, the judges in the majority of these cases have also been reluctant to look ahead and award damages for future lost income for women who have been raped, labelling both past and future losses of this sort as too speculative or too remote.[36] Such a conclusion has been reached even in cases where the judge also awarded monies for long-term therapy, which itself suggests recognition of the long-term nature of the psychological disability arising from the abuse (*Gray* v. *Reeves*). Only one judge has been prepared to give some recognition to lost income, both past and future.[37]

Fourth, some of the therapeutic aspects of a tort action are undermined by the fact that the woman is required to claim 'damage' – even the word plays upon the social view of the harm of rape – by emphasizing the effects of rape on her life; to forestall her own life reorganization process in a lengthy adversarial ordeal; and to have this experience translated into medical and psychological terms in the courtroom by an 'expert' who can authenticate her trauma and put a price on her losses.

Fifth, certain judicial statements made in the context of damages awards reinforce heterosexuality as the norm and compensate women for lost opportunities for heterosexual relationships. In *Gray v. Reeves*, the court in assessing damages stated that 'the problem of establishing a good relationship with a man is a matter which should be considered in an award of general damages,' and in fact used this head to double the general damage award, from $20,000 or $25,000 to $45,000 (320–1). In *Myers v. Haroldson* the judge also compensated the woman for lost opportunities to pursue heterosexual relationships (611). This presumption of heterosexuality was not unrelated to the judge's notions about appropriate female behaviour: 'Now she does not trust men and resents them. At work when she deals with men and finds them rude, she is rude right back' (609). The uncritical notions that heterosexual relations are otherwise non-coercive and that they represent a 'loss' render these decisions of questionable value in terms of both public education and challenge to gender relations.

Sixth, in terms of judicial articulation of harm through damages awards, I note that the racial identity of the women and girls in most of these cases has 'disappeared' (Duclos 1992). We are deprived of information that might assist us in understanding the interplay of race and gender in the power relations of rape and sexual abuse; we are also impoverished in our understanding of the dimensions of 'harm.'

In the two cases where the racial identity of the plaintiff emerges, the judges have failed to comment upon racism as part of the harm of the assault. In *Myers v. Haroldson* the plaintiff was called names by the assailant as part of the attack, including the pejorative 'squaw.' The judge failed to comment upon the racist aspect of this sexual attack, which is a serious omission, particularly given the harm to the woman's self-esteem when her Aboriginality was so clearly part of the defendant's effort to dominate her.

The plaintiff in *Jane Doe v. Awasis Agency of Northern Manitoba et al.* was also of Aboriginal descent. As a result of her removal from her community for a period of several years and the government agencies' failure to protect her once she had been returned to her community, the plaintiff 'was in no way accepted into the community and led the life of an outcast' (740). This young woman was so vulnerable in this context that she was subjected to repeated rape. Although the judge was only asked to approve Minutes of Settlement, it is important to recognize the harm this plaintiff suffered as including the impact of racially motivated state intervention, loss of familial and community relations, and damage to her pride in her Aboriginal heritage (Monture 1989).

Finally, the judges in these tort cases also continue to understand the harm of rape from their own standpoint, which is one that sees rape as 'dirty' and 'degrading,' rather than as an experience that brings a woman face-to-face with her own death. Even the judges who think that they are being generous with the plaintiffs before them express their decisions in terms that suggest they still hold views and values that support myths about rape and about women's sexuality. In *Harder* v. *Brown* the judge said that 'the plaintiff was highly vulnerable to the very evil which the defendant visited upon her. Driven by his perverted lusts' (94). Another judge framed the plaintiff's rape in this way: 'We have a young woman who, without provocation, enticement, invitation or consent was violated' (*Myers* v. *Haroldson*, 610). In several cases, including *Myers*, judges felt compelled to note that the plaintiff was attractive (610), as if this 'fact' had anything to do with the rape or the woman's damages.

Each plaintiff had to put herself up for judgment as a 'deserving victim.' While the women in the recent cases ultimately 'passed,' not all withstood judicial scrutiny unscathed. For example, in *Lyth* v. *Dagg* the judge held that the 15-year-old student had consented to subsequent sexual contact because he failed to inform anyone of the sexual overtures and because he did not stop the contact. Lyth has to live with this judicial appraisal of his behaviour: 'One of the matters which is of concern to Lyth and a contributor to his inner conflict is the question why he permitted the relationship to continue for such a long time' (33).

In *M. (M.)* v. *K. (K.)*, although the plaintiff was ultimately successful at the Court of Appeal, she initially lost at the British Columbia Supreme Court level because the judge held that the 15-year-old's two-and-one-half-year relationship with her foster father was consensual: 'She demonstrated before and after the relationship that she participated because she wanted the attention of the defendant and not because she was coerced into it' (105).

In *Storrie* v. *Newman and Insurance Corporation of British Columbia* the woman's evidence that she experienced great fear of men after the rape and an ongoing inability to engage in any relations with men, let alone sexual relations, was met by allegations from a witness produced by the defendant that Ms. Storrie had engaged in sexual intercourse with him, a 16-year-old boarder, after the rape. While it is unclear exactly how this evidence influenced the judge's assessment of the damages, it is apparent that Ms. Storrie must have been affected by this tactic and by the judge's acceptance of its veracity: '[Her] complaints ... were highly exaggerated and so far as her relationships with men were concerned, completely unreliable' (387).

Many of the judicial comments on the behaviour of the plaintiff in *Norberg* have already been reproduced. In addition to the assessment of her conduct as 'immoral,' one judge stated that 'while he capitalized on her addiction, she took advantage of his age and loneliness' (B.C.S.C., 313). Another judge clearly could not comprehend the emotional trauma associated with sexual abuse: 'I do not regard it as reasonably foreseeable on the facts of this case that the defendant could ever reasonably have thought that the other party to this transaction would be so overtaken by these human feelings as to sustain mental damage' (B.C.C.A., 59).

Finally, claims in negligence for sexual abuse will rarely carry the same advantages as the claims against abusers. Negligence actions will be against corporations or institutions such as schools, Children's Aid Societies, and provincial child welfare departments. Suits of this nature are less likely to succeed for many reasons, including a lack of clarity regarding the exact nature of the responsibilities of these institutions and problems with proof of the element of fault on the part of the institution (*Lyth* v. *Dagg*, 35; *M. (M.)* v. *K. (K.)*, 284–6). In *Q. et al.* v. *Minto Management Ltd. et al.*, the woman succeeded against the landlord corporation because its behaviour presented an obvious and shocking risk to her physical safety.[38] In the one case where Minutes of Settlement had been signed by government agencies in a claim on behalf of a girl who had been raped repeatedly after removal and return to her Aboriginal community, the judge approved what he considered to be a low settlement ($75,000 general damages) on the basis in part that the liability of the defendants was 'arguable' (*Jane Doe* v. *Awasis Agency of Northern Manitoba et al.*, 741).

Criminal Injuries Compensation

Women have a second option of applying for criminal injuries compensation from the province in which the rape or sexual abuse occurred. Every province now has a legislative scheme to compensate victims of crime.[39] Only two of these schemes are administered through the judicial system;[40] the remainder are processed by criminal injuries compensation boards, with occasional appeals to or judicial review by the courts. The decisions of these boards are generally not available to the public; my discussion of the law will therefore be limited to the relevant statutes and regulations, the annual reports of the provincial boards, and any judicial decisions interpreting the law.

Criminal injuries compensation offers a different configuration of advantages and disadvantages than does tort compensation. Relative to a tort claim, criminal injuries compensation is expedient and inexpensive. The tort cases described above took anywhere from three to eight years between date of assault and award, whereas criminal injuries claims are often resolved within a year of filing.[41] This time frame for resolution will be quite important to claimants whose recovery and life reorganization process is disrupted by constant reminders of the rape or abuse.

The criminal injuries acts, with one exception (Manitoba, s. 6(2)(a)), have a limitation period of one year from the time of the offence for the filing of a claim, although these statutes expressly contemplate extensions,[42] and certainly the one-year period will not run against a child until the age of majority is reached (*Gordon* v. *Commissioner of N.W.T.*). Although I could not locate any criminal injuries compensation claims that raised a comparable issue of timeliness, as was the case in *Marciano*, one might expect a more favourable resolution in the criminal injuries arena than in the realm of torts because of the clear statutory authority to disregard the limitation.

The filing of a criminal injuries application and the claims process itself carry no financial costs to the claimant. If she requires legal assistance, legal fees may or may not be recoverable as part of the claim.[43]

The criminal injuries process also offers privacy as compared with the tort action. These claims are adjudicated without publicity and, in fact, most of the provincial acts provide for *in camera* hearing of sexual assault claims.[44] The annual reports of the boards exclude names and details of the offence.[45] While it is possible for a plaintiff in a tort claim to achieve similar anonymity, she must apply to a judge to exclude her name from her claim (see *Jane Doe* v. *Metropolitan Toronto Police*). She may not succeed at keeping her identity private, as one recent case in which the woman's name was reported on the front page of *The Lawyers' Weekly* demonstrates.[46]

In addition, the offender is usually not involved in, let alone even notified of, the criminal injuries compensation process.[47] The woman does not need to confront him as she might need to do in a civil action. Thus, while the privacy of the criminal injuries compensation process means that the public education value of the criminal injuries compensation process is quite limited, the process may be safer for the claimant, both physically and emotionally.

Disadvantages to the criminal injuries claim route will be readily apparent. The schemes are provincial and therefore each uses different eligibility criteria and scales of compensation: some provinces are quite miserly with women who have been raped.

The lump-sum awards for criminal injuries are much lower than those one might receive under the tort system: the *highest* cap under the criminal injuries legislation is now at $30,000,[48] and, depending on the province, the awards (1989–90) can be as low as $1300.[49] However, some of the criminal injuries awards are substantially higher, as in Ontario where there have recently been two awards in the $18,000 range.[50] The lower range of awards for criminal injuries must be balanced against the faster rate of resolution, and the fact that this process offers something the tort system does not, which is the possibility of periodic payments in addition to any lump sum award.[51] All provinces also allow for reassessment and variation of the award in recognition of residual disability and of claimants' changing circumstances.[52]

Access to information about the process can be difficult. Each province produces an annual report, but these reports contain a minimum of information about certain matters that will be of concern to a woman who has been raped, such as the amount of money she can expect to receive. Further, in many provinces there is no legislative requirement that the board provide written reasons for its decision.[53] Therefore, even if she is awarded compensation, the woman may not receive a clear validation (and certainly will not receive a public one) of her loss. Criminal injuries compensation is thus an individualized and insulated process that may meet some minimum of women's income needs, but is unlikely to produce much by way of political or social transformation.

Women who have been raped and who seek criminal injuries compensation face further barriers. These barriers are rooted in two premises upon which these schemes are based: the notion that only the 'deserving' victim should be compensated, and the notion that the criminal justice system should be used by persons who have been victimized by violence. I will discuss each premise and its implications in turn.

The first premise, that only worthy victims should be compensated, is not unique to criminal injuries schemes, but rather is a pervasive though often unarticulated undercurrent in torts decisions (Glasbeek and Hason 1977, Ison 1967). This notion reaches its zenith in criminal injuries compensation where the claimant has been the subject of criminal, not simply tortious action, and where the idea is unabashedly stated as principle, not sentiment. In fact, at least one predecessor statute was entitled *The Innocent Victim Compensation Act!*[54]

This underlying idea that only 'good' victims deserve compensation is played out in the informational materials provided for the public and for potential claimants by provincial boards. The boards assert a distinction between the blameless and the culpable victim:

The Board is not inclined to compensate persons who have been drinking to a considerable extent and may have impaired their faculties, thereby rendering themselves as attractive targets for assault or as being incapable of resisting.[55]

The use of good investigatory techniques and close cooperation with police forces have resulted in sound file management, and claims from purported victims with no real right to benefits are detected.[56]

Generally the Board will assess contribution where the victim had adopted a lifestyle or voluntarily engaged in an activity in which the risk of injury was reasonably foreseeable.[57]

Given that our culture is imbued with rape myths that assign blame to women for their own victimization, and given that women who have been raped must struggle against blaming themselves (and most do not succeed),[58] such an identifiable punitive stance in the materials surely must warn off some number of women who have been raped. Quite noticeable in the annual reports is the low rate at which women claim for criminal injuries compensation as compared with men in nearly every province.[59]

The notion of the deserving victim is also manifested in the statutory requirements of every provincial act. Claimants are either denied compensation or their awards are reduced in proportion to their own 'fault' or contribution to the occurrence of the offence.[60] In one province, even the victim's 'character' is to be taken into account![61] In some provinces, as many as 43.21 per cent of claims are denied on this ground,[62] although unfortunately the annual reports give neither a gender nor a criminal offence breakdown for this figure.

This legislative mandate to blame the victim gives free reign to an entire range of pernicious opinions about women and rape. While the annual reports do not reproduce in full the decisions of the boards, the application of the 'victim fault' principle is in evidence in the case summaries:

It must be noted that the claimant had accepted a drink and then a ride from the assailant who was a total stranger to her. The claimant admits that she did so while partially under the influence of alcohol. It is considered that by doing so the claimant had placed herself in a position of some jeopardy and certainly extremely susceptible to such an incident as did ultimately occur. It is determined that the claimant has contributed substantially toward the circumstances in which she was ultimately attacked and that contribution shall be taken into account in the assessment of the award.[63]

A 27-year-old single, female bookkeeper was sexually assaulted by her former boy-friend and suffered mental trauma. Her assailant was charged and convicted of two offences ... The Board invoked Section 25 of the Act and reduced the award by one-third because of the contributory actions of the victim.[64]

The 'principle' of 'victim fault' has been applied with a particular vengeance to women who are assaulted while working as prostitutes in the province of British Columbia:

No award was granted [to a 17-year-old claimant] as ... claimant had contributed so substantially toward the entire occurrence as to disentitle her to any award of compensation. Claimant by acting in the capacity as prostitute had assumed a substantial risk of harm and was in no position to seek compensation in this particular case when such harm materialized.[65]

Québec applies this harsh principle even when the claimant has been *murdered*!

After sexually assaulting her, the offender beat her and then left her under the Metropolitan Autoroute.

The Commission concluded that the claimant had relinquished the advantages of the law by engaging in unlawful activities ... that entailed risks that the victim normally was, or should have been aware of.

In addition, given that communication for the purpose of prostitution is unlawful, the victim had shown evidence of serious fault characterized by extreme lack of concern for the consequences of her acts. In terms of serious injury to her physical integrity, the extent of her fault would or should normally have made her realize the probability or even strong likelihood of danger to her physical integrity. Thus, the victim contributed to her own death by *gross fault* (emphasis in original).[66]

Two points must be made here regarding the 'victim fault' rule. First, not all of the provinces interpret their mandate so as to blame women for their own rapes. For instance, Saskatchewan and the Yukon seem to disregard behaviour that others might describe as blameworthy.[67]

Second, in several provinces where claimants have sought judicial review of the application of this rule by criminal injuries compensation boards, the courts have narrowed the boards' authority to disentitle claimants based on their own 'contribution' to the commission of the offence. In *Poholko* v. *Criminal Injuries Compensation Board* the Nova Scotia Supreme Court reversed the Board's denial of compensation where the claimant had been kidnapped and assaulted over two days:

She was not performing as a prostitute when Mr. Burchell threatened her with a knife, struck her on the head and face with a hammer; locked her in the trunk of his car, and forced her to walk through the woods to a camp and then confined her under circumstances that he admitted (by his guilty plea) amounted to the offence of kidnapping.

...

Her conduct or behaviour did contribute to the injuries she received ... but certainly such conduct was not the sole cause of such injuries (18–20).

Similarly, the Ontario High Court has reversed a denial of compensation by the Ontario Board in *Dalton* v. *Criminal Injuries Compensation Board* where the victim had accepted a ride home from two men with whom she had been drinking. When one of them attempted to rape her and she fought back, she was thrown out of the moving vehicle onto the highway:

We agree that the Board erred in law in the way it purported to apply s. 17(1). This is a complex section which *requires* the Board to consider all the relevant circumstances, including the behaviour of the victim that contributed to the injury, in determining whether to order compensation or whether to make a reduced award ... In this case the Board failed to consider a significant circumstance ... the severity of the injuries suffered by the claimant ... In our view, certain contributing behaviour of a claimant might be sufficient reason to deny her an award if her injuries are slight, but would not be enough to bar her, if she is severely injured or killed ... Further, the Board did not properly consider the issue of the contribution to her injury by the behaviour of Mrs. Dalton ... By going with these two men in the circumstances she incurred a risk, that is true. But she surely could not have expected that, as a result, she would be pushed out of a moving truck on a highway so brutally. Although the Board could properly find that her behaviour *contributed* to her injury, to hold that she was the *exclusive* cause of this particular injury was legal error (emphasis in original).[68]

Whether the boards of Nova Scotia and Ontario have begun to interpret the 'victim fault' rule in light of these judicial decisions remains to be seen. Clearly these cases have not influenced provinces such as British Columbia and Québec. I note as well that in spite of this apparent judicial distaste for the harshness and extremity of the 'victim fault' rule, no provincial legislature has yet abandoned or tempered its governing statute. This means that even those provincial boards that do not give full range to victim-blaming ideas in rape cases may in fact shift as appointments to the board change. Furthermore, the annual reports do not clearly state the bounds of the 'victim fault' rule, which means that many women may decline to apply for criminal injuries compensation because they cannot risk such an assignment of blame.

The second underlying premise, that victims of violence should resort to the criminal justice system and that this system will respond appropriately, is also evident in the governing statutes and annual reports. One of the foundational requirements for a successful criminal injuries compensation claim is that the board must make a finding, on the balance of probabilities, that a 'crime' has occurred. A criminal conviction will establish a crime under the acts,[69] and the boards are usually empowered to delay their decisions pending resolution of the matter in criminal court.[70] If the police have 'unfounded' the woman's allegation of rape or if the accused is acquitted, then the claimant may not be able to establish that a crime has in fact taken place.

The requirement of a finding that a 'crime' has occurred shows up in the statistics that break down rejections of claims. In Québec in 1989 this category (98 cases) comprised 26.63 per cent of the rejected claims,[71] and in Alberta 39 out of 87 claims were rejected in 1989–90 because of insufficient evidence of commission of a crime within the schedule.[72] The impact of this criterion is also evident in case summaries of claims denied for rape and incest.[73]

Again, the harshness of this barrier to women's claims has been somewhat tempered in several provinces. For instance, Manitoba's Information Manual notes that the Board is not bound by the court's determination of the matter.[74] In a judicial review of denial of compensation in a criminal negligence case, the Nova Scotia Court of Appeal has said that an acquittal cannot be conclusive of the question of whether a 'crime' has occurred because the burden of proof is lower for a criminal injuries application, and because the *mens rea* element of proof of an offence in the criminal courts is also not relevant to the compensation process.[75]

Another manifestation of the premise that the criminal law is the primary forum for rape complaints is the requirement that the victim must have reported the offence, within a 'reasonable' time period, to the law enforcement authorities as a precondition to entitlement to compensation.[76] This category of rejected claims is relatively large in some provinces.[77] In several provinces the reporting requirement is not formalized in legislative form,[78] but only the province of Nova Scotia has a policy of waiving the requirement in cases of sexual assault where fear or embarrassment is involved.[79] In addition, criminal injuries legislation may require that the victim have cooperated with the police,[80] and the woman may need to undergo a medical examination at the request of the board.[81]

It should be evident that the requirements of reporting to police and convincing authorities that a 'crime' has occurred will pose serious barriers for women who have been raped. A commonly cited statistic is that approximately one in ten women who have been raped will report the crime to the police (Temkin 1987), which should not be surprising, given that our police continue to 'unfound' rape complaints at the rate of 15 per cent (see Chapter 3 on recent national founding statistics).[82] Mentally and physically disabled women may simply not be in a position to report sexual violence to police, and may not be believed even if they do. Lesbians who do not conceal their sexual identities may be unwilling to subject themselves to police scrutiny, disbelief, and harassment, and they may also legitimately fear additional abuse at the hands of officers to whom they report sexual violence (Petersen 1991). Aboriginal women and women of colour may likewise decide to protect themselves against racism and police scepticism by not reporting to police.[83] The response of the criminal courts will be equally discouraging for women who do report: the conviction rate for rape seems to range from 18.0 to 51.2 per cent in Canada.[84]

Several of the provinces have additional requirements that will pose difficulties for women who have been raped. For instance, Newfoundland bars claims based on crimes committed by family members,[85] which will quite obviously exclude most sexual abuse and all marital rape claims. In Manitoba, the attorney general can require that the claimant sue the offender to recoup the compensation.[86] In several of the provinces, the offender may be notified of the claim and requested to appear.[87] In New Brunswick, the applicant must also identify the names of others who have been victimized by the same offender.[88]

In sum, the 'victim fault' rule and the link to the criminal justice system means that criminal injuries compensation, usually, will be an option only for those women who are already seeking criminal prosecution; it is therefore an additional, not an alternative course of action for women who have been raped.

Conclusion

Are these two forms of compensation positive for women who have been raped? For individual women, tort and criminal injuries compensation offer the possibility of recovery of financial losses and of some degree of recognition that a wrong has occurred. In particular, a tort suit offers a greater opportunity for a woman who has been raped to publicly air the event; she is also likely to be awarded a higher sum in damages, although she in fact may not receive the money.

My tentative conclusion, however, is that in their present forms, both tort and criminal injuries compensation are available to a limited group of women: those whose conduct is relatively 'blameless,' who have found their 'voice' to speak about their abuse and survival through therapy or a feminist community, who have been willing and able to utilize the structures of the criminal justice system such as the police, and who have access to legal services. Even these women, who may be relatively privileged in our current social structure by being heterosexual, able-bodied, white-skinned, and not poor, face barriers in these processes and risk having their losses minimized and their selves exposed. Tort suits and, more significantly, criminal injuries claims present serious risks to the woman's recovery because of systemic victim blaming and because cooperation with the criminal justice system is required in situations may be neither possible nor safe for her.

Can these forms of compensation be conceptualized as progressive for women as a group? Both tort and criminal injuries compensation individualize rape: the structures and ideologies that support and reproduce coercive sexuality are hidden by the focus on the individual defendant as rapist. As well, the legal processes and doctrines leave out important dimensions of sexual violence such as male retaliation against lesbians, the expression of racial superiority, and the denial of the sexuality of mentally and physically disabled women, and their consequent vulnerability to secretive abuse. Sexual assault as part of women's lives is also rendered invisible by the private aspect of the criminal injuries compensation process and resulting decisions. By its nature, the criminal injuries compensation process offers almost no opportunity to challenge and transform the structures that contribute to sexual assault in Canada.

It is difficult to imagine how we might transform these systems to make them available to a broader group of women and to render them a radical challenge to gender relations in Canada. A fault-based, publicly funded tort action could be made widely available to women who have been raped, and we could instigate an insurance fund from which women could draw their unsatisfied judgments in much the same way as we now do for victims of uninsured motorists. We would of course need to consider how the fund would be created – against whom would we levy a 'sexual coercion' fee? Feminists could also engage in law reform efforts with respect to the provincial criminal injuries schemes to rid them of the obvious barriers identified.[89] If women flooded the boards with their claims, and if provincial governments responded with legislative reforms and public hearings, perhaps some degree of public education could be achieved. However, we still need to address the underlying structures that impede differentially women's access to compensation. Tort suits such as *Jane Doe* v. *Metropolitan Toronto Police* and *Jane Doe* v. *Awasis Agency of Northern Manitoba et al.* offer a stronger possibility of challenge to institutional structures of racism and beliefs about women and rape.

In the meantime, the decision as to whether to pursue compensation, and the forum in which to pursue it rests within an individualized framework. It is the woman herself who bears the personal and financial costs of pursuing compensation. The decision therefore remains a very difficult and personal one for women who have been raped.

As this chapter has illustrated, the criminal law response to a sexual assault does little or nothing to address the needs of the victim of the assault. In the next chapter, Adelyn Bowland discusses one of the most difficult aspects of a criminal trial for assault victims – the admissibility of evidence of the victim's past sexual history.

Notes

1 While this Chapter deals with compensation for all forms of sexual assault against women, girls, and boys, I frequently use the term 'rape' to signify a particular experience, and I employ 'women' as my reference point to both reflect the reality of who gets raped and to ground my discussion.

 I gratefully acknowledge the assistance of Uzma Ihansullah, Barbara Main, Teressa Nahanee, and Deborah Palumbo with the research and footnotes for this chapter. I also wish to thank Christine Boyle, Lucie Léger, and Elizabeth Pickett for their insightful comments on earlier drafts of this chapter.

2 The research for this chapter was current as of August 1992. Readers should be aware that the discussion around limitation periods should now be read in light of the Supreme Court of Canada's decision reversing the Ontario Court of Appeal in *Marciano* v. *Metzer*, decided in November 1992: *M. (K.)* v. *M. (H.)* (1993), 96 D.L.R. (4th) 289 (S.C.C.).

3 For accounts of the operation of the criminal law with respect to women who have been raped, see Lorenne Clark and Debra Lewis, *Rape: The Price of Coercive Sexuality* (Toronto: The Women's Press 1977); Rita Gunn and Candice Minch, *Sexual Assault: The Dilemma of Reporting, the Question of Conviction* (Winnipeg: University of Manitoba Press 1988).

4 For instance, it is estimated that 19 per cent of women who are raped attempt sui-
   cide: Pat Marshall, 'Sexual Assault, The Charter and Sentencing Reform' (1988),
   63 C.R. (3d) 216, 227.

5 While authors such as Sharon Batt and Lisa Freedman (see text, infra) and the
   lawyers quoted below make this claim, I do not think that we can assess it without
   the experiences of women who have pursued compensation. In 'Manitoba Woman
   Awarded $170,000 for Sex Assaults by Father During Childhood,' *The Lawyer's
   Weekly*, (12 April 1991), 1, the woman's lawyer stated that it wasn't the money
   that was the issue. She wanted to make her father answerable for what he had
   done to her. Secondly, she had, over the years, become aware that many, many
   other people were abused like her and no one was coming forward. And she felt
   that if she came forward, and took a step like this, then maybe others would have
   the courage to do so as well
      See also the words of the lawyer in *Kunz* v. *Kunz*, reported in 'Sex Assault Vic-
   tim Wins $125,000 Award against Father,' *The Lawyer's Weekly* (15 September
   1989), 8: 'She was after the ability to speak out and disclose the matter publicly.'

6 I am thinking here of Jane Doe, whose lawsuit, *Jane Doe* v. *Metropolitan Toronto
   Police* (1990), 74 O.R. (2d) 225 (H.C.J.), leave to appeal denied, (1991), 1 O.R. (3d)
   416 (C.A.) is in the service of other women and a direct challenge to the structure of
   policing. Jane Doe was raped by a serial rapist. Her claim is that the police failed to
   adequately investigate prior reports of rape with respect to the same assailant, and
   that this inaction is systemic in terms of the police response to violence against
   women. Women's equality rights under section 15 of the Charter are thus
   infringed by police failure to protect women's physical integrity. Ms. Doe also
   argues that the police had in fact pinpointed a suspect, that she was used as 'bait' to
   catch the rapist, and that the police failed to meet a tort law duty to warn women
   who were identifiable as potential victims of the rapist.

7 This group and its litigation tactics are described in Batt (1984), 60–2

8 See, for instance, the lawyer's comment in 'Sex Assault Victim Wins $125,000
   Award against Father,' *The Lawyer's Weekly*, (15 September 1989), 8: 'I think the
   conventional $50,000 award which we're seeing over and over again is inappropri-
   ately low.'

9 Canadian Charter of Rights and Freedoms Constitution Act, 1982, as enacted by
   Canada Act (U.K.), 1982, c. 11, Sched. B.

10 See 'Churches Buy Liability Insurance to Cover Sexual Abuse Lawsuits,' *The
   Ottawa Citizen*, (21 January 1989), H7.

11 For examples see the following acts: Statute of Limitations, R.S.P.E.I. 1974, c. S-7, s.
   2(1)(d); Limitations of Actions Act, S.N.B. 1990, c. L-8, s. 4; Limitations of Actions
   Act, R.S.M. 1987, c. L-150, s. 2(1)(e); Limitation Act, R.S.B.C. 1979, c. 236, s. 3; Limitation of Actions Act, R.S.Y.T. 1986, c. 104, s. 2(1)(d); Limitations of Actions Act, S.S.

1981, c. L-15, s. 3(1)(d); Limitations of Actions Ordinance, R.O.N.W.T., 1974, c. L-6, s. 3(1)(d); and Limitations of Actions Act, R.S.A. 1980, c. L-15, s. 55 [am. 1983, c. O-10, s. 82; 1984, c. C-9.1, s. 88; 1986, c. 27, s. 3; 1989, c. 17, s. 14(b)].

12 For a comparison with a recent, progressive decision of the Supreme Court of Canada regarding the question of whether an accused has been unfairly prejudiced by a complainant's rape charge 30 years after the assault, see: *R. v. L. (W.K.)* (1991), 64 C.C.C.(3d) 321 at 328 (S.C.C.) (Stevenson J.):

> For victims of sexual abuse to complain would take courage and emotional strength in revealing those personal secrets, in opening old wounds. If proceedings were to be stayed based solely on the passage of time between the abuse and the charge, the victims would be required to report incidents before they were psychologically prepared for the consequences of that reporting.

13 Subsections 6(3), (4), and (5) of the British Columbia Limitation Act, discussed in *Gray v. Reeves* (1992), 64 B.C.L.R. (2d) 275, 311 (S.C.).

14 Bill 198, An Act to Amend the Limitations Act, Ont., 1988, cl. 45(a)(2): 'Ten years after the time the person bringing the action discovers that the injury was caused by the sexual abuse or sexual assault and the injury no longer renders the person unable to bring an action.'

15 The bill was approved in principle in January 1989: Mary Gooderham, 'Bill on Sexual Abuse Clears Hurdle,' *The Globe and Mail* (13 January 1989), A9. The principles and concerns contained in Bill 198 have now been incorporated into a larger law reform effort: Consultation Group on the Limitations Act (Allan Shipley, Convenor), 'Recommendations for a New Limitations Act' (Toronto: Ministry of the Attorney General, 1991). In fact, this report recommends *no* limitation period if one of the parties was in a special relationship to the person who was sexually assaulted: ibid., 21.

16 See for example, Public Authorities Protection Act, R.S.O. 1980, c. 406, s. 11.

17 Wins: *Pie v. Thibert*, [1976] C.S. 180, plaintiff was sexually assaulted and was awarded $2400 in damages; *S. v. Mundy*, [1970] O.R. 764 (Co. Ct.), plaintiff was awarded $1500 in exemplary damages where the defendant had indecently assaulted and beaten her quite severely; *Radovskis v. Tomm* (1957), 9 D.L.R. (2d) 751 (Man. Q.B.), damages in the amount of $2000 to the plaintiff for physical injuries, but nothing for emotional suffering since the judge was of the view that the child was too young to have sustained mental suffering and that a broken hymen was not of serious importance given that the child had not been 'deformed'; *Hopkinson v. Perdue*, [1904] 8 O.L.R. 228 (Div. Ct.), unsuccessful motion by the defendant to set aside the judgment in favour of the plaintiff. Losses: *M. v. P.*, [1921] 14 Sask. L.R. 117 (C.A.), in an action for damages for assault and for seduction, the court held in favour of the defendant – the plaintiff was not believed regarding her non-consent and, since the plaintiff had sworn that she was

not a consenting party, she could not recover for seduction which imports consent on her part!; *MacKenzie and Palmer,* [1921] 62 S.C.C. 517, plaintiff failed in an action for assault amounting to rape since her evidence of force exerted and resistance on her part was discredited, but the court did find that there was seduction, thereby restoring the trial judgment.

No final decision: *E. v. E.* (1905), 10 O.L.R. 489 (Div. Ct.) suit by father for the seduction of his daughter wherein a motion was made for judgment dismissing the action and a new trial was ordered; *Lapalme v. Beaudoin,* [1948] R.P.363 (C.S.), an action for damages for attempted rape wherein the court decided that certain prejudicial paragraphs would be deleted from the plaintiff's pleadings.

18 *Storrie v. Newman and Insurance Corporation of British Columbia; Norberg v. Wynrib,* [1988] 6 W.W.R. 305 (B.C.S.C.), affirmed (1990), 44 B.C.L.R.(2d) 47 (C.A.), reversed [1992] 4 W.W.R. 577 (S.C.C.); *M. (M.) v. K. (K.)* (1987), 11 B.C.L.R. (2d) 90 (S.C.), reversed (1989), 38 B.C.L.R. (2d) 273 (C.A.); *Harder v. Brown* (1989), 50 C.C.L.T. 85 (B.C.S.C.); *N. (J.L.) v. L. (A.M.),* [1989] 1 W.W.R. 438 (Man.Q.B.); *Q. et al. v. Minto Management Ltd. et al.* (1985), 49 O.R. (2d) 537 (H.C.J.); *Lyth v. Dagg* (1988), 46 C.C.L.T. 9 (B.C.S.C.); *Myers v. Haroldson,* [1989] 3 W.W.R. 604 (Sask.Q.B.); *Jane Doe v. Metropolitan Toronto Police; B. (A.) v. J. (I.),* [1991] 5 W.W.R. 748 (Alta.Q.B.); *Gray v. Reeves; B. (K.L.) v. B. (K.E.)* (1991), 7 C.C.L.T.(2d) 105 (Man.Q.B.); and *Jane Doe v. Awasis Agency of Northern Manitoba et al.* (1990), 72 D.L.R.(4th) 738 (Man.Q.B.).

19 *C. (M.) v. M. (F.)* (17 September 1990), No. 1862 Action No. 323349/88 (Ont.Ct.J.); *D.T. and M.O. v. F.A.* (21 December 1990), No. 1088/88 (B.C.S.C.); *Marciano v. Metzger; Kunz v. Kunz; Beaudry v. Hackett* (28 June 1991) (B.C.S.C.); *G. v. R.* (3 January 1991), No. 1088/88 (B.C.S.C.) and *A.K.M. v. M.B.* (22 June 1990) (Ont.Ct.J.).

20 See *B. (K.L.) v. B. (K.E.);* but see the reference made in the article, 'Sex Assault Victim Wins $125,000 Award against Father,' *The Lawyer's Weekly* (15 September 1989), 8, to a $475,000 jury award in an unidentified case.

21 At the lower court level: 'By apparently voluntarily submitting ... the plaintiff gave her implied consent ... there is no evidence that she was under the influence of the drug, or that her addiction interfered with her capacity to consent to the sexual activity which took place. She was not at any time deprived of her ability to reason' (*Norberg v. Wynrib,* 309 (B.C.S.C.)).

22 See, e.g., comments made by defence counsel at a conference and reported as follows: Cristin Schmitz, '"Whack" Sex Assault Complainant at Preliminary Inquiry,' *The Lawyer's Weekly* (27 May 1988) 22.

23 See David Doherty (now Justice Doherty), '"Sparing" the Complainant "Spoils" the Trial' (1984), 40 C.R. (3d) 55.

24 For discussions of the state of the law regarding the admissibility of 'rape trauma syndrome' evidence see Elizabeth A. Sheehy, *Personal Autonomy and the Criminal*

Law: Emerging Issues for Women (Ottawa: Canadian Advisory Council on the Status of Women 1987) 24–7; and Anne-Marie Delorey, 'Rape Trauma Syndrome: An Evidentiary Tool,' *Canadian Journal of Women and the Law* 3:2 (1989–90) 531.

25 For instance, experts testified as to the plaintiff's trauma in the following cases: *N. (J.L.) v. L. (A.M.)*, 440–1; *Lyth v. Dagg*, 30–1; *Brandner v. Brandner*, 4–5.

26 See *C. (M.) v. M. (F.)*, 6. Keenan J. had this to say regarding expert evidence: 'To permit evidence in support of such an inference [that the plaintiff must be a rape victim] would open the door to serious mischief. It would serve only to bolster the credibility of a complainant who recites a list of complaints which are common to rape victims.'

27 Ibid., 11.

28 See also the statement in the case with the high award of $170,000: 'Accordingly, following conventional and arbitrary standards, I allow, including an allowance for interest, non-pecuniary loss at $150,000' (*B. (K.L.) v. B. (K.E.)*, 112.

29 *N. (J.L.) v. L. (A.M.)*, 441. Also see *D.T and M.O. and F.A.*, 5: 'Experience tends to show that children who suffer this type of trauma are 2 to 4 times more likely to be re-victimized in adulthood. They are more pre-disposed to bouts of depression, anxiety, and the infliction of harm upon themselves. They have more suicidal tendencies than members of the general population who have not gone through such an ordeal. They are often sexually maladjusted. Abuse by fathers has a more negative impact on a child than abuse by other perpetrators. The longer the child is abused, the more likely it will make the child feel damaged and without control over her life and the more likely these factors will become a permanent and predominant feature of her personality.' See also *B. (A.) v. J (I.)*, 753.

30 *D.T. and M.O. and F.A.*, 5: 'Today, DT does not want to take counselling. Over time she may forget what happened to her, yet it seems likely she will need some psychiatric assistance in the future. She is presently repressing her memory of the assaults although she may not be able to do this forever.'

31 *B. (K.L.) v. B. (K.E.)*, 111. See also the statement in the case with the high award of $170,000: 'Accordingly, following conventional and arbitrary standards, I allow, including an allowance for interest, non-pecuniary loss at $150,000' (*B. (K.L.) v. B. (K.E.)*, 112. See also *Gray v. Reeves*, 322.

32 *Myers v. Haroldson*, 615. See also *Harder v. Brown*, 99 ($10,000 in punitive damages); *Kunz v. Kunz* ($25,000); *Gray v. Reeves* ($12,500); and *Norberg v. Wynrib*, ($10,000) (S.C.C.).

33 *B. (K.L.) v. B. (K.E.)*, 112. For other aggravated damages awards see also *N. (J.L.) v. L. (A.M.)*; *C. (M.) v. M. (F.)*.

34 *B. (A.) v. J. (I.)*, 756, 757 ($50,000 in punitive damages for each of the three plaintiffs)

35 *Gray v. Reeves*, 318, 320

36 *Gray* v. *Reeves*, 323, 324; *B. (K.L.)* v. *B. (K.E.)*, 111

37 See *Beaudrey* v. *Hackett*, as discussed in 'B.C. Woman Awarded $85,000 for Child-hood Sexual Assaults,' *The Lawyer's Weekly* (10 April 1992), 8.

38 The landlord had been apprised of an earlier rape in the plaintiff's apartment complex by someone who used a master key. The landlord failed to investigate its employees, to limit access to the master keys, or to warn tenants in the complex.

39 Criminal Injuries Compensation Act, R.S.A. 1980, c. 33; Criminal Injuries Compensation Act, R.S.B.C. 1979, c. 83; The Criminal Injuries Compensation Act, R.S.M. 1987, c. C-30S; Compensation for Victims of Crime Act, R.S.N.B. 1973, c. 14; The Criminal Injuries Compensation Act, R.S.N.F.L.D. 1970, c. 68; Criminal Injuries Compensation Ordinance, R.O.N.W.T. 1974, c. 23; Compensation for Victims of Crime Act, S.N.S. 1975, c. 8; Compensation for Victims of Crime Act, R.S.O. 1980, c. 82; The Criminal Injuries Compensation Act, S.S. 1981, c. 47; Compensation for Victims of Crime, R.S.Y.T., 1986, c. 27; Victims of Crime Act, S.P.E.I. 1988, c. 67; Loi Sur l'Indemnisation Des Victimes d'Actes Criminels, L.Q.R. 1977, c. I–6

40 Northwest Territories; Prince Edward Island

41 For examples of claims resolved within a year of filing see *The 15th Annual Report of the Criminal Injury Compensation Act of British Columbia*, January 1, 1986–December 31, 1986, 10–13; *The 16th Annual Report of the Criminal Injury Compensation Act of British Columbia*, January 1–December 31, 1987, 13.

42 See Ontario, s. 6: 'the Board may extend the time for such further period as it considers warranted.'

43 Legal costs are awardable in the following provinces: Alberta, s. 11(2); Northwest Territories, s. 18 (up to 75 per cent of the taxable costs); Nova Scotia, s. 23; Saskatchewan, s.41; Yukon, s. 20 (up to 75 per cent of taxable costs); New Brunswick, s. 8(5)(b) (but only in a case of application to the Court of Appeal).

44 The following provinces provide for *in camera* hearings: Alberta, s. 4(2)(b); Manitoba, s. 8(2)(b); Newfoundland, s. 20(b); Northwest Territories, s. 11(b); Nova Scotia, s. 15(b); Ontario, s. 12(b); Quebec (all are *in camera*); Saskatchewan, s. 16(b); Yukon, s. 14(b).

45 See Nova Scotia Criminal Injuries Compensation Board, *Annual Report for the Fiscal Year April 1, 1988 to March 31, 1989*, 11–26; Commission de la santé et de la sécurité du travail, *Direction de l'Indemnisation des Victimes d'Actes Criminels*, in 1988 and 1989, 26–33, 30–36 respectively; *The 15th Annual Report of the Criminal Injury Compensation Act of British Columbia*, January 1, 1986–December 31, 1986, 14–22; *The 16th Annual Report of the Criminal Injury Compensation Act of British Columbia*, January 1–December 31, 1987, 14–18.

46 *B. (K.L.)* v. *B. (K.E.)* was originally reported using the woman's name: 'Manitoba Woman Awarded $170,000 for Sex Assaults by Father during Childhood,' *The Lawyer's Weekly*, (12 April, 1991), 1.

47 The only provinces wherein the offender is given notice of the hearing are as follows: Northwest Territories, s. 6; Nova Scotia, s. 9(1); P.E.I., s. 21 (although it is not required by the Act); Yukon, s. 7(c).

48 Nova Scotia, s. 28(2). A ceiling of $25,000 is used in British Columbia, s. 13(1)(a), and Ontario, s. 9(1)(a). Other provinces have much lower ceilings for lump-sum payments; i.e., New Brunswick has a maximum of $5000: s. 17(2)(b).

49 See claim No. 022-3105 (incest) in Commission de la santé et de la sécurité du travail, *Direction de l'Indemnisation des Victimes d'Actes Criminels*, 1989, 31.

50 See file Nos. 922-016506 and 922-018489 in Ministry of the Attorney General, *Ontario Criminal Injuries Compensation Board 1988–89*, 28,30.

51 Alberta, s. 12(1); British Columbia, s. 3(1)(a)(b); Manitoba, s. 15(1); New Brunswick, s. 22(1); Newfoundland, s. 27(1); Northwest Territories, s. 21; Nova Scotia, ss. 27, 28(2); Ontario, s. 18; Saskatchewan, s. 22(1); Yukon, s. 22; Prince Edward Island, s. 26(1)(a) (Minister has the right to set terms and conditions with respect to payment, disposition, allotment or appointment of compensation); and Quebec, s. 16

52 Alberta, s. 17(1)(2); British Columbia, s. 20(3); Manitoba, s. 20(1); New Brunswick, s. 22(4); Newfoundland, s. 31(1)(2); Northwest Territories, s. 17(1)(2); Nova Scotia, s. 22(1)(2); Ontario, s. 25(1)(2); Saskatchewan, s. 27(1)(2); Yukon, s. 19(1)(2); Prince Edward Island, s. 30(1); and Quebec, s. 8.

53 Alberta, s. 13(1); Manitoba, s. 16(2); Northwest Territories, s. 14(1)(2); Nova Scotia, s. 18; Ontario, s. 4; and Yukon, s. 16(1)(2).

54 Compensation for Victims of Crime Act, New Brunswick, name changed from *Innocent Crime Victims Compensation Act*, 1973, c. 747.

55 Nova Scotia Criminal Injuries Compensation Board, *Annual Report for Fiscal Year April 1, 1988 to March 31, 1989*, 9.

56 Commission de la santé et de la sécurité du travail, *Direction de l'Indemnisation des Victimes d'Actes Criminels*, 1989, 9

57 The Criminal Injuries Compensation Board – Manitoba, *Information Manual*, 3(e)

58 Gunn and Minch (1988), 39: 'It is instructive to note that almost all respondents (87 percent) believed they were entirely or partly to blame for the offence.' See also Robin Warsaw, *I Never Called It Rape* (New York: Harper & Row, 1988).

59 For example, in 1988 only 45 of 129 hearings were for women's claims in Nova Scotia: *Annual Report for Fiscal Year April 1, 1988 to March 31, 1989*, 10. Although one could explain this discrepancy as simply reflective of the differential rate at which women are victimized by violence, one notes that both the absolute numbers and percentages of caseloads of sexual assault claims or awards vary widely from province to province. In some provinces these claims are infrequent: in Alberta 1988–9, of 293 claims that received a first hearing, 23 were for some

form of sexual assault: Crimes Compensation Board of Alberta, *Annual Report, March 31, 1989,* 13. In other provinces such as British Columbia, they accounted for 758 out of 1973 claims (excluding 379 claims for sexual touching!): *The 17th Annual Report of the Criminal Injury Compensation Act of British Columbia,* January 1–December 31, 1988, 8. Variation of this degree is not simply related to provincial differences in population size and offence rate. For instance, British Columbia has experienced significant yearly fluctuation in the percentage of rape claims, which suggests that there are other factors at play.

60 Alberta, s. 8(1); British Columbia, s. 4(1); Manitoba, s. 11(1); New Brunswick, s. 16(1); Newfoundland, s. 14(a); Northwest Territories, s. 20(1); Nova Scotia, s. 25(1); Ontario, s. 17(1); Saskatchewan, s. 11(a); Yukon, s. 5(2); Prince Edward Island, s. 23(1); Quebec, s. 20(b)

61 Manitoba, s. 11(1)

62 Commission de la santé et de la sécurité du travail, *Direction de l'Indemnisation des Victimes d'Actes Criminels,* 1989, Table 44.1, 16

63 *The 16th Annual Report of the Criminal Injury Compensation Act of British Columbia,* January 1–December 31, 1987, 13

64 Nova Scotia Criminal Injuries Compensation Board, *Annual Report for Fiscal Year April 1, 1988 to March 31, 1989,* file No. 4/88-843, 17

65 *The 15th Annual Report of the Criminal Injury Compensation Act of British Columbia,* January 1, 1986–December 31, 1986, file No. 867-66, 22

66 Commission de la santé et de la sécurité du travail, *Direction de l'Indemnisation des Victimes d'Actes Criminels,* 1988, file No. 9754-733, 30. See also a 1989 case, file No. 023-1404, 34.

67 See *Saskatchewan Criminal Injuries Compensation Board Fiscal Year End Report 1989–90,* file No. 2139/89, 27 wherein the victim was sexually assaulted after she had accepted a ride home with a man who had posed as a photographer and had asked to take photos of her. The victim was awarded $2367.50. Also see Compensation for Victims of Crime Act – Yukon, 20 July 1991, File No. 1989-12. The victim, who had lived common-law with the offender for several years, had been sexually abused by the latter for over a period of approximately six years. The board did not reduce her compensation award by finding that she had contributed to her own injuries in continuing to reside with the aggressor. Also in the Yukon, another claimant who had been sexually assaulted was not penalized for having lost consciousness as a result of drinking heavily. She was awarded a total of $9470.00. Compensation for the Victims of Crime Act – Yukon , 21 March 1990, File No. 1987-1.

68 *Dalton* v. *Criminal Injuries Compensation Board* (1982), 36 O.R. (2d) 394, 397, 398. See also *Foy* v. *Crimes Compensation Board of Saskatchewan* (1985), 44 Sask. R. 108 (C.A.) and *Lévesque* v. *Crimes Comp. Bd. (Sask.),* [1989] 6 W.W.R. 359, (Sask.

Q.B.) both Saskatchewan cases wherein judicial review was sought where female victims of assault were denied compensation on the grounds of their own 'fault.'

69 Alberta, s. 6(2); British Columbia, s. 8(3); Manitoba, s. 10(2); Newfoundland, s. 24(2); Northwest Territories, s. 10(1); Nova Scotia, s. 12(5); Ontario, s. 11; Yukon, s. 13(1); Prince Edward Island, s. 22(5); Quebec, s. 19; Saskatchewan, s. 21(2)

70 British Columbia, s. 8(1); Northwest Territories, s. 15(1); Nova Scotia, s. 20(1); Yukon, s. 17(1); Prince Edward Island, s. 22(4)

71 Commission de la santé et de la sécurité du travail, *Direction de l'Indemnisation des Victimes d'Actes Criminels,* 1989, 16

72 Manitoba Criminal Injuries Compensation Board, *Annual Report 1989–90,* 25

73 *The 17th Annual Report of the Criminal Injury Compensation Act of British Columbia,* January 1–December 31, 1988, file No. 870193, 19: 'According to police, claimant had been the source of a number of other similar stories all of which had been determined to be 'unfounded.' Claimant not considered to be a credible witness.' See also *The Third Report of the Nova Scotia Criminal Injuries Compensation Board,* January 1, 1983 to December 31, 1983, file No. 1/83-178: 'The Board secured the attendance of a police constable, who gave evidence that she was unable, as a result of numerous interviews with the applicant and witness, to convince herself that the rape complained of had actually taken place. The Board declined to make an order for compensation.'

74 The Criminal Injuries Compensation Board – Manitoba, *Information Manual,* 3(b)

75 *Re Flynn and Criminal Injuries Compensation Board* (1988), 49 D.L.R. (4th) 619 (N.S.C.A.). See also *Re MacDonald* (1975), 64 D.L.R. (3d) 755 (N.W.T.S.Ct.) (no requirement that conviction be entered before compensation awarded).

76 Alberta, s. 2(3)(b); Manitoba, s. 6(2)(b); New Brunswick, s. 15(1)(b); Newfoundland, s. 15(1)(b); Nova Scotia, s. 25(3); Ontario, s. 17(2); Saskatchewan, s. 12(1)(b)

77 See, for example, Manitoba where in 1989, 29 of 87 claims and in 1990, 40 of 79 claims were rejected for this reason: Manitoba Criminal Injuries Compensation Board, *Annual Report 1989–90,* 25.

78 Quebec, the Northwest Territories, P.E.I., and the Yukon do not require outright reporting although apparently failure to do so will be taken into account: see Yukon Workers' Compensation Board, *Survey Results,* 1989, 16.

79 Ibid., 17

80 For example, see New Brunswick, s. 15(1)(b.1).

81 Alberta, s. 8(2)(a); British Columbia, s. 18(2)(b); Manitoba, s. 11(2)(a); New Brunswick, s. 11(2); Nova Scotia, s. 25(2)(a); Yukon, s. 6(2)(a)

82 Gunn and Minch (1988), provide a higher figure of 27 per cent – see Table 2, Chapter 5.

83 For example, the Consultation Collective on Bill C-49 recognized the unequal

access to criminal justice experienced by aboriginal women and women of colour who have been raped: correspondence from Sheila McIntyre to Justice Minister Kim Campbell, 2 February 1992, and Preamble to *Proposed Amendments, Unanimously Endorsed*, January 28, 1992.

84 Clark and Lewis, 56. See also the low conviction rates cited by Temkin (1987), 15.

85 Newfoundland, s. 15(1)(c)

86 Manitoba, s. 17(2)

87 Nova Scotia, ss. 9(1), 10(1); Yukon, ss. 7(c), 9

88 New Brunswick, s. 6(c)

89 The Advisory Board on Victims' Issues has now reported to the attorney general on reform of the legislation: *Victims of Crime in Ontario: A Vision for the Nineties* (June 1991). Note that LEAF is involved in a Charter challenge to the 'victim fault' rule in a wife assault claim in Saskatchewan: see 'Woman Denied Full Compensation in Spousal Assault,' *Leaflines* 5 (March 1991), referring to *Lévesque* v. *Criminal Injuries Compensation Board*, [1989] 6 W.W.R 359 (Sask. Q.B.).

References

Backhouse, Constance. 1986. 'The Tort of Seduction: Fathers and Daughters in Nineteenth Century Canada.' *Dalhousie Law Journal* 10:45

Batt, Sharon. 1984. 'Our Civil Courts: Unused Classrooms for education about Rape.' In *Feminism Applied: Four Papers*. Ottawa: Canadian Research Institute for the Advancement of Women, 57, 62

Boyle, Christine. 1981. 'Married Women – Beyond the Pale of the Law of Rape.' *Windsor Yearbook of Access to Justice* 1:192

Bumiller, Kristin. 1987. 'Victims in the Shadow of the Law: A Critique of the Model of Legal Protection.' *Signs: A Journal of Women in Culture and Society* 12:421

Dawson, Brettel. 1984. 'Legal Structures: A Feminist Critique of Sexual Assault Reform.' *Resources for Feminist Research* 13(3):40

Duclos, Nitya. 1992. 'Disappearing Women: Racial Minority Women in Human Rights Cases.' *Canadian Journal of Women and the Law* 6:1

Finley, Lucinda M. 1987. 'A Break in the Silence: Including Women's Issues in a Torts Course.' *Yale Journal of Law and Feminism* 90:473

Freedman, Lisa. 1985. 'Civil Courts: A Powerful Tool for Education.' *Status of Women News* 10(3):12

Glasbeek, Harry J., and Reuben A. Hasson. 1977. 'The Great Hoax.' In Lewis Klar, ed., *Studies in Canadian Tort Law* Toronto: Butterworths, 395

Ison, Terence. 1967. *The Forensic Lottery*. London: Staples Press

MacKinnon, Catherine A. 1983. 'Feminism, Marxism, Method, and the State: Toward

Feminist Jurisprudence.' *Signs: A Journal of Women in Culture and Society* 8:635
Monture, Patricia A. 1989. 'A Vicious Circle: Child Welfare and the First Nations.'
  Canadian Journal of Women and the Law 3:1
Peterson, Cynthia. 1991. 'A Queer Response to Bashing: Legislating Against Hate.'
  Queen's Law Journal 16:237
Temkin, Jennifer. 1987. *Rape and the Legal Process.* London: Sweet and Maxwell, 8–11
West, Nora. 1992. 'Rape in the Criminal Law and the Victim's Tort Alternative: A
  Feminist Analysis.' *University of Toronto Faculty of Law Review* 50:96
Wright, Cecil A., Allen M. Linden, and Lewis N. Klar. 1985 *Canadian Tort Law.*
  Toronto: Butterworths, 3-1, 3-2, 3-3, 3-16

Cases Cited

A.K.M. v. *M.B.*, (22 June 1990) (Ont.Ct.J.)
B. (A.) v. *J. (I.)*, [1991] 5 W.W.R. 748 (Alta.Q.B.)
B. (K.L.). v. *B. (K.E.)*. (1991), 7 C.C.L.T.(2d) 105 (Man.Q.B.)
Beaudry v. *Hackett*, (28 June 1991) (B.C.S.C.)
C. (M.) v. *M. (F.)*, (17 September 1990) Action No. 323349/88 (Ont.Ct.J.)
Central Trust v. *Rafuse*, [1986] 2 S.C.R. 147
Dalton v. *Criminal Injuries Compensation Board* (1982), 36 O.R.(2d) 394 (H.C.J.)
D.T. and M.O. and F.A. (21 December 1990) No.1088/88 (S.C.B.C.)
G. v. *R.*, (3 January 1991) No.1088/88 (Vict.)
Gordon v. *Commissioner of Northwest Territories*, [1987] N.W.T.R. 180 (S.C.)
Gray v. *Reeves* (1992), 64 B.C.L.R.(2d) 275 (S.C.)
Harder v. *Brown* (1989), 50 C.C.L.T. 85 (B.C.S.C.)
Jane Doe v. *Metropolitan Toronto Police* (1990), 74 O.R.(2d) 225 (H.Ct.), appeal denied
  (1991), 1 O.R.(3d) 416 (C.A.)
Jane Doe v. *Awasis Agency of Northern Manitoba et al.* (1990), 72 D.L.R.(4th) 738
  (Man.Q.B.)
Kunz v. *Kunz, The Lawyer's Weekly*, 15 September 1989, 8
Lyth v. *Dagg* (1988), 46 C.C.L.T. 25 (B.C.S.C.)
M. (M.) v. *K. (K.)* (1987), 11 B.C.L.R.(2d) 90 (S.C.)
Marciano v. *Metzger*, (14 November 1989) (Ont.C.A.)
Murphy v. *Welsh* (1986), 33 D.L.R.(4th) 762 (Ont.H.C.J.)
Myers v. *Haroldson*, [1989] 3 W.W.R. 604 (Sask.Q.B.)
N. (J.L.) v. *L. (A.M.)*, [1989] 1 W.W.R. 438 (Man.Q.B.)
Norberg v. *Wynrib*, [1988] 6 W.W.R. 305 (B.C.S.C.), affirmed (1990), 44 B.C.L.R.(2d) 47
  (C.A.), reversed [1992] 4 W.W.R. 577 (S.C.C.)
Pie v. *Thibert* [1976] C.S. 180

Poholko v. *Criminal Injuries Compensation Board* (1983), 58 N.S.R.(2d) 18 (S.C.)

Q. et al. v. *Minto Management Ltd. et al.* (1985), 49 O.R.(2d) 537 (H.C.J.)

Rothwell v. *Raes* (1989), 59 D.L.R.(4th) 319 (Ont.H.C.J.)

S. v. *Mundy* (1969), [1970] O.R. 764 (Co.Ct.)

Storrie v. *Newman and Insurance Corporation of British Columbia* (1982), 39 B.C.L.R. 376 (S.C.)

10

ADELYN L. BOWLAND

Sexual Assault Trials and the Protection of 'Bad Girls': The Battle between the Courts and Parliament

In August 1991, the Supreme Court of Canada struck down a law directed at reducing the trauma for complainants testifying in sexual assault trials.[1] This provision, part of the 1983 amendments to the Criminal Code (see Chapter 1), was one of two provisions designed to limit the admissibility of evidence of the sexual history of the complainant. In the Seaboyer *decision, the highest court in the country struck down the law restricting the admission at trial of evidence of the sexual conduct of the complainant with named parties other than the accused. The reason was that in the opinion of the majority, this provision limited the right of the accused to a fair trial as required by the Canadian Charter of Rights and Freedoms.[2] In this chapter, Adelyn Bowland discusses the strengths and limitations of past and present rules regarding the relevance and admissibility of a complainant's sexual history.*

By the time *Seaboyer* was before the Supreme Court of Canada, Parliament had twice changed the rules regarding evidence of a woman's sexual history: in 1976 and 1983. In 1976, Parliament first recognized that the common law rules then in place made testifying in sexual assault cases extremely hard for complainants. Unfortunately, when the Supreme Court of Canada dealt with this provision in 1980 and 1983,[3] it interpreted the provision so that the situation for women in court was worse than it had been under the old common law rules. The 1983 amendments were passed to overcome these decisions of the Supreme Court of Canada.

Thus, the *Seaboyer* case was the third opportunity the Supreme Court of Canada has had to interpret provisions limiting the evidence of a complainant's sexual history. For a third time, this court gave a decision with a particularly negative impact upon sexual assault complainants and upon women.

242 Confronting Sexual Assault

As a result of the *Seaboyer* decision, the position of complainants in sexual assault cases was worse than it had ever been. From the perspective of complainants and of women, this decision made the old common law rules regarding sexual history look good in retrospect.

Culminating with the recent passage of Bill C-49, the evidentiary rules regarding sexual character evidence in sexual assault trials have been the subject of a battle between the courts and Parliament since 1976. Parliament said all women should be protected from sexual assault; the courts replied: no, not 'bad girls.' In this chapter, I will examine the *Seaboyer* decision in the context of this battle and the resulting development of the law defining the role of sexual character evidence in sexual assault trials. As part of this analysis, I will analyse how Bill C-49 will reduce the damage caused by the *Seaboyer* decision. Rather than refer to the provisions as 'rape shield laws,' since the provisions did not shield women from rape, I will use the term 'sexual character provisions.' The evidence relates to the complainant's character and is sexual in nature. I will begin by reviewing the history of the sexual character rules.

The Previous Rules Regarding Sexual Character Evidence

THE COMMON LAW RULES

The sexual character rules developed parallel to the rule regarding general character evidence in criminal matters. In the common (or judge-made) law, there were two types of evidence concerning the complainant's sexual character: evidence of the complainant's *sexual reputation* and evidence of the complainant's *sexual conduct*. Sexual reputation evidence referred to a reputation for prostitution and/or promiscuity, while evidence of sexual conduct was divided into conduct involving the accused and conduct involving men other than the accused.

The early common law rules regarding character evidence of a witness other than the accused made three distinctions between offences of sexual aggression and other criminal offences. First, in all offences except rape, evidence of the general character of a Crown witness was relevant to the credibility of that witness, not to the guilt of the accused. Second, the *sexual* character of a witness was relevant to his or her credibility only where the witness was the female victim of an offence involving sexual aggression; victims in early sexual assault law were always female.[4] Finally, there was a special rule with regard to sexual offences that permitted the sexual character of the victim to define the guilt of the accused, that is, *whether there was, indeed, a sexual assault*. If a woman had a reputation as a prostitute, her consent to sex with the accused was presumed and there could be, in law, no sexual assault. The same was true if she had engaged in previous sexual activity with the accused.[5]

The defence could ask the victim of sexual assault all manner of questions regarding her sexual character; these questions could range from specific instances of the victim's sexual activity to her reputation for prostitution and sexual activity. But after that point in the trial process, the rules were different regarding the two types of evidence of sexual character.[6]

All evidence of the complainant's sexual character was relevant to her credibility in early English and Canadian law. The sustaining question in cases dealing with rape from the early nineteen century under the common law rules was which evidence of the complainant's sexual character was also relevant to consent.[7] If evidence went only to a complainant's credibility, then the rule with regard to general character evidence applied; that is, the defence could not call witnesses to contradict the complainant. From early rape cases, there was also a restriction that in matters regarding the credibility of the complainant, the judge had discretion to order that the complainant need not answer the question put to her by the defence. If the evidence went to consent, however, the complainant had to answer the question and the defence could lead independent evidence to contradict a complainant who denied particular sexual experience. Thus the distinction between the two types of evidence was crucial.[8]

In the development of the common law in nineteenth- and twentieth-century England and Canada, rarely were issues relating to sexual character formally addressed and even more rarely were they addressed by the appeal courts.[9] With regard to specific instances of sexual activity involving the complainant *and the accused*, the principle was clear: it was relevant to consent.[10] But the evidence of sexual conduct involving the complainant and third parties gave the courts some problems.

The question of which sexual activity evidence went to consent was contested such that English appeal courts considered it twice, in 1812 and 1871. The principle stated in both these cases was that a complainant need not answer questions regarding specific instances of sexual activity involving her and third parties nor could evidence be called on this issue.[11] In commenting on this restriction in 1887, Lord Coleridge, Chief Justice of the Court of Queen's Bench, indicated, in *Riley*, that to allow evidence regarding specific instances of a complainant's sexual conduct with men other than the accused would 'be unfair and a hardship to the woman ... the result of admitting such evidence would be to deprive an unchaste woman of any protection against assaults of this nature.'[12] Moreover, in *Holmes*, Kelly, Chief Baron, stated:

If such evidence ... were admitted, the whole history of the prosecutrix's life might be gone into; if a charge might be made as to one man, it might be made as to fifty, and that without notice to the prosecutrix. It would not only involve a multitude of collateral issues, but an inquiry into matters as to which the prosecutrix might be wholly unprepared, and so work great injustice.[13]

This was the law in Canada, too, followed by the Supreme Court of Canada in the 1877 case of *Laliberté*. Not until 1969 did an English court permit the admission of evidence of a complainant's sexual conduct. It was a trial level court, however, so it did not set a precedent, and the conduct involved acts of prostitution only.[14]

In spite of the fact that reputation evidence is based on hearsay, gossip, and innuendo, early English appeal courts found some evidence of sexual reputation relevant to consent. However, only in *obiter* (that issue was not before the court and therefore this statement held very little weight as an authority for that proposition) did the early English appeal courts deal with the question of reputation evidence of prostitution. In these two cases, it was stated that the defence could call reputation evidence of the complainant's prostitution.[15]

With regard to reputation evidence of 'unchastity,' in two nineteenth-century decisions of the English appeal courts, this evidence was disallowed.[16] It seems that as women became freer sexually, some of the early English trial courts strained to expand the scope of the rule relating to evidence of sexual reputation, to include a reputation for 'promiscuity.' But it would appear that not until 1973 did an English appeal court endorse this approach.[17] This issue has never been settled by the Supreme Court of Canada.[18]

Thus, in the early English decisions, there were few authorities with regard to evidence of the complainant's sexual character. Clearly, evidence of sexual conduct involving the complainant and the accused was admissible. But when the appeal courts permitted reputation evidence, they did so only in *obiter*, referring solely to prostitution. Although in the twentieth century courts began to allow in more types of sexual character evidence, the expansion of the definition of reputation evidence to include 'promiscuity' did not occur, in England, until 1973. While sexual conduct evidence involving prostitution was permitted in 1969, this was pursuant to an English trial level decision, which did not set a precedent.

By the twentieth century, according to the appeal courts of England and Canada, the following was admissible: evidence of sexual conduct involving the complainant and the accused as well as evidence of the complainant's sexual reputation for prostitution and 'promiscuity.' Yet the common law rules provided *some* protection to sexually experienced women, or in patriarchal terms, 'bad girls.' *Evidence of sexual conduct involving the complainant and third parties was not admissible because of the hardship this would cause to the complainant, the effect it would have on the administration of justice, and the resulting lack of protection for women with sexual experience.*

THE 1976 STATUTORY PROVISIONS

In the early 1970s, many feminists, particularly in North America, argued that the common law evidentiary provisions regarding sexual offences were unfair to women. Objections were also voiced within the traditional legal community: In 1971, the Evidence Project of the Law Reform Commission of Canada found that the common law did not afford sufficient protection to complainants and because of this many rapes were not reported and prosecuted; it thus recommended an amendment to the Criminal Code to prohibit evidence regarding the complainant's sexual conduct with men other than the accused, whether through questioning of the complainant or other witnesses, including the accused. A judge of the Ontario Supreme Court as well as an assistant Crown attorney in Ontario echoed these concerns.[19]

In 1976, Parliament responded by amending s. 142 of the Criminal Code. The 1976 provision started with a prohibition ('No question shall be asked ... as to the sexual conduct of the complainant') and permitted the judge a very broad discretion: The judge should admit evidence if, considering its weight, its exclusion would prevent the making of a just determination of an 'issue of fact, including the credibility of the complainant.'[20]

Contrary to Parliament's intention, the lower courts and the Supreme Court of Canada interpreted this provision to expand the rights of the accused compared with the common law rules. As a result, it was still the case that the judicial process could be almost as agonizing to a victim of sexual assault as the offence itself.[21]

Analysing this state of affairs in her dissent in *Konkin*, Wilson J. stated that rather than minimizing the embarrassment to complainants, the 1976 legislation (s. 142) increased it. First, she pointed out that under the common law, the accused could not ask questions regarding the sexual activities and reputation of the complainant after the time of the offence. Under s. 142 these inquiries could be made.[22] In addition, with regard to specific sexual activities of the complainant with third parties, under the common law, the accused had the right only to *ask questions* and did not have the right to expect answers. In contrast, under s. 142, the complainant had to answer all questions of this nature in the *voire dire*. The purpose of the *voire dire* was to

246 Confronting Sexual Assault

permit the judge to decide whether the accused could pursue these questions before the trier of fact (judge or jury) and whether the accused could lead evidence to rebut the denials of the complainant.[23]

Even the procedural protections of s. 142 were minimized. The defendant had to make an application to the court to admit this evidence, on reasonable notice to the Crown; in one case, the Ontario Provincial Court allowed the defence to make an application to introduce this evidence where notice to the Crown was given on the afternoon of the day before the 10 A.M. hearing. In addition, the courts (including the Supreme Court of Canada, in *Forsythe*) found that the defendant had the right to call the complainant as *his* witness, thus forcing her to testify twice, at the s. 142 hearing and at trial.[24]

At all levels, courts took the 1976 provision, designed to improve upon the common rules, and made the ordeal of testifying in sexual assault trials even worse for complainants than it had been under the common law rules. As a result, the credibility of sexually experienced women was dramatically reduced and the law could offer little protection to these women if they were sexually assaulted. 'Bad girls' were on their own.

THE 1983 STATUTORY PROVISIONS

When Parliament responded to the failure of the 1976 amendment to fulfil its purpose, it did so in the context of a complete overhaul of the law governing sexual offences; both the substantive and procedural laws governing these offences were significantly revised.[25] In contrast to the earlier legislation, which referred to the 'sexual conduct of the complainant,' the 1983 provisions were more specific and divided sexual character evidence into two types: 'sexual activity of the complainant with any person other than the accused' (formerly s. 276) and 'evidence of sexual reputation, whether general or specific' relating to the complainant (s. 277).

The distinction between the two types of sexual character evidence is important historically. As noted above, the common law rules restricted the rights of the accused far more where the evidence related to specific incidents between the complainant and a third party, in contrast to reputation evidence. The 1983 legislation left in place the common law rule permitting evidence of sexual conduct involving the complainant and the accused.

The relevant part of section 276 stated:

(1)   In proceedings in respect of an offence under section 271, 272 or 273 (sexual assault), no evidence shall be adduced by or on behalf of the accused concerning the sexual activity of the complainant with any person other than the accused unless

(a) it is evidence that rebuts evidence of the complainant's sexual activity or absence thereof that was previously adduced by the prosecution;

(b) it is evidence of specific instances of the complainant's sexual activity tending to establish the identity of the person who had sexual contact with the complainant on the occasion set out in the charge; or

(c) it is evidence of sexual activity that took place on the same occasion as the sexual activity that forms the subject-matter of the charge, where that evidence relates to the consent that the accused alleges he believed was given by the complainant.[26]

This is the provision that was struck down by the Supreme Court of Canada. It *expanded* the common law rights of the accused. The common law gave the accused no right to even expect answers to questions of the complainant regarding her sexual activities with named third parties, let alone call witnesses to describe specific sexual activities they had engaged in with the complainant.

Section 276 *required* that a judge permit questioning of the complainant and allow the accused to introduce evidence in three specific situations: to rebut claims made by the complainant in her testimony, to establish the identity of the person who committed the sexual assault, and to set up the defence of mistaken belief as to the complainant's consent if the evidence was of sexual activity that took place on the same occasion as the alleged sexual assault. The exclusionary scope of the general rule in s. 276 extended to all purposes of the evidence; that is, evidence of specific sexual acts involving the complainant and third parties was equally restricted, no matter what defence the accused was claiming. However, by means of three exceptions to the general rule of admissibility, the legislation addressed the purpose of the evidence where it related to the issues set out in the exceptions.

On the other hand, s. 277, still in place, limits the introduction of evidence of sexual reputation only with regard to credibility. In addition, it applies to both defence and Crown in that the evidence of a complainant's sexual reputation is not admissible for the purpose of challenging or supporting the credibility of the complainant. Section 276 applied only to the defence. In further contrast to section 276, section 277 restricted the common law rights of the accused. Section 277 states:

In proceedings in respect of an offence under section 271, 272 or 273 (sexual assault), evidence of sexual reputation, whether general or specific, is not admissible for the purposes of challenging or supporting the credibility of the complainant.[27]

Thus, the structure of the rules was very different. This structural difference, along with the use of a separate rule for each type of sexual character evidence and the different manner of referring to the purpose of the evidence, proved to be important in the ruling of the court.

The *Seaboyer* Decision

THE COURT'S REASONING

The court first had to decide whether the sexual history provisions breached sections 7 and 11(d) of the Charter. Section 11(d) is a type of section 7 right.[28] These provisions state:

7. Everyone has the right to life, liberty and security of the person and the right not to be deprived thereof except in accordance with the principles of fundamental justice.

11. Any person charged with an offence has the right

(d) to be presumed innocent until proven guilty according to law in a fair and public hearing by an independent and impartial tribunal.

In arriving at their decision, the majority of the Supreme Court of Canada focused on three issues in traditional legal doctrine; these issues provided the terms of reference for the outcome and, in some ways, dictated the result. First, the bottom line principle in criminal law is that the innocent should not be convicted. Second, they upheld the traditional authority of the judge to exercise discretion in deciding what evidence is relevant. Finally, they considered the nature of 'relevant' evidence of the complainant's sexual character.

Convicting the Innocent

The interest in preventing the punishment of the innocent is not merely individual (that of the accused), but also societal, since 'no just society can tolerate the conviction and punishment of the innocent,' according to McLachlin J. for the majority. This is the starting point of the decision.[29] This fundamental principle requires that the accused have the right to present full answer and defence: it requires that *the defendant have the right to call the evidence necessary to establish a defence and to challenge the evidence called by the prosecution.* A denial of this right constitutes the denial of the right to rely on a defence to which the law says the accused is entitled. From this principle flows the entire decision. Anything which, in the opinion of the majority, unnecessarily blocks the defendant's right in this regard is unacceptable.[30]

Judicial Discretion to Admit Evidence

A second concern was the judicial discretion to admit evidence. This is a cornerstone of Commonwealth and United States law, although some rules limit this discretion on the grounds of policy or of law. Nevertheless, the majority indicated that these rules are becoming far more flexible, so that judicial discretion has actually increased in the last few years. For this reason, the rigid limitation on judicial discretion provided in section 276 was all the more unacceptable. In the opinion of the majority, it is impossible to predict relevance in advance by a series of rules or categories; judges must have sufficient latitude to determine relevance in each individual case.[31]

Relevant Evidence of the Complainant's Sexual Character

The final guiding principle was the traditional notion of relevance. Based on this, the court made a judgment of whether sections 276 and 277 prohibited relevant evidence of a complainant's sexual character.

The majority dealt little with the definition of relevance, except to quote from an American author: 'Relevant evidence ... is evidence that in some degree *advances the inquiry*, and thus has probative value.'[32] The focus was the purpose for which evidence is introduced, since it forms the basis on which relevance is decided; relevance must be determined in relation to some issue in the trial.[33] Rather than state general principles regarding evidence of sexual character, the court dealt with sections 276 and 277 separately. Evidence of sexual conduct was governed by 276 and evidence of sexual reputation, by section 277.[34]

Dealing with section 276, the court cited several examples of relevant evidence of the complainant's sexual conduct that would be excluded under section 276. Moreover, this evidence has evidentiary value that is not clearly outweighed by the danger it presents to the trial process. Therefore, section 276 breached sections 7 and 11(d) of the Charter.[35] As the court saw it, unlike section 277, the general rule in section 276 did not restrict evidence of sexual history based on the purpose of the evidence; that was the first problem in the legislation. The court went on to say:

While there is some concession to the need to permit evidence of sexual activity for legitimate purposes, the exceptions exclude other purposes where the evidence would not be merely misleading, but truly relevant and helpful.[36]

When the court looked at section 277, it focused on the fact that this provision restricts sexual reputation evidence based on the purpose for which it is adduced. Section 277 says that evidence of a complainant's sexual reputation cannot be used to attack or support her credibility. Since the court agreed that this purpose is illegitimate, without qualification, section 277 is constitutional.[37] Section 277 passed constitutional muster; but because the court decided that section 276 breached the Charter, it next had to consider whether that provision was saved by section 1 of the Charter.

Striking Down Section 276

Legislation that breaches a substantive provision of the Charter may be saved by section 1 of the Charter if social interests require that the Charter guarantees be set aside; thus, social interests may justify an otherwise unconstitutional law. In criminal matters, a balancing of the interests of the accused and society is required at this stage. The text of section 1 is as follows:

The Canadian Charter of Rights and Freedoms guarantees the rights and freedoms set out in it subject only to such reasonable limits prescribed by law as can be demonstrably justified in a free and democratic society.

The majority review of section 1 was brief, a mere two pages. The court first considered the purpose of the legislation in question. The majority defined the purposes of the legislation as follows: to preserve the integrity of the trial by eliminating evidence that has little or no relevance but prejudices judges or juries against the complainant, to minimize the invasion of the complainant's privacy, and to encourage victims of sexual assault to report. They said these purposes are laudable.[38] But the *effect* of the provision is to exclude relevant defence evidence having value that outweighs its potential prejudice. Therefore, the purposes are not so important that section 276 could be saved by section 1 of the Charter; these purposes cannot prevail over the risk that an innocent person may be convicted. Section 276 'strikes the wrong balance between the rights of complainants and the rights of the accused.'[39] At the same time, the court said clearly that evidence of the complainant's sexual conduct should not be introduced to prove the complainant's consent or attack her credibility. This is an illegitimate purpose.[40]

NEW GUIDELINES FOR THE ADMISSION OF SEXUAL CHARACTER
EVIDENCE

Recognizing that in the absence of section 276, there was no law to govern
evidence of the complainant's sexual conduct, the court devised the following
guidelines:

1 As a general rule, evidence that the complainant has engaged in consensual
   sexual conduct on other occasions with anyone, including the accused, is
   not admissible for the purpose of inferring that the complainant is more
   likely to have consented to the sexual conduct at issue in the trial or less
   worthy of belief as a witness.
2 However, this type of evidence may be admitted 'for purposes other than
   an inference relating to the consent or credibility of the complainant where
   it possesses probative value on an issue in the trial and ... that ... value is
   not substantially outweighed by the danger of unfair prejudice flowing
   from the evidence.'
3 The following are *examples* of admissible evidence, but do not limit other
   possible instances of admissible evidence. Evidence relating to:
   a. the identity of the assailant and the physical consequences of the assault;
   b. the complainant's bias or motive to fabricate;
   c. the defendant's honest belief in the complainant's consent;
   d. the reception of similar act evidence; that is, evidence of past sexual con-
      duct of the complainant which is similar enough to the facts as the
      accused paints them to lend credibility to the accused;
   e. rebuttal of proof introduced by the prosecution regarding the complain-
      ant's sexual conduct[41]

   In addition, the court stated that where a jury is present, the judge should
remind them not to allow the allegations of past sexual activity to lead them
to see the complainant as less worthy of credibility and more likely to consent to sex.[42]

REDUCING THE PROECTION OF COMPLAINANTS

The most important impact of the *Seaboyer* decision is the reduction of the
protection of complainants such that their position is dramatically worse than
it was at common law. The decision did not merely strike down section 276
and return the state of the law that existed under the old common law rules

regarding sexual assault trials. *It removed even the protections provided by the common law rules.* These old rules absolutely prohibited any evidence regarding specific incidents of sexual relations between the complainant and men other than the accused. The *Seaboyer* decision provides no such restriction. On the contrary, the discretion of judges to allow in evidence regarding a complainant's sexual history is limited only by section 277, that is, the prohibition of reputation evidence introduced for the purpose of attacking the complainant's credibility. Thus, from the point of view of complainants in sexual assault cases, the news was bad.

Through the back door, *Seaboyer* reinstated the assumptions underlying the early common law rules: a sexually experienced woman is more likely to consent to sexual activity; a sexually experienced woman is less likely to tell the truth under oath; and the implied corollary of this, that only 'chaste' women are entitled to protection from sexual assault.[43] While disclaiming any support for these assumptions, the court made way for them to take the most prominent position they have had in legal history. At the same time, the court removed the limitations on sexual character evidence, and consequent protection for complainants, which the old common law rules provided.

Under the common law rules, the accused was limited in the witnesses he could call regarding the sexual history of the complainant with third parties; only with regard to the complainant's sexual reputation could he call witnesses regarding a woman's sexual experience with third parties. The *Seaboyer* decision permits him to call witnesses to describe their personal sexual experience with the complainant; what they did and when. Although the *Seaboyer* decision prohibits the use of evidence of a complainant's sexual conduct for the purpose of attacking her credibility or to prove she consented, it makes this evidence admissible to support a defendant's defence that he *believed* the complainant consented. So while, supposedly, the law does not allow the past sexual behaviour of a complainant to be used to indicate a propensity to engage in sex or a type of sex, it allows an accused to believe in this propensity and use it as a defence.

Moreover, the *Seaboyer* decision permits evidence of a complainant's sexual conduct to show her propensity to have sex through its enunciation of the application of the similar fact evidence rule. With regard to similar fact (or act) evidence of the complainant's sexual conduct, the court gave the example of a woman who is a prostitute and has on other occasions forced a man to pay her more than the agreed-upon fee after sexual activity between them by threatening him with a charge of sexual assault. The court found that section

276 would have excluded this type of evidence supporting the man's defence that there was a modus operandi of the complainant which she used against him, as well.[44] In the view of the majority, the law

now permits evidence of similar prior acts, *notwithstanding the inference of disposition or character which may drawn from them,* provided their relevance to a specific feature of the case outweighs their prejudicial value.[45]

Extortion is one thing, but ordinarily, as Madam Justice L'Heureux-Dubé points out in her dissent in *Seaboyer,* consent is to a particular person at a particular time, not to a circumstance.[46] Have courts fallen for the argument that 'women consent to sex based upon such extraneous considerations as the location of the act, the race, age or profession of the alleged assaulter and/or considerations of the nature of the sexual act engaged in'?[47] It was precisely these sorts of arguments which one of the defendants in the *Seaboyer* case wished to make, and the gates were wide open for other defendants.[48] According to L'Heureux-Dubé, these arguments are 'implicitly based upon the notion that women will, in the right circumstances, consent to anyone and, more fundamentally that "unchaste" women have a propensity to consent.'[49] None of this evidence would have been admitted under the common law rules.

What does this decision mean with regard to the two other types of evidence: evidence of sexual conduct involving the complainant and the accused and reputation evidence of the complainant's sexual experience?

Seaboyer means that all evidence of *sexual conduct* involving the complainant is to be judged on the same basis: is it relevant? No longer does the accused have the automatic right to introduce evidence of sexual relations between him and the complainant, as he did under the common law and under the 1976 and 1983 provisions. Nevertheless, relevance is to be judged on a patriarchal basis.

On the other hand, with regard to *reputation* evidence of the complainant's sexual character, the decision appears to leave in place two separate rules. Section 277 only restricts the defence's use of sexual reputation evidence in order to attack a complainant's credibility. Since the court found this provision to be acceptable, it did not consider other purposes for which evidence of the complainant's sexual reputation might be used. But the common law permits sexual reputation evidence to be introduced for the purpose of proving a complainant's consent. Thus, *Seaboyer* leaves open the question of whether the defence could introduce sexual reputation evidence for purposes other than that prohibited by section 277; not only the complainant's consent but also, for example, the defendant's belief in the complainant's consent.

All in all, the *Seaboyer* decision left complainants in sexual assault trials in a very disadvantaged position. They had no way of predicting what they would have to endure at trial, and very limited formal protection from the unfair use of evidence regarding their sexual character. In the year between the *Seaboyer* decision and Bill C-49, the rights of complainants were at the pleasure of judges and juries. 'Bad girls' were again on their own.

INTERPRETING SEXUAL ASSAULT LAW OUT OF CONTEXT

In making the decision on two occasions, in 1976 and 1983, to pass legislation protecting complainants from harassment during sexual assault trials, Parliament considered social science evidence as well as submissions by community, interest, and professional groups and recommendations of the Law Reform Commission of Canada. Parliament viewed the law in the context of sexual assault as a social problem and also in relation to women's equality, even though the 1976 amendment was made before the Charter became law. In addition, in 1983, it considered the history of the laws dealing with sexual assault and the manner in which the courts had interpreted section 142.[50]

Thus, Parliament did not consider the law governing sexual assault merely as a matter of legal doctrine. Rather it saw sexual assault as a pervasive social problem for which the criminal justice system was almost completely inadequate. It was not only the legislation that was the issue, but also the judicial interpretation of the legislation.[51] In contrast, the majority of the Supreme Court of Canada judges did not cloud their minds with the issue of context when they decided to strike down the sexual character provision. Rather, they relied on narrow interpretations of legal doctrine to justify their decision. In doing this, the court ignored its mandate under the *Charter* to consider the law in its social and political context, particularly with regard to section 15 which guarantees equality rights to women.[52]

Context and the Charter

It is not only section 1 of the Charter that requires the consideration of social context. The very decisions of the Supreme Court of Canada indicate that sections 7 and 11 of the Charter require reference to societal interests, not just the interests of the accused.[53] While the *Seaboyer* majority briefly acknowledged this, they saw society's interest in a fair trial for the accused as the main societal interest; for them the right of the accused to a fair trial is paramount. Therefore, the parliamentary goals of the legislation are comparatively lesser considerations. The societal interest stacked up on the side of the accused.[54]

The court could have considered the effect of section 15 of the Charter and its implications for the interpretation of sections 7 and ll(d); this it failed to do. Because of the submissions of the Women's Legal Education and Action Fund, the court was aware that almost all the accused are men and the vast majority of those assaulted are female, whether adult or child; however, it failed to make the connection between that fact and the implications of sexual assault law for the equality of women.

In fact, it almost completely failed to consider the social science evidence placed before it with regard to the problem of sexual assault. True, it did acknowledge that juries tend to be biased against complainants who are sexually experienced.[55] It had no evidence that the perceptions of judges are any different. But, in the end, that did not seem to particularly trouble the majority. Even as they admitted that it would be the rare case where the sexual history of a complainant would be relevant in the trial of an alleged sexual assault, they constructed guidelines that opened the evidentiary gates wide for the harassment of complainants in sexual assault trials to an unprecedented degree.[56]

Relevance, Context, and Perspective

Whether evidence is relevant is the first question in the decision of whether to admit the evidence. If evidence is relevant, the next question is whether it is excluded due to some evidentiary rule and, if not, whether the prejudicial effect of the evidence outweighs it probative value. The court said there should be only one, very limited, special exclusionary rule regarding sexual character evidence, as stated in section 277.

The evaluation of the prejudicial effect and probative value of sexual character evidence is strongly affected by the values informing the judgment of whether the evidence is relevant in the first place. These values provide the context in which the actions of women and men are interpreted. But in *Seaboyer*, the majority of the Supreme Court of Canada saw concepts of relevance as timeless, neutral, and unrelated to their historical context or the ideology that is dominant in legal theory.

Moreover, the court said there is a presumption in favour of permitting the defendant to introduce all relevant evidence; the burden of proving prejudicial effect is thus far greater where the Crown opposes the introduction of defence evidence. The prejudice caused by Crown evidence is considered to have a more negative effect on the trial process than that caused by defence evidence.[57]

The court's failure to consider the ideological context of the rules regarding sexual character evidence is particularly troubling because by the time the court heard *Seaboyer*, it had begun to see evidentiary law in a much less 'rationalist' way, to consider the context of evidentiary rules as well as differing perspectives on the facts.[58] For example, in *Lavallée*, a decision made before *Seaboyer*, the Supreme Court of Canada pointed out that there is 'popular mythology about domestic violence.'[59] It has not recognized that there is a popular mythology (patriarchal) about sexual assault: that women lie about sexual assault; if a woman is *really* sexually assaulted, she will immediately raise a 'hue and cry'; women would fabricate evidence of similar sexual assaults committed by an accused in order to frame him through the use of similar fact evidence; a woman has a propensity to consent to sex if she is 'unchaste' and a propensity to make false claims of sexual assault, as well. Now these assumptions are not openly expressed; they merely form the implicit backdrop of legal reasoning about relevance.[60] In the 1991 case of *L. (W.K.)*, decided just before *Seaboyer*, the Supreme Court of Canada rejected the 'hue and cry' assumption; and it claimed to face the assumptions regarding the credibility of 'unchaste' complainants in sexual assault cases in the *Seaboyer* case.[61] Yet the majority in *Seaboyer* failed to see these assumptions as part of a constellation of views regarding women and sexuality that affects notions of relevance in sexual assault trials.[62] The court did not acknowledge that there is more than one way to see sexual relationships between women and men or that legal theory regarding sexual assault is dominated by patriarchal ideology.

While many men and women still hold the patriarchal view of sexual relations, they are aware that there is another view of women, an egalitarian paradigm that promotes a single standard of sexuality for women and men. This is the paradigm that Parliament was attempting to support when it passed the evidentiary provisions of 1976 and 1983. The equality guarantees in the Charter were intended to foster this perception of the women. Unfortunately, the patriarchal view of sexual relations has dominated the decisions of the Supreme Court of Canada with respect to the protection of 'bad girls.' The very decisions of the Supreme Court of Canada regarding sexual character evidence show the problem Parliament was trying to address: judges do not consistently consider the interests of women who complain of sexual offences.

No More Protection for 'Bad Girls'

Women fought hard and long for the amendments to the Criminal Code regarding sexual character; much that was gained by this fight was wiped out by the *Seaboyer* decision. In addition to reducing the legal rights of complainants in sexual abuse and sexual assault trials, the decision was bad news for women, generally, since it struck a blow against more egalitarian sexual relations between women and men.

Because of this decision, most women lost the right to the protection of the law when they were sexually assaulted. The vast majority of Canadian women are 'bad girls' or reputed to be 'bad girls.' Pursuant to *Seaboyer*, the right to legal redress in the criminal justice system following sexual assault was, in effect, contingent on the sexual character of the complainant (real or imagined) or rumours about her sexual character.

From August 1991, until Bill C-49 came into force, in August 1992,[63] women attempting to use the criminal justice system following their sexual assault could only hope that if their case actually reached the trial stage, they would have a sympathetic judge (and jury) at the trial. The *Seaboyer* case so dramatically reduced the scope and effect of the law regarding sexual assault and child sexual abuse that only virgins and those reputed to be virgins or matrons who were 'chaste' and reputed to be 'chaste' before marriage could expect a fair hearing when they were the complainant in a sexual assault trial. This was not an acceptable state of affairs.

Bill C-49: Parliament Tries Again

A third time, in 1992, Parliament reacted to the judicial negation of legislation governing sexual character evidence in sexual assault trials. Bill C-49 was designed to reduce to a *minimum* the occasions on which evidence of a complainant's sexual character will be relevant in sexual assault trials. Using a combination of substantive and procedural rules, the bill is a detailed set of instructions to the courts.

SUBSTANTIVE PROVISIONS

Ensuring the Rights of Complainants Are Respected

The preamble to Bill C-49 addresses the problem of context in the *Seaboyer* decision. In order to ensure that the courts consider the rights of the complainant as well as the gender equality rights set out in section 15 of the Charter, the preamble requires that the bill be interpreted in the light of these rights. Moreover, the courts are instructed to be cautious in admitting evidence of the complainant's sexual history because it is rarely relevant and inherently prejudicial in sexual assault trials. Included for more emphasis is the purpose of the legislation: Parliament is concerned about the incidence of sexual violence against women and children and wishes to encourage the reporting of incidents of sexual violence or abuse and provide for the prosecution of these offences.

Consent Defined

Consent has only been defined in the negative in the Criminal Code. Now, in section 273.1, it is defined in a positive way with examples of non-consent which are not exhaustive. In relation to the effect of the *Seaboyer* decision, the most important aspect of the definition of consent is that it *requires the voluntary agreement of the complainant to engage in the sexual activity* in question at the trial. There is no consent where the complainant expresses by words *or conduct* her lack of agreement and, in addition, a woman can express a lack of agreement to continue in sexual activity after her initial consent. This expresses the principle stated by L'Heureux-Dubé, in dissent, in *Seaboyer* that consent is to a person, at a specific time and to a specific activity; it is not a generalized consent to a particular man, types of men, or sexual activity.

This provision should have the effect of limiting the occasions on which sexual character evidence would be relevant. What is important is the agreement between the accused and the complainant at the time of the sexual activity in question at trial, not the complainant's sex life or gossip about her sex life.

The Defence of Belief in Consent

The defence of belief in consent has also been amended. Pursuant to section 273.2, the accused must take 'reasonable steps' to ascertain that the complainant is consenting. In addition, the accused must show grounds for his interpretation of the woman's behaviour as consent by referring to her conduct *at the time of the encounter in question*. Thus an accused now has to show he took reasonable steps to find out whether a woman was consenting and then he must base his judgment as to her consent solely on the woman's behaviour at the time. This provision, combined with s. 273.1, will remove, or at least considerably reduce, occasions on which the accused could claim belief in consent based on his knowledge of the sexual history of the complainant. This would apply to evidence of both sexual reputation and sexual conduct of the complainant.

Evidence of Sexual Conduct

With regard to evidence of the complainant's sexual conduct, in the new section 276, the bill repeats the *Seaboyer* principle that evidence of the complainant's sexual conduct is not admissible to support an inference of her propensity to consent or to reduce her credibility. A defendant trying to use this evidence must show that specific instances of sexual activity are relevant to a particular issue at trial and that the evidence 'has significant probative value that is not substantially outweighed by the danger of prejudice to the proper administration of justice.' To ensure the rights of complainants, the bill indicates that in exercising its discretion to weigh probative value against prejudice, the court must consider:

society's interest in encouraging the reporting of sexual assault offences; whether there is a reasonable prospect that the evidence will assist in arriving at a just determination of the case; the need to remove from the fact-finding process any discriminatory belief or bias; the risk that the evidence may unduly arouse sentiments of prejudice, sympathy or hostility in the jury; the potential prejudice to the complainant's personal dignity and right of privacy; and the right of the complainant ... to personal security and to the full protection and benefit of the law.'

These factors, along with the preamble, definition of consent, and the limits on the defence of belief in consent, should substantially reduce the occasions on which sexual character evidence is admitted and minimize the negative impact of the *Seaboyer* case.

PROCEDURAL PROVISIONS

Applications for the Admission of Sexual Character Evidence

The procedural provisions regarding the application to decide whether character evidence is admissible are a vast improvement over both the 1976 and 1983 provisions. Both fairness to the complainant and clarity in decision-making should follow from the procedural requirements. Moreover, the process of decision-making regarding the application has been structured to focus judges on substantive as well as procedural fairness to the complainant.

The defendant has to first apply for a hearing to make submissions regarding evidence of the complainant's sexual character. The notice requirement is expressly stated as a minimum, in contrast to the 1976 and 1983 requirement that notice only be 'reasonable,' which was open to abuse. Now notice must be given seven days prior to the hearing, in writing to the Crown and the court. This notice must contain detailed particulars of the character evidence and the relevance it has to a specific issue at trial.

But hearings are not to be automatically granted because the technical requirements are met, unlike the rules under the 1976 and 1983 provisions. The judge must be convinced that 'the evidence sought to be adduced is capable of being admissible' under section 276. Moreover, like the 1983 legislation, if a judge grants a hearing under section 276, the complainant is not compellable and therefore she cannot be forced to testify as a witness of the accused.

The process of this decision is a private one. Thus, the jury and the public must be excluded during the hearing. For further protection, during the application and the hearing, newspapers cannot publish, nor can the media broadcast, any information relating to the application or the hearing itself. Nevertheless, once evidence is found to be admissible or if a judge makes a special order, newspaper publication and broadcast of the reasons and the decision will be permitted. The latter will open to public scrutiny all court decisions permitting sexual character evidence.

To ensure that judges direct their minds to the factors set out in section 276, the rules require judges to give reasons for their decision and to state which of these factors affected the determination. If judges admit evidence, they must indicate why it will be relevant to an issue at trial. This improves upon both the 1976 and 1983 provisions, as does the necessity for a record of the reasons for decisions. The latter means that judicial decisions can be reviewed for possible publication in law reports and thus will be available to researchers monitoring the effect of the law. In addition, the bill permits appeals of the decisions, so jurisprudence will develop in this important area.

The Trial

At the trial stage, to further reinforce the principle that a woman's sexual history is not to determine the court decision as to whether she was, in law, sexually assaulted, a special instruction to the jury is now required if sexual character evidence is admitted. The judge must instruct jury members 'as to the uses that the jury *may and may not make* of that evidence' (section 276.4, emphasis added). This suggests that the instruction must be detailed and admonitory. (Let's hope the courts take that instruction to heart, as well.)

A POSSIBLE CONSTITUTIONAL CHALLENGE

Now the courts will have a chance to deal with this legislation. It will not be long before defence counsel begin to raise anew Charter violations of sections 7 and 11(d). They could claim that these provisions violate the necessity for a definition of the offence that does not require punishment of the 'morally innocent.'

Moral innocence is an emotive term for the standard of intent, or the guilty mind, which the law requires of an accused for conviction. The question is whether the law should attribute criminal responsibility where the accused did not intend harm defined by the offence because he or she failed to consider certain factors. In Canada and England, there has been a debate for the last fifteen years regarding the judicial development of an increasingly objective standard of guilt or *mens rea.* Before that time, in most true criminal offences the standard was subjective, requiring that the accused fully intend the harm defined in the offence.

The debate may have been settled by recent decisions of the Supreme Court of Canada; it appears that criminal responsibility has been defined as a constitutional issue. In its decisions between 1987 and 1990, the Supreme Court of Canada moved toward an emphasis on the social stigma and penalty attached to conviction for an offence as the determining factors regarding the necessary *mens rea,* so that a subjective *mens rea* would be required for almost all criminal offences. Lamer C.J.C. found theft to be an offence requiring full *mens rea* partly because of the stigma attached. Considering this, would sexual assault offences also require full *mens rea*?[64] The earlier decisions left open the possibility that the courts would see the new definition of consent not merely as an attempt to criminalize the failure to ensure consent but also to apply criminal sanctions where the accused is unaware of the factors making his actions criminal, that is, where subjective *mens rea* was lacking.[65] If so, this would be a breach of sections 7 and 11. For the same reason, the amendment to the belief in consent defence, which requires an accused to take reasonable steps to ascertain that the complainant was consenting, would be problematic. The objective standard that is imported into the mistake of belief defence through the use of the word 'reasonable' would be questioned because it would mean that sexual assault requires less than full *mens rea.*

However, with its recent decisions in *Nova Scotia Pharmaceutical Society* and *DeSousa*, the court has backtracked. Section 7 now only requires that there be a minimum fault requirement; that is, either subjective or objective *mens rea*, but not absolute liability, which imposes a penalty where there is no intent to commit the crime at all. The exception to that is where there is a special stigma attached to the offence, that is, for offences analogous to murder. Nevertheless, it seems that now unreasonable behaviour in any context can be criminalized as long as it does not carry a stigma analogous to murder. In terms of *mens rea*, this could leave the sexual assault provisions home free, at least with respect to the offences requiring a lesser penalty, sexual assault and sexual assault with a weapon or causing bodily harm, where the victim is an adult.[66]

In addition to the issue of *mens rea*, there is the question of punishment. The Supreme Court of Canada has yet to consider in what circumstances the possibility of imprisonment following a finding of guilt breaches section 7. However, its 1990 decision in *Martineau* indicated that punishment must be proportionate to the moral blameworthiness of the offender and those causing harm intentionally must be punished more severely than those causing harm unintentionally. These principles remain intact. With regard to the sexual assault offences, because of the new requirements for consent and belief in consent, the same prohibition carrying the same penalty criminalizes a person who was deliberately aware of the risk and one who was acting unreasonably. This is true with respect to all three tiers of sexual assault. On the basis of *Martineau*, the court could strike down the requirements for consent and belief in consent, or read them down to conform with the *Martineau* principles on punishment.[67]

We will have to see how the consent and belief in consent provisions of the bill survive constitutional challenges on these grounds.

Equal Protection for 'Bad Girls'

In patriarchal terms, most Canadian women are bad girls. Most of us have had sex outside marriage with at least one partner. The law should guarantee all women, including prostitutes, virgins, and those of us in between, the same protection from sexual assault. Over a sixteen-year period, Parliament has tried, three times, to guarantee equal protection to all women, regardless of their sexual experience or rumours about their sexual experience. Equally, the courts have thwarted Parliament's intentions, assisted, most recently, by interpretations of the Charter of Rights and Freedoms.

The world is no longer divided into virgins and whores, as it was when the sexual character rules developed in the nineteenth-century. Yet the courts have insisted on this division in their interpretation of the sexual character rules in trials of sexual assault. The effect of the early sexual character rules was to enforce the notion that only 'good girls' were entitled to protection from sexual assault. These rules were also a warning to women that they better be good, or else they would fall into a no woman's land. It was as if the law were saying that a woman who had no chastity worth protecting did not exist legally in sexual assault law. The justifications for this legal theory have become more complex, culminating with the *Seaboyer* decision. But underneath was the same admonition: you girls better be good.

The sexual freedom of women is key to our full humanness. The high incidence of sexual assault forces us to see sex in a negative way: we want to be free to *refuse* sex. In a society in which we were truly equal, we would see sex in a positive way. We would be thinking about *choosing* sex. We must be free to choose many partners or no partner, conventional sexuality or practices considered 'deviant' by mainstream society. As long as we are not protected from sexual assault by virtue of our 'unchastity,' we will continue to be held hostage by the old ways, concerned about what people think, ever more fearful of our own sexual aspirations.

The development of the law governing sexual character evidence shows Parliament determined with each attempt to provide greater detail about what the courts can and cannot do. There is no other Canadian law that has been the subject of such a tug of war between Parliament and the courts. Again and again, Parliament has indicated that complainants in sexual assault trials should not be classified as bad girls or good girls.

All of us who value the full sexual expression of women hope that Bill C-49 will mean that women are freer to fully choose their sexual partners, the occasion on which they will engage in sexual activity with their partners, and the nature of the conduct involved. We wish for a society in which women are no longer under some legal duty to endure forced sex with a man because they have had sexual partners in the past or have had sex with the assailant in the past. No longer should a sexually experienced woman be 'fair game' for sexually aggressive men. Law reform cannot guarantee this, but it can certainly help. Is this too much to expect, considering the intransigent patriarchalism of the courts? I hope not.

Notes

1 The Department of Justice completed studies of police records of sexual assault complaints in six Canadian cities; an average of 90 per cent of the complainants were females while 99 per cent of the alleged assailants were males. See Tables 12

(p. 43) and 14 (p. 46), Department of Justice, *Overview, Sexual Assault Legislation in Canada, Report No. 5*, Ottawa, 1990

2 Constitution Act, 1982, enacted by Canada Act 1982, (U.K.) c. 11. The decision was particularly strong: the full court of nine judges sat and the majority was seven justices, with agreed upon reasons. It is all the more strong because in many recent decisions of the Supreme Court of Canada, judges of the majority have differed as to the reasons for making their decision, so there have been two or more judgments for the majority. It also noteworthy that both the majority and minority judgments were written by the two women on the court.

3 *Forsythe v. R.*, [1980] 2 S.C.R. 268; *R. v. Konkin* (1983), 3 C.C.C. (3d) 289 (S.C.C.)

4 Included here are rape, indecent assault, and offences involving 'seduction' and sex between male adults and female children where the 'chastity' of the child was considered part of the definition of the offence.

5 J. Temkin, 'Regulating Sexual History Evidence – The Limits of Discretionary Legislation,' 33 *International Comparative Law Quarterly* 942 (1984): 943–6; R. Delisle, *Evidence: Principles and Problems*, (Toronto: Carswell 1984), 161–6

6 Ibid.

7 Delisle, supra n. 5, 166–7, Temkin, supra n. 5 ibid.

8 Ibid.

9 Temkin, supra, n. 5, 942–3; *Laliberté v. R.* [1877], 1 S.C.R. 117

10 *R. v. Riley* (1887), 18 Q.B.D. 481 (Queen's Bench Div.)

11 *R. v. Hodgson* (1812), 1 Russ. & Ry. 211; *R. v. Holmes* (1871), L.R. 1 C.C.R. 334

12 Supra n. 10, 483

13 Supra n. 11, 336

14 *Laliberté*, supra n. 9; *R. v. Bashir* (1969), 3 All E.R. 692 (Leeds Assizes)

15 *Riley*, supra n. 10, *Holmes*, supra n. 11; see also *R. v. Clay* (1851), 5 Cox C.C. 146 (Salop Spring Assizes). But a lower court decision indicated that evidence of convictions for prostitution could not be led by the defence because this involved specific sexual activity. *R. v. Barker* (1829), 3 Car. & P. 588 (Oxford Assizes).

16 As early as 1812, in *Hodgson*, supra n. 11, the court said the question 'whether she (the complainant) had not before had connection with other persons?' was improper. A century later, King's Bench Division, Court of Criminal Appeal, said that the defence could not tender evidence to show that the complainant was of 'bad and light character' because it was not relevant [*R. v. Cargill* (1913) 2 K.B. 271]. In the same time period, three *trial* courts stated that the defence could call evidence of the complainant's 'light character' (*Barker*, supra n. 15) 'general want of decency' [*R. v. Tissington* (1843), 1 Cox C.C. 48 (Nottingham Summer Assizes)], 'loose and indecent' habits [(*R. v. Ryan* (1846), 2 Cox C.C. 115 (Central Crim. Ct]. In *Barker*, the principle was *obiter*.

17 Temkin, supra n. 5, 945–6
18 In *Forsythe*, supra n. 3, decided in 1980, the Supreme Court of Canada said *obiter*, that evidence of a complainant's 'general reputation for chastity,' as opposed to specific instances of her sexual activities, went to consent. It did not define 'general reputation for chastity' (at p. 274). It relied on only one Canadian case, decided by the Ontario Court of Appeal in 1906 (*R. v. Finnessey* (1906), 10 C.C.C. 347); but the principle stated in *Finnessey* was *obiter*. It would appear that only one other Canadian case on this issue, decided at trial level, has been reported, *R. v. Bishop* (1906), 11 C.C.C. 30 (N.S.S.C.). The sources of the cases cited on the history of the common law regarding sexual character evidence are Temkin, supra n. 5, N. Brooks, 'Rape and the Laws of Evidence,' (23) *Chitty's Law Journal* 1 (1975), 5, 6; and the *Laliberté* decision, supra n. 9
19 Unfortunately, the Canada Law Reform Commission failed to adopt the recommendation of the Evidence Project after hearing submissions from the legal profession. See M. Stanley, *The Experience of the Rape Victim with the Criminal Justice System Prior to Bill C-127, Sexual Assault Legislation in Canada: An Evaluation, Report No. 1* (Ottawa: Department of Justice, July 1985), 77–86; Law Reform Commission of Canada, *Character*, A Study Paper Prepared by the Law of Evidence Project (Ottawa: 1972), 5–6; Mr. Justice Haines, 'The Character of the Rape Victim,' (23) *Chitty's Law Journal* 57 (1975); S. Leggett, 'The Character of Complainants in Sexual Charges,' (21) *Chitty's Law Journal* (1973): 132
20 Criminal Law Amendment Act, 1975, S.C. 1974–75–76, C. 93
21 Law Reform Commission of Canada, *Sexual Offences*, Working Paper Number 22 (Ottawa: 1978), 35, 36; Stanley, supra, n. 19, 86–98
22 Supra n. 3, 295–96
23 Ibid. See also *R. v. LeGallant* (1987), 54 C.R. (3d) 46 (B.C.C.A.), 58; *Forsythe v. R.*, supra n. 3, Law Reform Commission of Canada, supra n. 21, 35, 36.
24 Stanley, supra n. 19, 88–90
25 An Act to amend the Criminal Code in relation to sexual offences and other offences against the person, S.C. 1980–81–82–83, c. 125 s. 5–s. 19
26 In 1988, this provision, as well as section 277, was amended to apply to new offences regarding child sexual abuse, as well as assorted other sexual offences, such as anal intercourse with a person under 18 and incest. An Act to amend the Criminal Code and the Canada Evidence Act, S.C. 1987, c. 24.
27 This provision has been amended to apply to other sexual offences; see n. 26.
28 *R. v. Askov* (1991), 75 O.R. (2d) (S.C.C.), 689–692; *B.C. Motor Vehicle Reference*, [1985] 2 S.C.R. 486, 502, 503
29 *Seaboyer v. R.*, [1991] 2 S.C.R. 577, 607
30 Ibid., 608
31 Ibid., 609–11, 618, 621–3

32 Ibid., 610, emphasis added
33 Ibid., 609, 618
34 Ibid., 612–13
35 Ibid., 613–16, 623, 625
36 Ibid., 619
37 Supra n. 34, Ibid.
38 Ibid., 604–5, 627
39 Ibid., 627
40 Ibid., 618
41 Ibid., 634–6
42 Ibid., 634, 636
43 Brooks, supra n. 18, 5, 6
44 Supra n. 29
45 Ibid., 623, emphasis added
46 *Seaboyer,* supra n. 29, 685
47 Ibid.
48 Ibid., 599
49 Ibid., 685–6
50 Ibid., 670–8, Stanley, supra n. 19, 87
51 *Seaboyer,* n. 29, 670–8
52 Ibid., 665–78
53 *R. v. Beare,* [1988] 2 S.C.R. 387, 403–7; *R. v. Lyons,* [1987] 2 S.C.R. 309, 327–9; *Askov,* supra n. 28, 689–92; *B.C. Motor Vehicle Reference,* supra n. 28, 502, 503
54 Ibid., 605, 620–1
55 Ibid., 605
56 Ibid., 605, 634, 648–65
57 Ibid., 611, 679–81
58 See M. MacCrimmon, 'Developments in the Law of Evidence: The 1989–90 term, Evidence in Context,' 2 *Supreme Court Law Review* (2d) 385 (1991), (1991) esp. 386–388
59 *R. v. Lavallée* (1990), 55 C.C.C. (3d) 97 (S.C.C.) at 113, noted in *Seaboyer* dissent, supra n. 29, 654; MacCrimmon, supra n. 58, 415–19
60 MacCrimmon, supra n. 58, 415–19
61 *L.(W.K.) v. R.* (1991), 64 C.C.C. (3d) 32
62 *Seaboyer,* supra, n. 29, 678–94
63 An Act to amend the Criminal Code (sexual assault), S.C. 1992, c. 38
64 R. Way, 'Constitutionalizing Subjectivism: Another Way' (1990), 79 C.R. (3d) 260, 264; D. Stuart, 'Further Progress on the Constitutional Requirement of Fault, but Stigma Is Not Enough' (1990), 79 C.R. (3d) 247, 254–5; D. Stuart, 'The Supreme Court Drastically Reduces the Constitutional Requirement of Fault: A

Triumph of Pragmatism and Law Enforcement Expediency' (1992), 15 C.R. (4th) 88, 88, 89

65 R. Wiener, 'Shifting the Communication Burden: A Meaningful Consent Standard in Rape,' *Harvard Women's Law Journal* 143 (6) (1983): 158

66 Stuart (1992), 91–4, 98, 99

67 Ibid., 88–89, 100

11

DIANA MAJURY

Seaboyer and *Gayme*: A Study InEquality

The ways in which judges interpret legislative language, rules, and laws were explored in the last four chapters. One of the themes in the exploration of judicial decision-making is the way in which 'who' the judge is informs how he or she constructs or defines the issue or problem. Christine Boyle, Renate Mohr, Teressa Nahanee, and Elizabeth Sheehy all reveal the ways in which the legal construction of sexual assault – whether in substantive law, sentencing decisions, or tort claims – is informed by the judge's gender, race, class, and other characteristics. What feminist scholars have long referred to as the 'maleness' of law is also the critical starting point for this chapter. In this chapter, Diana Majury explores the interpretive nature of judicial decision-making through an analysis of the majority and dissenting judgments in the Supreme Court of Canada decision in Seaboyer and Gayme. Majury explores the sex equality implications of the Supreme Court of Canada's interpretation of the 'rape shield' laws in Seaboyer. The very different approaches of the majority and the dissenting judgments to the legal construction of sexual assault are carefully set out for the reader. The author examines the meaning of 'equality' through the language used in the Seaboyer decision as well as through an examination of the judicial process itself. Ultimately the limitations of traditional legal analysis that is both abstract and decontextualized, are revealed as a central impediment to a challenge of the current 'assumption of equality.'

Male violence against women is such a blatant example of women's inequality that it is almost difficult to recognize it as such. The fact that violence is inflicted upon women as women, that is, because we are women, both expresses and reinforces women's unequal status in Canadian society. Offences of violence against women – rape, female partner assault, sexual incestuous assault, pornography, and prostitution[1] – are gen- s; they are rooted in male dominance and female subordination (MacKinnon 1987, Rush 1980, Russell 1984). An examination of any of these forms of violence can tell us a great deal about sexual inequality. Any legal judgment dealing with these issues can tell us a great deal about the court's perspective on sexual (in)equality, on women, and on sexuality.

In this chapter, I will explore the sex equality implications of the Supreme Court of Canada's decision in *Seaboyer* and *Gayme* (1991). In this case, the two accused challenged the constitutionality of the Criminal Code restrictions on the admissibility of evidence of the past sexual history of the women who were raped.[2] The majority of the Court held that the restrictions on past sexual history evidence breached the accuseds' section 7 right to life, liberty, and security of the person and their section 11(d) right to a fair trial and that the breaches were not justified under section 1 of the Charter. Madam Justice L'Heureux-Dubé wrote a strong dissent, concurred in by Mr. Justice Gonthier.

From the perspective of the majority in *Seaboyer*, this was not a case about equality for women and the meanings of women's inequality. For them, it was a case about fairness and the rights of the accused. However, if one accepts that rape is a gendered crime, which the dissenting judges did accept, then this case is, at its core, a sex equality case and the issues of fairness and the rights of the accused need to be examined in the context of sex equality. The majority and the dissenting judgments each have a lot to tell us about women's inequality and about the underlying assumptions that frame the law's response to male violence against women. I will look at this decision in terms of how the equality issues are presented, or ignored, and what the case reflects of current legal meanings of, and approaches to, equality.

The differences between the dissent and the majority judgment, in terms of approach and analysis, are dramatic. They demonstrate major differences in understandings of gender equality and inequality. In simple terms, McLachlin's majority judgment can be described as operating from a presumption of gender equality while L'Heureux-Dubé's dissenting analysis flows from her recognition of gender inequality.

While I recognize that there are serious problems inherent in choosing a single case as reflective of anything more than the case itself, the Anglo-Canadian system of *stare decisis* is premised on the understanding that decisions, and particularly decisions of the Supreme Court of Canada, have significance beyond the particularities of the case before them. Exposing some of the assumptions underlying even a single decision should provide some indication of where and how the court is currently situated.

Legal Background to the Case

The admissibility, in a rape trial, of evidence of the past sexual history of the woman who was raped[3] is an issue that has been the subject of a tug of war between the federal legislature and the courts in Canada for at least the past 15 years (Boyle 1981, Department of Justice 1987). More specifically, the issue has been with respect to evidence of the woman's past sexual history with persons other than the accused. Evidence pertaining to a sexual history with the accused has always been considered admissible without qualification.[4]

Historically, evidence of the past sexual history of the woman who was raped was admissible under common law as relating to both consent and credibility. In other words, sexually active women were considered less likely to be raped and more likely to lie about it. The concern that women lie about sex that was in fact consensual, or that women fabricate (sometimes described as fantasize) the sex as well as the lack of consent, stems from the myth that false accusations of rape are frequent occurrences (*Seaboyer*, 342). Despite the fact that these concerns are not grounded in reality, they continue to distort legal and social understandings of, and responses to, rape.

At common law, the type and range of sexual history questions that could be addressed to the woman who was raped, and the process of asking those questions, were largely unrestricted. Recognizing that such a free-ranging inquiry into a woman's past sexual history might be damaging to the woman and to the criminal trial process, Parliament, in 1975, passed legislation that set out some procedural safeguards to try to foreclose defence 'fishing expeditions' in search of the past sexual history of the woman who was raped. While these requirements might have mitigated to some small extent the ordeal of the trial process for the woman (or some women) who was raped, it did not in any way challenge the assumption of the relevance of past sexual history evidence. However, even this minor improvement for the woman who was raped was seen by the Supreme Court of Canada as too much, as evidenced by their decision in *R. v. Forsythe* (1980).

The Court in *Forsythe* clearly saw past sexual history evidence as an equality issue. However, it was seen, not as a sex equality issue, but as a matter of balancing between the 'complainant' and the accused. In the court's discussion of balancing, there is no mention of the gender imbalance that marks who is a 'complainant' and who is an accused. The *Forsythe* decision is premised on the assumption that the 'complainant' and the accused had been on an equal footing in a rape trial before the 1975 legislation. Thus, in order to retain the 'balance,' the protection seen to be accorded to women by the 1975 Code amendments had to be offset. Accordingly, the

Court interpreted the amendments as allowing the accused increased latitude in his questioning of the woman who was raped. The effect of the decision in *Forsythe* was to open up further both the questioning of the woman
who was raped and the admissible evidence pertaining to her past sexual
history.

The *Forsythe* decision exacerbated women's inequality in the name of balance. As will be seen in the discussion that follows, the same presumption of
sexual equality and concern with symmetry are central to the majority judgment in *Seaboyer*, a decision that similarly exacerbates women's inequality in
the name of balance.

In 1982, Parliament tried again to address the issue of past sexual history
evidence. This was part of a major revision of the rape law. While some of the
changes brought about by this new legislation did constitute improvements
for women, including the provisions at issue in *Seaboyer*, and especially the
elimination of the marital exemption for rape, many of the changes were
negative. The re-characterization of the gender-specific crime of rape as the
gender-neutral crime of sexual assault is misleading; it de-politicizes and de-
genders the issue, thereby masking the reality of the offence. The renaming
of the offence as sexual assault instead of rape diminishes the impact and significance of the crime. Rape is a word that holds meaning, power, and pain for
women in terms of describing what was done to them (Backhouse and Cohen
1980). In keeping with my objection to the name change, I continue to refer
to the crime as rape except when I am working very specifically with the provision.

The revised rape law included what is now section 276 of the Criminal
Code, the section challenged in *Seaboyer*. Section 276 places restrictions
on the admissibility of evidence pertaining to the previous sexual history of
the woman who was raped. Under the new law, such evidence was only
admissible to rebut evidence introduced by the Crown, to establish the identity of the accused, or to lay the foundation for the defence of honest but mistaken belief in consent where that evidence came from the same occasion as
the rape.

Section 276 has been the subject of innumerable Charter challenges by
men accused of rape who have argued that their section 7 right to life, liberty,
and security of the person and their section 11 right to a fair trial were
breached by this provision.[5] The result of all of these challenges has been a
slough of conflicting decisions at all levels of court, including provincial
courts of appeal. The *Seaboyer* case was the first time that these provisions
were before the Supreme Court of Canada and, in the continuing tug of war
with Parliament, the Supreme Court pulled back dramatically from any
movement toward equality.

The Judicial Process as an Equality Issue

This case raises issues of process that warrant comment in an equality analysis. Just as the decision in the case is gendered and has a differential gender impact, so, too, the process through which the particpants in the case have to go is a gendered process with differentially gendered impacts.

The incredible time and delay involved in bringing cases before the Supreme Court of Canada affects the women who were raped very differently than the accused. In both *Seaboyer* and *Gayme*, the constitutional challenge to the past sexual history provision arose in the context of a preliminary inquiry. The committals of the accused to trial were both quashed in November 1985, which means that the preliminary inquiries probably took place in 1984. The offences probably occurred in 1983, at the earliest. The trials on the sexual assault charges could not proceed until the final determination of the question of the constitutionality of section 276, which occurred on 22 August 1991.

It is generally acknowledged that unless an accused is in the unusual situation of being held in jail pending trial (which these accused were not), delay works to the advantage of the accused. Not only is he not incarcerated for that period of time, but the greater the lapse of time between the event giving rise to the charge and the trial, the lower the probability that he will be convicted. Conversely, delay can be very negative for a woman who has been raped and has decided to put herself through the ordeal of a rape trial. For most women, the prospect of the trial keeps the rape experience present and immediate. These women cannot start moving on from the rape until the trial and appeal periods are behind them. In addition, the increased likelihood of acquittal for the accused is extremely negative for the woman who has been raped.

When the Supreme Court of Canada decision on the constitutional question in *Seaboyer* was handed down, it had probably been at least eight years since the offences took place; and the actual trials had not yet begun. This was a painfully long time for the women who had been raped. I was not surprised to learn that the charges have been dropped in these two cases; the passage of so much time had made it too difficult to proceed.

There is no reference in the *Seaboyer* decision to the gendered and unequal impact of the legal process of this constitutional challenge. While delay of this magnitude would be difficult for any victim of a crime awaiting trial, the gendered specificity of rape, including the stigma that attaches to the woman who was raped and the emotional and psychological impact of crimes of male violence against women, makes delay disproportionately neg-

ative for the women in these kinds of cases. There is no easy or obvious solution to this problem. However, acknowledging the problem would seem to be
a first step toward addressing the inequality. There is no reference anywhere
in *Seaboyer* to the possible damage done to the women involved by the
extreme delay in proceeding to trial on their cases. In fact, these two women
are conspicuously absent from the judgment, which leads me to my second
issue of process – the abstractness of the legal proceeding.

With some exceptions, including the Ontario Court of Appeal decision in
Seaboyer, the constitutionality of any piece of legislation is not generally
seen to be specific to the situation that gave rise to the constitutional challenge. Accordingly, the admissibility of the particular evidence sought to be
introduced by the accused was not at issue in this case before the Supreme
Court of Canada. L'Heureux-Dubé in her dissenting judgment explicitly
refuses to discuss the facts of the two cases under appeal, and McLachlin, for
the majority, provides only a very brief description of the facts of the two
cases as background to her discussion of the issues. There is no further reference to those facts or to the evidence these two accused sought to introduce.
The very construction of this case as a Charter challenge reflects the privileg-
ing of the abstract 'rights' of men over the lived experiences of women.

If contextualization is critical to an equality analysis (Majury 1991), then
abstract Charter analysis is inimical to the equality process. Cases that focus
on the abstract will be less likely to address in any meaningful way the realities and complexities of women's inequalities. While the generalized nature
of a constitutional challenge renders it exceedingly vulnerable to the danger
of abstraction, constitutional challenges are not necessarily abstract. Much of
the Charter equality litigation in which the Women's Legal Education and
Action Fund (LEAF), for example, is involved is exactly about trying to contex-
tualize the understanding of equality and inequality and to bring the lived experiences of women into the court room (Razack 1991). L'Heureux-Dubé, in her
dissenting judgment in *Seaboyer*, relies very much on the lived experience of
women as the basis for her approach and her decision. Despite these efforts to
ground the analysis, the absence of the women whose particular experiences are
so much the issue of this case and whose lives are dramatically affected by this
decision decontextualizes the discussion and renders the whole process troubling.[6]

Language as an Equality Issue

The language employed in a judicial decision reflects the decision-maker, in
terms of her/his values and attitudes. The language used sets the parameters

and the focus for the reading and understanding of the case. The assumptions about sexual equality that underlie the decisions in *Seaboyer* are reflected in the language used in the judgments. An exploration of the gender implications of the language of the case discloses differences between the majority and the dissent, in terms of the approach taken to the issues in the case and the analysis undertaken.

THE CHARACTERIZATION OF THE WOMAN WHO WAS RAPED

Both McLachlin and L'Heureux-Dubé refer to the woman who was raped as 'the complainant.' But while L'Heureux-Dube struggles with the terminology, McLachlin uses the same term without any apparent recognition of its problems. McLachlin's only discussion of the word is toward the end of her judgment where she is adapting a proposal for guidelines as to what would constitute 'legitimate' uses of evidence of past sexual history. The word victim is used in the proposal and McLachlin replaces it with the word complainant, as being 'more compatible with the presumption of innocence of the accused than the word "victim"' (408).

The presumption of innocence similarly troubles L'Heureux-Dubé. She describes the problem in her discussion of the term 'alleged victim.' Having acknowledged that referring to the victim as 'alleged' undermines the victim and her story, L'Heureux-Dubé describes the qualification as necessary in order to preserve the presumption of innocence:

The ... description [alleged victim] is, however, accurate in that, in law, one cannot be the victim of the assaultive conduct of an accused until the accused has been found guilty beyond a reasonable doubt. In this sense, the phrase is accurate (excepting of course those cases where an assault has occurred but the accused successfully pleads the defence of honest but mistaken belief in consent) (333).

It is interesting that this dilemma of how to name the person against whom the crime was committed is raised almost exclusively with respect to crimes of male violence against women. It seems to me that for other crimes the term victim is used without any apparent problem about infringing the presumption of innocence. In other words, a person who has been robbed is comfortably referred to as such, or as a victim, without the reference being seen to say anything about the guilt or innocence of the person accused of having committed the robbery.

L'Heureux-Dubé is somewhat misleading when she states that 'in law, one cannot be the victim of the assaultive conduct of an accused until the accused has been found guilty beyond a reasonable doubt' (333). It is possible, in law, for an accused to be acquitted on a criminal charge of sexual assault and yet found liable civilly for the sexual assault. It is also possible, in law, to award damages to a woman who has been raped, under criminal compensation legislation, in the absence of any accused or defendant (See Chapter 10). According the woman who was raped the dignity of a label that does not by definition undermine her experience does not detract from the presumption of the innocence of the accused (see endnote 3).

Despite her perception of its legal accuracy, L'Heureux-Dubé rejects the term 'alleged victim' due to 'its overinclusiveness and presumptive character' (333). She chooses instead to use the term complainant, even though she recognizes that it too is problematic, particularly in terms of its harshness. Much as I dislike the term complainant, I appreciate the sensitivity to women who have been raped and the acknowledgment of the importance of language that L'Heureux-Dubé demonstrates in raising and discussing these issues.

The term complainant suffers from many of the same problems as 'alleged victim,' although the discrediting implicit in 'complainant' is somewhat less overt than with the qualification of the victim as 'alleged.' However, the term complainant has the additional disadvantage of trivializing the rape. One does not usually refer to serious crimes and acts of violence in terms of complaints, a word that denotes something minor, a nuisance, something troublesome. The word complainant invokes the stereotype of the complaining woman – the nag, the whiner, the woman who distorts a minor inconvenience into a catastrophe. It is easy to see the unrequited lover, the vengeful 'mistress,' the guilty 'adulteress' lurking just beneath the surface of the term 'complainant.' It is a word that invites us to see the woman who was raped as the problem.

While the language of both the majority and the dissent is problematic in this regard, L'Heureux-Dubé at least demonstrates an awareness that how one characterizes the woman who was raped is important and has an impact on how the woman and her story are accepted in the courtroom.

RAPE SHIELD

Both Madam Justice McLachlin for the majority and Madam Justice L'Heureux-Dubé for the dissent refer to the inappropriateness of the term 'rape shield' to describe legislation that limits the evidence the defence can introduce pertaining to the past sexual history of the woman who was raped. McLachlin notes in parentheses: 'that the term 'rape shield' is less than fortu-

nate; the legislation offers protection not against rape, but against the questioning of complainants in trials for sexual offenses' (386).

While this critique of the term is accurate in the literal sense, it ignores the
courtroom experience of many women who have been raped. Many of these
women describe the trial as a second rape or a continuation of the rape, or a
re-rape. A significant part of the experience of the trial itself as rape-like is
the questioning that the woman is put through by defence counsel, particularly questions about her past sexual history, questions that tend to imply
that she is a slut, a whore, that she is vindictive or indiscriminate, that she
asked for the rape, or consented to it (Berger 1977, Clark and Lewis 1977,
MacKinnon 1989). Limiting or eliminating these questions can be seen, to
some small extent, as shielding the woman who was raped from a rape-like
experience. However, despite its symbolic significance, the term is misleading
and overstated for the reason stated by McLachlin, that the evidentiary
restrictions do not protect women from rape.

The concerns expressed by McLachlin, however, do not lead her to discard
the term altogether. The term 'rape shield' does not appear very often in the
majority judgment, which may reflect a conscious effort on McLachlin's part
to avoid its use, but she does, in places, continue to refer to 'rape-shield provisions.'

L'Heureux-Dubé objects to the term on quite different grounds. At the
beginning of her analysis of the issues, she raises what she understands to be
the important question of language. In this context, she examines the
description of the provisions as 'rape shield' and explicitly refuses to use that
term:

The provisions that are the subject of the constitutional challenge in the present case
are commonly referred to as 'rape shield' provisions. Implicit in this description is a
presumption as to their purpose: that it is solely to shield a complainant from the
rigours of cross-examination at trial. As I hope to make clear through the course of
my reasons, although protecting the complainant may be one of the purposes of the
provisions, it is neither the only one, nor necessarily the most important. As a result,
I will not use this inaccurate shorthand in referring to these provisions (333).

The description of these provisions in terms of shielding the woman who
was raped sets the stage for the analysis of the issue as one of protection
against discomfort, and even pain, versus the possibility of convicting an
innocent man. The focus is thus less on the content and purpose of the questions and more on their impact on the person being questioned. The implicit
assumption is that these questions are unproblematic except for the pain and

discomfort they might cause the witness. It is not surprising that when the dichotomy is set up in this way, the conclusion reached is that the discomfort and/or pain are simply, as McLachlin refers to it, 'part of the price to be paid to ensure that only the guilty are convicted' (396).[7] The use of the passive voice – 'the price to be paid' – makes invisible that it is women in general and the woman who is being cross-examined in particular, who pay the price. McLachlin's ungendered analysis does not enable her to understand what that price is about; L'Heureux-Dubé's analysis starts from the recongition of that price.

SEXUAL HISTORY/CONDUCT/ACTIVITY

McLachlin uses the terms sexual conduct and sexual activity interchangeably to characterize the evidence under review, with a preference, in terms of frequency of use, for the former. L'Heureux-Dubé uses both of these terms but refers most frequently to a third term, past sexual history. There is no discussion of this terminology in either judgment.

I have reservations about the use of both sexual conduct and sexual activity. These terms imply the free, voluntary, and equal participation of the woman in the sex that makes up her sexual history; they ignore the reality that most women's histories include sexual coercion and abuse. This is exactly the danger in a rape trial – that the coercion and force will be invisible and the rape will be seen as free and voluntary sexual conduct or activity on the part of the woman. This synapse is particularly serious with respect to the issue of the admissibility of this evidence, because a woman's sexual history of coercion and abuse is often introduced as evidence of sexual activity that is then argued as providing the basis for a defence of motive to fabricate or of honest but mistaken belief.[8] While the term sexual history does not explicitly acknowledge the prevalence of rape as part of women's sexual histories, it does not negate it.

The language of past sexual conduct and activity in both judgments facilitates an uncritical reliance upon a woman's sexual past. While L'Heureux-Dubé's more frequent reference to past sexual history lessens this effect somewhat, her failure to examine this language allows assumptions of past consent to go unchallenged.

The Meanings of Equality: Different Centres, Different Ends

For McLachlin, this case is about truth and fairness; for L'Heureux-Dubé, it is about myth and stereotype. The accused is very much at the centre of

McLachlin's analysis; the spectre of an innocent man wrongly convicted of rape haunts her decision.[9] For L'Heureux-Dubé, it is the gendered experience of rape and the gendered social and legal responses to that experience that are at the centre. The very different focuses of the two judgments reflect very different assumptions about, and understandings of, sexual equality. In this section, I will explore some of the implications of these different meanings of equality as demonstrated by the different conclusions reached by each judge.

I do not intend to engage with the substantive issue of the relevance of the past sexual history of the woman who was raped except to the limited extent that I need to do so as part of my examination of the underlying assumptions about equality. I choose not to focus on the question of relevance for a number of reasons. First, my concern with equality is more general than the particularities of past sexual history evidence. Second, there are a number of excellent articles (Dawson 1988, Sheehy 1989) that explore this question in depth and which L'Heureux-Dubé canvasses fully and favourably in her dissent (341–372). I am not sure that I would have anything to add to these discussions.

Finally, it seems to me that in the course of trying to refute the relevance of past sexual history evidence, one runs the risk of entrenching belief in its relevance. As Sarah Hoagland says in her book, *Lesbian Ethics*:

I want to suggest that our strategy not be one of trying to prove oppressive values false, thereby working within the existing paradigm, since that merely affirms those values and habits. Rather our strategy can be one of transforming perception so that existing values cease to make sense (20).

This is one of the catch-22s of equality litigation – having to engage with the position of the dominant on the dominant's terms and the dominant's terrain. It is a major question whether litigation, or even the law more generally, can be used 'to transform perception so that existing values cease to make sense' or whether engaging with law per se affirms those values such that the more one struggles against those values within a legal context the more one affirms them (Razack 1991, Smart 1989). I choose to continue to engage with the law, but always with the nagging fear that I may be shoring up the patriarchy more than I am dismantling it (Lorde 1984, Rifkin 1980).

My position on the question of the relevance of past sexual history evidence is that such evidence is never relevant to the determination of the guilt of the accused. To the extent that any of us considers that any particular piece of past sexual history evidence or any type of past sexual history evidence meets the test of relevance, that it 'in some degree advances the inquiry'

(*Seaboyer* 390) or is a fact that 'according to the common course of events ... proves or renders probable ... the existence ... of [an]other fact [consent]' (356), we are relying upon myth and stereotype. It is ourselves and our own internalization of these myths and stereotypes that we need to question as we assess the relevance of particular pieces of information.[10]

McLachlin, however, considers much of the past sexual history evidence relevant. She is somewhat contradictory in her description of how much of this evidence should be admissible. At one point, she refers to 'numerous examples of evidence of sexual conduct which would be excluded by s. 276 but which clearly should be received in the interests of a fair trial' (393); she later states 'that while cases where such evidence will carry sufficient probative value will exist, they will be exceptional' (408). Her further description of what that evidence might be seems to accord more with her perception of numerous examples than with that of exceptional cases. She describes five categories of evidence that she considers relevant – evidence providing the foundation for the defence of honest belief; evidence of bias or motive to fabricate on the part of the woman who was raped; evidence to explain the physical condition of the woman who was raped; evidence that provides an explanation for the sexual knowledge of a young person who was sexually assaulted; similar fact evidence that shows a pattern of conduct on the part of the woman who was raped (393–4). These five categories are so broad and open-ended that it would seem that almost all evidence of past sexual history would be found admissible under at least one of these headings.

One of the categories McLachlin lists –similar 'act' evidence – is particularly problematic. Her discussion of this evidence is somewhat confused and confusing because she slips in her terminology between 'similar fact' and 'similar act' and in her references to the person against whom the evidence is being introduced between the woman who was raped and the accused (400). Similar fact evidence is a particular and specific category of evidence that is admissible in limited circumstances against the accused; there has been no such category of evidence pertaining to the victim of a crime. It is very telling that a categorization of evidence that has been developed in relation to the accused is now being applied, without acknowledgment or comment on the transference, against the woman who was raped in a rape trial. It certainly affirms the understanding that the woman who was raped is herself on trial in this process.

In addition to this egregious slippage between accused and the woman who was raped, there is an absence of any discussion of why in the particular circumstances of a rape charge the patterns of the prior sexual activity of the woman who was raped are seen as rendering consent more probable in the situation that gave rise to the charge when that situation otherwise resembles the pattern. The notion that consent can be inferred from, or at least that consent is more probable based on, a pattern of conduct is one of the most tenacious and fallacious leaps of logic that supports the equation of a woman's sexual activity with indiscriminate sex. It is no accident in this context that the example used almost always is that of a prostitute (falsely assumed to be a woman who engages in indiscriminate sex) who has a history of extorting money based on the threat of false accusation of rape. Why the prostitute? One clearly does not have to be a prostitute to attempt to extort money on the basis of a false accusation of rape; any woman could adopt this ploy. In fact it seems to me that if a prostitute were interested in extortion, she would be more likely to threaten to expose the john as a john than to threaten a rape charge that he would know that she, as a prostitute, would be unlikely to be able to carry through on. This hypothetical is one of the most frequently cited examples of clearly relevant evidence; yet no one ever refers to any case where this situation has actually arisen. The spectre of the manipulative powerful prostitute looms large; she is so marginalized that it seems that simply placing her in the scenario, however inappropriately, insulates the hypothetical from challenge. It is a hypothetical that plays on myths, fears, and assumptions about prostitutes that have no grounding in reality or even in common sense.

In setting out these categories, McLachlin is at great pains to distinguish the legitimate purposes, as categorized above, for which this evidence may be introduced from the illegitimate purpose of inferring 'that the complainant consented to the act or that she is an unreliable witness' (396). The problem is that this distinction collapses under scrutiny. With the exception of the first category relating to the honest belief defence where neither consent nor credibility is in issue, all of the categories of evidence that McLachlin sets out lead to an inference with respect to consent and/or credibility (MacCrimmon and Boyle 1991). The motive to fabricate evidence, for example, is clearly introduced to promote the inference that the woman lied either about the sex itself or about the person with whom she had the sex or about her consent. All that McLachlin's categories do is provide the stereotype that gives rise to the inference. The categories themselves are the myths and stereotypes that create the link between past sexual history and consent or credibility. Evidence introduced to show motive to fabricate, for example, relies upon the myth that women will lie and falsely accuse rape if caught in a 'compromising' situation. If the 'misuse of evidence of sexual activity for ... the inference that the complainant consented to the act or that she is an unreliable witness' is an 'irrelevant and misleading purpose'(396), as I would agree with McLachlin it is, then it is misleading and irrelevant for all of the categories of evidence that McLachlin so carefully lays out, because they are all introduced for the purpose of leading to inferences about consent and/or credibility.

McLachlin describes the inferred links between past sexual history and credibility or consent as 'twin myths' that 'have no place in a rational and just system of law' (406). She adopts, as her own, the words of Professor Galvin: 'our aim is "to abolish the outmoded, sexist-based use of sexual conduct evidence while permitting other uses of such evidence to remain"' (406). She then modifies Galvin's proposal to come up with a series of applicable principles to guide the case-by-case determination of the relevance of any piece of evidence the accused might seek to introduce. That she is able to recognize that some of the uses of the evidence are based on gendered myths and stereotypes and yet steadfastly cling to the 'truth' that underlies what she sees as other uses of the evidence is remarkably un–self-reflective. She talks about the need to adapt common law rules of evidence to conform to current reality, but it is not the 'reality' that has changed.

Not long ago, the equation of women's sexual activity outside marriage with sexual indiscriminateness and lack of credibility was seen by most legal decision-makers as logical and rational, as a 'truth.' The recognition that what was once considered 'truth' is a myth, a fabrication that is not grounded in reality, should surely lead one to question how one distinguishes myth from truth and where the myths come from and why they were once thought of as truths and what that might mean about what is now considered 'truth.' Once one has recognized that particular beliefs were a function of sexism and of gender inequality, it would seem incumbent upon one to do a gender analysis of the assumptions and beliefs underlying the evidence one wants to retain, to try to rout out the myths and stereotypes that might continue to inform one's own thinking.

But this is the sticking point. Somehow McLachlin assumes that the sexism that gave rise to those myths is no longer pervasive, that we have reached a stage where we can assess the relevance of this evidence without that process of assessment being riddled at every level with assumptions that flow from gender inequality. She assumes that the accused and the woman who was raped come before the court as gender equals and that the court can engage in its quest for 'truth' unhampered by the distortions of gender inequality. This perception that a criminal trial is a quest for truth and that the question of relevance is the question of what will assist in finding that truth is highly problematic. It assumes that there is a single, objective, verifiable 'truth' waiting to be found. In the context of a rape trial, presumably the truth being sought is the determination that this man did or did not rape this woman. It is as if our understandings of this question are not framed by how we define rape, our views on individual versus social accountability, our reading of the surrounding events, our perceptions about gender and other inequalities, and the list goes on. It is as if the determination of guilt somehow takes place outside the social context in which the act occurred and in which laws are made and interpreted.

But, while there is no single absolute truth, there is social context. There is a grounding in time and events that we then each interpret. The contemporary reality to which McLachlin refers, but which she fails to incorporate into her analysis, is a reality of gender inequality in which women are subjected to male violence at alarming rates. This violence is a function and a reflection of the sex-based, inequality-based myths and stereotypes that continue to define women and women's sexuality. 'Now something *men do to women* has become instead something that is a part of *women's nature*' (Hoagland 1988, 18; emphasis in original); what is done to women is no longer recognizable as a creation and reflection of gender inequality but has become a defining feature of women. In her approach of assumed gender equality, McLachlin not only renders women's inequality invisible she further entrenches it. The categorized linking of a woman's past sexual history to a current determination of her consent to sex is transformed into a gender-neutral truth that is somehow seen as distinguishable from previous gendered myths and stereotypes. Gendered reality becomes ungendered 'truth,' and courts are free, in the pursuit of that truth, to invoke with impunity a series of categorized myths and stereotypes about women and women's sexuality that are premised on and promote inequality.

L'Heureux-Dubé, in her dissent, starts at the other end of the spectrum, not with an assumption of sex equality but with an exploration of the evidence at issue within the context of gendered inequality. In her judgment, she gives primacy to 'a consideration of the prevalence and impact of discriminatory beliefs on trials of sexual offences' (332). She grounds her constitutional analysis in the 'broader political, social and historical context' and places gender at the centre of that context (332). Her approach is premised on a recognition of women's inequality and how that inequality is played out through rape, in terms of the incidence of rape, the demographics of rape, the impact of rape, the social and legal responses to rape, and the myths and stereotypes that inform those responses to rape.

While it is very affirming and important that L'Heureux-Dubé engages in a contextualized gender analysis, it is disconcerting that other forms of oppression do not form any part of the context that she analyses. Neither judge makes any reference to issues of race, class, disability, or sexual identity and yet these clearly are factors that operate in conjunction with gender in terms of the construction of rape and the legal and social responses to it. Myths and stereotypes about the sexuality and sexual practices of Aboriginal women, Black women, Asian women, and other women of colour, of women with disabilities, lesbians, poor women, and working-class women abound. Similarly, myths and stereotypes about the men who are oppressed on these same bases distort legal and social recognition of, and reaction to, rape (Davis 1981, Wriggins 1983).

The race and class implications of the conviction of Mike Tyson, the acquittal of William Kennedy Smith, and the confirmation of Clarence Thomas' appointment to the U.S. Supreme Court are enormous. Tyson was so easy to fit into the stereotype of the Black rapist that it was impossible for him to work his way out of it. While I do think that he was 'guilty' and should have been convicted, his case to me was a clear example where the presumption of innocence was not in operation, not because women lay false charges and then hide behind unfair protections, but because his race, class, and self-presentation made him an easy scapegoat for other high-profile men who rape and harass with impunity. I do not share McLachlin's concern that innocent men will be wrongly convicted; my concern is with the inequalities that determine which guilty men get charged, convicted, and sentenced.

The neglect of the impact of other forms of oppression is a major short-coming in L'Heureux-Dubé's analysis. It means that her gender analysis is only partial. However, she has begun seriously to apply a gender analysis, and one hopes that, in future cases, her analysis will be more complete. With respect to the gender issues that she does cover, her analysis is strong. She depicts the pervasiveness of rape and its systemic nature; she exposes the underlying social tolerance, even promotion, of rape. She critiques the gendered inequalities in the legal processes that cumulatively produce low founding rates, low charging rates, low conviction rates, and low sentences for rape, all of which factors then circle back upon themselves to produce low reporting rates. She unpacks the myths and stereotypes that are relied upon at each of these stages and that surface in the form of legal principles developed specifically to address crimes of sexual violence against women, as well as in the application of traditional legal principles to those crimes. She relies upon statistical data, on studies that have measured discriminatory beliefs pertaining to rape that prevail among the general population and studies that have examined the impact of these beliefs on the decisions of juries. She refers extensively to feminist writing that describes and analyses women's experience of rape and of the legal system's response. She quotes from recent rape decisions to demonstrate the currency of even the most overt rape myths.

This is the context from within which L'Heureux-Dubé examines the question of the relevance of the past sexual history of the woman who was raped. She recognizes that the subjective nature of the determination of relevance makes this an area that is particularly vulnerable to rape mythology and that the rape myths may be harder to detect in this context, either because they are better obscured or because the entrenchment of the beliefs makes the determination of relevance more automatic (356). I would say that both of these things – better obscuring of the myths and the promotion of more automatic determinations of relevance – are at work in and through the majority judgment. The hiving off of some past sexual history evidence as being clearly irrelevant and introduced for an illegitimate purpose facilitates the obscuring of the irrelevance and illegitimate purpose of other past sexual history evidence with respect to which the beliefs may be more deeply entrenched. The categories provided by McLachlin make the assumption of relevance more automatic within those categories.

L'Heureux-Dubé goes through each of the categories of relevant evidence set out by McLachlin and the hypotheticals she employs. In this process, L'Heureux-Dubé unpacks the underlying stereotypes and false analogies that shore up the perceived links between the past sexual history of the woman who was raped and her current consent and/or credibility. She comes to the conclusion that

the evidence which is excluded by the provision is simply irrelevant. It is based upon discriminatory beliefs about women and sexual assault. In addition, the impugned provision provides wide avenues for the introduction of sexual history evidence that is relevant. Paradoxically, some of the exceptions may be cast overly broadly with the unfortunate result that a large body of evidence may still be improperly admitted on the basis of specious relevancy claims (364).

I disagree with L'Heureux-Dubé to the extent that she considers any evidence of the woman's past sexual history relevant. The prohibition against this evidence should be absolute. In my view, none of the exceptions created by section 276, the section struck down in this decision, warrant retention. In terms of the first exception allowing the defence to rebut sexual history evidence introduced by the Crown, such evidence is equally irrelevant for the prosecution as for the defence. I would circumvent the need for this exception by prohibiting the introduction of evidence of the past sexual history of the woman who was raped by the prosecution as well as by the defence. The second exception is for evidence relating to the identity of the offender. As discussed above, mistaken identity evidence relating specifically to the rape in question would always be admissible and has nothing to do with past sexual history. Other 'identity' evidence stemming from the woman's prior sexual history is as suspect as any other evidence of this type and is made relevant only through the invocation of stereotype or myth. Finally, in terms of the third exception for evidence introduced to support an honest belief defence, this evidence simply allows an accused to rely upon myth and stereotype to excuse his criminal behaviour.

L'Heureux-Dubé arrives at the conclusions that she does through an inequality-based, contextualized analysis. The evidence at issue is evidence about women and accordingly it is women and women's experience that she places at the centre of her discussion. Unlike McLachlin, her focus has not been on abstract notions of fairness and truth, whether that be with respect to the accused or the woman who was raped. She does not agree with the characterization of section 276 as a protection for the woman who was raped, or a protection of her privacy, or a means to encourage reporting of rapes. For L'Heureux-Dubé, this is about relevance and the distorted connections that render information relevant with respect to evidence by and about the woman who was raped in a rape trial. The distortions are rooted in women's inequality and function so as to perpetuate that inequality.

Conclusion

While I assume that McLachlin, in speaking for the majority of the Court, would not say that we have attained gender equality in all aspects of our lives and at all levels, she clearly thinks that we have divested ourselves of the gendered inequalities of rape, or at least of the gendered myths and stereotypes that hold the woman responsible for her rape or redefine rape as consensual sex. McLachlin's judgment treats rape as a gender-neutral offence. She approaches the issues with an assumption of gender equality that assumes away the gender problems. Her focus on the abstract, the primacy she gives to fairness and truth, her rights-based analysis and her concern for hypothetical people and situations that have no grounding in reality enable her to maintain the illusion of gender equality upon which her whole judgment is predicated.

My fear is that this assumption of equality is increasingly the starting point for judges, as it is in society more generally (Faludi 1991). Traditional legal analysis, which is both abstract and decontextualized, does not provide the grounding to challenge this initial assumption of equality. This is bad news for all oppressed groups, women among them. It becomes increasingly likely that the Charter, including the equality guarantees, will be used to shore up women's inequalities rather than to challenge, reduce, or eliminate them. This is of course not new; the equality provisions of the Charter have been used against women from the beginning (Brodsky and Day 1989). It is also true that assumed equality will not always work against women and also that the courts will be able to recognize some gender inequalities in some contexts (*Lavallée* 1990, *Butler* 1992, *Norberg* 1992).

While presumed equality may currently be the prevailing approach, the dissent of L'Heureux-Dubé provides the assurance that it is not the only approach judges are taking. While things seem to be getting worse at the assumed-equality, abstract end of the spectrum, they are simultaneously getting better at the inequality-based, contextualized end of the spectrum. L'Heureux-Dubé's dissent is one of the strongest, most overtly inequality-based, contextualized judgments I have read. This gives me hope and the strength to keep arguing that we can and must continue to struggle within the legal forum. At the same time, the majority judgment increases my concern that we not privilege this forum in terms of its potential for social change and that we ensure that our work continues on the political and social levels, as well as the legal.

The Supreme Court of Canada's judgment in *Seaboyer* was a turning point in the criminal law response to sexual assault. As a result of the decision, the Federal Department of Justice had to draft new legislation regarding the admissibility of evidence of the sexual history of victims of sexual assault. As Sheila McIntyre documents in the next chapter, this legislative drafting process itself was an historical occasion.

Notes

1 The inclusion of prostitution as male violence against women is highly contentious among feminists. While some regard prostitution as a form of women's employment made more oppressive by state harassment, I think that the abuse, degradation, and lack of control that characterize the working conditions of most prostitutes are so extreme and inherent as to render prostitution a form of violence against women.

2 The constitutionality of the prohibition against sexual reputation evidence (section 277) was also at issue in this case. Section 277 was upheld, with little discussion or analysis, on the basis that the evidence excluded under that section was clearly not related to any legitimate purpose and thus the exclusion did not

infringe the right to a fair trial (*Seaboyer* 392). The focus of the Supreme Court of Canada was almost exclusively on past sexual history evidence. Accordingly, my discussion of the decision treats past sexual history as the issue of the case.

3 I continue to struggle with the question of how to refer to the woman in the context of a rape trial. Along with many other feminists, I choose not to use the term 'victim' because it denotes passivity and helplessness, female stereotypes that are used against women. The term victim ignores the strength and resistance of women who have been raped and may even promote the interpretation of some forms of that strength and resistance as helplessness and/or passivity. I also choose not to use the term, 'survivor.' Many feminists adopted the term 'survivor' as a way to acknowledge the ordeal that the woman has lived through and to support and honour whatever coping mechanisms she has relied upon in that process. The focus of the word survivor is on the woman and her positive action, as opposed to victim which focuses on what was done to her.

However, the term survivor is not without problems. For one, it distinguishes between women who do survive the experience of rape and those who do not in a way that may be seen to attach some blame to those who do not survive. Additionally, it raises the question of what constitutes 'survival.' Further, I assume that the genesis of the use of survivor in this context was use of the term survivor with respect to the Holocaust. This raises the difficult question as to whether the term rape survivor is a respectful derivative or an appropriating false analogy. While rape was one of the forms of violence and degradation to which the victims of the Holocaust were subjected, sexual aggression was a vehicle for the expression of Jew hatred, gay and lesbian hatred, and gypsy hatred that were the focus of the Holocaust.

I am choosing to use what I consider a more accurate and less problematic, if somewhat awkward, phrase – 'the woman who was raped.' I like this term because it is not gender-neutral; it clearly marks the fact that it is women who are raped. However, the phrase 'the woman who was raped' is not without problems. It is a very individualistic characterization; I would prefer a term that denotes the systemic, as well as the individualized, nature of rape and other forms of male violence against women. In addition, some people may be concerned that this terminology undermines the presumption of innocence of the accused. I do not think that it does. The presumption of innocence does not say anything about the actual guilt or innocence of the accused; it simply provides a starting point that is respectful of the dignity and worth of the accused as a person. The presumption, in law, is about the burden of proof and the degree of proof required. An acquittal does not necessarily mean that the accused did not commit the crime, only that the Crown did not prove beyond a reasonable doubt that he did. In much the same way, referring to the woman who was raped does not say anything about who raped her or in what circumstances. In other words, it does not say anything about the guilt or innocence of the accused; it simply respects the dignity and worth of the woman who was raped by not negating her description of the experience. Despite its limitations, the term, the woman who was raped, remains preferable to me. Because of its directness and simplicity, the respect that it accords the woman, and because of its gender specificity, using the phrase 'the woman who was raped' is more consistent with my understanding of, and approach to, equality.

4 One of the few positive aspects of McLachlin's majority decision in *Seaboyer* is that she raises the admissibility of this evidence as an issue – 'I question whether evidence of other sexual conduct with the accused should automatically be admissible in all cases' (408). This is an important question that warrants much more attention than it has received to date. I hope that Crown attorneys will follow through on this issue by challenging the admissibility of evidence of past sexual history with the accused.

5 Little energy has gone into testing and defining the scope of these restrictions. The focus has instead been on the more general attempt to eliminate the restrictions altogether (Department of Justice 1987). If defence counsel had attempted to test the ambit of the restrictions, I expect that they would have found the courts willing to give very wide definitions to the three exceptions to the inadmissibility of past sexual history evidence. The choice to pursue elimination of the section rather than first try to test its boundaries seems to me a reflection of men's sense of their own power and entitlement, their sense that the law is or should be for and about them.

6 This is not, I hasten to note, in any way an endorsement of the decision of the Ontario Court of Appeal in this case in which the majority of the Court held that section 276 of the Code might on rare occasions violate the accused's Charter rights and thus the constitutionality of the section would have to be determined on a case-by-case basis. While a decision that provides for the possibility of a case-by-case determination of constitutionality may at first glance seem to support a contextualized approach, context can become individualized to an extent that ultimately has the effect of decontextualizing. What becomes decontextualized through individualization is the systemic gender inequalities that provide the background to the individual case. My disagreement with the Court of Appeal decision is that, in my view, there is no context that could render this evidence relevant.

7 McLachlin is here quoting from David Doherty's article '"Sparing" the Complainant "Spoils" the Trial.' I cannot allow this to pass without comment. While one cannot equate McLachlin with the sources that she relies on, just as one cannot collapse an author into the title that he chooses for an article, I find McLachlin's

uncritical references to Doherty's article most troubling. In a judgment that is premised on the belief that the negative myths and stereotypes that have for so long distorted rape trials and traumatized and stigmatized women who have been raped have largely been eradicated, McLachlin favourably refers to an article whose title is less reflective of myth and stereotype than it is of overt, deliberate violence against women. The evocation of the old saying 'sparing the rod spoils the child' clearly likens women to children and rape to a form of discipline necessary to keep women in line. The existence of such a title written in 1984 should have made McLachlin seriously reconsider, if not abandon, her optimism with respect to contemporary attitudes toward rape; her unreflective reliance on the article makes me question to what extent Mclachlin herself is free of the negative myths and stereotypes that surround women who have been raped.

8   This may have been the situation in *State* v. *Jalo* (1976), a case referred to by McLachlin as an example of motive to fabricate evidence that would be improperly excluded under s. 276. In this case, the accused father sought to introduce evidence of his daughter's sexual relationship with her brother as the basis for the father's defence that her charges against him were in retaliation for his having discovered and put an end to that relationship. I have serious questions as to whether the sexual relationship between the brother and sister, if there was one, was consensual.

9   In this connection, McLachlin invokes the 'public revulsion felt at the improper conviction of Donald Marshall ... or the Birmingham Six' as evidence of the depth of our society's commitment to the precept that the innocent must not be convicted. This invocation of Marshall and the Birmingham Six is problematic on at least two levels. First while there may now be public support and sympathy for Donald Marshall, both were a long time coming. Marshall was adamant about his innocence throughout his trial and the 10 years of his incarceration. He had to fight for his release every step of the way, and he did so with great difficulty and with little assistance. Even after he was cleared by the Nova Scotia Court of Appeal, it was a major uphill battle for Marshall to get compensation. The 'public revulsion' was rather low-key and short-lived and has not resulted in any meaningful changes in the criminal justice system to reduce the likelihood of a recurrence. For a full account of the Marshall case, see Michael Harris, *Justice Denied* (Toronto: Macmillan, 1986).

Second, the Donald Marshall case was not simply about an innocent man being convicted; it was about a First Nations man being an easy suspect and assumed to be guilty at every level of the process; it was about the racism that permeates our criminal justice system. To invoke his case in the name of fairness, truth, and the precept of presumed innocence is not only an insult to Donald Marshall but to all of the aboriginal people and people of colour who have been and are abused, mistreated, and denied justice in the criminal legal process. To refer to his case and that of the Birmingham Six without mention of racism and oppression, dominance and subordination, power and politics is to individualize what happened to Donald Marshall and the Birmingham Six and to make invisible the underlying and over-riding systemic issues of racism, domination, and power. In similar ways, the gender issues and the dominance and subordination that underlie the issue of past sexual history evidence are invisible in the majority judgment.

10 Even those of us who do not believe that past sexual history evidence is relevant may have particular examples with which we struggle as to whether or not that piece of information does make it more probable in our minds that the woman under scrutiny did consent to the sex. According to the legal test of relevance, this process of our linking, in our heads, her sexual history to her present consent renders that information about her past relevant to the determination of the accused's guilt. However, to me that mental linking between past consent and present consent reflects the particular myths or stereotypes that continue to hold sway with us. It is these links that need to be acknowledged and unpacked as myth and stereotype. The struggle should not be about relevance but about exorcising the ingrained untruths about women's sexuality.

References

Backhouse, Constance, and Leah, Cohen. 1980. 'Desexualizing Rape: A Dissenting View on the Proposed Rape Amendments.' *Canadian Women's Studies* 2:99

Berger, Vivian. 1977. 'Man's Trial, Women's Tribulations: Rape Cases in the Court-room' *Columbia Law Review* 77:1

Boyle, Christine. 1981. "Section 142 of the Criminal Code: A Trojan Horse?" *Criminal Law Quarterly* 23:253

Brodsky, Gwen, and Shelagh Day. 1989. *Canadian Charter Equality Rights for Women: One Step Forward or Two Steps Back?* Ottawa: Canadian Advisory Council on the Status of Women

Clark, Lorenne, and Debra Lewis, 1977. *Rape: The Price of Coercive Sexuality.* Toronto: Women's Press

Criminal Code, R.S.C.1985, c.C-46

Criminal Law Amendment Act, 1975, S.C. 1974–75–76, c.93, s.8

Davis, Angela. 1981. 'Rape, Racism and the Myth of the Black Rapist.' *Women, Race and Class.* New York: Random House

Dawson, Brettel. 1988. 'Sexual Assault Law and Past Sexual Conduct of the Primary Witness: The Construction of Relevance.' *Canadian Journal of Women and the Law* 2:310–34

Department of Justice. 1987. *The New Sexual Assault Offenses: Emerging Legal Issues.* Report prepared by Gisela Ruebat. Ottawa: Supply and Services Canada

Doherty, David. 1984. '"Sparing" the Complainant "Spoils" the Trial.' *Criminal Reports* (3d) 40:55

Faludi, Susan. 1991. *Backlash: The Undeclared War against American Women.* New York: Crown

Hoagland, Sarah. 1988. *Lesbian Ethics: Toward New Value.* Palo Alto, CA: Institute of Lesbian Studies

Lorde, Audre. 1984. 'The Masters Tools Will Never Dismantle the Master's House.' *Sister Outsider.* Freedom, CA: Crossing Press

MacKinnon, Catharine. 1987. *Feminism Unmodified.* Cambridge, MA: Harvard University Press

– 1989. *Toward a Feminist Theory of the State.* Cambridge, MA: Harvard University Press

MacCrimmon, Marilyn, and Christine Boyle. 1991. 'R. v. Seaboyer: A Lost Cause?' *Criminal Reports* (4th) 7:225–32

Majury, Diana. 1991. 'Equality and Discrimination According to the Supreme Court of Canada.' *Canadian Journal of Women and the Law* 4:407–39

Razack, Sherene. 1991. *Canadian Feminism and the Law: The Women's Legal and Education Action Fund and the Pursuit of Equality.* Toronto: Second Story Press

Rifkin, Janet. 1980. 'Toward a Theory of Law and Patriarchy.' *Harvard Women's Law Journal* 3:83–95

Rush, Florence. 1980. *The Best Kept Secret: Sexual Abuse of Children.* New York: McGraw-Hill

Russell, Diana. 1984. *Sexual Exploitation: Rape, Child Sexual Abuse and Workplace Harassment.* Beverly Hills: Sage

Sheehy, Elizabeth. 1989. 'Canadian Judges and the Law of Rape: Should the Charter Insulate Bias?' *Ottawa Law Review* 21:741

Smart, Carol. 1989. *Feminism and the Power of Law.* London: Routledge

Spender, Dale. 1980. *Man-Made Language* London: Routledge

Wriggins, Jennifer. 1983. 'Rape, Racism and the Law.' *Harvard Women's Law Journal* 6:103

Cases Cited

Norberg v. *Wynrib*, [1992] 4 W.W.R. 577 (S.C.C.)
Re Seaboyer and the Queen; Re Gayme and the Queen (1991), 66 C.C.C. (3d) 321 (S.C.C.)

Re Seaboyer and the Queen; Re Gayme and the Queen (1987), 37 C.C.C. (3d) 53 (Ont. C.A.)

R. v. Butler (1992), 70 C.C.C. (3d) 129 (S.C.C.)

R. v. Lavallee, [1990] 1 S.C.R. 852

R. v. Forsythe, [1980] 2 S.C.R. 268

State v. Jalo (1976), 557 P.2d 1359 (Or. C.A.)

12

SHEILA MCINTYRE

Redefining Reformism: The Consultations That Shaped Bill C-49

In the last chapter, Diana Majury explored what she refers to as the 'assumption of equality' that many judges share. Her analysis of the major-ity decision of the Supreme Court of Canada in Seaboyer *revealed the ways in which this assumption undermines the possibiltites for true substantive equality for women. So long as judges remain uncritical of the ways in which sexual assault is an issue of equality for women, the Charter of Rights and Freedoms will be used to further deprive women of their few existing legal protections. Although an erosion of rights for victims of sexual assault was the result of the decision in* Seaboyer, *the legislative amend-ments that followed the decision signalled some hope for a new law that rec-ognized the reality of the gendered nature of sexual assault and its equality implications for the status of women in Canada. In this chapter, Sheila McIntyre provides her perspective on the consultation process that led to the 1992 legislative changes to Canadian sexual assault laws. She focuses on the feminist principles and practices that animated the coalition of women's groups. Although it is too early to examine the legal interpretations of the new legislation, one thing is sure – 'for sectors of the women's community who have never before so influenced power politics, there will be no going back.'*

Introduction

This chapter chronicles the history of the coalition of Canadian women that participated in the framing of Bill C-49, Canada's new sexual assault legisla-tion.[1] My hope is that the story of the coalition will provoke new thinking about old debates concerning whether and how women and other historically disempowered groups should pursue egalitarian social change through law. I argue for a particular model of feminist law reform whose measure of achievement is not the reform's particular substantive legal yield or its potential as a building block for changing other laws, but the degree to which it translates principles of accountability to, inclusion of, and genuine power sharing among the broad women's community into feminist legal practice. The record of the coalition suggests that fidelity to such principles not only generates far less compromised legal and political results but generates resources without which systemic egalitarian change can never be achieved.

A secondary goal of this account is to amend the partial and incomplete record of our enterprise. What was unprecedented about the coalition and its achievements has largely been erased in public accounts of the bill's evolution. Although then Justice minister Kim Campbell has celebrated the consultation process behind the bill,[2] she has been reticent in acknowledging the degree to which Bill C-49 directly incorporates the coalition's work.[3] Likewise, media reports have distorted history. Their routine format featured (male) 'lawyers' (gender-neutral, legally objective) debating 'women's groups' (partisan and non-legal) on the merits of the legislation.[4] Because Black and disabled women who addressed the media on behalf of the coalition never showed up in film or print coverage, they were defined out of the meaning of 'women's groups' in the public discourse surrounding the bill. Similarly, the consistent emphasis all coalition spokeswomen placed on remedying the ways that systemic inequalities based on race and class and disability compound violence, sexual inequality, and diminished access to justice was rarely found newsworthy.[5] Neither the media nor the bill's critics cared to mention that the coalition's legal approach was rooted in and justified by Charter equality guarantees.

Removing from public view the conscious strategies chosen by the coalition to avoid replicating the historic failures of mainstream feminism and to breathe inclusive, substantively egalitarian politics into legal (re)form, ensures that equality-seeking communities cannot learn from our successes and defeats or hold Parliament accountable for what it knowingly refused to incorporate in the bill.

Mitigating Known Risks: The Animating Strategy

The impetus behind the creation of Bill C-49 was the Supreme Court of Canada decision in *R. v. Seaboyer; R. v. Gayme*[6] issued on 22 August 1991. Seven of the Court's nine judges held legislated restrictions on the use in sexual assault trials of evidence of a complainant's prior sexual history with individuals other than the accused to be an unconstitutional violation of an accused's right to a fair trial. Determinations of the admissibility of such evidence would be left to individual judges: the majority was confident that the 'reality in 1991' was that judges could be trusted to function free of rape myths and gender bias.[7]

According to a Department of Justice official[8] no other legal decision or event has ever generated so much public outrage or such public pressure on Justice Minister Campbell to act. And agree to act she did. Within two weeks, Campbell announced her intention to introduce legislation to counteract the chilling effect of *Seaboyer* on potential complainants by October of the same year. She immediately initiated consultations with provincial and territorial justice ministers, bar associations, and prominent women's groups soliciting advice on how to proceed. However, deciding whether to participate in the reform project both at this early stage and later as the consultations became more protracted was extremely difficult for most feminists. Whether the master's tools can ever dismantle the master's house remains a perennial question for those struggling for social change.[9] In the wake of *Seaboyer*, the risks were plain.

The government sponsoring the reforms was Conservative, enjoyed majority status in Parliament, and pursued programs consistently indifferent or harmful to women and disadvantaged men.[10] There was little reason to believe that even modest reforms[11] would survive subsequent Charter[12] challenge. *Seaboyer* was the third time in less than 20 years that a Supreme Court had subverted legislation designed to reduce gender bias in sexual assault adjudication.[13] Worse, the Charter equality jurisprudence[14] that should have protected the old rape shield rules and that provides the legal rationale and imperative for rape laws that actually work for women has yielded few returns for equality-seeking groups[15], and is being steadily eroded by the current Court.[16]

For many grassroots and minority women, the global question whether women should attempt to combat sexual violence through legislators and/or courts, was cross-cut with and tested by a less abstract and more urgent question: whether to work with white women lawyers. No thinking feminist can now be unaware of the many legitimate criticisms of the failures of white/ professional/academic feminism:[17] persistent refusal or inability to acknowledge and own the obligations and oppressive habits of race, class, heterosexual, and other privilege or how they result in under-inclusive practices and theories; strategies based on false universals; deep divisions among women that have undermined effective coalition politics and reforms that deliver trickle-down equality of little relevance or benefit to the majority of women.[18]

How individual women weighed these varied risks when deciding whether to participate in the consultations remains their story to tell. What distinguished those who did participate was their fierce desire not to be used by anyone – the minister of Justice, the governing Conservative party, white feminists, or *any* constituency within the women's movement – to subordinate some women's inequality in the interests of others'. The collective commitment that resulted is easily enough stated: to be responsive and accountable, not to government or law's norms, but to each other, the constituencies we represented, and the broader women's community. In practice, this commitment often took the form of resistance: to Kim Campbell's stated timetable, to under-inclusive consultations, and to the Justice Department's approach to reform. At each stage in the process, those who had political leverage used their willingness to boycott and denounce publicly the government's agenda to expand the constituent base of the consultative body[19] so that the amendments would not only be shaped but tested by the diverse knowledge, experience, and needs of all women sexual assault law should serve. Although the coalition's shifting leadership was tested internally,[20] the more constant challenge came from powerbrokers who sought to divide women against each other.[21]

The Consultations

The challenge of conceiving sexual assault reforms that would meaningfully advance women's safety, liberty, and equal benefit and protection of criminal and constitutional law was formidable. It required persuading a Conservative and male-dominated legislature of two things. First, even if binding, *Seaboyer* was wrongly decided as a matter of constitutional equality law.[22] To conform to s. 15, amendments must therefore step outside *Seaboyer's* framework to reform the substantive law that allows male-centred stereotypes and myths about women and women's sexuality to define the criminality of male violence. Second, amendments must recognize, name, and face down the problem of judicial gender bias, including that revealed in the majority's reasons.

Early on, the Justice Department apparently concluded that in terms of the Constitution, it had little room to manoeuvre.[23] At the September 5 meeting of all justice ministers, Kim Campbell indicated she hoped to introduce legislation to 'clarify and make more precise the procedures to be followed' in decisions about the admissibility of sexual history evidence in order to provide protection for complainants 'consistent with the Supreme Court's decision.'[24] Provincial ministers viewed judicial education programs as the remedy for *Seaboyer*.[25] By 21 September the National Action Committee (NAC), the Women's Legal Education and Action Fund (LEAF), and the National Association of Women and the Law (NAWL), as well as the Canadian Bar Association (CBA) held a press conference urging the Minister to slow down and allow experts five or six weeks to explore a number of legal alternatives.[26] She agreed to a short delay and scheduled a consultation with a variety of lobby groups, professional organizations, and provincial officials for 23 October 1991.

In the next four weeks, women's organizations continually caucused with each other and with Crown lawyers and feminist bureaucrats about post-*Seaboyer* strategies.[27] A consensus was developing in the women's community against focusing on evidentiary exclusions alone because they would benefit few women, leave unaddressed far more fundamental problems with sexual assault[28] (and constitutional) law, and fail to capitalize on the public support for a sexual assault law that actually works to curb violence against women and children.[29]

Because of LEAF's unparalleled expertise and successes in constitutional equality litigation,[30] particularly in cases concerning sexual violence,[31] and because it had so recently developed in concert with the violence-against-women's movement, a powerful constitutional critique of the role of sexual assault law in legitimating both sexual violence and women's social inequality,[32] the women's community delegated primary responsibility to LEAF to come up with a legal strategy for sexual assault law reform. Prior to the October meeting with Justice, LEAF began researching the Charter implications of several reform options including requiring exculpatory mistakes to be honest *and* reasonable, making consent a defence the accused must prove and using a preamble to frame the new law with reference to women's constitutional rights. Fortuitously, a meeting of the National Legal Committee was scheduled for 19–20 October.[33]

Having reviewed preliminary research on a variety of post-*Seaboyer* options, LEAF's national legal committee reached a consensus in support of pursuing substantive (rather than simply evidentiary) amendments to sexual assault law such as redefining or altering the *mens rea* of sexual assault and codifying circumstances that negate consent (and thereby converting rape myths into errors of law),[34] both of which would narrow the availability of the defence of mistake. Because the individual and combined merits of such fundamental changes could not be assessed before the meeting with Justice, the legal committee elected to press for a further delay before new legislation was drafted and tabled. The only legal opinions LEAF could confidently advance at that point were that any amendments that simply codified

Seaboyer would fail to conform with women's constitutional rights to security of the person and equal protection and benefit of the law, and that any
law designed to advance women's rights must be developed through meaningful consultations with the women it purports to serve.

22 OCTOBER 1991

On 21 October, representatives of several women's organizations met in Toronto with staff of the Ontario Women's Directorate (OWD) and the Ministry
of the Attorney General (AGO). All agreed that piecemeal interim reforms to
sexual assault law would be worse than useless and that Justice should be
urged to delay tabling reforms in order to allow for broad consultations
among affected communities to strategize effective legal approaches. Prior to
meeting with Justice, that consensus had been endorsed by LEAF, NAC, NAWL,
OWDAGO, the Canadian Association of Sexual Assault Centres (CASAC), the
Disabled Women's Network of Canada (DAWN), the National Organization of
Immigrant and Visible Minority Women (NOIVM), and the Native Women's
Association of Canada (NWAC)[35]

The meeting with Justice got off to a very bad start. There were no spokeswomen for organizations representing women of colour or immigrant or
francophone women, and only one voice for disabled women.[36] Many participants had never seen an 'Issues Paper' prepared by Justice that summarized
the majority reasons in *Seaboyer* and identified questions left unresolved.[37]
No one had seen the detailed list of legal questions Justice proposed for the
day's discussion and, in any event, the questions addressed highly technical
evidentiary and procedural issues which grass roots women's groups were ill-
equipped to understand and legal groups were ill-prepared to answer.[38] Of
the 23 questions posed, only two concerned possible changes to the substantive criminal law.[39] There was no express proposal for requiring mistakes to
be reasonable; no suggestion that the definition of consent itself was on the
table; no reference to s. 15 of the Charter or how it might be used proactively
to rework discriminatory components of sexual assault law; and no mention
of a preamble.

From the outset, then, the Department of Justice and most of the groups
consulted were on different wavelengths. Justice took *Seaboyer* as its starting
point and outside limit and sought to advance complainants' interests[40] by
reinstating protections or clarifying provisions not clearly foreclosed by the
majority decision. In perceiving its task as accommodating women's 'interests' to existing jurisprudence on accused's rights without regard to the sexism embedded in that jurisprudence, or its assailability pursuant to s. 15

guarantees, Justice's replication of the backward-loo'ing and gender-blind legal method adopted by the *Seaboyer* majority promised to replicate *Seaboyer's* flaws. Its allegiance to established precedent also rendered the expertise of non-lawyers, particularly rape crisis workers and multiply oppressed women, as irrelevant to the consultation process as the material reality of systemic inequality had been to the *Seaboyer* majority.

By contrast, women participants other than representatives of REAL Women uniformly rejected *Seaboyer* on the ground that sexual history is never relevant to whether a particular woman consented to a particular man on a particular occasion and/or that most judges cannot be trusted to determine relevance or to weigh relevance against prejudice in a manner free of stereotypes about women's sexuality and credibility. Again excepting REAL Women's representatives, every participant agreed that piecemeal tinkering with evidence and procedure within the parameters of *Seaboyer* would legislatively entrench the gender bias of *Seaboyer* and would leave unaddressed the discriminatory substance of a body of law that had never protected or delivered impartial justice to the majority of women. In different ways and with differing emphases, women's groups (other than REAL Women) sought to persuade an unreceptive triad of lawyers from Justice that their approach was backwards and, as a result, emptied s. 15 of all meaning. Endorsing and amplifying upon LEAF's position,[41] women's groups insisted Justice should use women's constitutional rights to security of the person and to equal protection and benefit of law as a sword, not a shield, by building from the reality of systemic inequality to construct law tailored to redress it. Furthermore, LEAF urged the government to accept the authority of women, not man-made precedent, on the ways that sexual violence, social inequalities, and existing legal doctrine interact to deprive women of constitutional rights and, supported by a detailed legislative record and a preamble invoking women's s. 7 and 15 rights, to make equality (the) law. Such (in)equality-driven laws necessitated an equality-driven approach: meaningful consultations among and with all sectors of the women's community. Even the CBA, the Canadian Civil Liberties Association (CCLA), and several provincial governments' representatives urged Justice to respect the consensus among women's groups for further delay, broader consultations, and an approach to reforms that looked beyond *Seaboyer*. REAL Women again stood alone in opposition.

Notwithstanding this unexpected and powerful consensus, the approach urged by nine national women's groups was rejected as 'informative' but 'irrelevant' to the 'legal' task at hand, 'utopian' and too time-consuming when 'women' were demanding the Justice Department act quickly. Women in the Justice Department urged women's groups to accept a 'reasonable' compromise: immediate interim amendments to offset the chilling effect of *Seaboyer* on the reporting of assaults, followed by a broader substantive overhaul at a later date. The feminist response was simple, if incomprehensible to Justice. When the majority of women did not report assault pre-*Seaboyer*, procedural tidying of a decision which *expanded* judges' discretion to admit sexual history evidence would neither cure *Seaboyer's* damage nor address other reasons why women will not report, particularly racism and class bias in the law enforcement process. Accordingly, enacting in the name of 'women' reforms that are of real benefit only to a minority of women and at the real cost legitimating male and legal violence against most women is not only misguided, but politically and constitutionally unacceptable.

20 NOVEMBER 1991

Several organizations[42] responded to the October consultations by requesting a face-to-face meeting with the minister in order to advocate a holistic, constitutionally driven approach rather than cosmetic tinkering. Although the minister set up a meeting for 20 November, she also held a press conference announcing her intention to introduce legislation in November to be passed before the Christmas recess. She was quoted as saying that her sense of 'obligation to Canadian women' in responding urgently foreclosed any approach 'where we think and mull for months and months.'[43] In response, the coalition caucused and reached a crucial agreement that was probably the turning point in Bill C-49's history: if Campbell could not be persuaded of the wrongheadedness of purporting to serve 'women's' interests through reforms that feminist legal experts, rape crisis workers, and multiply oppressed women had concluded would perpetuate legalized inequality, the coalition's institutional members would publicly oppose the proposed legislation and recommend its defeat.

The potential short- and long-term risks to individual organizations of publicly opposing one of Parliament's most prominent feminists and one of the Tories' only pro-woman initiatives were significant.[44] Nonetheless, no organization balked or counselled compromise on the basis of its own material interests, or the belief that some reforms were better than nothing or the possibility we could use our leverage to secure a public commitment from the minister to initiate a comprehensive overhaul of sexual assault law in exchange for not opposing interim amendments. The seven groups scheduled a press conference to follow the 20 November meeting and notified the press that national women's groups might come out in opposition to the minister's proposed amendments.

Meanwhile, LEAF finalized a preliminary legal opinion consistent with, but elaborating upon, the approach proposed to Justice on 23 October. It was to be circulated only if the minister proved open to more comprehensive amendments and the extra time they would require. The opinion advanced four options but stated that their assessment

should be done only after extensive consultations with a wide variety of groups representing a cross-section of women in Canada, both within and without the legal community, and in particular those groups who work with and advocate for victims of assault. LEAF can offer our expertise in sex equality and constitutional law to participate in these consultations. But no new law will meet its policy objectives unless it persuades women that they will receive equal justice. The voices of Canadian women must be heard on that question.[45]

On 20 November, representatives of CASAC, the Church Council on Justice and Corrections (CCJC), the Canadian Nurses' Association (CNA), DAWN, LEAF, NAC, NAWL (NOIVM was delayed by fog) met with the minister and some of her staff. The minister explained the politics of her decision to proceed immediately with *Seaboyer*-specific amendments, indicated her commitment to initiate a considered review of the entire law thereafter, and insisted that the immediate amendments would not be mere tinkering. They would (as predicted) eliminate the 'vagaries' within the majority judgment, re-enact non-compellability and *voir dire* provisions and codify guidelines to govern the exercise of judicial discretion in determining the admissibility of sexual history evidence. The minister then dropped a bombshell. Justice was also 'considering' four additional amendments: a mixed subjective/objective standard for the mistake defence; a codified definition of consent to include circumstances that do not constitute consent; a preamble; and a presumption that sexual history evidence is irrelevant. The coalition then threw away its script.

Having grimly approached the meeting ready to dissociate from Campbell's reforms, the assembled women's groups switched gears to embrace the new proposals enthusiastically and to expand on their necessity. We indicated that if such substantive amendments were made we could support early legislation and were ready to lend Justice our expertise in assisting in that project. While feminist lawyers in the room were preoccupied with the legal possibilities of this apparent breakthrough on substantive law, CASAC's Lee Lakeman pursued the coalition's process concerns. Insisting that community presentations at the committee stage could not cure the absence of expertise and input from front-line rape crisis workers including aboriginal, disabled, poor, and racial minority women in the drafting process, she bluntly demanded further consultations in which the unparalleled expertise of such women concerning current law's defects had primacy of place. More, she stated that CASAC and other representatives of the grassroots women's movement must have the opportunity and funding to meet with LEAF and NAWL for legal guidance in transforming women's real needs into legal form. Accordingly, she called for two further consultations – one before tabling with at least the seven groups then present and another with a national and representative cross-section of the women's community after tabling but before the bill went to committee. NAC immediately endorsed CASAC's proposal. The minister's special adviser asked Lee to flesh out the parameters of the second consultation. On the spot, she calculated we would need a three-day meeting of 60 women from across the country, with travel, accommodation, and meal expenses paid by Justice. Those invited would discuss the tabled amendments for two days among themselves and then meet with the minister on the final day to present the results of our collective deliberations. The minister not only agreed, but made a further concession: although Justice staff would fund and organize the necessary administrative arrangements,[46] CASAC, and not the government, would control the agenda invitation list.[47]

At her own press conference following the meeting, Campbell informed the media she was 'considering' defining consent in the new bill as well as other proposals recommended by 'a coalition of women's groups.'[48] Immediately thereafter, the women's groups held their press conference, announcing that a breakthrough appeared to have been made: definitions of consent and non-consent as well as mistake were on the table and further consultations prior to and following the bill's tabling were to take place. The coalition stated that if, but only if, such amendments were tabled, the proposed bill would have our enthusiastic support. Pushed to be specific about the kind of consent clause we would support, part of the LEAF opinion was offered: 'overt words or gestures which, to a reasonable observer, unequivocally communicate voluntary agreement.' Asked to explain its meaning, NAC's Judy Rebick articulated the phrase that made national headlines: 'I think what we're talking about is a law that says "no" means "no" and "yes" means "yes" and before you initiate sexual contact it's your responsibility to find out whether it's yes or no.' Thereafter, Bill C-49 was consistently called the 'No means No Law.'

It was never clear whether these four new substantive proposals were being seriously pursued by the minister and her staff, or were mentioned in order to buy time and support. (The press release circulated by the minister immediately following the meeting makes no mention of any of the four new 'considerations.'[49]) But by early afternoon she confirmed in the House of Commons that the proposed legislation 'would contain a definition of consent that would be clear and unambiguous.'[50] The story made national news and launched a public debate on the meaning of 'consent' that has not yet abated.

27 NOVEMBER 1991

The pre-tabling consultation was scheduled for one week to the day after the definitions of consent and mistake were put on the table. At the coalition's request, two new organizations were invited, Intercede, an organization of immigrant domestic workers, and Regroupement québécois des centres d'aides et de lutte contre les agressions à caractère sexuel (CALACS). Because suspicion remained that Justice had, at best, the sketchiest of ideas about redefining consent, and because in any case, the minister could not be budged on her December deadline or pushed to consider further substantive changes, the coalition agreed the one-day consultation should focus on definitions of consent and non-consent. LEAF was delegated the task of drafting legal proposals for discussion. This effectively required LEAF to rank and reformulate its preliminary proposals and to secure National Legal Committee approval of such proposals within less than one week.[51]

LEAF's goal was not to draft what would become the law,[52] but to articulate a constitutionally sound legal framework whose basic components respected women's constitutional rights and reflected the expressed concerns of the women's community in understandable terms. The basic framework also had to be sufficiently simple to be translated into legislative drafting without delay. Should the proposal be approved by the coalition and improved during the day of consultations, a number of things followed. If the minister rejected a proposal endorsed by the coalition, the legislative committee would not likely repudiate her approach and adopt the coalition's proposal because her party had the majority of committee seats. The option of publicly opposing flawed amendments with our concrete proposal in hand remained open but more politically credible. If the minister were persuaded by the coalition approach and tabled a bill reflecting its basic elements, coalition members would have a month to refine its contents before the January consultations when the proposals could be tested and perfected by the different women's constituencies assembled. Amendments and additions backed by so unprecedented an assembly of women stood a greater chance of being adopted through the committee process, because the tabled bill would already reflect its equality-driven structure.

By 26 November, the National Legal Committee had developed two options designed to focus the adjudicative process on the actual events and communications between the accused and the complainant that resulted in a sexual assault charge (rather than on stereotypes about women and their sexuality), to reduce significantly the possible relevance of sexual history evidence and to convert most 'honest' mistakes into errors of law. The first option defined consent according to a reasonableness standard along the lines discussed at the press conference one week earlier. It was to be backed up by detailed legislative objectives justifying the rationales behind the amendment and its terms. The second option defined consent as the 'unequivocal communication of voluntary agreement to the sexual activity or activities between the accused and the complainant which form the subject matter of the charge' and then enumerated a non-exclusive list of situations that indicated lack of voluntary agreement or that foreclosed the operation of discriminatory assumptions about women's sexuality, credibility or nature as the basis for mistaken beliefs in a particular woman's consent.[53] In addition LEAF identified the types of supporting documentation required as part of the legislative record to support equality-based objectives underlying the amendments. Three pages in length, this set of proposals became the working document for the consultations.

The minister attended the first half-hour of the consultation. She summarized the intent of the amendments, emphasized her desire for clear, simple terms and provisions likely to survive constitutional scrutiny and her aspiration that the amendments promote 'inclusive justice' and be mindful of and responsive to the particular vulnerabilities of multiply oppressed women. After she left, the deputy minister added that the minister supported amendments that would place greater responsibility on men to take reasonable steps to secure consent and would like to find language to address sexual violence in the context of unequal power relationships.

By about 10:30 A.M., the coalition was ready to work and asked all government officials to leave. With reference to LEAF's working proposals, individual women's groups responded with a number of quite disparate concerns grounded in their particular constituencies' interests. My recollection is that some generated more group discussion than others but that all were quite quickly endorsed for reasons that ultimately reduce to the establishment and maintenance of mutual trust and respectfulness among the different players. In 20 years of political activism I have never experienced group dynamics so untainted by egotism, posturing, dogma, or rank-pulling.

Almost all the players were strong, self-respecting women with longstanding roots in community-based movements for social change.[54] Assured in their particular expertise but thoughtful and honest about its limits, they had the political maturity to recognize, value, and rely upon the distinctive expertise, leadership, and authority of others. Equally important, they knew how and why to manifest that they did. The commitment to an inclusive consultative process that reflected these qualities also mandated that when the delegated spokeswoman of a particular community articulated her constituency's concerns and priorities, she was presumed to know what she was talking about and her argument was credited.

The agreements on legal content, which were reached in under two hours, were as follows. The law should require consent to be explicitly sought and obtained. Requiring consent to be communicated by 'words or overt gestures' did not adequately accommodate the realities of women with disabilities who rely on a wider range of communicative methods. The law's language must explicitly mention the role of inequalities based on race, class, and disability wherever pertinent. There must be language addressing consent coerced by abuses of power. No new categories of sexual assault should be added to the existing three,[55] but assaults proven to be motivated by racism or other group bigotry should be subject to greater sanction. If reference to s. 15 of the Charter appears in any of the amended provisions of the law, it should not suggest that equality guarantees are relevant only to those provisions. The preamble must explicitly refer to s. 7 and s. 15 and the links between sexual violence and racism/classism/disability, etc.

Having agreed on the outlines of the law we wanted, we then agreed to ask Justice staff to return after lunch and to advise us on the kind of content they planned to include in the preamble, what they had already done to address compound inequality, and what their responses were to LEAF's working paper. All we learned about the preamble was it would address 'the nature of the problem.' Further questions revealed Justice staff would need help in that project. When Justice lawyers indicated that the preamble would be in gender-neutral language, coalition opposition was unanimously expressed and explained. Justice officials invited our help on compound inequality language. Male Justice officials raised patently male-centred objections to both of LEAF's suggested consent clauses: they set too high a threshold for consent; required communication to be too explicit, particularly for longstanding relationships where communication is (on their view) minimal or subtle or unspoken; put too much responsibility on men; risked criminalizing sex under ambiguous circumstances, and so on. Discussion was heated and the two sides were worlds apart.

After Justice staff again left us to work on our own, women of colour broke into a separate caucus to strategize how best to ensure race inequality was fully incorporated into the reforms. On their return we divided into two groups, each composed of lawyers and non-lawyers. One group tried to sketch out a preamble with particular sensitivity to the compounding effects of race and sex inequality; the other adapted LEAF's proposal to develop wording for all the substantive concerns raised by coalition members. By the end of the day we had completed the text of the consent clauses we unanimously recommended be incorporated in the new amendments and a preliminary outline for the preamble. The former addressed all but two concerns expressed during the day – language responsive to the needs of women with disabilities and a provision dealing with unwanted sexual advances in situations characterized by substantial inequality between the parties. Less than 24 hours later the outline of a recommended preamble was faxed in. Both appear in Appendix B of this chapter.

BILL C-49: FIRST READING

On 12 December 1991 Kim Campbell tabled Bill C-49.[56] Its innovative content reflected the basic framework proposed by the coalition two weeks earlier with one glaring exception. Its preamble was gender-neutral and silent on the relationship between sexual violence and sexual inequality.[57] Not surprisingly then, neither the preamble nor the bill's substantive amendments explicitly addressed compound inequality as a problem.[58] Aside from this significant flaw, the remaining components of the tabled bill met the coalition's fundamental goals.

The preamble referred to s. 15, stated sexual history evidence is 'rarely relevant' and 'inherently prejudicial,' and contained language that, if clarified, would bolster the chances that the bill's innovations would survive any constitutional challenge.[59] The consent clauses did not go as far as urged by the coalition, but five of our proposals did appear in the tabled legislation. Section 273.1(1) positively defined consent to require 'voluntary' (but not 'unequivocal') agreement to engage in the sexual activity in question, thereby underlining that consent requires active, hence verifiable (not projected) conduct freely chosen (not coerced or presumed) and focusing law enforcement on the specific sexual interaction in dispute, not on past history or self-serving myths. Three non-consent clauses along the lines recommended by the coalition appeared: a no means no clause, a clause stating that consent can be revoked, and an abuse of trust/authority clause [s. 273.1(2)(c),(d) and (e)]. As we had urged, the bill contained a clause stating that the codified circumstances in which no legally recognized consent exists are not closed [s. 273.1(3)].[60] Justice had not included coalition proposals stating consent shall not be presumed on the basis of a complainant's consumption of alcohol or drugs, or on the basis of a complainant's membership in a historically disadvantaged group.

Justice narrowed the availability of the mistake defence in two respects. It foreclosed acquittal altogether where an accused's mistake about consent (meaning a woman *was* raped) was based on self-induced intoxication, recklessness or wilful blindness. Additionally, unless an accused had taken 'all reasonable steps' in the circumstances known to him at the time of the assault 'to ascertain that the complainant was consenting,' mistakes resulting in sexual violence would be found legally unjustifiable. This revision effectively set a legal standard of care for sexual aggressors in conformity with the law's definition of consent. It credits women with full humanity – that is, the right to and capacity for self-determination; and credits men with the capacity for rational self-control. Here, consent is something a particular woman does, not something a man desires to the point of not caring enough to check whether his wishes are her desires.

Bill C-49 also introduced detailed guidelines for judges governing the procedures and substantive principles to be used in determining the admissibility of sexual history evidence in sexual assault trials.[61] The guidelines apply to all sexual offences, not just sexual assault, cover the complainant's prior history of non-consensual as well as consensual sex,[62] and prohibit use of sexual history evidence to support *any* inference that such history renders the complainant more likely to have consented to the alleged assault or less worthy of belief.[63] Beyond this general prohibition, Bill C-49 limits admissible evidence to specific instances of sexual activity that are relevant to an issue to be proved at trial and have 'significant' probative value that is not 'substantially outweighed by prejudice to the proper administration of justice.'[64] In striking that balance, judges are directed to consider a number of specific factors (s. 276(3)) including the elimination of discriminatory beliefs or biases from fact-finding and the risk of 'unduly' arousing prejudice, sympathy, or hostility in the jury. Thereafter follow formal procedural rules governing applications to admit sexual history evidence, which largely affirm the pre-*Seaboyer* status quo.[65]

Immediately following the minister's press conference explaining the objectives and content of the amendments, public debate along fairly predictable lines ensued. The *Globe and Mail's* headline summarized it perfectly: 'Political battle looms over sex-assault bill: Women's groups pitted against defence lawyers.'[66] The coalition and other women's groups endorsed the law's structure, particularly the preamble, the codification of the meaning of consent, and the detailed evidentiary guidelines that by implication conveyed that judges are in need of such instruction. The defence bar opposed the intoxication and mistake clauses and expressed alarm about ambiguous communication of non-consent.[67]

The ensuing media attention served women's interests well by fostering a quality of public education few advertising campaigns promoting 'no means no' principles could hope to replicate. Because the terms of this law are very easy to understand and explain, public debate focused on the content of the law, not lawyers' conflicting predictions about its constitutionality. This, in turn, generated widespread discussion of the social meaning of rape, gender(ed) differences in perceptions of consent, the rights and responsibilities of sexual partners, and what kinds of 'mistakes' should be justifiable. Even the defence bar's scaremongering about breathalyzers and signed affidavits by the bed and the number of 'innocent' men who may now be convicted for deciding that 'maybe' means 'yes'[68] have served a public interest. Most men are aware that, whether they agree or not, the rules have changed.[69] They have absorbed three messages: Unless a woman's consent is clearly communicated, proceeding with sex may result in criminal charges and possibly conviction; drunkenness is no excuse for mistakes about a woman's willingness to engage in sex; and consent on a previous occasion or to another act is not a grant of perpetual access. This law gives a woman the right to change her mind. Notwithstanding the defence bar's stated opposition to using the criminal law for purposes of public education,[70] the bill has already served a significant educative function.

CONSULTATIONS 27–29 JANUARY 1992

During December 1991, Lee Lakeman worked on assembling a genuine constituent assembly of women from across the country with expertise to contribute to the process of reviewing and proposing amendments to Bill C-49. About half of those invited represented national, autonomous (i.e., woman-only) women's organizations whose leadership is drawn from the constituency it is designed to serve.[71] The other half were front-line rape and transition house workers from across the country. The resulting assembly was truly representative of women on two counts: the national leadership of the women's movement was present and grassroots workers included women of colour, poor women, disabled women, lesbians, and sex trade workers.

Prior to the consultations, all participants received an information package designed to equip newcomers to the coalition for meaningful partnership in the consultations. For instance, the package contained the comprehensive proposals submitted to Kim Campbell following the Vancouver Symposium[72] and an annotated, clause-by-clause translation of Bill C-49's strengths and weaknesses designed for non-lawyers. The agenda scheduled time for women to caucus, respond to C-49 and strategize responses to legislation other than C-49 that increases or entrenches women's vulnerability to violence.

A full account of those three days is beyond the scope of this chapter. Their formal product was unanimous endorsement of the approach and most of the content of the 27 November coalition's proposals, revision of the preamble,[73] and a two-page summary of federal legislation whose role in facilitating violence against women, particularly multiply oppressed women, requires urgent review and amendment. Their more important harvest was the unforgettable experience of what power-sharing through genuine diversity can feel like and achieve. Some fragments of that literally indescribable dynamic may prove instructive.

The audience with the minister was used to confront her with our diversity, not the consensus we had reached. Those voices – Black women, lesbians, sex trade workers – who had not been at the table in the earlier meetings with Campbell, held the floor. Their failure to reach the minister on the inadequacy and unacceptability of generic drafting and false universals spawned the most innovative clauses of our final proposals.

Resources were devoted before, during, and after the January consultations to providing non-lawyers with sufficient knowledge to speak with assurance about the law that had been tabled, the legal meaning of the amendments the coalition was proposing, and the arguments being advanced by defence lawyers against the bill.[74] This made for amazing press conferences and committee hearings because it was simply assumed that the women lawyers would talk law and the non-lawyers, politics. But it has also empowered front-line workers to make the law accessible to their staff, public audiences, local bureaucrats, and so on. And it taught grassroots activists that law can be accessibly explained (or drafted) and to demand no less, particularly from feminist lawyers.

Following the January consultations, those organizations with the most resources prepared information packages to allow participants to engage women in their communities in the campaign to secure amendments to Bill C-49. Members of the press seeking interviews with the more prominent members of the coalition were referred to the less prominent. METRAC compiled and mailed a summary of our work and organized a community forum in Toronto. CACSW produced a detailed handout on everything a novice needs to know to appear before a legislative committee. Of the 14 organizations that appeared before the legislative committee, 8 had been coalition partners: CACSW, DAWN, LEAF, NAC, NAWL, NWAC, NOIVM and POWER.[75] Typically, at least some coalition members attended the hearings to provide support for other coalition presenters. When LEAF alone was invited to represent the coalition in the Senate hearings, their spokeswoman brought NAC and NOIVM representatives and all three addressed the committee.

Bill C-49 received Royal Assent on 23 June 1992. Although not all the coalition's recommendations were adopted, the preamble did become gender-specific and was resequenced exactly as we urged. The addition of 'abuse of power' to s. 273.1(2)(d) offers enormous promise for combatting the inequalities that foster sexual assault. The defence bar successfully had the mistake clause watered down to require less than 'all' reasonable steps to secure consent for legally blameless rapes, but the reasonableness requirement offers far more than the procedural fixes promised by Justice in November. The single, most stunning repudiation of the coalition's vision was politicians' refusal to incorporate the preamble in the Criminal Code, or to embrace the need to explicitly enumerate those classes of women that police officers, lawyers, judges, and juries have systematically deemed unworthy of law's protection.[76]

I am of the view that what is good about the bill is women's doing and that because the word is out within women's communities and the public sphere,[77] the individual women, the organizations they represented, the coalitions they built, and the principled feminism they made real will be heard from again. There is already evidence that for sectors of the women's community who have never before so influenced power politics, there will be no going back.[78]

The containment of law reform turns on rationalizing modest token change as the best that can be expected from 'the system' at a given time. This rationalization works best if the rationalizers are the visible tokens of change within the system, knowledgeable about – that is, socialized in – the limits of working within its norms. Co-optation is the process by which tokens feel useful, even daring, rather than used and tamed, in this process. For the same reasons that top-down process or theory will never address, much less end, systemic inequalities, political theorizing about how to prevent 'the system' from co-opting reform movements will never end legitimating compromise. Compromise must be checked by the concrete practices of mutual accountability through which the agents of change keep each other honest.

Abandoning law altogether is a luxury of theory and/or privilege from the perspective of those long abandoned by reformers and reformism.[79] The precondition of any reform initiative must be adequate consultations among a constituency-based assembly of all who will or should benefit from legal change to ensure that when reformers conclude that something is better than nothing, those for whom nothing has been law's historic yield concur.

Appendix A

Acronyms for Organizations in the Coalition

CACSW	Canadian Advisory Council on the Status of Women
CASAC	Canadian Association of Sexual Assault Centres
CBA	Canadian Bar Association
CCJC	Church Council on Justice and Corrections
CCLA	Canadian Civil Liberties Association
CNA	Canadian Nurses Association
DAWN	DisAbled Women's Network
LEAF	Women's Legal Education and Action Fund
METRAC	Metro Toronto Action Committee on Violence Against Women and Children
NAC	National Action Committee on the Status of Women
NAWL	National Association of Women and the Law
NCW	National Council of Women
NOIVM	National Organization of Immigrant and Visible Minority Women
NWAC	Native Women's Association of Canada
POWER	Prostitutes and Other Women for Equal Rights

Appendix B

Coalition Proposal, 27 November 1991

PREAMBLE

The preamble should have three components:

1. A powerful definition of the problem of violence against women and, in particular, sexual violence against women, as a gendered problem. This should contain a description of the scope of the problem; the history of women's disadvantage and oppression – to include the relationship between colonialism and the oppression of women of colour and aboriginal women, and the resulting nexus between race and sex inequality which has led to the sexual objectification and stereotyping of women from non-European cultures; and the role of law, including common law, with respect to women's disadvantaged status.

2. An explicit naming of the particular vulnerability to violence of certain classes of women on the basis of race, class, disability and other enumerated and analogous grounds found in s. 15 of the Charter. This should address the implications for s. 7 and s. 15 rights of the problem of sexual violence against women, not just in relation to sex, but also in relation to race, class, culture, disability and other enumerated or analogous grounds; the role of myths and stereotypes in relation to women's inequality on the basis of sex, race, class and disability; and the particular vulnerability occasioned by relationships of intimacy.

3. An express and comprehensive statement of the objectives of the legislation along the lines set out in the working paper.

4. The preamble should avoid any language that portrays women in terms of victimization or dependency.

SUBSTANTIVE LAW

Section 265(2)(a): For the purposes of sections 271, 272 and 273 consent shall be sought and obtained and shall mean words or gestures which unequivocally express or manifest voluntary agreement to the sexual activity or sexual activities between the accused and the complainant which form the subject matter of the charge.

265(2)(b): Without limiting the generality of s. 265(2)(a) but for greater certainty,

i) There is no voluntary agreement where the complainant has, by words or gestures, expressed unwillingness to participate in the sexual activity or activities which form the subject matter of the charge. In this respect, words such as 'no,' 'stop,' 'don't,' 'I don't want to' or like expressions in any language constitute such lack of voluntary agreement.

ii) Actual or rumoured sexual activity with the accused or with another individual or individuals on prior occasions does not constitute voluntary agreement to the sexual activity or activities with the accused which form the subject matter of the charge.

iii) Voluntary agreement to specific sexual activities with the accused on the occasion culminating in criminal charges does not constitute voluntary agreement to any or all further or subsequent sexual activities with the accused. Once the complainant has, by words or gestures, communicated unwillingness to continue sexual contact with the accused or to engage in particular sexual activities with the accused, prior voluntary agreement, if any, is negated.

iv) Voluntary agreement to sexual activity shall not be presumed from the complainant's economic class, sexual identity or membership in any class enumerated or recognized as an analogous ground in s. 15 of the Charter.

v) Voluntary agreement to sexual activity shall not be presumed on the basis that the complainant consumed alcohol or drugs prior to the sexual activity subject to charges.

vi) Words or gestures which unequivocally express voluntary agreement to sexual activity constitute consent except where such apparent agreement is elicited by:

amend [additions in bold] existing s. 265(3)(c) and (d) to read:

c) fraud **or false representation or any significant lie which influenced the decision to agree to the sexual activity or activities which form the subject matter of the charge;**

d) the exercise of authority **or the abuse of trust or of social, economic or institutional power to secure sexual compliance on the basis of the accused's power**

to deny the complainant or a person other than the complainant significant benefits or necessities of life or to impose upon the complainant or a person other than the complainant significant harm;

e) we were unable to find wording for a situation where there are no concrete quid pro quos such as expressed in d) above, but where a powerholder exploits his privilege and the complainant's subordinate position (doctor-patient, employer-immigrant, etc.) Here the problem isn't threats but that the complainant was propositioned or pursued at all under circumstances where she may fear saying no, may be isolated and vulnerable etc. But we don't want to deny her agency, or invoke dependency language.

f) conduct by the accused subsequent to obtaining the complainant's voluntary agreement to sexual activity which voids the conditions under which her agreement was offered.

g) other circumstances which may legally vitiate consent.

265(4): we are unable to offer a position on the mistake defence because we believe most, if not all, factual mistakes will be precluded by these changes. We could support a mixed subjective/objective test, but only so long as the amendments codify the definition of consent (and non-consent) along the lines above. We all agree, however, that the mistake provision must contain explicit reference to the difference between mistakes of fact and of law as to consent such that an accused who excuses assault on the basis of honest belief that consent means less than this law requires has made a mistake of law.

The law should specifically codify that intoxication provides no defence to sexual assault.

We emphasize that new Code language should not attribute dependency or vulnerability to women or particular classes of women or deny women's agency.

Appendix C

Proposals of January Coalition for Preamble

1. Print the preamble in the Criminal Code.
2. Add a clause before the sexual assault provisions as follows:

> The sexual assault provisions of the Criminal Code and, in particular, ss. 265–278 inclusive, shall be interpreted and applied in accordance with this Preamble.

3. Resequence and amend text as follows (passages in bold indicate recommended revisions; existing paragraph in the draft of Bill C-49 tabled 12 December 1991 indicated in parentheses).

> Whereas the Parliament of Canada intends to promote **and ensure** the full protection of the rights guaranteed under sections 7 and 15 of the Canadian Charter of Rights and Freedoms; (C-49's para 5)

> Whereas the Parliament of Canada is gravely concerned about the incidence of sexual violence and abuse in Canadian society **and, in particular, the prevalence of sexual assault against women and children;** (C-49's para 2 with new addition)

> Whereas the Parliament of Canada recognizes the unique **historical role** of the **laws** of sexual assault, **of actual assault** and of fear of assault **in denying and restricting the constitutional rights of women;** (C-49's para 3 with additions and revisions)

> **Whereas the Parliament of Canada recognizes that vulnerability to sexual assault and diminished access to justice are directly related to social inequalities such as those experienced by aboriginal women, Black women and women of colour, elderly women, immigrant women, Jewish women,**

lesbians, poor women, refugee women, sex trade workers, women without full citizenship, women who have a disability, and children; (new clause)

Whereas Parliament recognizes that the continued operation of sexist myths about sexual assault and women's sexuality is inconsistent with the promotion of the rights and freedoms enshrined in the Charter; (new)

And whereas the Parliament of Canada believes that at trials of sexual offences, evidence of the complainant's sexual history is rarely relevant and that its admission should be subject to particular scrutiny, bearing in mind the inherently prejudicial **effect** of such evidence;

Notes

1 An Act to amend the Criminal Code. First Reading 12 December 1991, 3rd Sess., 34th Parl., 40–41 Eliz. II; approved with amendments by House of Commons, 15 June 1992; approved by Senate and given Royal Assent 23 June 1992. The bill was proclaimed by Cabinet in 1992.

2 See, e.g., Campbell (1992, 13–16) and Department of Justice (1992).

3 By contrast, the bill's most virulent opponents maintain Kim Campbell turned over the law's drafting to 'radical feminists' (the REAL Women version) or 'bourgeois feminists' (the male left version). See, e.g., REAL Women (1992): 'Bill C-49 is radical feminist legislation for feminists drafted by feminists ... LEAF decided what the law will be ... The legislation ... should be called the "detest men amendment" ' (at 2:32–3); and Martin (1992): 'So who makes our laws now – Parliament or LEAF?'

4 See, e.g., Sallot (1991) whose headline, 'Lawyers Win Concessions from Ottawa on Rape Bill: Women's Groups Pitted Against Defence Lawyers' expunges feminist lawyers and their criticisms of the concessions from the record.

5 A dramatic (and unsavoury) exception was the press swarm around two sex trade workers who presented the brief of Prostitutes and Other Women for Equal Rights (POWER) to the legislative committee on 2 June 1992.

6 See Seaboyer (1991) and Diana Majury's chapter in this volume.

7 Seaboyer (1991:258, 278). The majority also assumes wise instruction by bias-free judges can effectively rid jury deliberations of discriminatory fact-finding: ibid., at 279–81.

8 Rick Mosley, Senior General Counsel, Criminal and Family Law Policy Directorate, 23 October 1991. Mr. Mosley had primary responsibility for Bill C-49.

9 Lorde (1984:110–13). See also Fudge (1987 and 1990), Smart (1989), and Sheehy (1991).

10 For instance, economic policies promoting deunionization and high unemployment; cuts to the federal transfer payments subsidizing provincial and municipal social services; inaction on child care and effective employment and pay equity legislation; and the termination of the Court Challenge Program, which subsidized the costs to disadvantaged groups of Charter litigation.

11 The law struck down had benefitted only a small minority of women: few victims reported sexual assault under its regime and only a minority of reported rapes went to trial. Section 276 had imposed no statutory limits on admission of prior sexual history with the accused. The majority of rapes are committed by acquaintances, or present or former lovers of the complainant. They are the least reported. Studies assessing whether the 1983 Code reforms were effective in encouraging greater reporting are inconclusive. See Department of Justice Research Section (1990).

12 Canadian Charter of Rights and Freedoms (1982).

13 See L'Heureux Dubé's discussion of 'the larger legal context' for the history of judicial bias against sexual assault victims and courts' subversion of legislation designed to redress such bias: *Seaboyer* (1991:217–27).

14 Rape shield rules were enacted before Charter equality guarantees came into force and before the Supreme Court interpreted equality rights broadly and purposively as measures to eliminate and redress deliberate, unintentional, and systemic discrimination. See, e.g., *O.H.R.C.* v. *Simpsons Sears* (1985), *Action Travail des Femmes* v. *C.N.R.* (1987) and *Andrews* v. *Law Society of B.C.* (1989). Three of the judges who gave substance to equality rights (Dickson, McIntyre, and Wilson) have now retired.

15 For the most comprehensive account, see Brodsky and Day (1989).

16 Tellingly, whether equality arguments prevail (e.g., *R.* v. *Butler* (1992) – criminal obscenity laws justifiable limits on free speech – and *Norberg* v. *Wynrib* (1992) – in relations of unequal power, there may be no legally recognized consent) or lose (e.g. *Seaboyer* (1991) and *Canadian Council of Churches* v. *The Queen* (1992) – public interest standing), the Supreme Court does not explicitly cite s. 15.

17 The literature is vast and growing in every discipline, including law. The kinds of criticism documented in the academic literature and the women's press has also been articulated since day one in the post-'60s women's movement at conferences, rallies, public meetings, student caucuses, union meetings, and so on. Within legal literature, I consider Mary Eaton, Patricia Monture-Okanee, Sherene Razack, Esmerelda Thornhill, Mary Ellen Turpel and Toni Williams powerful and eloquent Canadian voices (oral or written); in the United States, Kimberle Crenshaw, Angela Harris, Ruthann Robson, and Patricia Williams. I choose not to cite particular written works because orally delivered critiques have been at least as profoundly transformative in my own education and the broader women's movement. As well, to the extent the Bill C-49 coalition achieved genuine inclusivity and power-sharing, it was not because anyone read, cited, or applied certain texts.

18 The most troubling illustration in my view is pay equity legislation. For sophisticated critiques of its political costs, see Fudge and McDermott (1991) and Lewis (1988).

19 It is true, as REAL Women protested in the legislative and Senate committee hearings, that no efforts were made to include them. See Minutes, 2:32-50 and Proceedings, 29:54-70. Aside from the overt anti-feminism of the organization, it was excluded for the simple reason it opposed consultations at the only group meeting it attended on 22 October 1991.

20 What was generally in issue was whether power would be acknowledged and shared and whether credibility with the minister, politicians, the press, or the public would be bought by silencing particular voices or issues.

21 For documented examples, review the Minutes of the legislative committee hearings to see how often women's organizations were asked whether they would support the bill if the preamble were not amended to name those women, especially sex trade workers, most vulnerable to assault and least served by law.

22 McLachlin's decision does not even list s. 15 among its catalogue of statutory provisions described as 'relevant' to the decision. In the two very brief passages in her judgment that refer to constitutional equality rights, equality guarantees become 'interests' subsumed under other Charter rights. See *Seaboyer* (1991:257, 275).

23 The majority decision suggested that codifying an expanded list of inadmissible classes of evidence would not survive future challenge (ibid.:269–70).

24 See News Release following the Annual Conference of Federal/Provincial/Territorial Ministers Responsible for Justice Issues from Yellowknife, 5 September 1991 (on file with author).

25 Ibid., at 3

26 Vienneau (21 November 1991)

27 The Nova Scotia, British Columbia, and Ontario attorney general offices conducted local consultations with a variety of women including local LEAF lawyers.

28 So long as the term 'consent' is sufficiently uncertain as to accommodate culturally constructed discriminatory stereotypes based on sex, race, class, disability, and so on, what counts as relevant or prejudicial will always be problematic and the evidence grounding the sexual aggressor's beliefs about consent will always be over-broad.

29 Public alarm about sexual violence has been acute in Canada since the Montreal massacre and the explosion of public inquiries into pervasive child sexual abuse within orphanages, training schools, and religious institutions. Shortly following the release of *Seaboyer* came the William Kennedy Smith trial, the Clarence Thomas hearings, the Kingston date rape case, the public crossbow murder of Patricia Allen, and the Mike Tyson trial.

30 See, e.g., *Andrews* v. *Law Society of B.C.* (1989), *R.* v. *Keegstra* (1990), and *Brooks* v. *Canada Safeway Ltd.* (1987).

31 See, e.g., *A.G. Canada* v. *Canadian Newspapers Co.* (1988) (publication ban on identity of rape complainants); *Janzen and Govereau* v. *Platy Enterprises* (1989) (sexual harassment); and *R.* v. *Butler* (1992) (pornography).

32 See S.C.C. factum of LEAF and five other co-intervenors in *Seaboyer*. That factum was the product of two years of cross-country consultations with the leadership of the violence against women movement, especially front-line workers.

33 Both lawyers who argued *Seaboyer* were members of the legal committee at the time, as were members of the *Seaboyer* sub-committee.

34 The inspiration for this approach was the Dworkin-MacKinnon legislation, which

characterizes pornography as a vehicle of sex discrimination. The law defines pornography by describing common scenarios found in pornography. See Dworkin and MacKinnon (1988). As well, the approach drew on Vandervort (1987–8).

35 See Appendix A for organizations here referred to by acronyms.

36 Some absences were caused by other federal consultations scheduled on the same date(!). Groups represented were: CACSW, CASAC, CBA, CCJC, CCLA, CNA, DAWN, Elizabeth Fry, LEAF, NAC, NAWL, NCW, NWAC, the Panel on Violence against Women, REAL Women, and the Aids Committee of Ottawa. Additionally there were about 15 officials from the federal and provincial Justice ministries and status of women offices.

37 Copy on file with author. Issues left unresolved were: whether s. 276(2) (notice of intent to adduce sexual history evidence), s. 276(3) (non-compellability of complainant on *voir dire*), and s. 276(4) (publication ban on *voir dire* evidence) survived; whether the majority guidelines (including a *voir dire*) applied to prior sexual history with the accused as well as with third parties; whether admissible evidence was restricted to past *consensual* sexual activity; whether the *voir dire* must be *in camera* (the majority guidelines state that it 'may' be *in camera*); and whether the guidelines apply to sexual offences other than ss. 271, 272, and 273.

38 On file with author

39 Both queried whether and how the mistake of fact defence might be restricted where, for instance, a mistaken belief was based on information from third parties or from consensual sex remote in time from the alleged assault or based on intoxication.

40 This is to say, it only served that minority of women who do report, whose complaints police consider 'founded' and whose assailants do not plead guilty to sexual assault or a lesser offence. For the attrition rate from assault to conviction, see *Seaboyer* (1991:206–17).

41 LEAF argued: it is impossible to reinstate rape shield rules in a manner which effectively secures women's s. 7 and s. 15 rights; codification of the majority guidelines leaves fundamental constitutional shortcomings in sexual assault law intact; amendments must overhaul the definition, available defences and rules of evidence of sexual assault law, as well as police and trial procedures, and scope of judicial discretion; no legal strategy will meet s. 15 goals without widespread consultations that address women's diversity and build from their lived experience. Justice should fund such consultations, review and incorporate relevant recommendations from the Vancouver conference, proceed with initiatives for mandatory judicial education, review judicial selection and promotion processes, and build a strong legislative record for the purpose of justifying amendments under s. 1 of the Charter. (Copy on file with author.)

42 CNA, CCJC, DAWN, LEAF, NAC, NAWL and NOIVM

43 Bindman (1991)

44 Some organizations had grant applications pending; some were currently lobbying the government or the Justice Department on other issues; some had barely secured recognized standing to represent their constituencies in public affairs; all faced fundraising fallout from unfriendly media coverage of feminists opposing rape law reforms.

45 'LEAF Preliminary Position Paper on Rape Shield Reform' (copy on file with author)

46 The administrative coordination of the January consultation was pulled off notwithstanding short notice, holidays, and last-minute changes by Bea Cleary, one of the most gifted facilitators I have ever met.

47 I do not believe feminist lawyers on their own would have had the wit, the acute sense of accountability to the women's community, or the non-deference to professionals and their socialized professionalism to demand what Lee did. It took a seasoned activist to insist that feminist lawyers no less than Justice officials must defer to the expertise of front-line workers and the women they serve when attempting to reform sexual assault law. Because the consultations and their results constitute what is worth replicating about this feminist history, the women's community has Lee Lakeman to thank. I am utterly persuaded that no future feminist law reform should proceed unless veteran activists in that field outnumber lawyers, assume leadership of the project, and have adequate time and resources to engage in consultations at every stage in the reform process.

48 Sallot (1991:21 November). She qualified her announcement somewhat. According to Sallot, 'Campbell said she agrees with the concept of putting some form of consent test into the law, but it is not easy to write a new provision that does not infringe on the right of an accused person to present a full defence.'

49 Undoubtedly prepared before the meeting, the press release refers only to procedural reforms and *voir dire* protections in legislation slated for December and states that such immediate amendments do not 'preclude a more comprehensive review and reform of sexual assault laws ... undertaken in consultation with women's groups' at some future date. One sentence does state that the minister had undertaken to 'facilitate further consultations' in mid-January. This sentence may have been a late addition or reflect a process planned for second stage amendments. (On file with author.)

50 Vienneau (1991:21 November). The Canadian Press wire service story reports she said the law would have 'an unequivocal and objective' definition of consent: Cox (1991).

51 Under normal circumstances, no legal and/or feminist organization would agree to such deadlines. However, years of theorizing and litigating sexual violence cases as sex equality issues had created an exceptional pool of legal minds on which LEAF could draw in reworking its existing research.

52 Nor did LEAF or the coalition actually draft the law, REAL Women's claims to the contrary. See Minutes, 2:33.

53 The second option was pursued by the coalition. Its final form and language are set out in Appendix B of this chapter.

54 The 'almost' should be qualified. The process restored the term 'empowering' to my vocabulary. Individual women's strengths and self-respect multiplied as a result of interaction.

55 The submissions made to the legislative and Senate committees by Professor Stuart would not have had the coalition's support. See Minutes, 6:21-42 and Proceedings, 4 June 1992, 29:9–20 and 40–1.

56 Bill C-49 is reproduced in Appendix B to this volume.

57 The preamble on first reading expressed Parliament's concern about 'the incidence of sexual violence and abuse in Canadian society' and its recognition of how actual and feared sexual assault affect the lives of the *people* of Canada.

58 The preamble, for instance, declares Parliament's wish to promote 15 Charter rights. Section 15, of course, refers to several grounds of discrimination other than sex. Tabled s. 173.1(2)(c) states that no consent is obtained where the complainant engages in sex 'by reason of the accused's abuse of a position of trust or authority.' This clause would be of particular help to immigrant, poor, disabled, or elderly women, sex trade workers, and/or women of colour wherever they rely on state officials for their citizenship status, social benefits, or legal assistance or on public or private caregivers. Among the considerations to be weighed when judges determine the admissibility of sexual history evidence are elimination of 'any discriminatory belief or bias' (s. 276(3)(d)) and the risk that evidence will 'unduly' arouse jury 'prejudice' or 'hostility' (s. 276(3)(e)).

59 The third paragraph of the December preamble refers to the 'unique character' of the offence of sexual assault. This echoes the *Seaboyer* dissent: 'Sexual assault is not like any other crime' (at 205) and the analysis of the LEAF factum. See Appendix C for revisions that would have given content to this uniqueness and bolstered Bill C-49 against Charter challenges assailing its innovations precisely because they are unlike the old law.

60 Two additional non-consent provisions were conceived by Justice alone. See s. 273.1(2)(a) and (b).

61 Aside from promising greater uniformity in adjudication than the McLachlin guidelines, the new guidelines, used thoughtfully by prosecutors, promise to confront and curb judicial bias far more effectively than occasional, voluntary weekend seminars in gender bias.

62 The *Seaboyer* guidelines (at 281–2) apply only to sexual assault trials and only to prior history of consensual sex.

63 By contrast, the McLachlin guidelines (ibid.) prohibit use of such evidence only

where it is used 'solely' to support such inferences. This means such evidence could have been tendered in part to support illegitimate inferences.

64 It is unclear whether this formulation would exclude more evidence than McLachlin's dicta because her analysis is less than clear. She states that judges should exclude evidence relevant to the defence only where its prejudicial effect 'substantially outweighs' its value (at 263). Her analysis is vague and inconsistent in defining prejudice and probative value.

65 The only innovation is the creation of a two-stage process. See s. 276.1.

66 See Sallot (1991:13 December).

67 For detailed outlines of the most frequent arguments by proponents and opponents of the bill, see Schmitz (1991) and Bureau of National Affairs (1992).

68 The most offensive version of the breathalyzer/affidavit argument appeared in a half-page letter to the editor by Richard Gassenbeek in *The Lawyer's Weekly* on 31 January 1992. See also remarks by the president of the Criminal Lawyers' Association of Ontario, Brian Greenspan, reported by Vienneau (1991:21 November).

69 Rape crisis workers in Vancouver and Toronto have told me that since the bill was tabled they hear entirely new questions and comments in public rape education workshops. Men and women believe the law has changed and men bear more responsibility for securing clear consent. This confirms my own observations from numerous press conferences, radio phone-in programs, and public addresses about the bill. See, too, Fine (1992).

70 See, e.g., brief of Criminal Lawyers' Association of Ontario: Minutes, 1:41–2 and 1A:16.

71 Where no organization meeting all three criteria exists to represent a vital constituency of women, exceptions were made. Accordingly, regional organizations of prostitutes, lesbians, women's centres, and battered women's shelters were recruited and the woman's caucus of a national labour organization was invited.

72 The Symposium on Women, Law and the Administration of Justice was held in June 1991. The proposals drafted by a caucus of women lawyers and law activists offer concrete measures to end systemic inequalities in the legal system within and across particular doctrinal fields with particular attention to race, class, and aboriginal oppression. Copy on file with author.

73 See Appendix C of this chapter.

74 This is not to suggest lawyers were not educated by non-lawyers to speak with assurance about how the law on the books fails women in practice.

75 The others were: the B.C. Civil Liberties Association, the CCLA, the CBA, the Canadian Association of Journalists, the Ontario Criminal Lawyers' Association and REAL Women.

76 See paragraph four of preamble in Appendix C of this chapter. For the reasons offered by the minister against embracing language unanimously urged and

explained by the January assembly and pressed by every coalition member in
the legislative hearings, see Minutes, 6:50–2 and 60, and Proceedings, 29:27–8.
77 The practices of accountability to women modelled in the Bill C-49 process have
been widely discussed and endorsed or followed as a blueprint in all gatherings of
equality seeking groups I have attended in 1992: LEAF's Symposium on Sex Equality Litigation, consultations concerning forthcoming amendments to the Canadian
Human Rights Act (both in February), the NAC annual meeting (June), lobbies
attempting to secure for national women's organizations representation during
politicians' constitutional negotiations and continuing efforts to redress the under-
inclusive structure and approach of the Canadian Panel on Violence Against
Women. See also note 3, supra.
78 Indeed, when the committee hearing oral submissions on the bill initially excluded
NOIVM, NOIVM, supported by other coalition members, successfully demanded
access. When one committee member repeatedly challenged explicit mention of
sex trade workers in the preamble, presenters from DAWN, CASAC and NOIVM urged
the committee to invite sex trade workers to speak for themselves. POWER also
demanded that the hearings be extended and that POWER be heard. They succeeded. It has been DAWN, NOIVM, the Congress of Black Women, CASAC and NAC
who have maintained public pressure on the Panel on Violence to be more
accountable to women's communities.
79 Villmoare (1991:391–2). On the impasse of the 'impossibilism' of legitimation
theory, see Currie et al. (1992:6–8).

References

Bindman, S. 1991. 'Campbell to Introduce New Law in November.' *Ottawa Citizen*
(29 October) A3
Boyle, C. 1984. *Sexual Assault.* Toronto: Carswell
Brodsky, G., and S. Day. 1989. *Canadian Charter Equality Rights for Women: One
Step Forward or Two Steps Back?* Ottawa: Canadian Advisory Council on the Status
of Women
Bureau of National Affairs. 1992. 'Canada's Proposed Rape Law Rewrites Rules of
Evidence.' *Criminal Practice Manual* 6:51–4
Campbell, K. 1992. 'Judicial Review and the Role of the Courts: Challenges in Defin-
ing a Post-Charter Political Culture: Remarks on 10th Anniversary of the Charter.'
Ottawa: April 14, 1–18
Canadian Charter of Rights and Freedoms, Part I of the Constitution Act, 1982, being
Schedule B of the Canada Act 1982 (U.K.) c. 11
Cox, B. 1991. '"No" Will Mean No, Say Women.' *Ottawa Citizen* (21 November)

Criminal Lawyers' Association of Ontario. 1992. 1992 Brief to Legislative Committee on Bill C-49. *Minutes of Proceedings and Evidence* 1A:13–26

Currie, D., et al. 1992. 'Three Traditions of Critical Justice Inquiry: Class, Gender, and Discourse.' In Currie and MacLean, eds., *Re Thinking the Administration of Justice.* Halifax: Fernwood Publishing

Department of Justice, Research Section. 1990. 'Sexual Assault Legislation in Canada: An Evaluation.' Ottawa: Department of Justice

Department of Justice. 1992. 'Rape Shield Legislation Receives Royal Assent.' Communiqué. Ottawa: June 24

Dworkin, A., and C. MacKinnon. 1988. *Pornography and Civil Rights: A New Day for Women's Equality.* Minneapolis: Organizing Against Pornography

Fine, S. 1992. 'Yes and No not Black and White, According to Bar Patrons.' *Globe and Mail* (16 June), A-8

Fudge, J. 1987. 'The Public/Private Distinction: The Possibilities of and the Limits to the Use of Charter Litigation to Further Feminist Struggles.' *Osgoode Hall Law Journal* 25:485–554

– 1990. 'What Do We Mean by Law and Social Transformation?' *Canadian Journal of Women and the Law* 5:47–69

Fudge, J., and P. McDermott. 1991. *Just Wages: A Feminist Assessment of Pay Equity* Toronto: University of Toronto Press

House of Commons, Canada. 1992. *Minutes of Proceedings and Evidence of Legislative Committee on Bill C-49* Issues 1–7

LEAF factum in *Seaboyer* (1991)

– 1992. Brief to the Legislative Committee on Bill C-49, *Minutes of Proceedings and Evidence,* 2A:1–63

Lewis, D. 1988. 'Just Give Us the Money: A Discussion of Wage Discrimination and Pay Equity.' Vancouver: Women's Research Centre

Lorde, A. 1984. *Sister/Outsider: Essays & Speeches.* Freedom, CA: The Crossing Press

Martin, R. 1992. 'Proposed Sex Assault Bill an Expression of Feminist Hatred.' *The Lawyer's Weekly* 31 (January): 9

Pickard, T. 1980. 'Culpable Mistakes and Rape: Relating *Mens Rea* to the Crime.' *University of Toronto Law Journal* 30:75–98

REAL Women. 1992. Brief to the Legislative Committee on Bill C-49. *Minutes of Proceedings and Evidence*: 2A:64–81

Sallot, J. 1991. 'Planned Law May Revive Rape Shield: Campbell Hears Women's Plea for Fresh Approach in Sex Cases.' *Globe and Mail* (21 November):A-1

– 1991. 'Political Battle Looms over Sex-Assault Bill.' *Globe and Mail* (13 December):A-4

Schmitz, C. 1991. 'Criminal Lawyers Fear Consent Concept in New Sex Assault Bill.'
　　The Lawyer's Weekly (17 January):1

Senate of Canada. 1992. *Proceedings of the Standing Committee on Legal and Consti-
　　tutional Affairs* 29:5–70

Sheehy, E. 1991. 'Feminist Argumentation before the Supreme Court of Canada.' In
　　'*R. v. Seaboyer; R. v. Gayme*: The Sound of One Hand Clapping.' *Melborne Law
　　Review* 18:450–68

Smart C. 1989. *Feminism and the Power of Law.* London: Routledge

Stuart, D. 1992. Brief to Legislative Committee on Bill C-49. *Minutes of Proceedings
　　and Evidence Committee* 6B:7–32

Vandervort, L. 1987–8. 'Mistake of Law and Sexual Assault: Consent and *Mens Rea*.'
　　Canadian Journal of Women and the Law 2:233–309

Vienneau. D. 1991. 'Proposed Rape Law: "No means No"' *Toronto Star* (21 Novem-
　　ber):A-1

– 1991. 'Beware Mixing Drink, Sex, Top Defence Lawyer Warns.' *Toronto Star* (13
　　December):A-15

Villmoare, A. 1991. 'Women, Differences, and Rights as Practices: An Interpretive
　　Essay and a Proposal.' *Law & Society Review* 25:385-410

Cases Cited

Action Travail des Femmes v. *C.N.R.* (1987), 40 D.L.R.(4th) 193 (S.C.C.)

A.G. Canada v. *Canadian Newspapers Co.*, [1988] 2 S.C.R. 122

Andrews v. *Law Society of British Columbia*, [1989] 1 S.C.R. 143

Brooks v. *Canada Safeway Ltd.* (1987), 59 D.L.R. (4th) 32 (S.C.C.)

Canadian Council of Churches v. *The Queen* (1992), 88 D.L.R. (4th) 193 (S.C.C.)

Janzen and Govereau v. *Platy Enterprises*, [1989] 1 S.C.R. 1252

Norberg v. *Wynrib*, [1992] 2 S.C.R. 318

Ontario Human Rights Commission v. *Simpsons-Sears Ltd.* (1985), 23 D.L.R. (4th) 32
　　(S.C.C.)

R. v. Butler (1992), 89 D.L.R. (4th) 193 (S.C.C.)

R. v. Keegstra, [1990] 3 S.C.R. 697

R. v. Seaboyer (1991), 83 D.L.R. (4th) 193 (S.C.C.)

13

JULIAN V. ROBERTS AND
RENATE M. MOHR

Sexual Assault: Future Research Priorities

The planning of this volume began in the summer of 1990. Since then, a great deal of research has been conducted, much of which appears in this book. But much remains to be done; as academic researchers, we attempt, in this concluding chapter, to point toward some of the issues that need to be explored in the area of sexual assault. The contributions to this volume have examined the criminal justice response to sexual assault from a diversity of perspectives. But if there is a single theme that emerges from these chapters, it is that while the 1983 legislation may have resolved some of the problems identified in the 1970s, many remain to be addressed. As well, it is unfortunately becoming clear that the sexual assault legislation has also created some new problems that require resolution. Reform legislation, then, must be seen as only the first step in a longer-term process, that of improving the way in which the criminal justice system, and in fact Canadian society itself, responds to crimes of sexual aggression. This latter point is critical; to date there has been an excessive emphasis upon criminal justice remedies for sexual assault (see the chapter in this volume by Elizabeth Sheehy). There is general agreement now that sexual assault is not simply a criminal justice problem; it is a problem for us all. Ten years ago Jeanne Marsh and her colleagues (1982) published a major evaluation of a rape reform initiative in the United States. It was called *Rape and the Limits of Law Reform*. There clearly is a limit to what legislative action can achieve.

It is not our intention in this concluding chapter to attempt a summary or synthesis of the preceding chapters. We leave readers to draw their own conclusions about the issues raised by the contents of this volume. Instead, we shall attempt to draw attention to some research priorities that need to be addressed. In this task we have also drawn upon discussions with the contributing authors to this volume, as well as other colleagues working in the field.

Research in the area of sexual assault is critical to the process of criminal law reform. After all, it was the rape research conducted and published in the 1970s and 1980s (e.g., Clark and Lewis 1977) that provided much of the impetus for the rape reform legislation that followed in 1983. We hope that these suggestions will be of utility in focusing researchers' attention in the immediate future. Some of these areas require investigation by sociological methods, some entail legal case analyses. As we have attempted to demonstrate in this volume, the two traditions are far from incompatible. Indeed, it is only through an integrated sociolegal approach that we are going to approach an understanding of the phenomenon of sexual assault, and the nature of the criminal justice response.

Victimization Surveys

One of the principal goals of Bill C-127 was to improve the treatment of victims of sexual assault. There is some evidence from surveys of small numbers of victims (e.g., Nuttall 1989) that treatment of victims by the system has improved, but no systematic national survey exists. In this respect Canada lags behind other countries, where victimization surveys are a routine component of criminal justice research programs. For example, in Great Britain the British Crime Survey is conducted approximately every two years. It consists of a detailed survey of a large, random sample of the adult population (see Mayhew, Elliott, et al. 1989). Similar surveys are also conducted in the United States (see U.S. Department of Justice 1988). In Canada, the last victimization survey was conducted in 1982 (but published in 1984 – see Solicitor General), just prior to passage of the rape reform legislation.[1] Thus our only systematic[2] source of information about victimization experiences comes from the period in which crimes of sexual aggression involved rape and indecent assault. We have no national information about victims' experiences with the new sexual assault offences. This will change once the results of the Violence Against Women Survey (see earlier chapters) are available.

What would a victimization survey tell us about sexual assault? It would provide invaluable information about a number of issues. First, it would give us a more accurate idea of the true incidence of crimes of sexual aggression. At the present we can only know about the incidence of sexual assaults reported to the police (see Chapter 3). Estimates of the real incidence of these crimes vary considerably. Second, a victimization survey would clarify a related but distinct issue: the reporting rate. Of all sexual assaults that take place, what percentage are reported to the police? Are reported sexual assaults just the tip of the iceberg? In the pre-reform period, research suggested that most crimes of rape and indecent assault were not reported to the police (see Chapter 3). How does the reporting rate for sexual assault compare with the reporting rate for the earlier crime of rape? Only a national victimization survey can answer these questions. Beyond the question of the reporting rate, a victimization survey also generates answers to questions such as *why* some victims do not report to the police. Only a victimization survey can establish why this is the case; interviewing victims in the system is of little use in this respect.

Victimization surveys also provide insight into the phenomenon of sexual assault. At present, the image of what constitutes sexual assault is derived almost exclusively from cases that proceed to court (see Chapter 4, and Department of Justice 1990). But the cases of sexual assault that are processed by the criminal justice system may not be representative of all sexual assaults. In fact, one recent study in Nova Scotia (Yurchesyn et al. 1991)· found significant differences between sexual assault cases reported to community-based sexual assault centres, and cases of sexual assault that appeared in court. Cases appearing in court usually involved strangers and social acquaintances. The agency records however showed that the aggressor was, in an overwhelming number of cases, a family member. Similar research is required in order to obtain an accurate picture of the nature of sexual assault in this country.

Police Decision-Making

The national data summarized in Chapter 3 suggest one positive impact of Bill C-127: more victims of sexual assault are turning to the criminal justice system. And, since there has been no decline in the conviction *rate* as a function of this increased caseload, this means that the number of convictions has risen substantially since 1982. A greater percentage of the total sexual offender population is being convicted by the courts. Whether from the perspective of just deserts or general deterrence this is good news.

However, the national data also show that reports of sexual assault are almost always classified at the first level of seriousness (sexual assault I). If 96 per cent of reports of sexual assault are classified at level I, it seems inappropriate to regard sexual assault as a collection of three (or four) offences. In this respect the Canadian rape reform experience is unique: in other countries – the United States (see Marsh et al. 1982) and Australia (see New South Wales Bureau of Crime Statistics, 1991) for example – the introduction of multi-tiered sexual assault offences has resulted in a far more evenly balanced distribution (see Pires 1991, Roberts and Pires 1992).

The key to this lopsided distribution in reports (and charges) of sexual assault may lie in the 10-year maximum penalty associated with the first level of sexual assault. The fact that offenders can receive up to 10 years in prison might have encouraged police officers to classify, and Crown prosecutors to charge, almost all cases of sexual assault at the first level of seriousness. Whatever the cause, it seems highly likely that other critical actors in the criminal justice process – including and especially the victim – probably do not share the same perceptions as the police in terms of classifying reports of sexual aggression. We need, therefore, to know more about the way in which the police (and Crown counsel) make classification decisions. Very little research has been conducted upon this issue in Canada; we believe it to be a priority.

A second issue that comes to light as a result of the national Uniform Crime Data concerns provincial variation in sexual assault statistics. Criminal law is of course within the ambit of the federal government. It is reasonable therefore to expect national standards, and yet the data show that the criminal justice system responds to reports of sexual assault in very different ways, depending upon the province in which the report is recorded. Attempts to explain this kind of variation would also benefit from research into the behaviour of the police as they respond to reports of sexual assault.

Criminal Justice Processing of Sexual Assault Reports

ATTRITION RATES

A critical issue that has been raised by many researchers going back to Clark and Lewis (1977) concerns the issue of attrition (see Gunn and Minch, 1988, and the chapter in this volume by Gunn and Linden). It has long been argued that a higher percentage of cases of sexual assault are filtered by the criminal justice system. However, research that compares the attrition rates of cases of sexual assault with the attrition rates of other serious crimes of violence such as aggravated assault is rare. Recent research in progress at the time this volume goes to press (Roberts and Grossman 1994) has quantified the difference in attrition rates for a number of offences; it is clear that the attrition rate is higher for sexual assault. Thus 44 per cent of all reports of sexual assault result in the laying of a charge; 56 per cent of the initial reports do not result in the laying of a charge against a known suspect. This can be compared with the general category of crimes of violence: only 52 per cent of reports of these crimes are filtered out by the police. This research has also shown the stage at which this filtering occurs. It is not the clearance rates that differ, but the founding rates. Thus a significantly higher percentage of sexual assault reports are declared by the police to be unfounded. Why is this so? The consequences for the victim are serious: we need to know more about why this differential exists, and how to eradicate it. Otherwise victims of sexual assault are going to be, from the outset, at a disadvantage in terms of the criminal justice process (relative to victims of other crimes, such as assault).

A priority for criminal justice researchers then is the way in which police officers across the country respond to reports of sexual assault. The founding process has been addressed in part in previous research; it is clear that it needs to be the focus of a systematic research project.

CROWN DECISION-MAKING

One of the most pressing issues from the public's perspective is the issue of leniency, or perceived leniency, in sentencing trends. Although they have not always been accompanied by reliable data, many claims have been made that sentences imposed for the sexual assault offences do not reflect, in severity, the seriousness of the crimes. An important yet overlooked issue in the area concerns the hybrid nature of the first level of sexual assault. This means that if the Crown proceeds by way of summary conviction, the maximum penalty that can be imposed by a judge is six months in prison. It may surprise many people that the maximum penalty is so low; it may also help us to understand sentencing patterns for this crime. If the charge proceeds by way of summary conviction, then we can hardly criticise the judge for being excessively lenient when the offender receives a sentence of less than six months in prison. At present, we do not know, from national statistics, what percentage of convictions for sexual assault were indictable, but estimates suggest that it could be as high as one in three (see Roberts and Grossman 1994). If this estimate is correct, it raises some very important questions about the role of the Crown, and also means that we must view sentencing patterns with this statistic in mind. The issue of the hybrid nature of the first level of sexual assault is all the more important, since almost all charges (over 96 per cent in 1991) are laid at this first level (see Chapter 3 of this volume).

VICTIM RESPONSE TO CRIMINAL JUSTICE PROCESSING

We have heard a great deal in recent years about the importance of promoting the interests of the victim. One of the mechanisms that has been introduced to accomplish this is the Victim Impact Statement, in which the effects of the crime upon the victim are recorded and brought to the attention of the court. Has this innovation resulted in greater victim satisfaction with the judicial process? Has it accomplished the goal set out by the drafters of the legislation? These critical questions need to be addressed by future research. One of the central aims, it will be recalled, of the original rape reform legislation of 1983 was to reduce the secondary victimization of the rape complainant that took place in the courtroom. We need to know to what degree the innovations introduced in 1983 (and afterwards) have had a real impact upon the treatment of victims of sexual assault. What reactions do they have to their treatment by the police and by the Crown, and what do they think about the experience of testifying, in those cases that proceed to trial? A start has been made in this area by research conducted for the Department of Justice as part of the Bill C-127 evaluation initiative (Department of Justice 1990; see also Nuttall 1989), but a great deal more is needed. Only when we fully understand the needs of the victim can the system make the necessary reforms to procedures governing the actions of criminal justice professionals who deal with sexual assault cases.

Sentencing Trends

In Chapter 8, the sentencing of sexual offenders was discussed from a legal perspective. But the issue of sentencing has a much broader significance than reported sentencing decisions. To many members of the public, and to some advocacy groups, it is in the area of sentencing that the criminal justice system is most at fault; yet what do we know about sentences imposed for this offence? The answer is very little. This is in stark contrast to reporting statistics, which are published on a national basis annually, and have been for many years, thus permitting the researcher to make comparisons of reporting trends over time, as in Chapter 3. The Canadian Centre for Justice Statistics stopped publishing national sentencing data years ago. The Centre is currently in the process of assembling national sentencing statistics, but publication of such information is not a high priority from the perspective of the system, and is unlikely to take place within the next few years – that is, unless pressure is brought to bear upon the system to acknowledge that sentencing statistics are a priority. We are of course not the first to point this out; over five years ago the Canadian Sentencing Commission (1987) also lamented the absence of national sentencing statistics for all crimes, not just sexual assault. The report describing sentencing trends referred to earlier (Roberts and Grossman 1994) is but a small step toward the goal of annual sentencing publications.

Children as Victims

Another issue that cries out for attention is the relationship between the sexual assault legislation and the legislation addressing sexual assaults against children (Bill C-15; see Wells 1990), which was introduced in 1988. Much of the focus to date has been upon adult victims of sexual aggression, but this is changing. Part of the increase in sexual assault statistics can be explained by increasing numbers of cases involving children as victims (e.g., Yurchesyn et al. 1991). In fact there is substantial overlap between the sexual assault and the child sexual abuse sections in the Criminal Code. Evidence is accumulating that suggests that when a report involves a child victim, police are laying charges of both sexual assault and child sexual abuse (see Hornick and Bolitho 1992). The reasons for this are unclear, but one possibility is that the police have more familiarity with sexual assault cases, and are therefore more comfortable with laying sexual assault charges. The inter-relationship between the child sexual abuse and the sexual assault provisions needs further exploration.

Male Victims of Sexual Assault

The national reporting statistics for sexual assault do not specify the gender of the complainant. The Department of Justice research, conducted in several sites across Canada, suggests that approximately 90 per cent of sexual assault complainants were female (see Department of Justice 1990, Table 12). It is possible that the percentage of male victims is higher, but that male victims (who are frequently boys) are less likely to report to the police. This may well be changing, as several recent stories in the news media (see Chapter 1) indicate. Sexual assault is a gender-related offence, in that most victims are female, and almost all aggressors male, but these statistics are based on reports made to the criminal justice system. We should not lose sight of the fact that although males are invariably the perpetrators, they are sometimes victims of the same crime, particularly in environments that are seldom the object of research scrutiny, such as reformatories, prisons, and penitentiaries.

The Charter of Rights and Freedoms

Legal scholars have long questioned whether law can be an effective tool in bringing about social change. The recent decision of the Supreme Court in *Seaboyer*[3] is a painful reminder that, in spite of some advances in the legal arena, one step forward for women is often followed by two steps back.[4] The important research addressing who uses the Charter of Rights and Freedoms, and for what purposes, must be continued. Just as legislative changes require evaluation and analysis, so do judicial interpretations of those changes.

A construction and interpretation of the state's response to violence against women must always be carefully scrutinized. Whether the laws will help or hinder women in the quest for equality – the quest to 'take back the night' – remains to be seen. One thing is sure, law is powerful, whether constructed by legislators or judges, and we cannot afford to become complacent about its use.

Judicial Interpretation of Consent

A number of chapters in this volume have also raised questions and concerns about men who use their position of authority to coerce women and children into submitting to acts of sexual aggression. 'Submission' is often misunderstood by judges to mean 'consent.' Further research must identify the ways in which parental or professional power is experienced as coercion. The recent task force report on the sexual exploitation of patients by health professionals has brought this issue into the public arena. Cases like *Norberg*, discussed by Christine Boyle and Elizabeth Sheehy in their chapters, clearly underline the importance of examining the often unstated power of doctors. As well, the application of the new Criminal Code provision that criminalizes sexual aggression where children are abused by persons in authority must be studied. The judicial interpretations of consent that are beginning to follow the enactment of the 1992 consent provision in the Code must be carefully documented and critically analysed.

Expert Evidence

What counts as evidence is an issue with implications that go beyond the scope of *Seaboyer*. The legal construction of what constitutes an 'expert' has a large impact on what 'facts' about sexual assault are heard by a judge. What kinds of information about sexual assault are presented to the courts by psychiatrists and psychologists? Would judges better understand the phenomenon of sexual assault and its effects on survivors if survivors or rape crisis centre workers were constructed as 'experts'? What information should judges take 'judicial notice' of, that is, admit into evidence without proof? If some judges take judicial notice of the long-lasting trauma experienced by survivors of sexual assault, why not all? The list of questions is long, but most important is that writers in the legal arena begin challenging accepted rules and procedures.

Race, Ethnicity, Class, Disability, Sexual Orientation

The research and statistics that have been gathered on sexual assault often fail to address race, ethnicity, class, disability, and sexual orientation. How do these conditions affect risk, reporting and founding rates, and judicial interpretation of acts of sexual aggression? Although there have been attempts in this volume to explore these issues, a second volume written by people who are themselves able to tell their stories or whose research reveals how some sexist assumptions about sexual aggression also reveal racist, class-based, able-ist, and homophobic assumptions, is necessary to provide a full exploration of these issues. It follows that data must identify these conditions in order that we can more fully understand that symptom of coercive sexuality that we call sexual assault.

The stories of the women whose lives have been directly affected by the violence of sexual assault have not been documented in this book. These stories, as told by women from all walks of life – women of colour, women with disabilities, Aboriginal women, sex-trade workers, and immigrant women, to name but a few – must be documented to allow researchers, students, journalists, and criminal justice professionals to more fully understand this 'decade of legal and social change.' We are encouraged by the number of authors and publishers who are committed to printing these stories. Works such as this are crucial to increasing awareness and educating the public and criminal justice workers alike that, for example, the availability of rape-crisis centres is not the same for all women. Aboriginal women living on reserves and in remote communities rarely have access to such services. Nor do women with disabilities or immigrant women in urban centres.

In order for social and legal responses to be truly responsive to the women and children who have been sexually assaulted in the past or may be sexually assaulted in the future, the differences in the life experiences of women and children across the country must be heard. Although we can document the 'founding' statistics, little or nothing has been published on reporting or founding of charges on reserves. Little has been documented on why certain women are less likely to report sexual assaults than others, regardless of more 'victim-friendly' legislation and/or police policies. Due largely to the writings of feminist scholars, even judges have begun to document how the credibility of women is linked to their race, class, sexual orientation, legal status, and physical and mental ability. Women with disabilities, women of colour, Aboriginal women, immigrant women, and sex trade workers, and lesbians are all less likely to report crimes of sexual violence. Their reasons, however, are as varied as their circumstances. Until these reasons are better documented, no legislation or policy will change their practices or the response of state officials to their reports.

Although sexual assault has long been recognized by feminist scholars as a single point on a continuum of male violence, more must be written on the relationships between this form of male violence and other forms or threats of male violence. What is the relationship between rape, 'peeping Toms,' sexual harassment, flashers, obscene phone calls, pornography, and advertising that depicts women as 'rapeable'? What is the difference between an 'adoring sexual fantasy' and a threat to rape? As was illustrated by the judgments in *McCraw*,[5] to some judges there is no difference. In fact, some judges construct fact as law and their assumptions about rape define what is fact.

Unchallenged assumptions are often the basis of laws and their interpretation. These assumptions more often than not reflect the experience of a white, heterosexual, middle-class, able-bodied man. That is but one experience. Until the assumptions of police officers, law-makers, lawyers, judges, and criminal justice professionals are challenged, changes to the laws will neither reflect nor be responsive to the reality of acts of sexual aggression. Research must confront and be confronted on these assumptions. White, able-bodied, middle-class, heterosexual researchers have also to be reminded of the assumptions that inform their work. For those who engage with the law, it is critical to continue to demand that these challenges be heard.

There is much work yet to be done if we are ever to create a society in which women and children are safe in their own homes and on the street. Law is but one arena for change, and, as we have attempted to demonstrate, there is a great need for law to be informed by work from other disciplines. Sexual assault is not simply a topic of academic interest. It is a very real threat to women, children, and, in some cases, men, across this country. Research priorities must acknowledge this reality.

Notes

1 In 1988 Canada participated in a multi-nation victimization survey (see Van Dijk et al. 1989). However, the scale of the survey does not permit the kind of detailed analysis that was possible with the earlier Canadian Urban Victimization Survey.

2 As its name indicates, even the Canadian Urban Victimization Survey was not a truly national survey. It was conducted in only seven urban centres across Canada.

3 *Re Seaboyer and the Queen*, decision of Supreme Court of Canada (#20666, #20835) 22 August 1991

4 See Brodsky and Day (1989).
5 See LEAF factum in *Norberg* v. *Weinrib* (1991).

References

Brodsky, G., and S. Day. 1989. *One Step Forward or Two Steps Back?* Ottawa: Canadian Advisory Council on the Status of Women

Canadian Sentencing Commission. 1987. *Sentencing: A Canadian Approach.* Ottawa: Supply and Services Canada

Clark, L. and D. Lewis. 1977. *Rape: The Price of Coercive Sexuality.* Toronto: Women's Press

Department of Justice. 1990. *Overview. Sexual Assault Legislation in Canada: An Evaluation, Report No. 5.* Ottawa: Research Section, Department of Justice

Gunn, R., and C. Minch. 1988. *Sexual Assualt: The Dilemma of Disclosure, The Question of Conviction.* Winnipeg: University of Manitoba Press

Hornick, J., and F. Bolitho. 1992. *A Review of the Implementation of the Child Sexual Abuse Legislation in Selected Sites.* Ottawa: Supply and Services Canada

Marsh, J., A. Geist, and N. Caplan. 1982. *Rape and the Limits of Law Reform.* Boston, MA: Auburn House

Mayhew, P., D. Elliott, and L. Dowds. 1989. *The 1988 British Crime Survey.* London: Her Majesty's Stationery Office

New South Wales Bureau of Crime Statistics. 1991. *Crime and Justice Facts (1990).* Sydney, Australia: New South Wales Bureau of Crime Statistics

Nuttall, S. 1989. *Toronto Sexual Assault Research Study.* Ottawa: Ministry of the Solicitor General

Pires, A.P. 1991. *The Reform of Sexual Assault Laws in Canada: A Reconstruction of Juridical Categories and Their 'New' Symbolic Effect.* Working Paper #9101C. Ottawa: University of Ottawa, Faculty of Social Science

Roberts, J.V. 1990. *Sentencing Patterns in Cases of Sexual Assault. Sexual Assault in Canada: An Evaluation. Report No. 3.* Ottawa: Department of Justice

Roberts, J.V., and M.G. Grossman. 1994. *Criminal Justice processing of Sexual Assault Cases.* Ottawa: Canadian Centre for Justice Statistics

Roberts, J.V., and A.P. Pires. 1992. 'Le renvoi et la classification des infractions d'agressions sexuelles.' Criminologie 25:27–63

Sacco, V., and H. Johnson. 1990. *Patterns of Criminal Victimization in Canada.* Ottawa: Supply and Services Canada

Solicitor General. 1984. *Canadian Urban Victimization Survey: Reported and Unreported Offences.* Ottawa: Supply and Services Canada

Thornhill, E. 1985. 'Focus on Black Women.' *Canadian Journal of Women and the Law*

Toews, C. 1991. *Issues in Sexual Assault Sentencing in Nova Scotia.* Halifax: Nova Scotia Advisory Council on the Status of Women

U.S. Department of Justice. 1988. *Criminal Victimization. 1987.* Washington, DC: U.S. Department of Justice, Bureau of Justice Statistics

Vandervort, E. 1987–8. 'Mistake of Law and Sexual Assault: Consent and Mens Rea. *Canadian Journal of Women and the Law* 2:233–309

Van Dijk, J., P. Mayhew, and M. Killias. 1989. *Experiences of Crime Across the World: Key Findings of the 1989 International Survey.* The Hague: Research and Documentation Centre, Ministry of Justice

Wells, M. 1990. *Canada's Law on Child Sexual Abuse. A Handbook.* Ottawa: Supply and Services Canada

Yurchesyn, K., A. Keith, and E. Renner. 1991. 'Contrasting Perspectives on the Nature of Sexual Assault Provided by a Service for Sexual Assault Victims and by the Law Courts.' *Canadian Journal of Behavioural Science* (in press)

APPENDIX A

Sexual Assault in Canada: A Bibliography (1977–1991)

JULIAN V. ROBERTS AND MICHELLE G. GROSSMAN

This appendix contains references relating to sexual assault in Canada for the period 1977–1991. It is an abridged version of a larger, annotated report (see Roberts and Grossman 1991). The references are drawn from an electronic and manual search of the literature. It does not include publications dealing with child sexual abuse, sexual harassment or other such issues related to sexual assault (these have already been covered in other bibliographies). The project was supported by funds provided by the Department of Justice Canada.

Backhouse, C. 1983. 'Nineteenth-Century Canadian Rape Law (1800–92).' in D. Flaherty, ed., *Essays in the History of Canadian Law.* Toronto: University of Toronto Press
– 1987. 'Nineteenth Century Judicial Attitudes toward Child Custody, Rape and Prostitution.' In S. Martin and K. Mahone, eds., *Equality and Judicial Neutrality.* Calgary: Carswell
Backhouse, C., and L. Schoenroth. 1983. 'A Comparative Study of Canadian and American Rape Law.' *Canada–United States Law Journal* 6:48–88
– 1984. 'A Comparative Survey of Canadian and American Rape Law. *Canada–United States Law Journal* 7:173–213
Barbary, H. 1987. 'Alcohol/Drugs and Violence.' In J. MacLatchie, ed., *Insights into Violence in Contemporary Canadian Society.* Ottawa: John Howard Society of Canada
Baril, M., M. Bettez, and L. Viau, 1988. *Sexual Assault before and after the 1983 Reform: An Evaluation of Practices in the Judicial District of Montreal, Quebec.* Ottawa: Department of Justice Canada (WD1991-2a)
Baskin, C. 1983. 'Rape and Rape-Crisis Centres: An Interview.' *Canadian Women's Studies* 4:63–5
Batt, S. 1983. 'Our Civil Courts – Unused Classrooms for Education about Rape.'

Feminism Applied: Four Papers. Canadian Institute for the Advancement of Women. 7:56–8

Baylis, M. and A. Myers. 1990. 'Combating Sexual Assault: An Evaluation of a Prevention Program.' *Canadian Journal of Public Health* 81:341–4

Begin, P. 1987. 'Sexual Assault.' In J. MacLatchie, ed., *Insights into Violence in Contemporary Canadian Society.* Ottawa: John Howard Society of Canada

– 1989. 'Rape Law Reform in Canada: Evaluating Impact.' In E. Viano, ed., *Crime and Its Victims: International Research and Public Policy Issues.* Bristol, PA: Hemisphere Publishing

Bibby, R. 1983. 'The Moral Mosaic: Sexuality in the Canadian 80s.' *Social Indicators Research,* 13:171–84

Biesenthal, L. 1991. 'Sexual Assault Legislation in Canada: An Evaluation.' *Justice Research Notes* 3:1–9

Borins, E. 1987. 'The Women's Clinic: A Viable Psychiatric Clinic in the Canadian Context. Special Issue: Women, Power, and Therapy: Issues for Women.' *Women and Therapy* 6:333–40

Bowland, A. 1986. *Rape, The Family and the State: Controlling Female Deviance.* Toronto: Osgoode Hall Law School, York University

Boyd, S., and E. Sheehy. 1986. 'Feminist Perspectives on Law: Canadian Theory and Practice.' *Canadian Journal of Women and the Law* 2:1–52

Boyle, C. 1981a. 'Section 142 of the Criminal Code: A Trojan Horse?' Criminal Law Quarterly 23:253–6

– 1981b. 'Married Women – Beyond the Pale of the Law of Rape.' *Windsor Yearbook of Access to Justice* 1:192–213

– 1984. *Sexual Assault.* Toronto: Carswell

– 1985a. 'Sexual Assault and the Feminist Judge.' *Canadian Journal of Women and the Law* 1:93–107

– 1985b. 'Offences against Women.' In: J. Rusell, ed., *A Feminist Review of Criminal Law*

– 1989. 'Publication of Identifying Information about Sexual Assault Survivors: *R. v. Canadian Newspaper Co. Ltd.*' *Canadian Journal of Women and the Law* 3:602–14

– 1991. 'Sexual Assault: A Case Study of Legal Policy Options.' In M. Jackson and C. Griffiths, eds., *Canadian Criminology.* Toronto: Harcourt Brace Jovanovich

Boyle, C. and S. Rowley. 1987. 'Sexual Assault and Family Violence: Reflections on Bias.' In S. Martin and K. Mahoney, eds., *Equality and Judicial Neutrality* Toronto: Carswell

Brehaut, L., and R. Freeman. 1989. *Believe Her! A Report on Sexual Assault and Sexual Abuse of Women and Children.* Prince Edward Island Advisory Council on the Status of Women

Brickman, J., J. and Briere. 1984. 'Incidence of Rape and Sexual Assault in an

Brickman, J., J. Briere, M. Ward, M. Kalef, and A. Lungen. 1980. 'Preliminary Report of the Winnipeg Rape Incidence Project.' Paper presented at the annual meeting of the Canadian Psychological Association, Quebec City, June

Brown, M., ed., 1991. *Gender Equality in the Courts.* Winnipeg: Manitoba Association of Women and the Law

Brown, R.S., and R.W. Courtis. 1977. 'The Castration Alternative.' *Canadian Journal of Criminology and Corrections* 19:157–69

Bryant, A. 1989. 'The Issue of Consent in the Crime of Sexual Assault.' *Canadian Bar Review* 68:94–154

Cameron, R. 1988. *The Pre-trial Processing of Sexual Assault Cases in Scotland and Toronto: A Comparative Analysis.* Toronto: Osgoode Hall Law School

Canadian Advisory Council on the Status of Women. 1981. *Report on Sexual Assault in Canada.* Ottawa: Canadian Advisory Council on the Status of Women

– 1982. *A New Justice for Women.* Ottawa: Canadian Advisory Council on the Status of Women

Carrière, R. 1980. 'Victimology and Rape: An Accessory Discourse; La Victimologie et le viol, un discours complice.' *Criminologie*, 13:60–79

Cashman, M. 1981. *Proposed Changes in Sexual Offences Legislation (Bill C-53): Implications for Legal Aid.* Ottawa: University of Ottawa, National Legal Aid Research Centre

Chappell, D. 1984. 'The Impact of Rape Legislation Reform: Some Comparative Trends.' *International Journal of Women's Studies* 7:70–80

– 1989. 'Sexual Criminal Violence.' In N. Weiner and M. Wolfgang, eds., *Pathways to Criminal Violence.* Newbury Park: Sage

Chappell, D., G. Geis, and F. Fogarty. 1979. *Forcible Rape: Bibliography.* Ottawa: Supply and Services Canada

Chase, G. 1982–3. 'An Analysis of the New Sexual-Assault Laws.' *Canadian Women's Studies*, 4:53–4

Clark, L. 1989–90. 'Feminist Perspectives on Violence against Women and Children: Psychological, Social Service and Criminal Justice Concerns.' *Canadian Journal of Women and the Law* 3:420–31

Clark, L., and D. Lewis. 1977. *Rape: The Price of Coercive Sexuality.* Toronto: The Women's Press

– 1978. *A Study of Rape in Vancouver and Toronto.* Toronto: Centre of Criminology, University of Toronto

Cohen, L., and C. Backhouse. 1980. 'Desexualizing Rape: Dissenting View on the Proposed Rape Amendments. *Canadian Women's Studies*, 2:99–103

Collette-Carriere, R., and C. Lamontagne. 1979. 'Le viol au Canada, un débat renouvelé.' *Déviance et Société* 3:83–8

– 1980. 'La femme: victim designeé: La victimologie et le viol, un discours complice.'

– 1980. 'La femme: victim designeé: La victimologie et le viol, un discours complice.' In *Criminologie 1980: Regards sur la victime*. Montréal: Presse de l'Université de Montréal

Conway, E.R. 1987. *Wife Assault and Sexual Assault on Prince Edward Island: Results of a Victim Survey and a Police Survey*. Santa Monica, CA: Consortia

Cousineau, M., and S. Gravel. 1985–6. 'L'agression: ce qu'on en dit, ce qu'il en est.' *Resources for Feminist Research* 13:46–7

CS/RESORS Consulting Ltd. 1988. *The Impact of Legislative Change on Survivors of Sexual Assault: A Survey of Front Line Agencies*. Ottawa: Department of Justice Canada (WD1991-8a)

Dawson B. 1986. 'Legal Structures: A Feminist Critique of Sexual Assault Reform.' *Resources for Feminist Research*, 14:40–3

– 1987–8. 'Sexual Assault Law and Past Sexual Conduct of the Primary Witness: The Construction of Relevance.' *Canadian Journal of Women and the Law* 2:310–40

Dawson, D. 1984. 'The Abrogation of Recent Complaint: Where Do We Stand Now?' *Criminal Law Quarterly* 27:57–78

DeKeseredy, W., and R. Hinch. 1991. 'Rape and Sexual Assault.' In *Woman Abuse. Sociological Perspectives*. Toronto: Thompson Educational Publishing

Delorey, A. 1989. 'Rape Trauma Syndrome: An Evidentiary Tool.' *Canadian Journal of Women and the Law* 3:531–51

Department of Justice. 1980. *Information Paper: Sexual Offences against the Person and the Protection of Young Persons*. Ottawa: Department of Justice

– 1990a. *After Sexual Assault: Your Guide to the Criminal Justice System*. Ottawa: Department of Justice, Communications and Public Affairs

– 1990b. *Sexual Assault Legislation in Canada. An Evaluation. Overview Report Number 5*. Ottawa: Department of Justice

Department of Justice, Research Section. 1988. *An Analysis of Public Attitudes Toward Justice-Related Issues (1986–1987)*. Ottawa: Research Section, Department of Justice

– 1990. *Overview. Sexual Assault Legislation in Canada: An Evaluation, Report No. 5*. Ottawa: Department of Justice

– 1991. *A Review of the Sexual Assault Case Law, 1985–1988. Sexual assault legislation in Canada: An Evaluation, Report No. 6*. Ottawa: Department of Justice

Devon, S.A. 1984. *Rape and the Judicial System* [Microform]*: A Study of Social Control, Manitoba, 1965–1980*. M.A. Dissertation, University of Manitoba

Dickens, B. 1983. 'Sexual Aggression and the Law – Implications for the Future.' In S. Verdun-Jones and A. Keltner, eds., *Sexual Aggression and the Law*. Burnaby, BC: Simon Fraser University, Criminology Research Centre

Dominic, B., and J. Check. 1986. 'The Impact of Highly Aggressive Cues on Perceptions of Stranger and Acquaintance Rape Scenarios.' *Canadian Psychology*, 2:168

Ekos Research Associates Inc. 1988a. *Report on the Treatment of Sexual Assault Cases in Vancouver.* Ottawa: Department of Justice (WD1991-3a)

– 1988b. *Report on the Impact of the 1983 Sexual Assault Legislation in Hamilton-Wentworth.* Ottawa: Department of Justice (WD1991-4a)

Ellis, M. 1986. *Judicial Interpretation of the New Sexual Offences in Light of the Charter of Rights and Freedoms.* Unpublished manuscript

– 1988a. *Surviving Procedures after a Sexual Assault.* Vancouver: Press Gang Publisher

– 1988b. 'Re-defining Rape: Re-victimizing Women.' *Resources for Feminist Research* 17:96–9

– 1989. *An Analysis of Sexual Offence Sentencing in the B.C. Court of Appeal.* The Western Workshop

Fraser, D. 1979. *Effects of a Recent Law Change on the Verdicts of Simulated Jurors in Rape Offenses and the Effects of a Proposed Law Change on the Verdicts of Simulated Jurors.* Toronto: Centre of Criminology, University of Toronto

Fudge, J. 1989. 'The Effect of Entrenching a Bill of Rights upon Political Discourse: Feminist Demands and Sexual Violence in Canada.' *International Journal of the Sociology of the Law* 17:445–63

Fuller, D.L. 1988. *Perception and Violence* [microform]: *Competing Aspects of Serious Sexual Assault.* L.L.M. dissertation, Université Laval

Garley, K. 1989. *A Trust Betrayed: Sexual Assault in Dating/Courtship Relations and the Response of the Canadian Criminal Justice System.* M.A. thesis. Department of Criminology, Simon Fraser University

Geller, S. 1977. 'The Sexually Assaulted Female: Innocent Victim or Temptress?' *Canada's Mental Health* 25:26–9

Gendron, C. 1987. 'Silence: Rape Is Taking Place.' *Nursing Quebec* 7:26–32

Gibson, G., R. Linden, and S. Johnson. 1980. 'A Situational Theory of Rape.' *Canadian Journal of Criminology* 22:51–6

Gigeroff, A. 1980. 'Sex Offenders and the Sentencing Process.' In B. Grosman, ed., *New Directions in Sentencing.* Toronto: Butterworths

Giroux, J., et al. 1981. 'Les causes de viol entendues dans le district judiciare de Montréal entre 1975 et 1978: Une enquête rétrospective.' *Canadian Journal of Criminology* 23:173–90

Goldsberry, N. 1979. *Rape in British Columbia.* Vancouver: Ministry of the Solicitor General

Goode, M.R. 1983. 'Mens rea in corpore reo: An Exploration of the Rapists' Charter.' *Dalhousie Law Journal* 7:447–527

Gourgues, J., and M. Guay. 1980. *Le Viol.* Sainte-Foy, PQ: Ministère de la Justice

Gouvernement du Québec. 1987. *Une politique d'aide aux femmes violentées.* Édition révisée. Québec: Ministère des Affaires Sociales

Grant, Y. 1989. 'The Penetration of the Rape Shield: *R. v. Seaboyer* and *R. v. Gayme* in the Ontario Court of Appeal.' *Canadian Journal of Women and the Law* 3:592–601

Greenland, C. 1983. 'Sex Law Reform in an International Perspective: England and Wales and Canada.' *Bulletin of the American Academy of Psychiatry and the Law* 11:309–30

Grossman, M.G. 1990. *Canadian Legislative Changes in the Area of Sexual Aggression: An Experimental Survey.* Toronto: Centre of Criminology, University of Toronto

Guberman, C., and M. Wolfe. 1985. *No Safe Place.* Toronto: The Women's Press

Guenette, F. 1986. 'Onze femmes en colère. Confrontation d'un violeur.' *La vie en rose* 35:30–4

Gunn, R., and R. Linden. 1991. 'Factors Affecting the Disposition of Sexual Assault Cases before and after a Change in Sexual Assault Laws.' *Canadian Journal of Program Evaluation,* 6:71–82

Gunn, R., and C. Minch. 1985–6. 'Unofficial and Official Response to Sexual Assault.' *Resources for Feminist Research* 14:47–9

– 1988. *Sexual Assault: The Dilemma of Disclosure, The Question of Conviction.* Winnipeg: University of Manitoba Press

Hann, R., and F. Kopelman. 1987. *Assault: Custodial and Probation Sentences: 1984/ 85. (The Correctional Sentences Project).* Ottawa: Department of Justice

Harris, R.M., and L. Parsons. 1985. 'Expected Responses to Assault: The Effects of Circumstance and Locus of Control.' *Canadian Journal of Behavioural Sciences* 17:122–9

Heald, S. 1985. 'Social Change and Legal Ideology: A Critique of the New Sexual Assault Legislation.' *Canadian Criminology Forum* 7:117–28

Hegeman, N., and S. Meikle. 1980. 'Motives and Attitudes of Rapists.' *Canadian Journal of Behavioural Science* 12:359–372

Herold, E.S., D. Mantle, and O. Zemitis. 1979. 'A Study of Sexual Offenses against Females.' *Adolescence* 14:65–72

Hinch, R. 1985. 'Canada's New Sexual Assault Laws: A Step Forward for Women?' *Contemporary Crises* 9:33–44

– 1988. 'Inconsistencies and Contradictions in Canada's Sexual Assault Law.' *Canadian Public Policy* 14:282–94

– 1988. 'Enforcing the New Sexual Assault Laws: An Exploratory Study.' *Atlantis,* 14

Hutchinson, C.H., and S.A. McDaniel. 1986. 'The Social Reconstruction of Sexual Assault by Women Victims: A Comparison of Therapeutic Experiences.' *Canadian Journal of Community Mental Health* 5:17–36

J. and J. Research Associates Ltd. 1988. *An Evaluation of the Sexual Assault Provisions of Bill C-127, Fredericton and Saint John New Brunswick.* Ottawa: Department of Justice Canada (WD1991-5a)

James, B. 1982.' Breaking the Hold: Women against Rape.' In M. Fitzgerald et al., eds., *Still Ain't Satisfied.* Toronto: Women's Press

Johnson, S.D., L. Gibson, and R. Linden. 1978. 'Alcohol and Rape in Winnipeg, 1966–1975.' *Journal of Studies on Alcohol* 39:1887–94

Kasinsky, R. 1978a. 'The Anti-rape Movement in Canada.' In M. Gammon, ed., *Violence in Canada.* Toronto: Methuen

– 1978b. 'Rape: The Social Control of Women.' In W. Greenaway and S. Brickey, eds., *Law and Social Control in Canada.* Scarborough, ON: Prentice-Hall

Kinnon, D. 1981. *Sexual Assault in Canada – A Report.* Ottawa: Canadian Advisory Council on the Status of Women

Lacerte-Lamontagne, C. 1980. *Le viol: Acte de pouvoir et de colère.* Montréal: La Press

Lamontagne, Y., R. Boyer, C. Lamontagne, and J. Giroux. 1984. 'Two Person and Gang Rape in Montreal; Viols à deux et viols en bandes à Montréal. *Canadian Journal of Psychiatry* 29:564–9

Law Reform Commission of Canada. 1978a. *Sexual Offences.* Working Paper No. 22. Ottawa: Law Reform Commission of Canada

– 1978b. *Sexual Offences.* Report No. 10. Ottawa: Law Reform Commission of Canada

Legare, J. 1983. 'La condition juridique des femmes ou l'histoire d'une affaire de famille.' *Criminologie* 16:7–26

Lennon, E. 1990. 'Equality Rights and Violence against Women: LEAF's Approach.' *LEAF Lines* 4:1

Lessard, L. 1990. *Recherche sur les agressions sexuelles: revue de la littérature féministe.* Ottawa: Department of Criminology, University of Ottawa

Lewis, T. 1979. 'Recent Proposals in the Criminal Law of Rape: Significant Reform or Semantic Change?' *Osgoode Hall Law Journal* 17:445–58

Lewis, D. 1985. *The Impact of the Justice System on Sexual Assault Victims: A Feasibility Study.* Ottawa: Department of Justice Canada

Liddle, A. 1989. 'Feminist Contributions to an Understanding of Violence against Women – Three Steps Forward, Two Steps Back.' *Canadian Review of Sociology and Anthropology* 26:759–76

Lord, C. 1986. 'Comment les journaux traitent-ils le viol.' *Gazette des Femmes.* 7:23

Łoś, M. 1990. 'Feminism and Rape Law Reform.' In L. Gelsthorpe and A. Morris, eds., *Feminist Perspectives in Criminology.* Milton Keynes: Open University Press

MacFarlane, M. 1983. *Transition Houses and Rape Crisis Centres in Ontario.* Downsview, ON: La Marsh Research Programme, York University

Mahoney, K. 1989. R. v. *McCraw*: Rape Fantasies v. Fear of Sexual Assault.' *Ottawa Law Review* 21:207–19

Malcolm, P.B., P.R. Davidson, and W.L. Marshall. 1985. 'Control of Penile Tumescence: The Effects of Arousal Level and Stimulus Content.' *Behaviour Research and Therapy* 23:273–80

Manitoba Association of Women and the Law. 1991. *Gender Equality in the Courts. Criminal Law.* Winnipeg, MB: Manitoba Association of Women and the Law

Marshall, P. 1986. 'Sexual Assault, the Charter and Sentencing Reform.' *Criminal Reports,* (3rd series):216–35

McCormack, T. 1985. 'Deregulating the Economy and Regulating Morality: The Political Economy of Censorship.' *Studies in Political Economy* 18:173–85

McDonald, D. 1982a. *Rape and Consent – The Defense of Mistake of Fact.* Prepared for the Standing Committee on Legal and Constitutional Affairs. Ottawa: Library of Parliament

– 1982. *The Evolution of Bill C-127.* Prepared for the Standing Committee on Legal and Constitutional Affairs. Ottawa: Library of Parliament

McFadyen, J. 1978. 'Inter-spousal Rape: The Need for Reform.' In J. Eekelaar and S. Katz, eds., *Family Violence.* Toronto: Butterworths

McIvor, D., and C. Harting. 1990. 'Working with Female Adolescent Date-Rape Victims. *Canadian Journal of Psychiatric Nursing* 31:8–15

McTeer, M. 1978. 'Rape and the Canadian Legal Process.' In M. Gammon, ed., *Violence in Canada.* Toronto: Methuen

Minch, C., R. Linden, and S. Johnson. 1987. 'Attrition in the Processing of Rape Cases.' *Canadian Journal of Criminology* 29:389–403

Moscarello, R. 1990. 'Psychological Management of Victims of Sexual Assault.' *Canadian Journal of Psychiatry,* 35:25–30

Mosley, R. 1987. 'Approaches to Prevention and Treatment: An Overview.' In J. MacLatchie, ed., *Insights into Violence in Contemporary Canadian Society.* Ottawa: John Howard Society of Canada

Nadin-Davis, R. 1983. 'Making a Silk Purse? Sentencing: The "new" Sexual Offences.' *Criminal Reports (3rd)* 32:28–46

National Association of Women and the Law. 1979. *Recommendations on Sexual Assault Offences.* Ottawa: National Association of Women and the Law

– 1981. *A New image for Sexual Offences in the Criminal Code: A Brief in Response to Bill C-53.* Ottawa: National Association of Women and the Law

Nelson, S. 1978. 'An Experimental Study Concerning Jury Decisions in Rape Trials.' *Criminal Reports (3rd)* 1:265–83

Noone, J.A. 1986. 'The Indeterminate Sentence Option for Sex Offenders in Canada.' *American Journal of Forensic Psychiatry* 7:49–57

Nuttall, S. 1989. *Toronto Sexual Assault Research Study.* Ottawa: Ministry of the Solicitor General (User Report No. 1989-12)

O'Neill, P.,and M.P. Leiter. 1986. 'Shared Assumptions: A Citizen Action Group Simulation.' *Canadian Journal of Behavioural Science* 18:115–25

Ontario Provincial Secretariat for Justice. 1979. *Helping the Victims of Sexual Assault*. Toronto: Provincial Secretariat

Osborne, J.A. 1984. 'Rape Law Reform: The New Cosmetic for Canadian Women.' *Women and Politics* 4:49–64

Paciocco, D. 1989. 'The Charter and the Rape Shield Provisions of the Criminal Code: More about Relevance and the Constitutional Exemptions Doctrine.' *Ottawa Law Review* 21:119–49

Parker, G. 1983. 'The "new" sexual offences.' *Criminal Reports (3rd)*, 31:317–29

Pasquali, P. 1991. *Sexual Assault Sentencing in the Yukon*. Unpublished report

Pickard, T. 1980a. 'Culpable Mistakes and Rape: Relating Mens Rea to the Crime.' *University of Toronto Law Journal* 30:75–98

– 1980b. 'Culpable Mistakes and Rape: Harsh words on *Pappajohn*.' *University of Toronto Law Journal* 30:415–20

Pires, A. 1991. *The Reform of Sexual Assault Laws in Canada: A Reconstruction of Juridical Categories and Their 'New' Symbolic Effect*. Working Paper No. 9101C. Ottawa: Faculty of Social Sciences

Porteus, T., et al. 1986. *Working with Survivors of Sexual Assault*. Victoria: Victoria Women's Sexual Assault Centre

Price, M. 1984. *A Monitoring Project of the New Sexual Assault Legislation*. Report presented to the Alberta Law Foundation in conjunction with the Calgary Sexual Assault Centre

– 1984. *Canadian Sexual Offence Laws – A History*. Report to the Alberta Law Foundation. Calgary: Calgary Sexual Assault Centre

Quinsey, V. 1987. 'Sexual Assault.' In J. MacLatchie, ed., *Insights into violence in Contemporary Canadian society*. Ottawa: John Howard Society of Canada

Quinsey, V.L., and D. Upfold. 1985. 'Rape Completion and Victim Injury as a Function of Female Resistance Strategy.' *Canadian Journal of Behavioural Sciences* 17:40–50

Raphaneal, G. 1984. 'Justice and Sexual Politics: Legal Rights in the Charter of Rights and Freedoms.' *Socialist Studies: A Canadian Annual* 2:125–30

Regroupement provincial des maisons d'hébergement et de transition pour femmes victimes de violence.' (1987) *La sexualité blessée. Étude sur la violence sexuelle en milieu conjugal.*

Renner, K., and S. Sahjpaul. 1986. 'The New Sexual Assault Law: What Has Been Its Effect?' *Canadian Journal of Criminology* 28:407–13

Renner, K., and C. Wackett. 1987. 'Sexual Assault: Social and Stranger Rape.' *Canadian Journal of Mental Health* 6:49–56

Renner, K.E., C. Wackett, and S. Ganderton. 1988. 'The "Social" Nature of Sexual Assault.' *Canadian Psychology* 29:163–73

Resnick, G. 1979. *An Annotated Bibliography of Current Research on Rape and Other Sexual Offences*. Toronto: Provincial Secretariat for Justice

Rioux, M., and J. McFayden. 1978. 'Background Notes on the Proposed Amendments to the Criminal Code in Respect of Indecent Assault. Notes documentaires sur les modifications proposées au Code criminel en ce qui concerne l'attentat à la pudeur.' Ottawa: Le Conseil consultatif canadien de la situation de la femme.

Roberts, B. 1983. 'All Our Lives: Sexual Assault, A Normal Activity.' Canadian Women's Studies 4:7–10

Roberts, J. 1990a. Sentencing Patterns in Cases of Sexual Assault. Sexual Assault Legislation in Canada, Report No. 3. Ottawa: Department of Justice

– 1990b. An Analysis of National Statistics. Sexual Assault Legislation in Canada: An Evaluation, Report No. 4. Ottawa: Department of Justice

Roberts, J., and M. Grossman. 1991. Homicide and Sexual Assault. Sexual Assault Legislation in Canada: An Evaluation, Report No. 7. Ottawa: Department of Justice

Roberts, J., and R. Gebotys. 1992. 'Reforming Rape Laws: Effects of Legislative Reform in Canada.' Law and Human Behavior 16:555–74

Roberts, J., and A. Pires. 1992. 'Le renvoi et la classification des infractions d'agression sexuelle.' Criminologie 25:27–63

Robinson, D. 1989. 'Research on Sex Offenders: What Do We Need to Know?' Forum on Corrections Research 1:12–22

Roy, M. 1990. 'L'agression sexuelle, une blessure mieux comprise.' Justice. Québec: Ministère de la Justice

Ruebsaat, G. 1985. The New Sexual Assault Offences: Emerging Legal Issues. Sexual Assault Legislation in Canada: An Evaluation. Report No. 2. Ottawa: Department of Justice

Rule, G. 1984. Bibliographie sélective sur le viol. Québec: Ministère des Affaires Sociales du Québec, Service de la Documentation

Russell, M. 1980.'Les victimes du viol et le rapport du délit à la police.' Santé Mentale au Canada 28:16–18

Sacco, V. 1987. 'Perceptions of Violence.' In J. MacLatchie, ed., Insights into Violence in Contemporary Canadian society. Ottawa: John Howard Society of Canada

Sacco, V., and H. Johnson. 1990. Patterns of Criminal Victimization in Canada. Ottawa: Minister of Supply and Services

Sahjpaul, S., and K. Renner. 1988. 'The New Sexual Assault Law: The Victim's Experience in Court.' American Journal of Community Psychology 16:503–13

Sheehy, E. 1987. Personal Autonomy and the Criminal Law: Emerging Issues for Women. Ottawa: Canadian Advisory Council on the Status of Women

– 1989. 'Canadian Judges and the Law of Rape: Should the Charter Insulate Bias?' Ottawa Law Review 21:741–87

Sheehy, E., and S. Boyd. 1989. Canadian Feminist Perspectives on Law. Resources for Feminist Research. Toronto: Ontario Institute for Studies in Education

Siggins, M. 1984. *Brian and the Boys: A Story of Gang Rape.* Toronto: Lorimer

Silverberg, C.E. 1983. *Police Processing of Rape Complaints: Legal Constraint or Extra-legal Bias.* M.A. thesis. Centre of Criminology, University of Toronto

Snider, L. 1985. 'Legal Reform and Social Control: The Dangers of Abolishing Rape.' *International Journal of the Sociology of Law* 13:337–56

Solicitor General 1985. *Female Victims of Crime. Canadian Urban Victimization Survey No. 4.* Ottawa: Solicitor General, Communications Group

Stanley, M. 1985. *The Experience of the Rape Victim with the Criminal Justice System prior to Bill C-127. Sexual Assault Legislation in Canada: An Evaluation, Report No. 1.* Ottawa: Department of Justice

Streit-Forest, U., and M. Goulet. 1987. 'The Effects of Rape 6 Months after the Attack and Factors Associated with Recovery.' *Canadian Journal of Psychiatry* 32:43–56

Te Paske, B. 1982. *Rape and Ritual. A Psychological Study.* Toronto: Inner City Books

Toews, C. 1991. *Issues in Sexual Assault Sentencing in Nova Scotia.* Halifax, N.S.: Nova Scotia Advisory Council on the Status of Women

Toronto Rape Crisis Centre 1985. 'Rape.' In C. Guberman and M. Wolfe, eds., *No Safe Place: Violence against Women and Children.* Toronto: The Women's Press

Towson, S.M.J., and M.P. Zanna. 1983. 'Retaliation against Sexual Assault: Self Defense or Public Duty?' *Psychology of Women Quarterly* 8:89–99

University of Manitoba Research Ltd. 1988a. *Report on the Impact of the 1983 Sexual Assault Legislation in Winnipeg, Manitoba.* Ottawa: Department of Justice (WD1991-7a)

– 1988b. *Report on the Impact of the 1983 Sexual Assault Legislation in Lethbridge, Alberta.* Ottawa: Department of Justice (WD1991-6a)

Usprich, S. 1987. 'A New Crime in Old Battles: Definitional Problems with Sexual Assault.' *Criminal Law Quarterly* 29:200–21

Vandervort, L. 1985–86. 'Enforcing the Sexual Assault Laws: An Agenda for Action.' *Resources for Feminist Research* 14:44–5

– 1987–8. 'Mistake of Law and Sexual Assault: Consent and Mens Rea.' *Canadian Journal of Women and the Law* 2:233–309

– 1990. 'Consent and the Criminal Law.' *Osgoode Hall Law Journal,* 28:485–500

Victoria Women's Sexual Assault Centre. 1984. *Let's Talk about Sexual Assault.* Victoria, BC: Victoria Women's Sexual Assault Centre

– 1986. *Working with Survivors of Sexual Assault.* Victoria, BC: Victoria Women's Sexual Assault Centre

Voumvakis, S., and R. Ericson. 1984. *New Accounts of Attacks on Women – A Comparison of Three Toronto Newspapers.* Toronto: Centre of Criminology, University of Toronto

Watt, D. 1984. *The New Offences against the Person: The Provisions of Bill C-127.* Toronto: Butterworths

Wigmore, J., and M. Ward. 1986. 'Incidence of Ethanol and Acetone in the Blood and Urine of Sexual Assault Victims.' *Canadian Society of Forensic Science* 19:49–58

Yarmey, A. 1985. 'Attitudes and Sentencing for Sexual Assault as a Function of Age and Sex of Subjects.' *Canadian Journal on Aging* 4:20–8

– 1985. 'Older and Younger Adults' Attributions of Responsibility toward Rape Victims and Rapists.' *Canadian Journal of Behaviour Science* 17:327–38

Yurchesyn, K., A. Keith, and E. Renner. 1991. 'Contrasting Perspectives on the Nature of Sexual Assault Provided by a Service for Sexual Assault Victims and by the Law Courts.' *Canadian Journal of Behavioural Science* (in press)

APPENDIX B

Text of the 'Rape Shield' Legislation C-49

Third Session, Thirty-fourth Parliament,

40–41 Elizabeth II, 1991–92

THE HOUSE OF COMMONS OF CANADA

BILL-C-49

An Act to amend the Criminal Code (sexual assault)

AS PASSED BY THE HOUSE OF COMMONS
JUNE 15, 1992

An Act to amend the Criminal Code (sexual assault)

WHEREAS the Parliament of Canada is gravely concerned about the incidence of sexual violence and abuse in Canadian society and, in particular, the prevalence of sexual assault against women and children;

WHEREAS the Parliament of Canada recognizes the unique character of the offence of sexual assault of how sexual assault and, more particularly, the fear of sexual assault affects the lives of the people of Canada;

WHEREAS the Parliament of Canada intends to promote and help to ensure the full protection of the rights guaranteed under sections 7 and 15 of the *Canadian Charter of Rights and Freedoms*;

WHEREAS the Parliament of Canada wishes to encourage the reporting of incidents of sexual violence or abuse, and to provide for the prosecution of offenses within a framework of laws that are consistent with the principles of fundamental justice and that are fair to complainants as well as to accused persons;

WHEREAS the Supreme Court of Canada has declared the existing section 276 of the 25 Criminal Code to be of no force and effect;

AND WHEREAS the Parliament of Canada believes that at trials of sexual offenses, evidence of the complainant's sexual history is rarely relevant and that its admission should be subject to particular scrutiny, bearing in mind the inherently prejudicial character of such evidence;

NOW THEREFORE, Her majesty, by and with the advice and consent of the Senate and House of Commons of Canada, enacts as follows:

1. The Criminal Code is amended by adding thereto, immediately after section 273 thereof, the following sections:

273.1 (1) Subject to subsection (2) and subsection 265(3), 'consent' means, for the purposes of sections 271, 272 and 273, the voluntary agreement of the complainant to engage in the sexual activity in question.

(2) No consent is obtained, for the purposes of sections 271, 272 and 273, where
(a) the agreement is expressed by the words or conduct of a person other than the complainant;
(b) the complainant is incapable of consenting to the activity;
(c) the accused induces the complainant to engage in the activity by abusing a position of trust, power or authority;
(d) the complainant expresses, by words or conduct, a lack of agreement to engage in the activity;
or
(e) the complainant, having consented to engage in sexual activity, expresses, by words or conduct, a lack of agreement to continue to engage in the activity.

(3) Nothing in subsection (2) shall be construed as limiting the circumstances in which no consent is obtained.

273.2 It is not a defence to a charge under section 271, 272 or 273 that the accused believed that the complainant consented to the activity that forms the subject-matter of the charge, where

(a) the accused's belief from the accused's
(i) self-induced intoxication, or
(ii) recklessness or wilful blindness; or

(b) the accused did not take reasonable steps, in the circumstances known to the accused at the time, to ascertain that the complainant was consenting.

2. Section 276 of the said Act is repealed and the following substituted therefor:

276. (1) In proceedings in respect of an offence under section 151, 152, 153, 155 or 159, subsection 160(2) or (3) or section 170, 171, 172, 173, 271, 272 or 273, evidence that the complainant has engaged in sexual activity, whether with the accused or with any other person, is not admissible to support an inference that, by reason of the sexual nature of that activity, the complainant

(a) is more likely to have consented to the sexual activity that forms the subject-matter of the charge; or
(b) is less worthy of belief.

(2) In proceedings in respect of an offence referred to in subsection (1), no evidence shall be adduced by or on behalf of the accused that the complainant has engaged in sexual activity other than the sexual activity that forms the subject-matter of the charge, whether with the accused or with the any other person, unless the judge, provincial court judge or justice determines, in accordance with the procedures set out in sections 276.1 and 276.2, that the evidence

(a) is of specific instances of sexual activity;
(b) is relevant to an issue at trial; and
(c) has significant probative value that is not substantially outweighed by the danger of prejudice to the proper administration of justice.

(3) In determining whether evidence is admissible under subsection (2), the judge, provincial court judge or justice shall take into account.

(a) the interest of justice, including the right of the accused to make a full answer and defence;
(b) society's interest in encouraging the reporting of sexual assault offenses;
(c) whether there is a reasonable prospect that the evidence will assist in arriving at a just determination in the case;
(d) the need to remove from the fact-finding process any discriminatory belief or bias;
(e) the risk that the evidence may unduly arouse sentiments of prejudice, sympathy or hostility in the injury;
(f) the potential prejudice to the complainant's personal dignity and right of privacy;
(g) the right of the complainant and of every individual to personal security and to the full protection and benefit of the law; and

(h) any other factor that the judge, provincial court judge considers relevant.

276.1 (1) Application may be made to the judge, provincial court judge or justice by or on behalf of the accused for a hearing under section 276.2 to determine whether evidence is admissible under subsection 276(2).

(2) An application referred to in subsection (1) must be made in writing and set out
(a) detailed particulars of the evidence that the accused seeks to adduce, and
(b) the relevance of that evidence to an issue at trial,
and a copy of the application must be given to the prosecutor and to the clerk of the court.

(3) The judge, provincial court judge or justice shall consider the application with the jury and the public excluded.

(4) Where the judge, provincial court judge or justice is satisfied
(a) that the application was made in accordance with subsection(2).
(b) that a copy of the application was given to the prosecutor and to the clerk of the court at least seven days previously, or such shorter interval as the judge, provincial court judge or justice may allow where the interests of justice so require, and
(c) that the evidence sought to be adduced is capable of being admissible under subsection 276(2),

the judge, provincial court judge or justice shall grant the application and hold a hearing under section 276.2 to determine whether the evidence is admissible under subsection 276(2).

276.2 (1) At a hearing to determine whether evidence is admissible under subsection 276(2), the jury and the public shall be excluded.

(2) The complainant is not a compellable witness at the hearing.

(3) At the conclusion of the hearing, the judge, provincial court judge or justice shall determine whether the evidence, or any part thereof, is admissible under subsection 276(2) and shall provide reasons for that determination, and
(a) where not all of the evidence is to be admitted, the reasons must state the part of the evidence that is to be admitted;
(b) the reasons must state the factors referred to in subsection 276(3) that affected the determination; and
(c) where all or any part of the evidence is to be admitted, the reasons must state the manner in which that evidence is expected to be relevant to an issue at trial.

(4) The reasons provided under subsection (3) shall be entered in the record of the

proceedings or, where the proceedings are not recorded, shall be provided in writing.

276.4 (1) No person shall publish in a newspaper, as defined in section 297, or in a broadcast, any of the following:

(a) the contents of an application made under section 276.1;

(b) any evidence taken, the information given and the representations made at an application under section 276.1 or at a hearing under section 276.2;

(c) the decision of a judge, provincial court judge or justice under subsection 276.1(4), unless the judge, provincial court judge or justice, after taking into account the complainant's right of privacy and the interests of justice, orders that the decision may be published; and

(d) the determination made and the reasons provided under section 276.2, unless

(i) that determination is that evidence is admissible, or

(ii) the judge, provincial court judge or justice, after taking into account the complainant's right of privacy and the interest of justice, orders that the determination and reasons may be published.

(2) Every person who contravenes subsection (1) is guilty of an offence punishable on summary conviction.

276.4 Where evidence is admitted at trial pursuant to a determination made under section 276.2, the judge shall instruct the jury as to the uses that the jury may or may not make of that evidence.

276.5 For the purposes of sections 675 and 676, a determination made under section 276.2 shall be deemed to be a question of law.

3. This Act or any provision thereof, or any provision of the Criminal Code as enacted by this Act, shall come into force on a day or days to be fixed by order of the Governor in Council.